HIDDEN®
Colorado

D1330597

"Besides the obvious, author Richard Harris looks also to spots beyond
the tourist track."

—*New Orleans Times-Picayune*

HIDDEN®
Colorado

Richard Harris

SECOND EDITION

Ulysses Press®
BERKELEY, CALIFORNIA

Published by:
ULYSSES PRESS
P.O. Box 3440
Berkeley, CA 94703-3440

Library of Congress Catalog Card Number 98-84071
ISBN 1-56975-127-7

Printed in Canada by Best Book Manufacturers

10 9 8 7 6 5 4 3 2

MANAGING EDITOR: Claire Chun
PROJECT DIRECTOR: Natasha Lay
COPY EDITOR: James Donnelly
EDITORIAL ASSOCIATES: Aaron Newey, Lily Chou,
    Carol Delattre, David Wells
TYPESETTER: Steven Schwartz
CARTOGRAPHY: Stellar Cartography
HIDDEN BOOKS DESIGN: Sarah Levin
COVER DESIGN: Leslie Henriques
INDEXER: Sayre Van Young
COVER PHOTOGRAPHY: Front: Terry Donnelly
    Circle and back: Cheyenne Rouse
    Back: Markham Johnson
ILLUSTRATOR: Doug McCarthy

Distributed in the United States by Publishers Group West, in Canada by Raincoast Books, and in Great Britain and Europe by World Leisure Marketing

Write to us!

If in your travels you discover a spot that captures the spirit of Colorado, or if you live in the region and have a favorite place to share, or if you just feel like expressing your views, write to us and we'll pass your note along to the author.

We can't guarantee that the author will add your personal find to the next edition, but if the writer does use the suggestion, we'll acknowledge you in the credits and send you a free autographed copy of the new edition.

ULYSSES PRESS
P.O. Box 3440
Berkeley, CA 94703-3440
E-mail: readermail@ulyssespress.com

What's Hidden?

At different points throughout this book, you'll find special listings marked with a hidden symbol:

◄ HIDDEN

This means that you have come upon a place off the beaten tourist track, a spot that will carry you a step closer to the local people and natural environment of Colorado.

The goal of this guide is to lead you beyond the realm of everyday tourist facilities. While we include traditional sightseeing listings and popular attractions, we also offer alternative sights and adventure activities. Instead of filling this guide with reviews of standard hotels and chain restaurants, we concentrate on one-of-a-kind places and locally owned establishments.

Our authors seek out locales that are popular with residents but usually overlooked by visitors. Some are more hidden than others (and are marked accordingly), but all the listings in this book are intended to help you discover the true nature of Colorado and put you on the path of adventure.

Contents

Maps

OUTDOOR ADVENTURE SYMBOLS

The following symbols accompany national, state and regional park listings, as well as beach descriptions throughout the text.

▲	Camping		Snorkeling or Scuba Diving
	Hiking		Waterskiing
	Biking		Windsurfing
	Horseback Riding		Canoeing or Kayaking
	Downhill Skiing		Boating
	Cross-country Skiing		Boat Ramps
	Swimming		Fishing

ONE

Colorado

That first view of Colorado's 14,000-foot mountain summits stirs a traveler's soul with the kind of elation and awe that the "Pikes Peak or Bust" pioneers with their covered wagons must have felt. You're driving across the midwestern plains on a fast, straight interstate highway when suddenly Pikes Peak stands in massive solitude. Or you're crossing the piñon-studded redrock canyonlands of the Navajo country when the San Juans rise up in the hazy distance in jagged majesty like misplaced Swiss Alps. Or you look out the window of the plane taking you to Aspen, see that from horizon to horizon among the granite crags and evergreen slopes there is not a single road in sight and realize in that moment that there are still places in these mountains where no human has ever set foot.The Colorado Rockies are big in the way that an ocean is big. From any one place, the eye can see only a small part of them, and the unseen part tantalizes the imagination. They reach up high into a world apart from the one in which most of us live. Their alpine lakes and forest trails hold out the promise of cool respite from the humid summer heat of the flatlands, and in winter their high-speed slopes gleam with packed powder and their cross-country ski trails lead through crystal fantasies.

It's easy to think of Colorado as one huge public park. Thirty-six percent of the state is public land, much of it ideal for recreation. On any highway, many cars are clearly bound for the great outdoors, mounted with roof racks carrying skis, kayaks or mountain bikes, depending on the season. Horseback riders are a common sight along back roads and busy thoroughfares alike. Along a thousand creeks and lakeshores, fishing enthusiasts cast for rainbow trout. It is not unusual to spot deer, elk and pronghorn antelopes grazing within sight of the highway. Tourism brings more money into Colorado's economy than mining, and almost as much as cattle.

Yet tourism is just one of Colorado's multiple facets. The state boasts a diversified economy that runs the gamut from computer companies to llama and buffalo ranches. Colorado is the most prosperous state in the Mountain West as well as the most populous. Between the 1980 and 1990 censuses, the number of people in the state increased by 14 percent to 3.5 million residents. The vast majority of Coloradoans live in the cities of the Front Range Corridor, a narrow band of development that clings to Route 25 from Fort Collins in the north to Pueblo in the south. Denver, the state capital and commercial hub, has a population density of 3050 per square mile. Yet not far away lie several of the dozen Colorado counties that have fewer than two human residents per square mile.

Hidden Colorado is designed to help you explore every part of the state. It covers popular, "must-see" places, offering advice on how best to enjoy them. It also tells you about many off-the-beaten-path spots, the kind you would find by talking with folks at the local café or with someone who has lived in the area all his or her life. It describes the region's history, its natural areas and its residents, both human and animal. It suggests places to eat, to lodge, to play, to camp. Taking into account varying interests, budgets and tastes, it provides the information you need whether your vacation style involves backpacking, mountain biking, playing golf, museum browsing, shopping or all of the above.

This book covers Colorado in eight sections. Each region of the state is so different from the others that whether your taste in travel destinations runs to the sophistication of the big city, the glamorous seclusion of a chic year-round resort, the rugged majesty of 14,000-foot-high mountain peaks, the whisper of history through ghost-town streets, the solitude of redrock desert canyons or the pure relaxation of picturesque creeks and alpine lakes, you're bound to find a part of Colorado that fits your vacation dreams perfectly.

The traveling part of the book begins in Chapter Two with the sightseeing highlights of metropolitan Denver, the natural starting point for most Colorado explorations. Chapter Three expands the focus to the Front Range, the region along the eastern perimeter of the mountains that includes the booming university towns of Boulder and Fort Collins as well as the casinos of Central City and Black Hawk and the family-style resort town of Estes Park, gateway to Rocky Mountain National Park—all within an hour's drive of Denver.

Chapter Four takes you over the Continental Divide to North Central Colorado's world-renowned ski resorts, including Aspen, Vail, Steamboat Springs, Winter Park and Breckenridge in the heart of the Colorado Rockies, where they are easily reached via Route 70. Chapter Five continues the journey into Northwestern Colorado, beginning with a descent from the high country down Glenwood Canyon to the town whose claim to fame is the state's largest hot spring and follows the Colorado River westward through dramatic canyon and mesa country, best known for dinosaur bones.

The last third of this book covers the southern and far eastern part of the state, beginning in Chapter Six with the Colorado Springs and Pikes Peak Region, the state's oldest tourist area and still one of the most popular, where vacation fun can include such diverse options as mountain climbing, whitewater rafting, gold panning and blackjack. Chapter Seven broadens the look at South Central Colorado to take in such destinations as the spectacular Great Sand Dunes, the ghost-town-turned-ski-resort of Crested Butte and the remote mountain hideaways of Lake City and Creede. Chapter Eight presents the mystery and majesty of South-

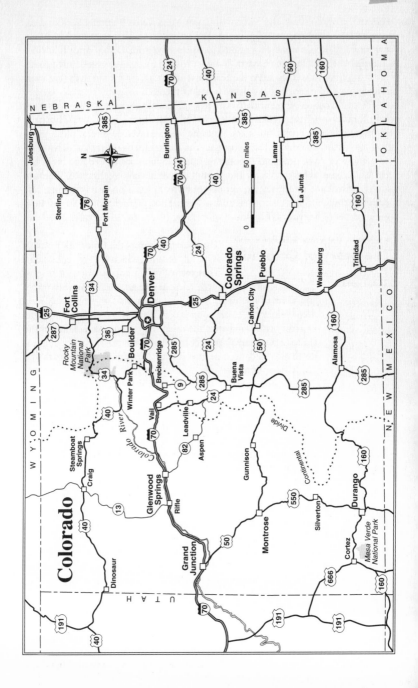

western Colorado, from the cliff dwellings at Mesa Verde National Park and an array of lesser known ancient ruins to the vast wilderness areas of the San Juans surrounding such unique mountain towns as Silverton, Ouray and Telluride. Chapter Nine examines the Eastern Plains, revealing an array of little-known roadside attractions as well as a few natural areas so far off the beaten path that even most native Coloradoans have never heard of them.

What you choose to see and do is up to you. The old cliché that "there is something for everyone" pretty well rings true in Colorado. In this book, you'll find free campgrounds with hiking trails and fantastic views as well as several plush playgrounds for the wealthy and well-known. You can take a chairlift to a high alpine ridge and then coast down on a mountain bike. Or check into a bed and breakfast that has delightful little galleries and boutiques within walking distance. Whether you're a first-time visitor setting out on your dream vacation or a long-time resident searching for that proverbial undiscovered spot, *Hidden Colorado* will help you experience for yourself a wealth of exciting places and adventures.

▼▼▼▼▼▼▼▼▼▼▼▼▼▼▼▼

The Story of Colorado

GEOLOGY

The rock that forms the Colorado Rockies is mainly granite, which is an igneous rock. That means it is a combination of several different minerals—quartz, feldspar and granite, along with traces and veins of metals such as gold, silver, lead and zinc—blended deep within the earth countless millennia ago under conditions of great heat. Long after the other major mountain chains in the United States had already been formed, the massive layer of granite that would become the Rocky Mountains lay beneath the sandy floor of a great sea.

Very slowly, inexorably, two tectonic plates that make up most of the North American continent—the Canadian Shield and the Pacific Plate—drifted toward each other, floating on molten rock far under the earth's surface. In a slow collision, the plates crushed against each other and started to crumple, pushing the granite layer upward. Dinosaurs, which were abundant in the area at that time, would have experienced this phenomenon as occasional earthquakes.

Sixty million years ago, around the time dinosaurs became extinct, the granite mass cracked through the red sandstone surface that had been beaches and marshy wetlands. In many places along the edges of the uplift, the fractured sandstone was thrust skyward to create the spires and hogback formations that characterize the Front Range of the Colorado Rockies today. The collision of tectonic plates and the uplifting of the granite rock continues even now, though the process is so slow that the mountains have only gained a few inches in height during the time humans have walked the earth.

The mountains as we see them today were shaped by glaciers. A series of Ice Ages, the last of which ended 10,000 years ago—a mere eyeblink in geological time—covered the high country in accumulations of snow and ice that flowed down the mountainsides slowly in solid frozen rivers that gouged deep valleys called moraines, creating steep mountain faces and marking the courses for the turbulent rivers that would slice canyons hundreds of feet deep.

The lofty mountains attract storm clouds like a magnet, making for rainfall and snowfall many times greater than in the deserts and arid prairies at the foot of the mountains. Runoff from the melting snowpack in spring and the thunderstorms of summer gives birth to several of the West's great rivers—the Colorado, Río Grande, Arkansas and South Platte. It is the rivers that give significance to the Continental Divide, the dotted line on maps that meanders through the wilderness connecting Colorado's highest mountain passes.

All precipitation that falls east of the Continental Divide flows eventually to the Gulf of Mexico or the Atlantic Ocean, while west of the Divide it flows to the Pacific. Elsewhere in the western states, the backbone of the continent may be marked by nothing more spectacular than a point-of-interest sign at a roadside rest area. But in Colorado the Continental Divide is a formidable barrier bisecting the entire state. Crossing it means either driving through a tunnel beneath the mountains or climbing a switchback road up a wall of granite to the summit of a pass more than two miles above sea level.

AMERICAN INDIANS Anywhere you go in Colorado, particularly in the southwestern part of the state, you'll find reminders of the American Indian people who used to roam the region's mountains, mesas and prairies. In the glass cases of Denver's big art, history, and natural history museums as well as in small-town historical museums across the state, you'll see 19th-century Indian artifacts. Then, too, you will find souvenir stores everywhere selling turquoise-and-silver Indian-made jewelry (state law prohibits displaying the ubiquitous "authentic Indian design" or "replica" Indian jewelry alongside the genuine item), as well as pottery, beadwork, and other arts and crafts. It's enough to make one wonder why visitors so rarely see a living American Indian in Colorado.

Indian petroglyphs (designs chipped into rock) and pictographs (paintings on rock) are found in several lowland areas of the state, particularly the southeast and northwest corners. Some of the images are thought to be as much as 4500 years old. Little is known of the early people who created them beyond the fact that they hunted large mammals using spears and throwing sticks with flaked flint points. Artistic differences suggest that the plains people on the east side of the Continental Divide and the desert people on the west side had little or no contact with one another.

HISTORY

Anthropologists are particularly puzzled by rock art found in the canyons of Colorado's southeastern plains, which bear an inexplicable resemblance to the system of writing used in ancient Ireland.

Civilization came to southwestern Colorado around 800 A.D., when the Anasazi (a Navajo name meaning "ancient enemies"), presumably descendants of early nomads, began growing corn and building permanent houses. They built monumental cliff dwellings and pueblos such as the ones visitors see today at Mesa Verde National Park, the Anasazi Heritage Center near Dolores, and the Ute Mountain Tribal Park. They accomplished impressive feats of astronomy and architecture, and they established trade networks that reached all the way to the Toltec cities of central Mexico. Mysteriously, around 1250 A.D., the Anasazi suddenly abandoned the region, moving south into New Mexico, where their descendants now live at Acoma Pueblo near Grants. Why they left the communities where their people had lived for more than 400 years remains one of the most puzzling questions in American archaeology.

For centuries, the Colorado high country was the domain of the Ute people, who touched the mountains lightly and with reverence. Living as nomads, they huddled around fires in bison-leather tents through thousands of long, brutal winters in the canyonlands of southwestern Colorado, waiting to follow the spring snowmelt into hidden canyons and ancient forests of the high country along the Continental Divide. The Indian population of the Colorado region was never large. The Utes laid claim to virtually all the mountain country of Colorado—yet numbered only about as many as there are year-round residents of Aspen today. With such a vast territory to roam, the mountain tribes rarely came into conflict with one another. In fact, they rarely encountered each other at all except on purpose, in intertribal powwows held at traditional times and places for purposes of trade, social contests, spiritual ceremonies and political diplomacy. At the same time the nomadic Cheyenne and Arapaho tribes followed the bison herds across the plains of northeastern Colorado, as they had since the dawn of memory.

Warfare among the Indian tribes took place mainly along the eastern edge of the mountains, where Plains tribes such as the Arapaho and Cheyenne would send hunting parties into the rich high-country valleys of the mountain people. Before the arrival of non-Indians, intertribal battles bore little resemblance to the bloodbaths that would come later. War parties were generally small and had no firearms, steel or horses. The limited supply of arrows a warrior could carry did not last long in battle, and it was better to save them for hunting if possible, since each handmade arrow represented many hours of work.

At least two non-Indian influences—horses and guns—began to change the Indian way of life long before the first white man set foot in the Rockies at the beginning of the 19th century. Horses first came into Indian hands in northern New Mexico in 1680, when Pueblo people revolted against their Spanish oppressors, looting and burning every settler's home. Navajo and Apache groups agreed to help the Pueblos drive the Spaniards out; in exchange, they could keep all the livestock they could round up from the Spanish ranches and farms—including thousands of horses. Many more horses driven off from the ranches were never captured, but instead went wild to spawn the herds of mustangs that inhabit remote areas of western Colorado even today. As neighbors of the Navajo, the Ute people got their first horses around 1700, and within the next sixty years, virtually every tribe in the Rocky Mountain West had bought, captured or stolen enough horses to breed its own herd.

> Horses let the Indians travel much farther and faster, bringing more frequent contact—whether friendly or hostile—between tribes.

Guns spread more slowly among the Indians. In the British and French settlements along America's east coast, armies of both colonial powers gave rifles to tribes that helped fight the Seven Years War (1756–1763), also known as the French and Indian War. Guns meant power to conquer other tribes to the west who did not have them. Fur traders on what was then the American frontier found that the self-defense needs of Indian tribes made guns extremely valuable as items of exchange, even as they empowered Indian hunters to hunt more efficiently and bring larger quantities of valuable furs to trade for more guns. As Indians got guns by trading with non-Indians from the east, they often turned the guns against rival tribes to the west in order to expand their hunting territory. In this way, firearms often made their way westward ahead of the first non-Indian explorers.

In 1851, as more and more non-Indian homesteaders came into the region, the Cheyenne and Arapaho people signed the Fort Laramie Treaty, granting them spacious reservation lands along the Front Range, including the land where Denver now sits. Ten years later, as the first settlers began homesteading in that area, the government canceled the treaty and relocated the Indians to an arid reservation near Las Animas in southeastern Colorado. Starvation set in, and parties of Indian men left the reservation to scour the countryside for food, alarming the non-Indian settlers, many of whom could not communicate with the Indians and feared them. In a solitary instance, a farm family south of Denver was killed by a small party of Indians.

Colorado was settled at the height of the U.S. government's military campaigns against the Indians, and with few exceptions, the Indians were either relocated or exterminated within a few years after Colorado became a state. Colonel John Chivington of the Colorado National Guard took punitive action against the Cheyenne and Arapaho people in November 1864, leading a cavalry company in a dawn raid on a reservation village and killing 123 people, mostly women and children. News of the raid, which is now remembered as the Sand Creek Massacre, was received with mixed emotions. Chivington was awarded a Medal of Honor by the Territorial Governor and hailed as a hero by some settlers, but he was simultaneously court-martialed by the U.S. Army and drummed out of military service. The Cheyenne and Arapaho people were relocated to reservations in Nebraska and South Dakota, but renegade Cheyenne "dog" soldiers terrorized the Colorado plains for five years before their leader, Tall Bull, was killed in a battle with the cavalry. Buffalo Bill Cody, then a 23-year-old army scout, was inaccurately given credit for killing Tall Bull in a best-selling dime novel that established Cody's spurious reputation as an Indian fighter.

Meanwhile, Kit Carson, a legitimately legendary Indian fighter who commanded the garrison at Fort Garland in southern Colorado's San Luis Valley, led actions in the southeastern plains against small, elusive parties of Comanche, Kiowa and Prairie Apache warriors who had been driven from their homelands in West Texas. There was no major, decisive battle. Little by little, the renegades were confined to reservation lands in Oklahoma— or killed.

In 1868, the U.S. government made a treaty with the Ute people granting them a magnificent 6000-square-mile reservation that contained all of the San Juan Mountains, including the sites of present-day Durango, Silverton, Ouray, Telluride and Montrose. Their leader, Chief Ouray, settled down on a farm that is now the site of Ute Indian Museum and Chipeta Park near Montrose and became one of the most eloquent spokesmen and negotiators for the Indian cause.

But five years later, in 1873, soon after gold was discovered in the San Juans, the government rescinded the treaty, and the Utes were forced to move—some to a reservation south of Vernal, Utah, others to the narrow bands of piñon-covered hills and mesas that lie between the desert and Sleeping Ute Mountain on the southern fringe of their former homeland. The Southern Ute and Ute Mountain reservations are now the only Indian lands in Colorado, and the instrument of retribution for past injustices seems to be at hand, for the Ute people now operate the only gambling casino in southern Colorado, the Ute Mountain Casino in Towaoc. When Colorado legalized casino gambling in Cripple Creek, Central City and Black Hawk in 1993, under federal law casinos automatically became legal on the Ute reservations.

EXPLORERS AND MOUNTAIN MEN   A vast area of North America, from the Mississippi River to the Pacific Northwest coast, including all of Colorado, was claimed sight-unseen as Spanish territory in 1769, even though no Spanish settlement was ever established beyond the port city of New Orleans. France acquired the Louisiana Territory from Spain by treaty in 1800, but except for small trading expeditions up the river, the French found it impossible to occupy—or even explore and map—the territory, and in 1803 they sold it to the United States for $12 million dollars. Two years later, the first French trapper/traders reached the Rocky Mountains; they had been in the wilderness so long that they did not know the region had been sold to America, nor did it matter much, since virtually all of the estimated 150 French frontiersmen who went west found homes among the Indians and never returned to civilization.

No American expedition reached Colorado until 1806, when the U.S. government sent an expedition under the leadership of Captain Zebulon Pike to trace the Arkansas River to its source. After seeing—and failing in attempts to climb—the peak that would later bear his name, Pike was arrested as a spy by the Mexican army and imprisoned in Santa Fe. He was released only after making an unauthorized agreement that henceforth the Arkansas River would be recognized as the border between U.S. and Mexican territory—an agreement that would hold in the Rocky Mountain region for the next 43 years.

As the Bent brothers and other entrepreneurs established trading posts along the Arkansas and South Platte rivers of eastern Colorado, hundreds of freelance adventurers set off to probe deeper into the mountains in search of pelts. These "mountain men," as they were called, explored virtually every valley in the Colorado Rockies during the next thirty years, bringing back more than half a million beaver pelts each year. In order to kill animals in such phenomenal numbers, the mountain men not only set their own traps but also traded gunpowder and bullets to the Indians for more furs. By the 1840s, beavers had become nearly extinct in the territory. The last of the old-time fur trappers either became guides for army expeditions and pioneer wagon trains or established their own trading posts, where they continued to sell ammunition to the Indians—a practice that would soon become controversial and then illegal.

PIONEERS AND PROSPECTORS   Colorado missed out on the great pioneer migrations of the 1840s and 1850s because its high mountain passes posed an impossible obstacle to wagon trains. Colorado was settled later than any of its neighboring states because mountain winters made it a hard place to survive in. But almost overnight, rumors of gold turned the eastern slope of the

Colorado Rockies into the region's main population center. A trickle of prospectors started arriving in the territory in 1849, a year after the discovery of gold at Sutter's Mill in California proved that gold existed in United States territory.

The gold find that touched off the 1858 "Pikes Peak or Bust" gold rush turned out to be a bust—a discovery of about $200 worth of gold flakes in Cherry Creek, where no more gold has been seen since. Large numbers of gold hunters made their way to Colorado's Front Range chasing exaggerated reports of the find, and many newcomers starved that winter.

But the following May saw the first of a seemingly endless string of fabulous finds in the canyon country along the route of present-day Route 70. Idaho Springs, Central City, Georgetown— boom towns appeared ever deeper in the forbidding mountains. By 1861, two years after the first find, claims had been staked along every foot of Clear Creek's banks, and the goldfields of Colorado were producing 150,000 ounces of gold a year (worth about $60 million today).

The gold rush only lasted for a few years. By the end of the Civil War in 1865, Colorado's gold production was already declining. By 1868, it had dwindled to almost nothing, leaving the miners to scramble after lesser minerals like silver, lead and even coal. In all, the "Pikes Peak or Bust" gold rush produced about one-sixteenth the amount of gold that came from California during the same years.

People had flocked to gold and silver boom towns such as Central City and Leadville, as well as the Front Range towns of Denver and Colorado City (now part of Colorado Springs) in such numbers that Colorado—a region previously inhabited only by Indians and fur traders—was declared a territory in 1862, just three years after the gold rush began, and a state 14 years later on the centennial of the Declaration of Independence, giving rise to the nickname, "the Centennial State."

The years following the Civil War saw the construction of four major railroads. The Santa Fe Railway followed the old Santa Fe Trail through Lamar, La Junta and Trinidad on its way to

THE COLOR OF MONEY

Gold hunters poked into every canyon and creek of the Rocky Mountain labyrinth. Wherever a trace of "color" was found, a gold camp would appear, and if the discovery proved significant enough to become a mine, the camp would instantly become a town complete with shops, saloons, hotels, newspapers and lots of lawyers.

New Mexico Territory. The Colorado Central connected Golden, Colorado, with the transcontinental Union Pacific Railroad at Cheyenne, Wyoming, and soon the Kansas Pacific linked Denver with the Union Pacific. Shorter railroad lines soon linked the main rail arteries to Denver and Colorado City (now part of Colorado Springs), and within a few more years a network of narrow-gauge railroads connected mining towns throughout the mountains. Finally, in the early 1870s, the Denver & Rio Grande began extending service between Denver and the communities of southern Colorado.

At the same time that bison were being exterminated to feed railroad work crews, leaving boundless empty grazing land, the new transportation network made cattle and sheep ranching feasible in the Rockies. Starting in the mid-1870s, vast cattle ranches that measured in the millions of acres were established on the northeastern plains under absentee ownership. These ranches thrived, employing thousands of cowboys and earning their owners bigger profits, in many cases, than the gold mines of Colorado had ever yielded. On some ranches, cattle came to number in the millions—on paper, at least. The unfenced rangeland was so big that actually counting the cattle—let alone rounding them up and branding them—was impossible.

In the 1870s, gold continued to lure prospectors into the mountains, from Leadville to the San Juan Mountains of southwestern Colorado, but once there, most would-be gold hunters found that the real fortunes were being made in silver and more mundane metals such as zinc and lead. Stories were common of newcomers buying fraudulent "salted" gold mines—where small amounts of gold were fired into an exposed wall with a shotgun to falsify assays—only to dig a little farther and find rich silver lodes.

THE DECLINE OF THE OLD WEST   The end of the great ranches came in the brutal winter of 1887–88, when a single blizzard heaped snow higher than cattle's heads and was followed by weeks of record cold temperatures. When the spring thaw came, few cattle could be found alive. Many ranch owners went bankrupt, leaving the former ranches unsupervised. Newcomers rushed in to seize pieces of the abandoned ranches. Many started their own ranches on a more modest scale. Legal title to lands that had been part of bankrupt ranches was vague at best, so violent clashes erupted between cowboys, sheepmen and farmers (known as grangers). The lawlessness was made worse by the fact that some cowboys from the early ranches turned to crime after losing their jobs, forming outlaw bands that lived by armed robbery. Rampant lawlessness continued into the early years of the 20th century. Eventually, when landholders had occupied their ranches and farms long enough to file for legal title under the law of adverse possession, the violence faded.

The mining districts of northern Colorado continued to flourish until 1893, when the U.S. Congress ended silver subsidies, bringing about a collapse in the silver market. Towns that depended mainly on silver mining, such as Aspen and Leadville, were all but abandoned within a few years. Many miners moved to the newfound goldfields of Cripple Creek, site of the West's last major gold boom.

Bob Womack, a cowboy living in a lonely line shack on the west side of Pikes Peak, found the first nuggets of gold in a stream called Cripple Creek on the back side of Pikes Peak in 1879, but it took eleven years for him to convince anyone that his find was genuine. By the time he finally found a backer and proved his gold find, he had become known as "Crazy Bob," and his credibility was so low that he was only able to sell his interest for $500; within the next year, it produced more than $200,000 in gold ore. Womack is memorialized today by the Cripple Creek casino named after him. Between 1890 and 1896, Cripple Creek grew to become—briefly—Colorado's second-largest city.

Still, gold mining was rarely a profitable business. Of nearly 100,000 people who flocked to the Cripple Creek goldfields, 28 became millionaires from their gold claims. Only one was a professional prospector and none were miners; most were shopkeepers, construction workers, lawyers, pharmacists and real estate agents. All made their millions by selling their claims to mining corporations, which rarely recovered as much gold as they paid for the claims.

The main reason mining companies were interested in Colorado gold at all was that it was easy to sell stock in gold mines. The United States was on the Gold Standard in those days, meaning that the nation's economy could only expand as fast as gold was produced. Even a money-losing mine was good for the national economy, inspiring eastern politicians to pour money into gold production. In Cripple Creek, of the 5000 exploratory holes that were dug, 700 became working mines. Yet more than 12,000 mining corporations were selling stock on the (now-defunct) Colorado Springs stock exchange.

Violence became commonplace in the Cripple Creek District as labor union organizers battled against enforcers hired by the mine owners. Dynamite was the weapon of choice, and the outcome of the conflict was inconclusive. The gold mining industry prospered until 1933, when it, too, came to an abrupt end as a change in federal law ruined the market for the precious metal. A lot of old-time Coloradoans believe the legendary gold veins of the Cripple Creek District were a mere offshoot of an immense mother lode hidden deep beneath the Pikes Peak massif. Amateur

and professional geologists have been debating this theory's likelihood for decades, since tunneling beneath the mountain to find
out would be so enormously costly that nobody is likely to actually do it. Even scoffers agree that there is probably more gold
under the hills of Cripple Creek today than the $412,974,848
worth of ore (that's about 1,200,000 ounces of gold, worth something like $5 billion today) mined there between 1890 and 1950.

MODERN TIMES   The introduction of the railroads made it easy
for vacationers to visit Colorado and the Rocky Mountains.
Tourism came to the Pikes Peak and Glenwood Springs areas
around 1885 and to Estes Park around 1900. In those days, however, the West was much more remote than the African veldt or
the Australian outback is today—the exclusive province of adventurers, tycoons and wealthy dilettantes. It was not until the 1920s,
when many Americans bought automobiles and the first main
highways were paved, that tourists began heading for Colorado
in large numbers. Tourism has become central to the economy of
Colorado and has increased steadily for more than a century now.

But as enticing to tourists as the wild, pristine Colorado mountains were already proving to be, other forces were less ecologi-
cally benign. As early as the 1880s, large seams of high-quality
coal had been discovered in Colorado, allowing Coloradoans to
cheaply heat the high-ceilinged houses that came into vogue at
that time and enabling the Rockefeller family to establish Colorado Fuel and Iron, which would become one of the nation's
leading steel producers, in Pueblo. Coal mining grew to become a
huge industry in Colorado—more profitable than gold, and more
destructive to the environment.

In 1933, the United States went off the Gold Standard but
still regulated gold prices at levels too low for profitable mining.
Nearly all gold mines in Colorado shut down. Gold prices were
deregulated in 1976 and instantly jumped from $35 an ounce to
around $400 an ounce. But because of the huge equipment invest-
ments required, few mines have been reopened. Instead, gold companies use high-tech cyanide leeching methods to extract more gold
from old mine and refinery slag heaps. Today, fortune-seekers are
more likely to play the Colorado Lottery (the odds are better) and
mining companies are content to leave most of Colorado's remaining gold in the ground—for now.

Energy booms have swept across 20th-century Colorado with
the frenetic but fleeting quality of earlier gold rushes. In the 1950s,
atomic bombs and the glowing promise of nuclear power made
a previously unheard-of mineral called uranium one of the most
valuable commodities known to humanity. Scattered deposits of
the stuff were found in the Colorado backcountry from Grand
Junction west to Utah and south to the New Mexico state line,
luring a new generation of prospectors driven by fantasies of strik-

ing it rich. Though there was still plenty radioactive ore waiting to be found, rising costs, lower prices and reduced government subsidies brought the collapse of Colorado's uranium industry around 1960.

Tourism got a major boost with the development of Aspen, Vail and a host of other ski resorts that have created a second tourist season in the winter, bringing millions of additional visitors to the state. These winter-season resorts, in turn, began to experiment with other kinds of facilities designed to stimulate the local economy during the roughly seven months of the year when the ski slopes were closed. Conference centers, golf courses and alpine slides popped up in every ski town. Finally, in the early 1980s, a single stunt—an impromptu race up a jeep road and over a mountain pass from Crested Butte to Aspen on battered old bicycles—spawned the mountain bike industry, which has since transformed summer sports in many areas of the Rockies, providing an ideal way to experience the mountain magnificence around many ski resort towns in the summertime.

With the late 1960s and early 1970s, population growth and development came to Colorado's Front Range in a big way, making it one of the fastest-growing areas in the United States. Many surrounding communities doubled in size in a year, then doubled again the next year. With this rampant development came skyrocketing prices for land in the nearby mountains, and soon formerly remote areas were being filled with paved roads, vacation homes and condominiums.

By the time the 1970s Energy Crisis came along, energy-aware prospectors had attracted the notice of major oil companies with a rock called oil shale, so permeated with petroleum that it could actually be set on fire. Huge-scale operations were undertaken in the canyons north of Parachute to prove that oil could be mined in the form of shale as cheaply as drilling for it. But soon the international chess game of petroleum made both oil wells and shale operations in the American West unprofitable, and Parachute, Colorado's last mining boom town, changed overnight into a modern-day ghost town just off the interstate.

Saving the natural landscape from real estate development and other forms of economic exploitation has become a primary concern in Colorado in recent years with some of the nation's strictest environmental laws, including the only statewide ban on clear-cutting in the national forests. The tension between developers and conservationists remains a polarizing reality in Colorado.

FLORA

Altitude makes all the difference when it comes to Colorado plant life. At lower elevations—low in this region meaning a mile or less above sea level—the environment consists of arid prairies with vegetation so sparse that it takes as much as 60 acres to graze a single cow. The reason is that the Rocky Mountains cast a "rain shadow"; as weather patterns move from west to east, clouds dump most of their rain or snow on the high, cool mountains, leaving little moisture to fall on the prairies. The closer the land is to the base of the mountains, the drier it is, with natural vegetation that consists mainly of thin veneers of grass punctuated by prickly pear cactus. In some areas, especially northeastern Colorado, farmers have transformed this seeming wasteland into fields of wheat, sugar beets and other crops made possible by irrigation wells that tap into huge underground aquifers fed by the moisture that falls in the mountains and then seeps into the earth.

The aspen is a delicate tree that cannot tolerate high or low altitude extremes. Attempts to use aspens for landscaping in lower places like Denver and Colorado Springs almost always end in failure.

The foothills along the Front Range are even drier than the prairies, since they are not only in the mountains' rain shadow but also steep enough so that whatever rain does fall quickly spills away like water off a duck's back. The foothills are just high enough, however, so that cooler temperatures let snow melt more slowly, seeping into the top layer of earth to sustain scrub, or small trees that may reach a mature height of only five or six feet. The most common scrub tree in the foothills is Gambel oak (commonly called "scrub" oak), a diminutive cousin of the stately oak trees found in lowland forests of the eastern United States. Other scrub trees include juniper and, in the southern foothills, piñon.

Mountain forests, too, change with elevation, forming three distinct bands. On the lower slopes of the mountains, ponderosa pine stand 50 feet tall and more. Douglas fir and blue spruce dominate the higher reaches of the mountains. Between the two bands of evergreen forest, shimmering stands of aspen trees fill the mountainsides and paint them bright yellow in early October. The aspen, perhaps the most intriguing and distinctive tree in the Colorado Rockies, is what forestry experts call an opportunistic species: stands grow wherever clearings appear in the evergreen woods—usually because of forest fires or pine beetle infestations. Gradually, over a span of centuries, the taller evergreens will crowd out old aspen stands as new stands appear elsewhere.

The upper boundary of the deep green forests of spirelike Douglas fir is known as timberline, the elevation above which temperatures drop below freezing at night year-round and trees can't grow. Timberline is around 10,500 to 11,000 feet in the southern Colorado Rockies and lower the farther north you go. Above timberline lies the alpine tundra, a delicate world of short grasses and other green plants rooted in permafrost where tiny flowers appear for brief moments each summer. At the highest elevations, around 14,000-foot mountain summits, summer freezing prevents even the small plants of the tundra from growing. Up there, clinging to the granite cliffs and boulders, grows lichen, a symbiotic combination of two plants that survive in partnership: a type of moss forms a leathery, sheltering shell that protects an algae, which in turn provides nutrients by photosynthesis to feed the moss. This ingenious arrangement is perhaps the ultimate tribute to life's amazing capacity for adapting to even the harshest environments.

FAUNA   The abundance of wildlife is one of Colorado's greatest attractions. You are most likely to get a good look at large animals in the national parks, where long-standing prohibitions against hunting have helped them lose their fear of humans. The wildlife populations are about the same in national forests, but sightings are much less common because animals generally keep their distance from roads, trails, and any human scent.

The eastern foothills, high plains and mountain parks (not the kind with rangers, but flat grasslands surrounded by mountain ranges) are a favorite habitat of jackrabbits, coyotes and pronghorn antelope, as well as prairie birds such as hawks, grouse and pheasants. Coyotes are abundant in Colorado; they are commonly seen not only in open grasslands but also on the outskirts of urban areas, including the suburbs of Denver. Intelligent and curious, coyotes can often be spotted observing humans from a distance. They are not dangerous to humans, though they may sometimes attack small pets.

Pronghorn antelope, once hunted nearly to extinction and until recently listed as a threatened species under the federal Endangered Species Act, have multiplied to the point that they are now a common sight on the high plains of eastern Colorado and in grassland areas in the northwestern part of the state. Although these tan, black and white deerlike creatures with short legs and large heads are commonly called antelope, they are not related to the true antelope of Africa and Asia. In fact, they are not related to any other living species.

◆◆

THE HIGHER THE PRESSURE, THE BIGGER THE LITTER

Coyote populations are on the increase just about everywhere in the West. Scientists have discovered that as the number of coyotes in an area declines, the number of coyote pups born in a litter increases to compensate; so although states have paid hundreds of thousands of dollars annually for nearly a century to eliminate these wild canines because ranchers believe they may pose a threat to livestock, there are now more coyotes than ever.

American bison, more often called buffalo although they are unrelated to Asian buffalo, once roamed throughout Colorado's eastern prairies and mountain parks. Today they are only found in captive herds, mostly on buffalo ranches, a growing industry along the Front Range.

There are also rattlesnakes in the foothills and high plains. The good news is that they rarely venture into the mountains. Snakes and other reptiles are cold-blooded and cannot function in low temperatures, so they are hardly ever found at elevations above about 7000 feet. When hiking at lower elevations, walk loudly and never put your hand or foot where you can't see it.

Deer, mountain lions and bobcats inhabit the western plateaus and, in lesser numbers, the eastern foothills. While deer may be spotted anywhere in the mountains, they prefer to graze in areas where scrub oak grows. Mountain lions hunt deer and prefer areas with high rocks, where they can spot both dangers and prey a long ways away. Since mountain lions are nocturnal and reclusive, it's a stroke of luck to glimpse one darting across the road in your headlights at night. They have not been known to attack humans in the Colorado Rockies, though several recent incidents in Southern California have proved that they can be dangerous. Wild horses also graze the remote plateaus and mesas of western Colorado.

In mountain forests and meadows, common small mammals include squirrels, chipmunks, raccoons and porcupines. Large animals include elk and black bears. Since elk prefer high mountain meadows in the warm months, they are usually seen in the summer only by serious hikers who venture deep into the wilderness. Sightings are more common in winter, when they descend to lower elevations where grass is easier to reach under the snow. In some areas, usually marked by signs and sometimes observation areas, herds of elk can often be spotted from the road in winter. Moose are rarely found in Colorado.

As for black bears, they are elusive but more common than most hikers realize. In times of drought, when food becomes scarce, it's not unusual for a bear to raid trash cans along the fringes of civilization. Black bears rarely attack people, but they are unpredictable and can be dangerous because of their size. Most injuries involving bears happen because campers store their food inside tents with them at night. When camping in the forest, it's a better idea to leave all food inside a closed vehicle or suspended from a tree limb. Grizzly bears are believed to be extinct, or at least very rare, in Colorado, though several unconfirmed sightings have been reported in the San Juan Mountains. Unconfirmed sightings have provided evidence to support rumors that timber wolves were also reintroduced surreptitiously to the San Juans by radical environmentalists in the 1980s.

Beavers once inhabited virtually every stream in Colorado. Trapped by the millions for their pelts in the early 19th century, these largest of North American rodents once stood on the brink of extinction. In more recent times, they have too often been considered pests because their habit of damming streams to create ponds surrounding their dome-shaped sticks-and-mud lodges floods the most desirable areas of mountain valleys. Landowners persisted for many years in poisoning the beavers or dynamiting their dams and putting up low electric fences to keep them away. Now a protected species in Colorado, beavers seem to be making a slow comeback. It's not unusual to discover beaver ponds on backcountry streams, and if you watch a pond near sunset, you may get a look at the animals themselves.

Above timberline, Rocky Mountain bighorn sheep are common and easy to spot in alpine meadows. Herds of ewes are protected by a single ram, while other males lead a solitary existence elsewhere until mating season, when the high crags echo with the crash of horns as young rams challenge their elders for dominance over the female herd. In areas with vehicle traffic, such as Pikes Peak, Mount Evans and Rocky Mountain National Park's Trail Ridge, the sheep vanished in the 1950s because the rams were so distracted by the noise of cars that they became impotent. New herds were brought from the Collegiate Range in central Colorado, which had become overpopulated with sheep, and they have made a successful comeback, particularly on Pikes Peak. Mountain goats—shaggy, snow-white and solitary, may also be seen in some high mountain areas, especially Rocky Mountain and Glacier National Parks. The smaller animals most commonly seen above timberline are golden marmots, large, chubby rodents nicknamed "whistlepigs" because they communicate with shrill whistles. Smaller rodents called picas colonize high-altitude rockpiles, where swarms of hundreds of them are sometimes seen.

Where to Go

Most visitors from out of state, whether they arrive by car, plane or train, begin their Colorado explorations in **Denver**, the region's largest city and main transportation center. The largest city in Colorado—and, indeed, within 600 miles in any direction—Denver has the biggest museums, the best shopping malls and the most restaurants in the state. Here you'll find such popular attractions as the Denver Art Museum and Elitch Gardens, as well as such lesser known sights as the old-time stagecoach station at Four Mile Historic Park and the Denver Museum of Miniatures, Toys and Dolls.

Chapter Three includes the cities of the **Front Range** and the nearby mountains. Just beyond the Denver metropolitan area you will find towering mountain peaks, old mining towns and plenty of scenery and history. Denver and most other Front Range municipal and county governments have cooperated to set aside vast expanses of mountain parklands, protecting their skylines from both mining exploitation and subdivision development and offering both popular and little-known wilderness getaways within a half-hour's drive of the city. Rocky Mountain National Park, adjoining the town of Estes Park, is the biggest tourist destination in the area. Visitors can also take their pick among dozens of other historic, scenic and entertainment attractions ranging from the old-time gold mines of Idaho Springs to the recently resurrected gambling casinos of Central City and Black Hawk. The region's main features also include the state's largest and liveliest university towns, Boulder and Fort Collins.

Chapter Four takes you through the Eisenhower Tunnel under the Continental Divide and directly into the heart of the mountains, home of such world-class ski resorts as Vail, Breckenridge, Aspen and Steamboat Springs. The scene of the great mid-19th-century gold and silver strikes, **North Central Colorado** is a region steeped in history and change, where within a span of a few generations entire cities of brick buildings and Victorian homes have appeared in the wilderness only to be abandoned as the mineral wealth played out. Travelers who choose to explore beyond the booming resorts of today can explore the historic mining town where such famous Colorado historical figures as Leadville Johnny Brown and Horace Tabor struck it rich. Other adventure options include watching for bighorn sheep on Guanella Pass, mountain biking on the old railroad bed over Boreas Pass, and hiking in the Eagle's Nest Wilderness. More vacationers come to this region of Colorado in winter than in summer. Millions of ski enthusiasts each year pay top dollar for lodging and lift tickets to experience the thrill of plunging thousands of feet down mountain slopes, while others put on cross-country skis to discover budget-priced exhilaration and the natural beauty of winter in the high country. Summer brings off-season bargains at northern Colorado's luxury megaresorts, as most ski areas keep chairlifts running, offering an amazingly easy way to climb mountains.

One of Colorado's fastest-growing tourist areas, Glenwood Springs, invites you to hike or bike on the newly created Glenwood Canyon Trail, then relax in one of the region's largest hot-springs pools. From here Chapter Five works its way down the Colorado River through **Northwestern Colorado** to Grand Junction, the largest city on the western slope of the Colorado Rockies. Along the way, short side trips from the interstate highway lead to some of the least-visited mountain scenery in the state, including the high, cool "islands" in the sky of Grand Mesa and the Flattops. A longer detour takes travelers into the rugged, unpopulated northwestern corner of the state to explore the backcountry of Dinosaur National Monument and Brown's Park.

The **Pikes Peak Region** just west of and including Colorado Springs, explored in Chapter Six, is an old-timer where tourism is concerned. Several sightseeing attractions have been in continuous operation since the end of the 19th century, when Aspen and Durango were forgotten, nearly abandoned mining towns and Vail had not yet been imagined. Tourists have been climbing the peak for more than 120 years. The Royal Gorge has been attracting visitors for nearly as long. In recent times, the face of tourism in the region has been transformed by river rafting on the Arkansas River, the most popular whitewater run in the world, and by the resurrection of the once-abandoned gold mining city of Cripple Creek as a casino gambling mecca. Hidden spots abound in this part of the state, from hot springs and hidden canyons to wild drives on mountain roads that were once narrow-gauge railroad beds.

Pikes Peak is named after the first American explorer to set foot in Colorado.

Chapter Seven covers **South Central Colorado** from Pueblo, Trinidad and the San Luis Valley to Alamosa, Creede and the area around Gunnison and Crested Butte. Although tourism in this part of the state happens on a much smaller scale than in northern Colorado, the Pikes Peak Region or the Durango area, the recreational options this area has to offer are impressive, from such awesome sights as the Great Sand Dunes and the Black Canyon of the Gunnison to scenic steam train trips on the narrow-gauge Cumbres and Toltec Railroad and boating on Colorado's largest lake in Curecanti National Recreation Area. The area around the skiing-and-mountain-biking town of Crested Butte boasts some of the West's most interesting ghost towns.

Southwestern Colorado, a region with a distinctly different character from any other part of Colorado, is the subject of Chapter Eight. The hub of the region is Durango, departure point of the Durango & Silverton Narrow-Gauge Railway, and starting point for driving tours on the San Juan Skyway, one of America's most scenic highway trips. The San Juan Mountains contain several of Colorado's largest and most spectacular wilderness areas, and though they are becoming increasingly well known, the picturesque towns of Silverton, Ouray and Telluride are certainly among Colorado's most "hidden" communities in the geographic sense. Durango is also a good base from which to explore the ancient cliff dwelling ruins at Mesa Verde National Park as well as less-visited sites such as Hovenweep and the Lowry Ruins.

Chapter Nine covers the three major highway routes across the **Eastern Plains**—Route 76, which follows the old Overland Trail along the South Platte River; Route 70, which traces the earliest railroad route straight across the plains; and Route 50, which follows the old Santa Fe Trail along the Arkansas River. This seemingly featureless farm and ranch country covers more than a third of the state, and hardly anybody would consider it as a potential vacation destination. In fact, just about the only way most people see the eastern plains is through a windshield. But the traveler who finds wide open roads thrilling, who takes time to seek out secret glimpses of the past and to appreciate the subtle natural beauty of this magnificent emptiness, will find that the prairie holds a few roadside surprises such as the Living Tree sculptures of Sterling, the County Carousel in Burlington, and the unexplained Celtic-style rock art found at Picture Canyon in the Comanche National Grassland.

When to Go

SEASONS

Though it may sound romantic, springtime in the Colorado Rockies is less than appealing in reality. Cold winds, occasional avalanches, brown vegetation and plenty of mud are a few of the reasons that most Coloradoans in the tourist business shut down their shops and motels in April and take their own vacations in more southerly climes. Just about any other time of year, however, the climate is ideal for one kind of outdoor recreation or another, giving rise to Colorado's distinctive summer-and-winter double tourist season.

The traditional summer tourist season, which runs from Memorial Day to Labor Day, is characterized by cool nights, mild days, colorful wildflowers and sudden, brief afternoon rainstorms. In all mountain areas, it's a good idea to start outdoor activities early and carry ponchos or waterproof tarps on all-day hikes, since rain is almost inevitable in the afternoon. In a common, peculiar phenomenon, wind currents called "waves" can carry precipitation for long distances from clouds hidden behind the mountains, causing "sun showers." Old-timers say that if it rains while the sun is shining, it will rain again tomorrow. This adage almost always holds true—but then, if it doesn't rain in the sunshine, it's still likely to rain tomorrow. The good news is, summer rains rarely last more than one hour, and skies generally clear well before sunset.

Along the Front Range, clouds typically build in the early afternoon and then burst into thunder, lightning, and sometimes hail. In mountain areas west of the Continental Divide, storms tend to be smaller, more scattered, and much more frequent. In the San Juan Mountains of southwestern Colorado, it's not unusual to encounter five or six brief rainstorms in a single day. Above timberline, temperatures fall below freezing at night through the whole summer and typically reach only 40° to 50°F at midday. High mountain roads such as the Pikes Peak Highway, Independence Pass and Rocky Mountain National Park's Trail Ridge Road may be closed by blizzards even in August, sometimes stranding motorists for an hour or two before snowplows clear the road.

Early fall—around the end of September—is one of the most delightful times to visit Colorado, as the turning of the aspens paints the mountainsides in yellow with splashes of orange and red, brilliant against a deep green background of evergreen forests. Mountain highways tend to be crowded with carloads of leaf-gawkers on weekends but not on weekdays, while hiking and biking traffic on forest trails is much lighter than during the summer. The weather is generally dry and cool at this time of year, making it a great time to take a long wilderness hike or mountain bike excursion. The first light snowfall can be expected in the high country around the first week of October and along the Front Range around the third week; the first heavy snow typically comes around Halloween. November is hunting season, a good time to keep out of the mountains unless you're armed and dangerous.

The official ski season in Colorado runs from Thanksgiving through March 15. This is the period for which all ski areas expect a reliable snow base. All ski events and package tours are scheduled within this time period, and if you're planning ahead for a major ski vacation, you'll want to schedule it between these dates, too. In reality, snowfall amounts, as well as winter temperatures in the mountains, can vary a lot from year to year, so the actual dates of operation at various ski areas are somewhat unpredictable. These days, the huge artificial snowmaking capacity of most ski areas almost always assures a Thanksgiving opening day. While snowmaking usually ceases after mid-March when advance-reservation business slows down, skiing continues until spring temperatures rise enough to erode the snow base. In some years, at some ski areas, late-season skiing may continue well into April, and even later in parts of the northern Rockies. Uncrowded ski trails, discount lift tickets and lots of sunshine make this late season a favorite time for many local ski enthusiasts.

CALENDAR OF EVENTS

JANUARY   **Denver**   The National Western Stock Show and Rodeo, the world's largest rodeo, features top-name country-and-western music concerts and a parade through the streets of Denver.

North Central Colorado   Ullrfest in Breckenridge honors the Norse god of snow with a fireworks, torchlight skiing and cross-country ski competitions. Aspen's five-day **Winterskol** features a parade, torchlight skiing, fireworks and skydiving. In Steamboat Springs, the **Cowboy Downhill** pits professional rodeo cowboys against each other in a unique triathlon of skiing, roping and horse racing.

Southwestern Colorado   The events of **Snowdown** are divided between Durango and nearby Purgatory Ski Area; besides ski competitions, they include a chili cook-off and odd events such as a waiter/waitress obstacle race.

Front Range   The city of Loveland observes St. Valentine's Day with the **Sweetheart Sculpture Show**, exhibiting works by local and nationally known sculptors with an emphasis on romance.

North Central Colorado   Fishermen compete for prize money at the **North Park Ice Fishing Contest**. The week-long **Steamboat Springs Winter Carnival** includes ski races, contests and street celebrations.

South Central Colorado   Walsenburg's municipal golf course is the scene of a **Groundhog Brunch** on Groundhog Day.

FEBRUARY

Denver   Denver's **St. Patrick's Day Parade**, the second-largest in the nation, features more than 5000 horses as well as floats and marching bands.

North Central Colorado   Leadville's **Crystal Carnival**, the oldest winter celebration in the West, features ski joring, an activity in which a skier is pulled by a horse and rider along snow-covered Main Street and goes off jumps in the road.

South Central Colorado   The **Monte Vista Crane Festival** celebrates the migration of sandhill and whooping cranes with art shows, naturalist speakers and bus tours of the Rio Grande Wildlife Refuge.

MARCH

Pikes Peak Region   Thousands attend the spectacular **Easter Sunrise Pageant** at Garden of the Gods in Colorado Springs.

South Central Colorado   Crested Butte marks the end of the ski season with **Flauschink**, featuring a parade and a coronation ball.

Eastern Plains   Birdwatchers flock to Wray to witness the **greater prairie chicken courtship dances** that take place on private land (info: 970-332-5063) in the area.

APRIL

Denver   Cinco de Mayo, Mexico's national patriotic celebration, is observed in Denver with fiestas downtown and along Santa Fe Drive.

Front Range   Boulder hosts the **Kinetic Conveyance Sculpture Race**. Later in the month, the **Bolder Boulder 10K Marathon** is the state's largest footrace, with more than 35,000 runners.

Northwestern Colorado   Craig celebrates **Grand Olde West Days** with bluegrass and country music contests and a "wild game and roadkill" cookoff.

Pikes Peak Region   **Territory Days** celebrates the era when Colorado Springs' Old Colorado City Historic District was the territorial capital. **Music and Blossom Festival and Royal Gorge Rodeo** packs Cañon City's Main Street with band performances, parades and a carnival; the rodeo is one of the oldest in Colorado.

MAY

South Central Colorado   Art shows, bluegrass music and samples of cuisine from local restaurants highlight **A Taste of Creede**.
Southwestern Colorado   Durango's **Iron Horse Bicycle Classic**, a grueling three-day series of bike races on roads and trails, draws more than 2000 competitors from around the world. The **Telluride Mountain Film Festival** focuses on mountain and outdoor adventure movies.
Eastern Plains   Rocky Ford celebrates **Cinco de Mayo** with food, street dancing and a mariachi Mass.

JUNE

Denver   Denver's **Capitol Hill People's Fair** showcases the work of more than 550 artists and crafters, along with live music on six stages.
Front Range   Evergreen kicks off the summer rodeo season in Colorado with **Rodeo Weekend**. Fort Collins hosts the **Colorado Brewers' Festival. The Greeley Independence Stampede** fills the two weeks leading up to July 4th with family fun, including foot races, fireworks, parades, street breakfasts and the world's largest Fourth of July rodeo. Weavers and wool producers from around the world meet in Estes Park for the annual **Wool Market**, with contests, exhibits and a livestock show of sheep, llamas and angora rabbits.
North Central Colorado   The three-day **Aspen Food and Wine Classic** features wine tastings, lectures and seminars, along with cooking demonstrations and a dessert extravaganza. Late June marks the start of the **Aspen Music Festival**, the premier music festival in the United States, with opera, jazz, classical and chamber music performances daily for nine weeks. The summer rodeo season kicks off with Steamboat Springs' PRCA **ProRodeo Series** and Walden's **Never Summer Rodeo**.
Northwestern Colorado   Glenwood Springs' **Strawberry Days**, Colorado's oldest town celebration, lasts three days and includes a rodeo, talent show, live entertainment and a parade followed by a street feast of strawberries and cream.
Pikes Peak Region   The high point of Colorado Springs' **Springspree** weekend is a bed race through downtown. Salida's **FIBArk Boat Race** is the oldest, longest and most famous kayak race anywhere; the four-day event also includes raft, foot and bike races, live entertainment and a parade.
South Central Colorado   **Fiesta del Rio** in Pueblo features bluegrass performances on the banks of the Arkansas River. In Trinidad, the **Santa Fe Trail Festival** features historical recreations, live entertainment and a quilt show. Monte Vista's **Sunshine Festival** features an arts and crafts fair, food booths and live entertainment.
Southwestern Colorado   The **Telluride Bluegrass Festival**, the granddaddy of Telluride festivals, fills the town with big-name

musicians and enormous crowds of festival-goers. Later in the month comes the **Telluride Wine Festival**, with formal tastings and connoisseurs' seminars and the **Telluride Theatre Festivals**, featuring new plays, theater arts workshops and seminars. The **Music in Ouray Chamber Concert Series** presents nine days of chamber music. Silverton's **Jubilee Folk Music Festival** focuses on bluegrass and folk music.

Eastern Plains   Fort Morgan sponsors the **Tin Man Triathlon**, a swimming, biking and running competition. Sterling hosts **Hay Days**, extolling the crop's virtues with exhibits, booths and baling demonstrations. Kit Carson, a small town an hour's drive southeast of Limon, hosts a **Mountain Man Rendezvous** with blackpowder shooting contests, tomahawk throws and buckskin-clad storytellers.

JULY

Denver   The **Cherry Creek Arts Festival** showcases nearly 200 Colorado artists and crafters as well as entertainment and cooking demonstrations. Later in the month, the **Denver Black Arts Festival** presents work by African-American artists and crafters.

Front Range   The small mountain town of Empire hosts its annual **Frog Rodeo** (no kidding). The **Greeley Independence Stampede** culminates on July 4th with myriad festivities. The renowned **Central City Opera Festival** begins, with three operas in English presented in rotation through August. Boulder fairly bursts with live cultural performances—the overlapping **Colorado Dance Festival**, **Colorado Music Festival** and **Colorado Shakespeare Festival**.

North Central Colorado   The hills are alive with the sound of music as the National Repertory Orchestry presents **The Breckenridge Music Festival**. Winter Park stages its **American Music Festival**, Aspen opens its six-week **Dance/Aspen Festival** and Vail presents the **Bravo Colorado Music Festival**. The **Carbondale Mountain Fair** features artists and crafters along with live entertainment and kids activities.

Northwestern Colorado   In Grand Junction, **Dinosaur Days** presents a dinosaur parade and paleontology lectures, and the public is invited to help dig for fossils.

Pikes Peak Region   In Colorado Springs, the **Pikes Peak or Bust Rodeo** kicks off with a street breakfast and parade. Woodland Park presents the **Ute Trail Stampede Rodeo & Parade**. Llama races as well as burro races highlight Fairplay's **Burro Days**.

South Central Colorado   **Aerial Weekend** in Crested Butte focuses on hot-air ballooning, hang gliding and skydiving events.

Southwestern Colorado   Silverton's **Kendall Mountain Run** is one of the top mountain running events in the state.

Eastern Plains   Fort Morgan sponsors a three-day **Festival in the Park**.

AUGUST   **Front Range**   Musicians come from all over the United States and Europe to participate in the three-day **Central City Jazz Festival**. Fort Collins' big local festival, **New West Fest**, features food, music, arts and crafts, and contests. Bluegrass, folk and country musicians break out their guitars and banjos for Estes Park's **Rocky Mountain Folks Festival**.

North Central Colorado   Hundreds of fine American wines, as well as cuisine from Colorado's top chefs, are available for sampling at Winter Park's **Rocky Mountain Wine and Food Festival**. Grand Lake is the site of one of the region's most improbable sporting events, the **Daven Haven Downs Turtle Race**. Celebrities flock to Vail for the **Ford Cup Golf Invitational**. Leadville celebrates **Boom Days** with a parade, carnival, street fair, 22-mile burro pack race and mining contests.

Northwestern Colorado   Palisade, near Grand Junction, celebrates the top local crop in the **Palisade Peach Festival** with a big parade.

Pikes Peak Region   Manitou Springs hosts a big bluegrass event, the **Mountain Music Festival**. The **Pikes Peak Or Bust Rodeo** is in Colorado Springs. Buena Vista's **Gold Rush Days & Burro Jamboree** offers burro pack races, outhouse and bed races, gold panning, street dancing and the area's largest rock and gem show.

South Central Colorado   Pueblo is the site of the **Colorado State Fair**. A street celebration, **Noche de Fiesta**, takes place the night before the opening of the fair. In Crested Butte, a five-day **Mountain Man Rendezvous** features period costumes, rough-and-tumble contests and music.

Southwestern Colorado   Telluride events include the **Telluride Chamber Music Festival** and the **Telluride Jazz Celebration**.

Eastern Plains   Colorado's oldest local fair, the **Arkansas Valley Fair**, held in Rocky Ford, features a Chicano fiesta and a watermelon feast.

SEPTEMBER   **Denver**   The **Festival of Mountain and Plain** marks the end of summer with food and entertainment.

Front Range   Golden celebrates **Goldenfest** in mid-September. Estes Park hosts a **Scottish-Irish Highland Festival** complete with bagpipes, dancing and traditional Celtic contests.

North Central Colorado   Oktoberfest livens up the Vail Valley with food, entertainment and children's activities. Steamboat Springs hosts the **Steamboat Vintage Auto Race and Concours d'Elegance** on Labor Day weekend.

Northwestern Colorado   Glenwood Springs' **Fall Arts Festival** has separate competitions for amateur and professional artists. Meeker hosts the **National Border Collie Finals**, America's top sheepdog competition.

Pikes Peak Region The Colorado Springs Hot-Air Balloon Classic, featuring more than 100 balloons, is the largest such event in Colorado.

South Central Colorado Crested Butte celebrates **Vinotok**, an Eastern European fall festival, with storytelling, polka dancing and a feast of traditional Slavic foods.

Southwestern Colorado Twenty-one southwestern Colorado communities join together to stage the spectacular **Colorfest**, with more than 70 special events plus hikes, jeep trips and auto tours to see the fall colors. The **Airmen's Rendezvous** is the world's largest and most spectacular hang gliding event. Also here is the **Telluride Film Festival**.

Eastern Plains Burlington holds an **Outback Hoedown** with food and western entertainment on Labor Day weekend. Limon holds its annual **James Dean Daze & Classic Car Show**. La Junta's **Early Settler's Day Celebration** features arts and crafts booths and street dancing. Sterling hosts an arts and crafts fair for **Sugar Beet Days**.

Denver The three-day **Colorado Performing Arts Festival** in Denver presents free music, dance and theater events. Later in the month, the city hosts the **Denver International Film Festival** and the **Great American Beer Festival**.

OCTOBER

Northwestern Colorado A farmers market, parade, live entertainment and an outdoor meat-and-potatoes feast are highlights of Carbondale's annual community festival, **Potato Day**. Cedaredge, a small fruit-growing town north of Montrose and Delta, celebrates the harvest with **Applefest**.

Southwestern Colorado Ouray hosts a lively **Oktoberfest**. The **Western Arts, Film and Cowboy Poetry Gathering** takes place in Durango.

Eastern Plains Haxtun, a small town east of Sterling, holds its annual **Corn Festival**, featuring a parade, crafts show, races and an ice cream social.

Denver Beginning around Thanksgiving and lasting through the National Western Stock Show in January, downtown Denver's city and county buildings are festooned with the World's Largest Christmas Lighting Display for **Winterfest**.

NOVEMBER

Front Range A standout among the Christmas lighting ceremonies on Thanksgiving weekend is Estes Park's **Catch the Glow**, which includes a parade.

North Central Colorado Georgetown has a **Christmas Tree Lighting** on Thanksgiving weekend.

Pikes Peak Region Victorian Christmas at Miramont Castle opens in Manitou Springs to run through Christmas.

South Central Colorado   Creede celebrates self-indulgence with its annual **Chocolate Festival**. Pueblo has a nighttime **Christmas Parade of Lights**, as well as a traditional Mexican-style **Las Posadas** procession.

DECEMBER   **Denver**   Winterfest continues in December with the **Larimer Square Christmas Walk**, re-creating the ambience of a traditional Victorian Christmas, and the downtown **Parade of Lights**, an illuminated nighttime parade with floats and marching bands.

North Central Colorado   Georgetown's **Christmas Market** features food, horse-drawn carriage rides and a Santa Lucia processional. Leadville sponsors an all-day **Victorian Christmas Home Tour** complete with an elegant brunch and a candlelight dinner.

Southwestern Colorado   In Silverton, local children and visitors are invited to take part in a traditional **Yule Log Festival**.

Eastern Plains   Burlington observes the holiday season with **Christmas in the Hayloft at Old Town**. Near La Junta, Bent's Old Fort re-enacts **Christmas 1846**.

▼▼▼▼▼▼▼▼▼▼▼▼
Before You Go

VISITORS CENTERS

For free visitor information packages including maps and current details on special events, accommodations and camping, contact the **Colorado Tourism Board**. ~ 1625 Broadway, Suite 1700, Denver, CO 80202; 800-433-2656. The state operates Welcome Centers that provide tourist information at major points of entry including Burlington, Lamar, Dinosaur, Trinidad, Fruita and Cortez. State and local tourist information centers are usually not open on weekends.

PACKING

The old adage that you should take along twice as much money and half as much stuff as you think you'll need is sound advice as far as it goes. Bear in mind, though, that even in the more remote reaches of Colorado you might come across a store selling something more substantial than beef jerky and country-and-western cassettes . . . well . . . every once in a while.

Westerners are casual in their dress and expect the same of visitors. Once you leave the Denver metropolitan area, restaurants with dress codes are few and far between, though major resort towns such as Vail and Aspen cater to such upmarket vacationers that you might want to wear sport clothes a little more chic than a plaid flannel shirt and old Levis. Then again, you might not. They'll never know if you might be an eccentric billionaire. These two ski areas in particular seem to fancy themselves the Paris and Rome of winter sportswear; otherwise, hardly anybody comes to the Rocky Mountains to show off their clothes.

When packing clothes, plan to dress in layers. Colorado's temperatures can turn hot or cold in a flash. During the course of a single summer vacation day in the mountains, you can expect to start wearing a heavy jacket, a sweater or flannel shirt and a pair of jeans, peeling down to a T-shirt and shorts as the day warms up, then putting the extra layers back on as the late afternoon shadows set in.

Other essentials to pack or buy along the way include a good sunscreen and high-quality sunglasses. Cool temperatures often lull newcomers into forgetting that thin high-altitude air filters out far less of the sun's ultraviolet rays; above timberline, exposed skin will get sunburned faster than it would on a Florida beach. If you are planning to camp in the mountains during the summer months, you'll be glad you brought mosquito repellent. Umbrellas are considered an oddity. You'll hardly ever see one, and you'll get funny looks from the locals if you carry one. The approved means of keeping chilly afternoon rain from running down the back of your neck is a cowboy hat.

For outdoor activities, tough-soled hiking boots are more comfortable than running shoes on rocky terrain. Even RV travelers and those who prefer to spend most nights in motels may want to take along a backpacking tent and sleeping bag for irresistible urges to stay out under Colorado's star-spangled skies. A canteen, first-aid kit, flashlight and other routine camping gear are also likely to come in handy. Both cross-country and downhill ski rentals are available everywhere you look during the winter, though serious skiers may find that the quality and condition of rental skis leaves something to be desired. In the summer, mountain bikes can be rented in just about any small town in the Colorado Rockies, but bike rentals are much harder to come by in other areas, so cycling enthusiasts who plan to explore the eastern plains or the northwest quadrant of the state should bring their own bikes. Other outdoor recreation equipment—a kayak, fishing tackle, golf clubs or a gold pan—generally cannot be rented, so you'll want to bring the right gear for your special sporting passion.

A camera is essential for capturing your travel experience; of equal importance is a good pair of binoculars, which let you explore distant landscapes from scenic overlooks and bring wildlife up close. And don't, for heaven's sake, forget your copy of *Hidden Colorado*.

LODGING

Lodgings in Colorado run the gamut from tiny one-room cabins to luxury hotels that blend traditional alpine lodge ambience with contemporary elegance. Bed and breakfasts can be found in almost all Colorado mountain towns you're likely to visit—not only chic destinations like Aspen and Telluride but also such off-the-beaten-path places as Sterling and Creede. They come in all types, sizes and price ranges. Typical of the genre are lovingly restored Victorian-era mansions comfortably furnished with period decor, usually with fewer than a dozen rooms. Some bed and breakfasts, however, are guest cottages or rooms in nice suburban homes, while others are larger establishments, approaching hotel size, of the type sometimes referred to as country inns.

In many parts of Colorado, you'll find lavishly restored historic hotels that date back to the gold boom days of the late 19th century. Many of these places combine affordable rates with plenty of antique decor and authentic personality.

The abundance of motels in towns along all major highway routes presents a range of choices, from name-brand motor inns to traditional mom-and-pop establishments that have endured for the more than half a century since motels were invented. While rather ordinary motels in the vicinity of major tourist destinations can be pricey, lodging in small towns away from major resorts and interstate routes can offer friendliness, quiet and comfort at ridiculously affordable rates.

At the other end of the price spectrum, peak season rates at leading ski resorts can be phenomenally high. Ways to skirt this problem include staying in more affordable lodging as much as an hour away and commuting in to the ski slopes during the day, or planning your ski vacation at the beginning or end of the season when rates are somewhat lower. Even though summer is a lively time in many ski towns, there is such a surplus of accommodations that room rates during the summer months are often a small fraction of winter rates.

Whatever your preference and budget, you can probably find something to suit your taste with the help of this book. Remember, rooms can be scarce and prices may rise during peak season, which is summer throughout most of the region and winter in ski resorts. Travelers planning to visit a place in peak season should

HOME ON THE RANCH

A vacation option can be found at guest ranches throughout the mountain areas of the state. Horseback riding is the common theme of all these ranches. Some offer luxury lodging, spa facilities and a full range of activities that may include fishing, boating, swimming and even tennis. Others operate as working ranches, provide lodging in comfortably rustic cabins and offer the opportunity to participate in roundups and other ranching activities. Rates at most guest ranches are comparatively expensive but include all meals and use of recreational facilities. Most guest ranches have minimum stay requirements ranging from three days to a week.

either make advance reservations or arrive early in the day, before the "No Vacancy" signs start lighting up.

Accommodations in this book are organized by region and classified according to price. Rates referred to are summer high-season rates; in ski resorts where rooms cost significantly more in winter than in summer, ranges are given for both seasons. If you're looking for off-season bargains, it's good to inquire. *Budget* lodgings generally run less than $50 per night for two people and are satisfactory and clean but modest. *Moderate* hotels range from $50 to $90; what they have to offer in the way of luxury will depend on where they are located, but they generally offer larger rooms and more attractive surroundings. At *deluxe*-priced accommodations, you can expect to spend between $90 and $130 for a homey bed and breakfast or a double in a hotel or resort. In hotels of this price you'll generally find spacious rooms, a fashionable lobby, a restaurant and often a bar or nightclub. *Ultra-deluxe* facilities, priced above $130, are the finest in the region, offering all the amenities of a deluxe hotel plus plenty of extras.

Room rates vary as much with locale as with quality. Some of the trendier destinations have no rooms at all in the budget price range. In other communities—those where rates are set with truck drivers in mind and those in out-of-the-way small towns—every motel falls into the budget category, even though accommodations may range from $19.95 at run-down, spartan places to $45 or so at the classiest motor inn in town. The price categories listed in this book are relative, designed to show you where to get the most out of your travel budget, however large or small it may be.

DINING

Fine dining in most Colorado towns tends to focus on the region's traditional cuisine—beef and trout. You can also count on finding Mexican restaurants in just about every town you come to. More unusual cuisine is to be found in the major resort areas, such as Aspen and Vail, for restaurant business is fierce. There you'll find menus featuring everything from duck *à l'orange* to grilled elk. In Denver and some other areas of Colorado, buffalo meat is emerging as a specialty thanks to a growing number of ranches that have turned to raising this tasty, lean, low-cholesterol alternative to beef. If your idea of an ideal vacation includes savoring epicurean delights, then by all means seize opportunities whenever they arise. When traveling in the Colorado Rockies, you can go for days between gourmet meals.

Within a particular chapter, restaurants are categorized by region, with each restaurant entry describing the establishment according to price. Dinner entrées at *budget* restaurants usually cost $8 or less. The ambience is informal, service usually speedy and the crowd often a local one. *Moderate*-priced restaurants range between $8 and $16 at dinner; surroundings are casual but pleasant, the menu offers more variety and the pace is usually slower. *Deluxe* establishments tab their entrées from $16 to $24; cuisines may be simple or sophisticated, depending on the location, but the decor is plusher and the service more personalized. *Ultra-deluxe* dining rooms, where entrées begin at $24, are often the gourmet places; here cooking has become a fine art and the service should be impeccable.

Some restaurants change hands often and are occasionally closed in low seasons. Efforts have been made in this book to include places with established reputations for good eating. Breakfast and lunch menus vary less in price from restaurant to restaurant than evening dinners.

DRIVING   Some first-time visitors to Colorado wonder why so many mountain roads do not have guard rails to separate motorists from thousand-foot drop-offs. The fact is, highway safety studies have found that far fewer accidents occur where there are no guard rails. Statistically, edgy, winding mountain roads are much safer than straight, fast interstate highways. Unpaved roads are another story. While many are wide and well-graded, weather conditions or the wear and tear of heavy seasonal use can create unexpected road hazards. Some National Forest Service and Bureau of Land Management roads are designated for four-wheel-drive or high-clearance vehicles only. If you see a sign indicating four-wheel drive only, believe it. These roads can be very dangerous in a standard passenger car without the high ground clearance and extra traction afforded by four-wheel drive—and there may be no safe place to turn around if you get stuck.

Some side roads will take you far from civilization, so be sure to have a full radiator and tank of gas. Carry spare fuel, water and food. Should you become stuck, local people are usually helpful about offering assistance to stranded vehicles, but in case no one else is around, for extended backcountry driving a CB radio or a car phone would not be a bad idea.

If your car does not seem to run well at high elevations, the solution is probably to have the carburetor adjusted at the next service station. The air at Rocky Mountain altitudes is "thin"— that is, it contains considerably less oxygen in a given volume than air at lower altitudes. The carburetor or fuel injection unit should be set leaner to achieve an efficient fuel-to-air mixture. Another common problem when climbing mountain passes is vapor lock, a condition in which low atmospheric pressure combined with high engine temperatures causes gasoline to evaporate in the fuel lines, making bubbles that prevent the fuel pump from functioning. The result is that your car's engine coughs and soon stops dead. The solution is to pull over to the side of the road and wait until the fuel system cools down. A damp rag held against the fuel line will speed up the process and get you back on the road more quickly.

The most serious hazard of mountain driving is brake failure. Drivers of motor homes and heavily loaded trucks must be constantly alert to this risk, which is why mountain passes have "Trucks Use Lower Gear" signs—and runaway truck ramps. It can happen in a passenger car, too, if the driver "rides" the brakes while going down a steep mountain road. With heat buildup from friction, brakes quickly "fade" and lose their stopping power. To avoid this, descend steep grades in a lower gear and keep your foot away from the brake pedal. When you do brake, as for a switchback curve, bring the car's speed way down quickly and let it start picking up momentum as you begin the turn, minimizing the time your foot is on the brake pedal. If the brakes start feeling questionable or you smell a strange odor, pull over and feel the temperature inside one of the wheels. Hot brakes? Let them cool down before proceeding.

TRAVELING WITH CHILDREN

Any place that has wild animals, cowboys, rocks to climb and limitless room to run is bound to be a hit with youngsters. Plenty of family adventures are available in Colorado, from manmade attractions to experiences in the wilderness. A few guidelines will help make travel with children a pleasure.

Book reservations in advance, making sure that the places you stay accept children. Many bed and breakfasts do not. If you need a crib or extra cot, arrange for it ahead of time. A travel agent can be of help here, as well as with most other travel plans.

If you are traveling by air, try to reserve bulkhead seats where there is plenty of room. Take along extras you may need such as diapers, changes of clothing, snacks and toys or small games. When traveling by car, be sure to take along the extras, too. Make

WHEN IT SNOWS

In the winter months, mountain passes frequently become snowpacked, and under these conditions tire chains are required by law in Colorado, even on main highways. The chain law goes into effect regularly on Route 70 west of Denver. State patrolmen will make you turn back if your car is not equipped with chains, so make sure you have them. In winter it is also wise to travel with a shovel and blankets in your car.

sure you have plenty of water and juices to drink; dehydration can be a subtle but serious problem. Most towns have all-night convenience stores that carry diapers, baby food, snacks and other essentials; national parks and some state parks also have such stores, though they usually close early.

A first-aid kit is a must for any trip. Along with adhesive bandages, antiseptic cream and something to stop itching, include any medicines your pediatrician might recommend to treat allergies, colds, diarrhea or any chronic problems your child may have. Mountain sunshine is intense, so take extra care. Children's skin is usually more tender than adult skin, and severe sunburn can happen before you realize. A hat is a good idea, along with a reliable sunblock.

Many national parks and monuments offer special activities designed just for children. Visitor center film presentations and rangers' campfire slide shows can help inform children about the natural history of an area and head off some questions. Still, kids tend to find a lot more things to wonder about than adults have answers for. To be as prepared as possible, seize every opportunity to learn more—particularly about wildlife, a constant curiosity for young minds.

TRAVELING WITH PETS

Colorado is big dog country, and you'll probably notice more travelers accompanied by their pets than in other regions. Pets are permitted on leashes in virtually all campgrounds. Most bed and breakfasts and guest ranches will not accept them, and more run-of-the-mill motels, particularly in Colorado tourist areas, seem to be adopting No Pets policies each year. Otherwise, the main limitation of traveling with a canine companion is that national parks and monuments prohibit pets on trails or in the backcountry. You are supposed to walk your dog on the roadside, then leave him in the car while you hike in the woods. Make sure the poor creature has adequate ventilation and water. Fortunately, dogs are free to run everywhere in national forests, and leashes are only required in designated camping and picnic areas.

Wildlife can pose special hazards for pets in the backcountry. At lower elevations in the plains and foothills, campers should not leave a cat or small dog outside at night because coyotes sometimes attack small pets. In remote forest areas, it's especially important to keep an eye on your dog at all times. Bears are upset by dogs barking at them and may attack even very large dogs. Porcupines, common in pine forests, are tempting to chase and slow enough to be easy to catch; if your dog *does* catch one, a mouthful of quills means painfully pulling them out one by one with a pair of pliers or making an emergency visit to a veterinary clinic in the nearest town.

In the greater Denver and Colorado Springs areas, the incidence of crimes against women is substantially the same as in other middle American cities of comparable size. Sexual assaults are rare but not unheard of in less populated parts of the state, including ski towns, gambling towns, wilderness areas and national parks.

WOMEN TRAVELING ALONE

Hitchhiking—or picking up hitchhikers—can be hazardous to one's personal safety on all Colorado highways and back roads. Personal security is one reason, though not among the most compelling ones, to avoid hiking or camping alone in remote areas. Unless your goal is absolute solitude—with its risks as well as its rewards—as a single traveler you can feel safer by sticking to larger established campgrounds and well-used trails. If you are hassled or threatened in some way, never be reluctant to scream for assistance.

It's a good idea to carry change for a phone call. Many Colorado organizations provide 24-hour help in case of emergency. In metro Denver there's **Comitis Crisis Center**. ~ Aurora; 303-343-9890. Other help lines include the **Rape Crisis Team of Boulder** (303-442-7300); **Fort Collins Helpline** (970-586-5050); and the **Durango Rape Intervention Team** (970-247-5400). When in doubt, dial 911 anywhere in the state.

Colorado achieved national notoriety in 1994 when it became the first state to pass an anti-gay rights law forbidding municipalities from enacting ordinances to protect gay and lesbian individuals from discrimination. The state supreme court ruled the new law unconstitutional, but not before public outrage resulted in a devastating tourist boycott. Today, Colorado's gay-unfriendly image lingers on.

GAY & LESBIAN TRAVELERS

Every story has two sides. Orchestrated by conservative religious groups, the anti-gay rights referendum was a backlash to the fact that several towns, including Boulder and Aspen, had just been among the first to pass progressive ordinances *protecting* gay and lesbian civil rights. These gay-rights ordinances, and others passed in other cities and towns since the referendum, remain in full force today, protecting against discrimination in employment and housing—including travelers' lodging.

In general, gay and lesbian travelers will find open, multilayered alternative communities in major cities, including Denver, Boulder and Colorado Springs, and friendly attitudes in most resort towns. Bigotry is not dead in this part of the Wild West, though, and if you find yourself surrounded by people wearing cowboy hats, "don't tell" is still the safest policy.

Leading gay and lesbian periodicals in Colorado are the biweekly **Out Front** (244 Washington Street, Denver, CO 80203; 303-778-7900) and the monthly **Quest** (430 South Broadway, Denver, CO 80209; 303-722-5965).

SENIOR TRAVELERS Colorado is a hospitable place for older vacationers, many of whom migrate from hotter climates to enjoy the cool summers. National parks and monuments invite persons age 62 and older to save considerable money with a Golden Age Passport, which allows free admission. Apply for one in person at any national park unit that charges an entrance fee. The passports are also good for a 50 percent discount on fees at most national forest campgrounds. Many private sightseeing attractions also offer significant discounts for seniors.

The **American Association of Retired Persons** (AARP) offers membership to anyone over 50. AARP's benefits include travel discounts with a number of firms. ~ 3200 East Carson Street, Lakewood, CA 90712; 562-496-2277.

Elderhostel offers educational courses that are all-inclusive packages at colleges and universities. In Colorado, Elderhostel courses are available in numerous locations including Boulder, Gunnison and Durango. ~ 75 Federal Street, Boston, MA 02110; 617-426-7788.

Be extra careful about health matters. High altitude is the biggest risk factor. Since many driving routes through the Colorado Rockies involve crossing mountain passes at 10,000 to 12,000 feet above sea level, it's advisable to ask your physician first. People with heart problems are commonly advised to avoid all physical exertion above 10,000 feet, and those with respiratory conditions such as emphysema may not be able to visit high altitudes at all. In the changeable climate of the Rockies, seniors are more at risk of suffering hypothermia. Many tourist destinations in the region are a long way from any hospital or other health care facility.

In addition to the medications you ordinarily use, it's a good idea to bring along the prescriptions for obtaining more. Consider carrying a copy of your medical record with you, including your history and current medical status as well as your doctor's name, phone number and address. Make sure that your insurance covers you while you are away from home.

DISABLED TRAVELERS Colorado strives to make public areas fully accessible to persons with disabilities. Parking spaces and restroom facilities for the physically challenged are provided according to both state law and national park regulations. National parks and monuments also post signs that tell which trails are wheelchair-accessible. Some recreation areas have Braille nature trails with marked points of interest appealing to the senses of touch and smell.

Golden Access Passports, good for free entry to all national parks and monuments as well as discounts at most federal public campgrounds, are available at no charge to persons who are blind or who have another permanent disability. Apply in person at any national park or monument that charges an entrance fee.

Information sources for travelers with disabilities include: the **Society for the Advancement of Travel for the Handicapped** ~ 347 5th Avenue, Suite 610, New York, NY 10016; 212-447-7284; the **Travel Information Center** ~ 215-456-9600; and **Mobility International USA** ~ P.O. Box 10767, Eugene, OR 97440; 541-343-1284. For general travel advice, contact **Travelin' Talk**, a networking organization. ~ P.O. Box 3534, Clarksville, TN 37043; 615-552-6670.

FOREIGN TRAVELERS

Passports and Visas   Most foreign visitors, other than Canadian citizens, need a passport and tourist visa to enter the United States. Contact your nearest U.S. Embassy or Consulate well in advance to obtain a visa and to check on any other entry requirements.

Customs Requirements   Foreign travelers are allowed to carry in the following: 200 cigarettes (1 carton), 50 cigars, or 2 kilograms (4.4 pounds) of smoking tobacco; one liter of alcohol for personal use only (you must be 21 years of age to bring in alcohol); and US$100 worth of duty-free gifts that can include an additional quantity of 100 cigars. You may bring in any amount of currency, but must fill out a form if you bring in over US$10,000. Carry any prescription drugs in clearly marked containers. (You may have to produce a written prescription or doctor's statement for the custom's officer.) Meat or meat products, seeds, plants, fruits and narcotics are not allowed to be brought into the United States. Contact the **United States Customs Service** for further information. ~ 1301 Constitution Avenue NW, Washington, DC 20229; 202-927-6724.

Driving   If you plan to rent a car, obtain an international driver's license before arriving in the United States. Some car rental agencies require both a foreign license and an international driver's license. Virtually all require a lessee to be at least 25 years of age and to present a major credit card. Seat belts are mandatory for the driver and all passengers. Children under the age of five or under 40 pounds should be in the back seat in approved child-safety restraints.

Currency   United States money is based on the dollar. Bills generally come in denominations of $1, $5, $10, $20, $50 and $100. Every dollar is divided into 100 cents. Coins are the penny (1 cent), nickel (5 cents), dime (10 cents) and quarter (25 cents). Half-dollar and dollar coins exist but are rarely used. You may not use foreign currency to purchase goods and services in the United States. Consider buying travelers checks in dollar amounts. You may also use credit cards affiliated with an American company such as Interbank, Barclay Card, Visa and American Express.

Electricity and Electronics   Electric outlets use currents of 110 volts, 60 cycles. For appliances made for other electrical systems, you need a transformer or other adapter. Travelers who use laptop computers for telecommunication should be aware that modem configurations for U.S. telephone systems may be different than their European counterparts. Similarly, the U.S. format for videotapes is different than in Europe; National Park Service visitor centers and other stores that sell souvenir videos often have them available in European format on request.

Weights and Measures   The United States uses the English system of weights and measures. American units and their metric equivalents are: 1 inch = 2.5 centimeters; 1 foot (12 inches) = 0.3 meter; 1 yard (3 feet) = 0.9 meter; 1 mile (5280 feet) = 1.6 kilometers; 1 ounce = 28 grams; 1 pound (16 ounces) = 0.45 kilogram; 1 quart (liquid) = 0.9 liter.

▼▼▼▼▼▼▼▼▼▼▼▼▼▼
Outdoor Adventures

CAMPING

RV or tent camping is a great way to tour Colorado during the summer months. Besides saving substantial sums of money, campers enjoy the freedom to watch sunsets from beautiful places, spend nights under spectacularly starry skies and wake up to find themselves in lovely surroundings that few hotels can match.

Most towns have commercial RV parks of some sort, and long-term mobile home parks often rent spaces to RVers by the night. But unless you absolutely need cable television, none of these places can compete with the wide array of public campgrounds available in national and state parks, monuments and forests. Federal campground sites are typically less developed: you won't find electric, water or sewer hookups in national forest, national monument or national recreation area campgrounds. As for national parks, the campground at Mesa Verde has some sites with full hookups, but Rocky Mountain National Park, with five large campgrounds totaling almost 600 sites, has no hookups. In Colorado, only a few state park campgrounds at major recreation lakes near cities have hookups; most do not. The largest public campgrounds, such as those in national parks, offer tent camping loops separate from RV loops, as well as hike-in backcountry camping by permit.

You won't find much in the way of sophisticated reservation systems in Colorado. In July and August, the largest campgrounds in Rocky Mountain National Park require reservations call 800-365-2267; credit card required. State park campgrounds accept reservations and are usually full on weekends but nearly empty on weekdays. Otherwise, the general rule in public campgrounds is still first-come, first-served, even though they fill up practically every night in peak season. For campers, this means traveling in the morning and reaching your intended campground by early afternoon. In many areas, campers may find it more convenient to keep a single location for as much as a week and explore surrounding areas on day trips. In a few resort areas where housing

Secrets of Wildlife Watching

Most of us are probably city dwellers who rarely encounter wildlife more exotic than park pigeons in our everyday lives. One of the things that makes a trip on Colorado's back roads and trails so special is the chance it provides to see abundant—and often large—wild animals in a variety of habitat.

The state has no less than nine distinct life zones, each shaped by altitude and water availability, and each with its own set of animal inhabitants. A drive of just a few hours can take you through most of these zones—from riparian wetlands with white-tailed deer and beaver, up into the subalpine forest domain of elk and black bears, then higher yet to alpine tundra where mountain goats and bighorn sheep roam free, then down into the semidesert shrublands of the western slope where coyotes and pronghorn antelope are common sights.

Hidden Colorado contains dozens of tips for particularly good places to watch wildlife. Spotting large mammals is easiest in state parks and national parks and monuments, because game species possess an uncanny sense of where they are safe from human hunters. Fall hunting is permitted in the national forests, including in designated wilderness areas, so forest inhabitants such as deer and bears usually avoid encounters with humans.

The National Forest Service has set up viewing stations in some areas where there is an exceptional likelihood of seeing elk, pronghorn antelope, bighorn sheep, and even moose. State and federal governments have also set aside wetland reserves for migrating birds, and many of these provide havens for deer and other animals. In backcountry areas, the best places to look for wildlife are in open meadows with streams or lakes. Campgrounds, too, attract deer, raccoons and other animals who forage for food there. Avoid feeding deer, who have lost their natural fear of humans. Human food quickly impairs their ability to digest the leaves and bark that are their natural food, leaving many deer to starve to death during the off-season in tourist areas.

The best time for wildlife viewing is the first hour after sunrise and the last hour before sunset. Armed with binoculars or a telephoto camera lens, sit quietly, motionlessly and, above all, patiently. Animals notice sudden movements the most, and often pay no attention to motionless objects. A car can provide an effective blind, concealing sounds, scents or small movements that could alarm wildlife.

is very expensive, particularly Aspen, don't expect to find a campsite no matter how early in the day you arrive; students working seasonal jobs and other long-term visitors monopolize the public campgrounds all summer, trading locations every two weeks to avoid maximum-stay limitations.

For a listing of state parks with camping facilities and reservation information, contact **Colorado State Parks.** ~ 1313 Sherman Street, Room 618, Denver, CO 80203; 303-866-3437. Information on camping in the national forests is available from **National Forest Service—Rocky Mountain Region.** ~ P.O. Box 25127, Lakewood, CO 80225; 303-236-9431. Camping information for national parks and monuments is available from **National Park Service—Rocky Mountain Regional Headquarters.** ~ P.O. Box 25287, Denver, CO 80225; 303-969-2000. A list of private campgrounds is available from the **Colorado Association of Campgrounds, Cabins & Lodges.** ~ 501 Pennsylvania Avenue, Boulder, CO 80303; 303-499-9343.

PERMITS   Colorado has well over two million acres in federally designated wilderness areas, most of which have been created quite recently. When the U.S. Congress passed the original Wilderness Act in 1964, only five areas in the state—La Garita, Mount Zirkel, Maroon Bells–Snowmass, Rawah and West Elk—were granted federal wilderness protection. They totaled less than 300,000 acres. Since then, wilderness protection has been expanded by the Colorado Wilderness Act of 1980, which set aside an additional 1.4 million acres, and the Wilderness Act of 1993, which extended wilderness protection to another 600,000 acres in the state. Today, Colorado boasts 33 designated wilderness areas, several of which are so new that they do not yet appear on most maps. Another 500,000 acres in 15 wilderness study areas enjoy temporary protection pending evaluation as future wilderness areas.

To be considered for federal wilderness protection, an area must consist of at least five contiguous square miles of public land without a road of any kind. Once it has been declared a wilderness area, its use is limited to uses that existed as of that date. Since most wilderness areas in the Rockies were created quite recently it is generally the highest peaks, where roads are few and far between, that qualify for wilderness status. Besides protecting ancient forests from timber cutting by newly developed methods like skylining or helicopter airlifting, the main significance of federal wilderness designation is that it prohibits all mechanized transportation—no jeeps, motorcycles or all-terrain vehicles and, after years of heated controversy, no mountain bikes. Wilderness areas usually have well-developed trail networks for hiking, cross-country skiing, and pack trips using horses or llamas.

You no longer need a permit to hike or camp in national forest or BLM wilderness areas, but plan to stop at a ranger station anyway for trail maps and advice on current conditions and fire regulations. Tent camping is allowed without restriction in wilderness areas and most other backcountry areas of national forests, except where signs are posted prohibiting it. Throughout the national forest in dry season and in certain wilderness areas at all times, regulations may prohibit campfires and sometimes ban cigarette smoking, with stiff enforcement penalties.

The Arkansas River is the most-used whitewater recreation river in the United States.

For backcountry hiking in most national parks and monuments, you must first obtain a permit from the ranger at the front desk in the visitor center. The permit procedure is simple and free. It helps park administrators measure the impact on sensitive ecosystems and distribute use evenly among major trails to prevent overuse.

BOATING

Many large manmade lakes in Colorado are administered as state parks, while others are National Recreation Areas supervised by the U.S. Army Corps of Engineers. Federal boating safety regulations may vary slightly from state regulations. Indian reservations have separate rules for boating on tribal lakes. More significant than any differences between federal, state and tribal regulations are the local rules in force for any particular lake, which are posted near boat ramps. Ask for applicable boating regulations at a local marina or fishing supply store or use the addresses and phone numbers listed in "Parks" or other sections of each chapter in this book to contact the headquarters for lakes where you plan to use a boat.

Boats, from small motorized skiffs to big, fast bass boats and sometimes even houseboats, can be rented by the half-day, 24-hour day or longer at marinas on many of the larger lakes. At most marinas, you can get a boat on short notice if you come on a weekday, since much of their business comes from local weekend recreation.

River rafting is a very popular sport in many parts of Colorado, notably the Arkansas River between Salida and Cañon City; the Roaring Fork River between Aspen and Glenwood Springs; and, for week-long backcountry float trips, the Yampa River in Dinosaur National Monument. Independent rafters are welcome, but because of the bulky equipment and specialized knowledge of river hazards involved, most adventurous souls stick with group tours offered by many rafting companies throughout the region. Rafters, as well as people using canoes, kayaks, sailboards or inner tubes, are required by state and federal regulations to wear life jackets.

FISHING   Colorado boasts 7000 miles of streams and more than 2100 lakes. The more accessible a shoreline is, the more anglers you're likely to find there, especially during the summer months. You can beat the crowds by hiking a few miles into the backcountry or, to some extent, by planning your fishing days during the week.

Fish hatcheries in Colorado keep busy stocking streams with trout, particularly rainbows, the most popular game fish throughout the West. More than 22 million rainbow trout are stocked annually. Many cold-water mountain lakes also offer fishing for cutthroat trout and kokanee salmon. Catch-and-release flyfishing is the rule in some popular areas, allowing more anglers a chance at bigger fish. Be sure to inquire locally about eating the fish you catch, since some seemingly remote streams and rivers have contamination problems from old mines and mills.

The larger reservoirs, especially those at lower elevations, offer an assortment of sport fish, including carp, crappie, channel catfish, largemouth bass, smallmouth bass, white bass, bluegill, bullhead, perch, walleye and northern pike.

For copies of state fishing regulations, inquire at a local fishing supply or marina, or contact the **Colorado Division of Wildlife**. ~ 6060 Broadway, Denver, CO 80216; 303-297-1192. State fishing licenses are required for fishing in national parks, national forests and national recreation areas, but not on Indian reservations, where daily permits are sold by the tribal governments.

TWO

Denver

Passengers arriving by plane at Denver International Airport first glimpse Denver as a hazy sprawl that blurs the boundary between the flat prairie that stretches eastward and the jagged granite peaks of the central Rockies rising like castle walls and parapets just west of the city's edge. To motorists arriving from the east, north or south, the city is usually hidden by its murky atmosphere until the last possible moment, when the freeway plunges headlong into the dirty urban air, and suddenly the mountains fade away, replaced by the plate-glass canyons and steel pinnacles of the downtown skyline.

In recent years, Denver has topped all other American cities in air quality improvement. The problem is the city's location; the same mountains that offer Denverites so much natural beauty so close at hand also create air inversions that trap the smog, preventing it from blowing away. Despite the pollution, heavy traffic, suburban sprawl and other big-city drawbacks, Denver is actually a fun and easy place to visit. Colorado's largest museums, skyscrapers and amusement parks are located here, and the range of shopping and nightlife possibilities is unrivaled in the entire Rocky Mountain region. To reduce Denver to a set of sightseeing highlights worth searching for on a quick visit is to overlook the essential nature of the place, for its vast expanse and complexity make the city as unique and awe-inspiring as any mountain range or wilderness area in this book.

Just as modern travelers bound for almost any place in the Colorado Rockies are likely to come through Denver first, the city served as the main gateway through which miners, traders and homesteaders made their way into the mountains and where they often returned—sometimes wealthy. The Victorian-era mansions of the fortunate few who struck it rich still stand in the stately, shaded residential neighborhoods around the city center. During its early growth years, Denver developed strictly segregated ethnic neighborhoods. This cowboy-style discrimination even led to a landmark school desegregation case in which the U.S. Supreme

Court outlawed Denver's practice of drawing district lines to create not only all-white and all-black schools but also separate Chicano, Asian, German, Italian and Jewish schools. Today, old prejudices have faded, and Denverites take considerable pride in the city's multiethnic heritage; yet visitors who explore the residential areas of the city will soon discover the traditional ethnic enclaves that remain a key part of the city's character.

Denver got its start 1858, when prospector William Green Russell made the first gold discovery in Colorado along a tributary of Cherry Creek. Although the amount of gold dust panned from the creekbed proved insignificant and early prospectors soon moved higher into the mountains, they were quickly replaced by hordes of settlers chasing exaggerated rumors of wealth for the taking. Developers who had chartered the towns of Denver and Auraria (now Aurora) on paper several years before, sight unseen, rushed in to take charge as founding fathers of the tent communities that had sprung up on opposite banks of Cherry Creek.

Although its promoters billed it as "The Queen City of the Plains," Denver was slow to emerge as a town of any special importance. In the early years, it had no apparent advantages over other Front Range communities such as Colorado City, Boulder and Greeley. Central City, not Denver, was generally expected to emerge as the main cultural, political and financial center of the territory. To make matters worse, Denver burned to the ground in an 1863 fire. The following year, a flood sent a "wall of water" down Cherry Creek, devastating the town. Denver's aspirations as a commercial center were dashed when the builders of the first transcontinental railroad decided to bypass Denver and go through Cheyenne, Wyoming, instead. Observers of the developing West dismissed Denver as "a city without reason for being." Newspaper editor Horace Greeley went so far as to assert that there were " . . . more brawls, more fights, more pistol-shots with criminal intent in this log city of one hundred and fifty dwellings, not three-fourths completed nor two-thirds inhabited, nor one-third fit to be, than in any community of equal numbers on earth."

Little by little, however, mainly by developing a network of short-line railroads to serve the mining towns and building smelters and foundries that manufactured the heavy equipment needed for large-scale gold and silver mining in the mountains, Denver emerged as the economic hub of the region. Growth has followed the same pattern of Western-style sprawl as Los Angeles, as independent municipalities including Aurora, Lakewood, Westminster, Brighton, Englewood, Commerce City and Wheat Ridge—many larger in themselves than almost any other city in the state—have grown together to produce a five-county megalopolis. Today, with a population of almost two million, the Denver metro area is home to 54 percent of all Coloradoans.

Downtown Denver

Set at a 45-degree angle to the conventional north–south streets and east–west avenues of the rest of the metropolis, downtown Denver dazzles visitors with a diversity of venerable Victoriana, '80s mirrored skyscrapers and stately government buildings. Best of all, it is tailor-made for walking. A few hours in the heart of the city provide

Denver Area

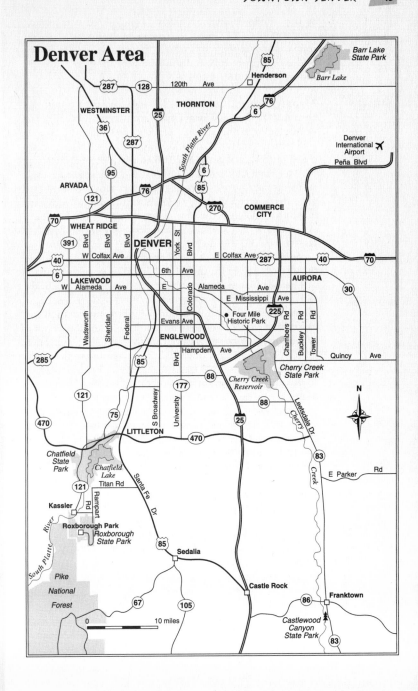

Barr Lake State Park

Barr Lake

85

Henderson

120th Ave

287   128

THORNTON

76

6

WESTMINSTER

25

36

Denver International Airport
Peña Blvd

287

95

South Platte River

6

ARVADA

85

121

76

270

COMMERCE CITY

70

WHEAT RIDGE

391   Blvd   Blvd   Blvd   DENVER   York St   Blvd   E Colfax Ave   287   40   70

W Colfax Ave

40

6

LAKEWOOD   6th   Ave

AURORA

W Alameda   Ave   E   Colorado   Alameda   Ave   30

E Mississippi   Ave

225

Wadsworth   Sheridan   Federal   Evans Ave   Four Mile Historic Park   Chambers Rd   Buckley Rd   Tower Rd   Quincy   Ave

ENGLEWOOD

Hampden   Ave

285   Blvd   Cherry Creek State Park

85   88   Cherry Creek Reservoir

121   177   Cherry Creek State Park

N

75   S Broadway   University   88   Ledistale Dr   Cherry

470   Creek

LITTLETON   25

470   83

Chatfield State Park   E Parker   Rd

Chatfield Lake   Santa Fe Dr   Titan Rd

121

Kassler   Rampart Rd

Roxborough Park   Roxborough State Park   85   Sedalia

South Platte River

Pike   National   Forest

67   105   Castle Rock   86   Franktown

0   10 miles   Castlewood Canyon State Park

83

an opportunity to admire Colorado's gold-plated state capitol, wander through the largest art museum in the Rocky Mountain region, stand in the room where "Unsinkable" Molly Brown held lavish society balls and stroll the steel-and-glass canyon of pedestrians-only 16th Street.

SIGHTS   A good landmark from which to begin exploring downtown Denver is the **Colorado State Capitol**, conventional in design but unique for its gleaming dome gilded with 303 ounces of 24-carat gold from the mines of Colorado, worth $4000 when it was completed in 1894, and nearly $120,000 today. Denver is known as the Mile-High City, and a plaque on the west steps of the capitol marks the elevation as exactly 5280 feet above sea level. Free tours start on the half hour, weekdays year-round and Saturdays in summer, and go all the way up into the dome, 180 feet above the ground floor. ~ Sherman Avenue between 14th and East Colfax avenues; 303-866-2604.

Stone lions flank the front door of the **Molly Brown House**, three blocks east of the capitol building. The mansion belonged to Leadville Johnny Brown, who struck it rich in the goldfields, and his wife, Molly, who achieved local fame as a survivor of the *Titanic* disaster. Their story became a hit Broadway musical and movie, *The Unsinkable Molly Brown*. Now restored to its turn-of-the-century glory, the house radiates conspicuous consumption from its gold-leafed parlor ceilings to its lavish third-floor ballroom. Admission. ~ 1340 Pennsylvania Street; 303-832-1421.

Another of Denver's stateliest homes, the **Grant-Humphreys Mansion** is an elegant example of the beaux-arts style, a conglomeration of European Renaissance and ancient Roman and Greek architectural features including tall columns and balustrade-edged balconies, which became popular in Denver at the beginning of the 20th century. Built in 1902 for former Colorado governor James Benton Grant and later sold to oil tycoon Albert Humphreys, the 30-room mansion is open for public tours; the tour schedule is changeable, so call ahead for current times. Admission. ~ 770 Pennsylvania Street; 303-894-2506.

West of the capitol building stand a group of municipal buildings collectively known as the **Denver Civic Center**, erected around a Greek amphitheater commonly frequented by picnickers and street preachers. Southeast of the Civic Center, the **Colorado History Museum** presents changing exhibits on the state's heritage assembled from the museum's large collection of documents and antiques. Permanent displays include Plains Indian artifacts and Mesa Verde pottery. The museum's centerpiece is a huge scale model of Denver as it looked in 1860 before the original wooden buildings were destroyed by fire. There are also models of cavalry forts and gold mines, along with real covered wagons and a full-size replica of a pioneer sod house. Admission. ~ 1300 Broadway; 303-866-3681.

The six-story free-form building gleaming with glass tiles at the south end of the Civic Center is the **Denver Art Museum**. It takes all day to see everything in this huge museum. Wings are devoted to pre-Columbian and Spanish Colonial art, Asian art, 19th-century art of the American West and decorative arts, among others. The museum's pride is an American Indian collection, said by many to be the finest in the world. A major renovation in 1997 added a floor of European paintings and textiles as well as a café. Admission. ~ 100 West 14th Avenue; 303-640-2793.

The bold design of the art museum must have been a hard act to follow, but the city rose to the challenge in its recent expansion of the **Denver Public Library**. Contrasting round and square elements, the architects used various colors of masonry to create a complex skyline of turrets, towers and pyramids that seems to mirror the kaleidoscopic character of Denver's downtown architecture. The largest library between Chicago and Los Angeles, it boasts 47 miles of bookshelves, including the seemingly boundless resources of the Gates Western History Reading Room. Rows of computers provide free public Internet access, a boon for travelers who keep in touch with the home front via e-mail. ~ 10 West 14th Avenue Parkway; 303-640-6200.

Located behind the art museum, the **Byers-Evans House** is the headquarters of the Colorado State Historical Society. Built in 1883 by William Byers, founder of the *Rocky Mountain News*, it was lived in until 1981 by the Evans family of Denver philanthropists, including Anne Evans, founder of the Denver Art Museum. The house has been restored to its pre–World War I opulence and contains the Denver History Museum as well as family heirlooms. Admission. ~ 1310 Bannock Street; 303-620-4933.

✔ **CHECK THESE OUT—UNIQUE SIGHTS**

- Watch 30 million coins a day being made at the **United States Mint**, the nation's second-largest gold repository. *page 48*
- Ride a golf cart to the manmade ski mountain at **Gart Bros. Sports Castle**, the world's largest sporting goods store. *page 57*
- Feel your stomach plummet on one of three roller coasters at **Lakeside Amusement Park.** *page 60*
- Tour a nuclear weapons factory turned wildlife refuge at **Rocky Mountain Arsenal.** *page 62*

A block west of the Civic Center, the **United States Mint** is where the government makes more than 30 million coins a day. Take the free 15-minute tour for an experience in small change that even Las Vegas can't match. Just in case the nation ever needs to start making gold coins again, the mint also serves as the United States' second-largest gold repository (after Fort Knox), and the tour includes a close-up look at some of the gold bars. Tours start every half-hour. ~ 320 West Colfax Avenue; 303-844-3582.

HIDDEN ►

Any present or former kid who has ever dreamed of becoming a firefighter can fuel that fantasy at the **Denver Firefighters Museum**, in Denver's old fire station near the mint. You'll see antique fire engines, photos of famous fires and the firefighters' dormitory, complete with the pole they used to slide down. Open weekdays year-round and Saturdays in summer. Admission. ~ 1326 Tremont Place; 303-892-1436.

Head west on Colfax Avenue across Cherry Creek to the **Auraria Higher Education Center**, a large college campus shared by the University of Colorado at Denver, Metropolitan State College and Denver Community College and used by 30,000 students. At the northwest edge of the campus is a shady block of beautifully restored older residences that were preserved when the rest of the neighborhood was demolished to make room for the college buildings. Known as **Ninth Street Historic Park**, the block contains 14 homes, each in a different architectural style from Denver's early days, with signs on the front lawns to tell visitors about them. Northwest of Ninth Street Historic Park, a small 1911 duplex owned by the colleges was once the home of Israeli leader Golda Meir and is being restored as a museum.

Skyscrapers turn the downtown streets into echoing canyons through which streams of humanity flow. The pedestrians-only **16th Street Mall**, the most people-friendly route through the heart of the city, starts at Broadway two blocks north of the Civic Center and runs northwest for the entire one-mile length of downtown. Cafés and shops line the mall, and free frequent shuttle buses run from one end to the other. Points of interest along the way include the **Paramount Theatre**, the city's only surviving motion-picture palace, now used for plays, rock concerts and Denver Chamber Orchestra performances, as well as several blocks of department stores and refurbished commercial buildings that date back to the late 1800s. ~ 1621 Glenarm Place; 303-534-8336. The **D & F Tower**, now dwarfed by skyscrapers nearby, was the tallest building west of the Mississippi when it was completed in 1909 as part of the Daniels & Fisher department store (which later merged with the May Company to create Denver's leading department store, May D & F). The tower is not presently open to the public. ~ 1601 Arapahoe Street.

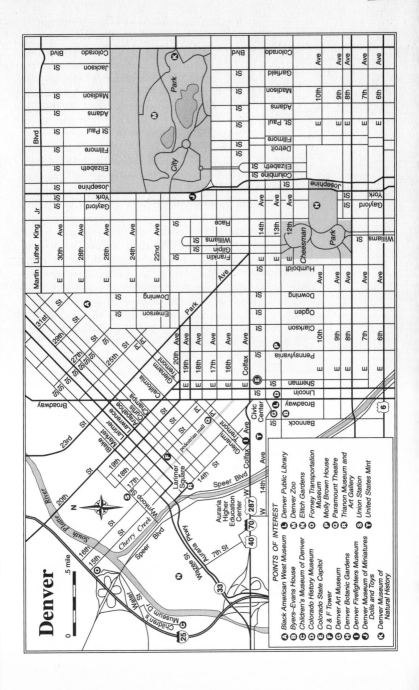

Denver

0 .5 mile

POINTS OF INTEREST

- A Black American West Museum
- B Byers–Evans House
- C Children's Museum of Denver
- D Colorado History Museum
- E Colorado State Capitol
- F D & F Tower
- G Denver Art Museum
- H Denver Botanic Gardens
- I Denver Firefighters Museum
- J Denver Museum of Miniatures Dolls and Toys
- K Denver Museum of Natural History
- L Denver Public Library
- M Denver Zoo
- N Elitch Gardens
- O Forney Transportation Museum
- P Molly Brown House
- Q Paramount Theatre
- R Trianon Museum and Art Gallery
- S Union Station
- T United States Mint

At the northwest end of the 16th Street Mall is Writer Square, a modern development that integrates retail, office and living space. It is the gateway to the **Lower Downtown Historic District**, usually referred to as "the LoDo." The area of historic buildings from the late 1800s starts at **Larimer Square**, Denver's oldest commercial block. Restored in 1964, it was one of the first officially designated historic districts in the United States. Today, Larimer Square is filled with restaurants and unique shops. The LoDo Historic District continues for about six blocks to grand old **Union Station**, still used by Amtrak and ski-train passengers.

In the basement of the station, one of the world's largest model-train collections is open to the public only on the last Friday evening of every month. ~ 1701 Wynkoop Street.

The **Trianon Museum and Art Gallery** contains French paintings and furniture from the 16th through 18th centuries in a 1910 mansion modeled after the palace of Marie Antoinette. The museum also has Asian art of the same period. A gun room exhibits dozens of ornately carved and filigreed antique black-powder firearms as well as a fair array of the weapons that won the West. Closed Sunday. Admission. ~ 335 14th Street; 303-623-0739.

Elsewhere in the downtown area, the **Black American West Museum** traces the roles African American pioneers, cowboys, miners, soldiers and politicians played in settling the West. The museum is housed in the former office and residence of Dr. Justina Ford, a black woman physician who practiced in Denver for 50 years. Admission. ~ 3091 California Street; 303-292-2566.

"Not to see Elitch's is not to see Denver" was the familiar slogan of the old Elitch Gardens, a Denver landmark that dated back to the 1890s and had not only amusement park rides but also lavish fresh-flower displays, a big-band ballroom and a theater where generations of Broadway stars performed. In 1993, however, Elitch's closed down and began the two-year task of disassembling its rides, including a 70-year-old carousel and parts of its original roller coaster (to be incorporated in a new, higher, faster roller coaster), and relocating to the present **Elitch Gardens Amusement Park**, located at the confluence of Cherry Creek and the South Platte River just west of downtown Denver. There are 21 major rides, six entertainment stages, four game arcades, six restaurants and a plethora of curio stands. Bereft of most of its historical charm, the new park has been receiving mixed reviews, and there no longer seems to be much reason to choose Elitch's over its long-time rival, Lakeside (see "Suburban Denver"). Admission. ~ Route 25 at Speer Boulevard; 303-595-4386.

Located just across the river from Elitch's, off Route 25 at the 7th Street exit, is the **Children's Museum of Denver**. Exhibits include CompuLAB, where visitors can create programs and access the Internet; Wild Oats Community Market, an interactive kid-size supermarket, and We All Live Downstream, focusing on the importance of clean water. The museum also offers children's inline-skating lessons spring through fall and ski and snowboard lessons year-round. Admission. ~ 2121 Children's Museum Drive; 303-433-7444.

North of Elitch's, the **Forney Transportation Museum** is housed in the former powerhouse for the electric streetcars that ran along Denver streets from the 1930s through the 1950s. Besides streetcars, the museum displays antique cars such as Theodore Roosevelt's Renault and Arab prince Aly Khan's Rolls-Royce, as well as railroad coaches and cabooses, the world's largest steam locomotive and a vintage McCormick reaper. Admission. ~ 1416 Platte Street; 303-433-3643.

LODGING

Although rates for lodging in downtown Denver tend to be very expensive, those traveling on minimal funds can find budget-priced beds at the **Denver International Youth Hostel**, a large AYH-affiliated hostel offering separate dormitory-style accommodations for men and women. There is a curfew, and guests must furnish their own sheets or rent them, but both the location and the prices are hard to beat. ~ 630 East 6th Avenue; 303-832-9996. BUDGET.

For low-budget private rooms with basic beds and bare walls, check out the YMCA. Though some areas are for men only, a new annex offers co-ed accommodations (no children allowed). ~ 25 East 16th Avenue; 303-861-8300. BUDGET.

Toward the other end of the lodging spectrum, the **Brown Palace Hotel** has enjoyed a reputation as Denver's finest hotel ever since it was built in 1892, when cattle barons and railroad tycoons made this their home away from home. In those days, the seven-story red stone structure with its distinctive triangular shape dominated the downtown skyline. Renovated for its 100th birthday in 1992, the 232-room hotel still stands proud among the steel-and-glass faces of neighboring skyscrapers. A lofty, six-story-high stained-glass atrium makes the hotel far more impressive inside than out. Guest rooms are individually decorated in a variety of styles spanning the lifetime of the hotel: gracious Victorian, lively art deco and bright contemporary. ~ 321 17th Street; 303-297-3111, 800-321-2599, fax 303-293-9204. ULTRA-DELUXE.

The architect of the Brown Palace also designed the smaller, 81-room **Oxford Hotel**, located in the LoDo historic district. It prospered for decades as the grand hotel closest to Union Station.

In the 1930s a top-to-bottom renovation transformed it into an art-deco masterpiece. The hotel deteriorated with the decline of train travel and finally was closed down for restoration in 1979. Today, the sterling-silver chandeliers have been stripped of layers of paint and faithful copies of the original carpets grace the hotel's corridors after a $12 million effort restored the glory of this elegant small hotel. Rooms have dark wood antique furnishings and soft-hued floral patterns; some have canopied beds and fireplaces. ~ 1600 17th Street; 303-628-5400, 800-228-5838, fax 303-628-5413. DELUXE TO ULTRA-DELUXE.

You wouldn't know it from its plain-Jane exterior, but the little **Cambridge Hotel** is one of the best bets in the downtown area for low-profile luxury. Just half a block from the capitol, the Cambridge offers 27 guest accommodations—all suites—ranging from parlor-style to two-bedroom. Each is individually decorated in a wildly unique style: Oriental, French traditional, English-country manor or futuristic. ~ 1560 Sherman Street; 303-831-1252, 800-877-1252. DELUXE TO ULTRA-DELUXE.

Most modern hotels in the downtown area are brand-name highrises geared toward business travelers. Room rates are high and reservations essential during the workweek, but on Friday and Saturday nights the cost typically drops by 50 percent or more, so you can realize significant savings if you make your Denver sightseeing visit on a weekend. For instance, the rates at the **Executive Tower Inn**, a 337-room skyscraper across the street from the Denver Convention Center, run in the ultra-deluxe range on weeknights but come down all the way to the moderate range on weekends for spacious, bright rooms with mountain or cityscape views. Guest facilities at this sleek, contemporary hotel include an indoor swimming pool, sauna and whirlpool, indoor and outdoor running tracks, exercise equipment and tennis, squash and

✔ **CHECK THESE OUT—UNIQUE LODGING**

- *Budget:* It's fun to stay at the YMCA—cheap, too, and there's even a swimming pool. *page 51*
- *Moderate to ultra-deluxe:* Beat the high cost of downtown lodging with a weekend stay at the highrise **Executive Tower Inn.** *page 52*
- *Deluxe to ultra-deluxe:* Bask in Victorian luxury at the romantic **Castle Marne**, site of Denver's first indoor bathroom. *page 53*
- *Ultra-deluxe:* Make yourself at home at the **Brown Palace Hotel**, just like wealthy oil- and cattle men of yore. *page 51*

Budget: under $50   Moderate: $50–$90   Deluxe: $90–$130   Ultra-deluxe: over $130

racquetball courts. ~ 1405 Curtis Street; 303-571-0300, 800-525-6651, fax 303-825-4301. MODERATE TO ULTRA-DELUXE.

Located near 16th Street Mall and the Denver Mint, the **Holiday Inn Denver Downtown** shows the results of a major renovation of the venerable Hotel Denver Downtown, which was the largest hotel in the city for many years. The 21-story highrise has spacious, modern rooms decorated in soft hues, many with views overlooking the capitol dome. Amenities include a complete fitness center and rooftop swimming pool, as well as such business conveniences as in-room data ports and secretarial service on call 24 hours a day. ~ 1450 Glenarm Place; 303-573-1450, 800-423-5128, fax 303-572-1113. DELUXE.

The **Comfort Inn Downtown Denver** offers somewhat lower rates for centrally located downtown lodgings. The 229 rooms are modern, with bright, contemporary furnishings, and hotel services include 24-hour room service and valet parking. The prices include a continental-plus breakfast. ~ 401 17th Street; 303-296-0400, 800-221-2222 fax 303-297-0774. DELUXE.

Located four blocks from downtown in Denver's Clement Historic District, the **Queen Anne Inn B&B** consists of two Victorian-era houses with porches, turrets, sundeck, hot tub, gardens and patio. Two of the 14 guest rooms have fireplaces and all are distinctively decorated with flowery motifs and four-poster brass beds to create a romantic ambience. ~ 2147 Tremont Place; 303-296-6666, fax 303-296-2151. MODERATE TO DELUXE.

Merritt House, in the Swallow Hill Historic District near the capitol, is a ten-room Queen Anne mansion furnished in turn-of-the-century antiques. Among the special features are a private jacuzzi in each guest room. ~ 941 East 17th Avenue; 303-861-5230, fax 303-861-9009. MODERATE TO DELUXE.

The brownstone **Holiday Chalet** was originally built in 1896 as the Bohm mansion, residence of one of Denver's first jewelers. Its ten rooms are furnished with heirloom antiques and have individual kitchens and baths. A recent renovation added new tile floors and decorative touches. Rates include a self-serve breakfast. ~ 1820 East Colfax Avenue; 303-321-9975, fax 303-377-6556. MODERATE.

One of Denver's best bed and breakfasts is **Castle Marne**, an 1889 Richardsonian Romanesque stone mansion five minutes from downtown. Among the curiosities found in this nine-room inn are the first indoor bathroom in Denver and a sunroom jacuzzi. Rooms are furnished with period antiques and decorated with vintage and local artwork; some rooms have balconies and private baths. Rates include a complete gourmet breakfast. ~ 1572 Race Street; 303-331-0621, fax 303-331-0623. DELUXE TO ULTRA-DELUXE.

The **Ramada Inn Downtown West** is located about two miles from downtown near Mile High Stadium, home of the Denver Broncos football team. The new Elitch's amusement park, successor to Denver's famous, century-old (and now defunct) Elitch Gardens, is located across the street. There is an outdoor pool and a restaurant; a complementary shuttle runs to and from downtown. Following a complete remodeling in 1996, the 167 rooms look brand-new in warm hues. ~ 1975 Bryant Street; 303-433-8331, 800-228-2828, fax 303-455-7061. MODERATE.

DINING

Cliff Young's tops the list of Denver's finest restaurants. Situated in a restored downtown storefront from the early 1900s, the restaurant is divided into several dining areas, one of which is the Amethyst Room, perhaps the most elegant dining room in Denver. The creative menu spotlights American nouvelle cuisine with such selections as a carpaccio of free-range veal and buffalo appetizer, lamb chops with shiitake mushroom caps, and medallions of pheasant. ~ 700 East 17th Avenue; 303-831-8900. DELUXE.

The **Wynkoop Brewing Company** is Colorado's oldest brewpub (a genre that has recently become ubiquitous in the Denver–Boulder area). Located in an old warehouse in the LoDo district, the establishment brews its own beer—more beer, they claim, than any other brewpub in the country—and serves it in a traditional tavern atmosphere along with English and Scottish food selections, such as shepherd's pie and black-and-tan dessert. ~ 1634 18th Street; 303-297-2700. MODERATE.

Many Denver gourmands contend that the **Imperial Chinese** is the best Chinese restaurant in the Rocky Mountain region. It certainly has the most elaborate decor, from the papier-mâché lions that guard the front entrance to the high-style Hong Kong glitz of the dining area. Seafood is the specialty. Try the Dungeness crab in hot Szechuan spices and scallops stir-fried with oriental vegetables. ~ 431 South Broadway; 303-698-2800. DELUXE.

In part of the historic building that was once Denver's grand Paramount Theatre, rescued from demolition with all artwork and original gilding still intact, **Paramount Café** is a lively bar and grill specializing in buffalo burgers and teriyaki chicken. Dining is either inside or on the patio. The café shares the premises with a new five-table pool room. ~ 511 16th Street; 303-893-2000. BUDGET.

A good low-priced eatery on 16th Street Mall is **Goldies Delicatessen,** a traditional New York–style deli open for lunch only. Here's where you can get lox and bagels or kosher pastrami on dill rye to eat there or take out for a picnic in the mountains (something you can't do in New York). ~ 511 16th Street; 303-623-6007. BUDGET.

You'll find Cajun cuisine reputed to be the best in town at **Bayou Bob's**. Plastic tablecloths highlight the decor, but no frills are necessary. Fried catfish and spicy seafood gumbo have made this place a favorite of the downtown weekday lunch bunch; it's also open for dinner. ~1635 Glenarm Place; 303-573-6828. BUD-GET.

The **Denver Buffalo Company** is an all-American steak-and-potatoes restaurant with a difference: only buffalo meat is served. (There are also a few vegetarian and fish entrées.) Try the cowboy fillet—buffalo pan-seared with peppers, onions and Southwestern spices. The restaurant raises its own buffalo on a ranch outside the city and has a gift shop that sells buffalo products. The decor features ranch memorabilia and bison motifs. ~ 1109 Lincoln Street; 303-832-0880. MODERATE TO ULTRA-DELUXE.

The quaint, Old World–style **Little Russian Cafe** on Larimer Square features authentic Russian food. Favorites are beef stroganoff and *pelmeni*, beef dumplings. Also available are European wines and beers and plenty of vodkas. Patio dining is available in summer. ~ 1424-H Larimer Street; 303-595-8600. MODERATE.

The affordable yet elegant **European Café**, located in a converted loft in Denver's historic LoDo district, serves an array of Continental cuisine guaranteed to wow even the most jaded palate. Menu highlights include lobster, veal, lamb and pasta creations plus downright sinful deserts. Most remarkable of all are the reasonable prices. ~ 1040 15th Street; 303-825-6555. MOD-ERATE.

The strangest decor in a downtown restaurant-and-bar is at the **Croc's Mexican Grill**, where a 20-foot-long artificial crocodile dangles from the ceiling and leers at diners. The scene is lively after five, as happy-hour sloshes its way toward the dinner hour. The menu features Mexican food along with sandwiches and seafood. ~ 1630 Market Street; 303-436-1144. BUDGET.

✔ CHECK THESE OUT—UNIQUE DINING

- *Budget:* Dine on enchiladas and beans with a 20-foot crocodile at **Croc's Mexican Grill**. *page 55*
- *Moderate:* Savor tandoori chicken or rich lamb curry at **India's**, a casual neighborhood eatery. *page 64*
- *Deluxe:* Enjoy a five-course feast in the Arabian Nights ambience of **Mataam Fez**. *page 64*
- *Ultra-deluxe:* Nibble an appetizer of rattlesnake meat at Denver's oldest restaurant, **The Buckhorn Exchange**. *page 56*

Budget: under $8 Moderate: $8–$16 Deluxe: $16–$24 Ultra-deluxe: over $24

Vegetarians are well-advised to steer clear of **The Buckhorn Exchange,** but other visitors discover a unique brand of Old-West elegance here. Denver's oldest restaurant, it was started in 1893 by a former frontier scout, who began decorating the restaurant with hunting trophies (still common practice in some parts of Colorado). The collection grew over the years until today the Buckhorn displays more than 500 stuffed animals and birds. The menu, too, may remind you of a museum of natural history, with its emphasis on wild game meats such as rattlesnake, alligator, pheasant and venison. ~ 1000 Osage Street; 303-534-9505. ULTRA-DELUXE.

SHOPPING   As the largest city in the Rocky Mountain states, Denver caters to many people who live in small ranch, mining and oil communities and come to "the big city," often traveling hundreds of miles, for special-occasion shopping sprees. Nowhere is this phenomenon more vividly apparent than along the **16th Street Mall,** a major downtown street that has been closed to traffic for its entire one-mile length. Amid fashion boutiques, Parisian-style sidewalk cafés, numerous sporting goods shops and outdoorsy clothiers, 16th Street still has some of Denver's longest-established retail stores—for instance, **Joslin's** is Denver's oldest department store. ~ 16th Street at Curtis Street; 303-534-0441. **Miller Stockman** has been selling Western accessories at this location since 1918. ~ 16th Street at California Street; 303-825-5339. Near the northwest end of 16th Street Mall is **Tabor Center,** a two-block-long, three-story atrium containing 65 upscale stores. ~ 16th and Lawrence streets; 303-572-6868. Also here is **Bridge Market,** where vendors sell such wares as T-shirts, imports, paintings and electronic novelties from pushcarts.

Larimer Street, at the northwest end of 16th Street Mall just past Tabor Center, was Denver's original main street. It had deteriorated into the city's skid row by the 1960s, when a massive urban-renewal effort transformed it into a showpiece historic district of red-brick Victorian restorations. Two shopping blocks, **Writer's Square** and **Larimer Square,** offer an ever-changing kaleidoscope of specialty stores ideal for gift shopping. Among the fine art galleries in Writer's Square are **Gallery One** (303-629-5005), with works by leading contemporary Western artists such as R. C. Gorman and Frank Howell, and **Third Canyon Gallery** (303-893-3936). ~ 1512 Larimer Street. In Larimer Square, check out **Earth Works, Ltd.** (1421-B Larimer Square; 303-825-3390), which features a wide array of made-in-Colorado arts and crafts. **John Atencio** (1440 Larimer Street; 303-534-4277) has the award-winning custom-designed jewelry of goldsmith John Atencio. ~ 14th and Larimer streets.

Just south of downtown, **Gart Bros. Sports Castle** is the world's largest sporting goods store. It has its own tennis court and ski mountain, and shoppers can ride around the huge store on golf carts. ~ 1000 Broadway; 303-861-1122.

The **Denver Performing Arts Complex,** commonly known as "The Plex," covers four city blocks and has 9000 seats in ten theaters and performance spaces, placing it second only to Lincoln Center in audience capacity. Within the arts complex, theater productions are presented at the **Helen Bonfils Theater Complex,** which is associated with the National Theatre Conservatory. Musical performances are offered at the Denver Center for the Performing Arts by the **Colorado Symphony Orchestra** (303-986-8742), the **Denver Chamber Orchestra** (303-825-4911)**, Opera Colorado** (303-778-6464) and the **Colorado Ballet** (303-298-0677). For a complete rundown on current performances at the complex, call 303-893-4000. ~ 14th and Champa streets; 303-893-4100.

NIGHTLIFE

As for nightclubs, Denver has plenty of them. **Comedy Works** features nationally known standup comics Wednesday through Sunday and has an open-mike night on Tuesday. Cover. ~ 1226 15th Street; 303-595-3637. **Comedy Sports,** downstairs from the Wynkoop Brewing Company brewpub, offers tag-team improvisational comedy Thursday, Friday and Saturday nights. Cover. ~ 1634 18th Street; 303-297-2111.

Mercury Café offers jazz Tuesday through Sunday, an open stage for drumming and storytelling on Wednesday and poetry readings and performance art on Friday. Cover. ~ 2199 California Street; 303-294-9281. **El Chapultepec** also features live jazz nightly. Cover. ~ 1962 Market Street; 303-295-9126.

Rock Island is a popular club for alternative dance music from hip-hop to slammin'. Cover. ~ Wazee and 15th streets; 303-572-7625.

A prime location on 16th Street Mall helps make **Rock Bottom Brewery** one of downtown's liveliest young professional happy-hour hangouts, presents live jazz later in the evening on Friday and Saturday nights. ~ 1001 16th Street; 303-534-7616. **Brendan's Market Street Pub,** located in the LoDo district, features live dance music Tuesdays through Saturdays and has 14 labels of premium beer on draft. ~ 1624 Market Street; 303-595-0609. Connoisseurs will find the widest selection of beers imaginable, along with big-screen TVs blaring sports events and a rowdy intergenerational crowd, at the peanut shell-strewn **Boiler Room,** located in the former Tivoli Beer Brewery. ~ 901 Larimer Street; 303-893-5733.

Probably *the* most anachronistic trend to appear on the Denver nightlife scene in decades is the "gentlemen's cabaret" concept.

The largest, conveniently located just a block from the Convention Center, is the **Diamond Cabaret**. With "over 100 of the world's most gorgeous entertainers," this place may not win any prizes for political correctness, but it's a far cry from the sleazy strip joints found farther east along Colfax Avenue. It has more in common with the Playboy Clubs of decades past. The club features an elegantly appointed dining area that specializes in steaks, along with a billiards room and sports bar. (There are no comparable clubs for gentlewomen around the Convention Center.) ~ 1222 Glenarm Place; 303-571-4242.

Charlie's offers country-and-western deejay dancing for a predominantly gay crowd nightly. ~ 900 East Colfax Avenue; 303-839-8890. The hot cruise bar for young professional men is **The Grand**. ~ 538 East 17th Street; 303-839-5390. **The Elle** is a popular lesbian dance club (gay men are welcome). Cabaret entertainment is featured on Thursday while local bands play on Wednesday and Sunday. Dancing takes center stage on Friday and Saturday nights when two dancefloors open for patrons. ~ 716 West Colfax Avenue; 303-893-3553.

▼▼▼▼▼▼▼▼▼▼▼▼
Suburban Denver

Hemmed in by mountains on its west side, the city of Denver has historically grown south and east, spreading from the banks of the South Platte River and Cherry Creek. For decades, the city's politicians annexed every new development that was built, so the city limits today enclose more than 300 square miles. Eventually, however, the city filled all the land in Denver County and could not expand farther. So when a population explosion hit the Denver area in the 1960s, when the completion of a pipeline tunnel through the Continental Divide greatly expanded the water supply, most newcomers settled in sprawling independent suburbs in neighboring Arapahoe, Jefferson and Adams counties. For the most part, visitors are likely to find Denver's 'burbs short on points of interest, with hotels geared for business travelers and restaurants designed for a local family trade. The older residential neighborhoods of Denver have more to offer in terms of parks, museums and historic sites.

SIGHTS

Foremost among Denver's sightseeing highlights located away from the downtown is **City Park**, in a pretty, shady old residential neighborhood about three and a half miles east of downtown, off Colorado Boulevard between 17th and 23rd avenues. There, the **Denver Museum of Natural History** displays everything from skeletons of dinosaurs and a great blue whale to a life-size Navajo hogan and Eskimo igloo, plus dioramas of wildlife from the plains and mountains of Colorado as well as other continents. The museum's gold collection features the largest gold nugget ever found in Colorado, weighing eight and a half pounds. Attached to the museum, **Gates Planetarium** (303-370-6487; admission), alternates astronomy presentations and laser light shows throughout the day, and an IMAX Theater (303-370-6300; admission) shows thrill-a-minute films on a wraparound screen. In another part of City Park, the **Denver Zoo** (303-331-4110; admission) has more than 1700 animals from around the world, some caged and others in open habitats. Admission. ~ 2001 Colorado Boulevard; 303-322-7009.

Just across the street from the west boundary of City Park, the **Denver Museum of Miniatures, Dolls and Toys** exhibits some of the largest and most lavish dollhouses ever created, including reproductions in miniature of Molly Brown's mountain shack near Leadville, an adobe Indian pueblo and a mansion complete with working electric lights. Visitors will also find collections of American Indian kachinas and teddy bears. Admission. ~ 1880 Gaylord Street; 303-322-1053.

In the same part of town, **Mizel Museum of Judaica** is the only cultural center in the Rocky Mountain States established to honor Jewish history, art and culture. The free museum presents lectures, films and changing displays from its archives of documents and photos tracing the roles of Jews and Judaism in the growth of Denver and the Rocky Mountain region. Also featured are touring exhibits from the Smithsonian Institution and the Israel Museum. Closed Friday and Saturday. ~ 560 South Monaco Parkway; 303-333-4156.

About a mile southwest of City Park is **Cheesman Park**, home of the **Denver Botanic Gardens**, with its array of indoor and outdoor environments including a Japanese garden, a habitat for nesting birds, a "Plants of the Bible" garden and a re-creation of a tropical rainforest. Of special interest is the alpine rock garden, which contains more than 3500 species of high-mountain plants from around the world. Admission. ~ 1005 York Street; 303-331-4000.

Farther toward the east side of town, little **Cranmer Park** is interesting for its large terrazzo model of the Continental Divide. The park also makes a peaceful spot for an urban picnic. ~ East 3rd Avenue at Bellaire Street.

The oldest building in Denver is the former stagecoach station at **Four-Mile Historic Park**. The station, which was in the middle of nowhere when it was built in 1860, is now surrounded by the affluent southeast Denver neighborhood of Glendale. Volunteers in period costume show visitors around the main travelers' inn as well as the barn and other outbuildings, some of which have been reconstructed with 19th-century tools and construction methods. Farm animals and peacocks wander through the 14-acre park. Traditional beekeeping techniques are demonstrated with active hives in a bee house. Admission. ~ 715 South Forest Street; 303-399-1859.

In the early 20th century, thousands of people migrated northward from Mexico and New Mexico to work in the Colorado sugar beet fields. Many stayed to make their homes in Denver's *barrio* southwest of downtown, and the Latino population soon grew to become the city's largest ethnic minority. Located in the heart of the traditional Spanish-speaking district, the **Museo de las Americas** presents changing exhibits on Latino art, history and cultural heritage in Colorado, the Southwest and Latin America. Closed Sunday and Monday. ~ 861 Santa Fe Drive; 303-571-4401.

HIDDEN ▶

With three roller coasters (including a classic Cyclone), 25 other major rides and 15 kiddie rides, **Lakeside Amusement Park** is the Colorado's largest. The quaint art-deco park hasn't changed much for half a century, and the cost of admission and rides is far lower than at the newer Elitch's. The miniature train ride around Sloan Lake has created sentimental memories for generations of native Denverites. Admission. ~ 4601 Sheridan Boulevard; 303-477-1621.

More than 85 percent of Denver metropolitan area residents live outside the Denver city limits in 13 adjoining suburbs— Aurora to the east; Englewood, Greenwood Village and Littleton to the south; Lakewood, Wheat Ridge and Arvada to the west; and Commerce City, Northglenn, Thornton, Federal Heights, Westminster and Broomfield to the north.

Aurora is Colorado's largest city in area and third-largest in population. It is quintessential suburbia on a vast scale. Besides miles and miles of lookalike houses, Aurora has its own freeway— Route 225—and one of the largest shopping malls in the state, Aurora Mall. It is somehow appropriate that the **Aurora History Museum** focuses on 1950s-era memorabilia. Artifacts on display here include everything from old-fashioned black-and-white TV sets and manual typewriters to Davy Crockett hats. Admission. ~ 15001 East Alameda Drive, Aurora; 303-340-2200.

Englewood, Greenwood Village and Littleton are part of an older suburban area, where most homes date back to the post-World War II era. The economy in these communities received a much-needed boost when General Dynamics Space Systems bought Martin Marietta, the largest employer in the area, creating thousands of new jobs. Englewood looks better than ever following an urban-renewal facelift, and Littleton has done a good job of historical preservation on its quaint small-town main street. The **Littleton Historical Museum** has developed two working farms into an open-air museum where 19th-century agricultural methods and lifestyles are preserved. Goats, sheep, cows, horses, pigs and chickens roam the grounds, as do friendly, informative staff members clothed in pioneer-era garb who do farm chores in between visitors' questions. The museum also has 19th- and 20th-century art galleries. Closed Monday. ~ 6028 South Gallup Street, Littleton; 303-795-3950.

Although Lakewood, Wheat Ridge and Arvada make up the most industrialized part of the greater Denver area, neighborhoods in this part of town are considered attractive because they are close to the mountains, making weekend escapes easy. The Denver Federal Center, located in Lakewood, is the largest employer in Jefferson County, and Lakewood is on the verge of surpassing Denver itself as Colorado's most populous city.

Sightseeing attractions are few in this part of town; the best bet is the art gallery at the **Arvada Center for the Arts and Humanities**, which features two exhibition halls of contemporary works by Colorado artists and crafters. The center also has an outdoor amphitheater and an auditorium that is used as a venue for a packed schedule of community and special-interest programs ranging from AIDS benefits and women's consciousness workshops to cowboy poetry readings. ~ 6901 Wadsworth Boulevard, Arvada; 303-431-3939.

The Rocky Mountain Arsenal contains a Superfund cleanup site said to be the most polluted square mile on earth.

Commerce City, Northglenn, Thornton, Westminster, Federal Heights, and Broomfield, on the north side, form Denver's most economically diverse area, where both smokestack and high-tech factories punctuate green farm and ranch lands along the fringes of the city's sprawl. **Rocky Mountain Arsenal**, a former U.S. Army chemical weapons complex, has become a de facto wildlife refuge since it was shut down; today, Denverites take the kids to ride the shuttle buses that run through the arsenal grounds on weekends and view bald eagles and the largest wild elk herd in the greater Denver area. ~ 303-289-0232. In Westminster, the **Arabian Horse Trust** has an art gallery and small museum dedicated to the breed many riders and breeders consider the world's most beautiful horses. Admission. ~ 12000 Zuni Street, Westminster; 303-450-4710.

LODGING

Loews Giorgio Hotel is an Italian-style hotel ten minutes from downtown in the Glendale area. Palms and hanging plants give the atrium lobby a tropical feeling; the columns and murals evoke an atmosphere of ancient Rome. The 187 rooms have balconies and either a king-size or two queen-size beds. Rates include a continental breakfast. ~ 4150 East Mississippi Avenue; 303-782-9300, fax 303-758-6542. DELUXE.

Aurora has a full complement of chain motor inns, most offering room rates that are a fraction of the price for comparable lodging in downtown Denver. Characteristic and conveniently located, the **Hampton Inn Denver/Aurora** has 132 modern, spacious mini-suites, some with refrigerators and microwaves. There is a large heated swimming pool. ~ 1500 South Abilene Street, Aurora; 303-369-8400, 800-426-7866, fax 303-369-0324. MODERATE.

In the Englewood/Littleton area, major hotels cluster around the Denver Tech Center off Route 25 at the south edge of the city. Not surprisingly, all of these hotels are oriented toward business travelers and are state-of-the-art modern and ultrastylish in a corporate way. A standout is the **Inverness Hotel and Golf Club**. The 302 guest rooms are so bright and seemingly brand-new that you'll almost feel as though you shouldn't touch anything. The sporting facilities, second to none in the Denver area, include lighted tennis courts, indoor and outdoor swimming pools, saunas and whirlpool spas, a complete fitness club and an 18-hole golf course that hosts the prestigious annual Colorado Open golf tournament. ~ 200 Inverness Drive West, Englewood; 303-799-5800, 800-346-4891, fax 303-799-5874. ULTRA-DELUXE.

Lakewood can be a convenient place for vacationers to stay while exploring the Denver area. Rates run much lower than in the city center, and Route 70 can put you downtown within a matter of minutes or, with equal simplicity, take you into the heart of the Colorado Rockies. **The Sheraton Four Point**, an attractive motor inn near the Denver Federal Center, has rooms that are large, modern and thoroughly conventional, as well as complete facilities including an exercise room, spa and outdoor swimming pool. A hotel shuttle offers free transportation within a five-mile radius. ~ 137 Union Boulevard, Lakewood; 303-969-9900, 800-222-8733, fax 303-989-9847. MODERATE.

One of the few notable lodgings in the north part of metro Denver, the **Radisson North Denver Graystone Castle**, is located at Route 25, Exit 223, and you can't miss it. The exterior styling of this five-story motor inn re-creates a medieval castle, and the motif is carried through the common areas of the hotel—restaurant, pub, pool and spa area—until you may start to feel as if you're spending the night in a theme park. Fortunately, though, you can leave the Arthurian ambience outside the door of one of the 136 large, thoroughly modern (if rather bland) guest rooms. ~ 83 East 120th Avenue, Thornton; 303-451-1002, fax 303-452-1962. MODERATE.

DINING   Strings serves imaginative contemporary cuisine à la carte and offers patio dining. Sample dishes include *penne bagutta* (a homemade pasta), steamed oysters and *champagne beurre blanc*. The clientele presents a striking cross section of Denverites—on any

Colorado's Financial Heartbeat

From the mirrored skyscrapers that form a canyon around downtown Denver's 17th Street financial district to the sprawling corporate complexes that fill the Denver Tech Center on the city's southern edge, it's plain to see that the Mile High City is Colorado's economic hub. Almost 90 percent of the wealth from all in-state sources—mining, ranching, tourism, manufacturing and all the rest—eventually finds its way inro Denver banks and boardrooms. What is less visible is the underlying economic shift that is presently transforming the state.

The get-rich-quick optimism of the gold rush days is long gone. Ornate mountain-town mansions built by silver barons a century ago survive, if at all, as local museums or bed and breakfasts. Mineral extraction has continued to play an important if volatile role in Colorado's economy. Growing environmental and safety concerns have combined with changes in market demand to end uranium prospecting, shut down molybdenum mining and slam the doors on the state's only steel mill. Oil shale, once touted as the key to national energy independence, turned out to be a bust, leaving a new crop of ghost towns in the 1980s. Even coal mining, the most resilient of the state's extractive industries, is on the decline.

Colorado's other traditional key industry, agriculture, has also seen hard times recently. Beginning with the early 1980s, a national recession hit Colorado's economy especially hard, and those who suffered worst were independent farmers and ranchers, who went bankrupt in record numbers. Even large agribusiness corporations, including the sugar-beet conglomerate Holly Sugar, have collapsed.

Closures of Cold War–era weapons facilities have reduced the flow of federal money into the state, and even growth in summer and winter tourist economies has leveled out. Statistics show that while more tourists visit Colorado each year, they are spending less on the average as more travelers eschew traditional resort areas in favor of less-known, "hidden" destinations where they get more adventure for less money.

Despite such bearish trends, Colorado's natural appeal as a place to live and work has attracted high-tech companies and other clean industries as fast as the old industries have faded. With this economic diversification, Colorado's urban population and standard of living are growing with the momentum of a new gold rush, and the state still reigns as the wealthiest in the Rockies.

evening you're likely to see diners wearing everything from T-shirts to tuxedos. ~ 1700 Humboldt Street; 303-831-7310. DELUXE

Looking for the best pizza in Denver? Locals, especially students at the nearby University of Denver, agree that the place to find it is the **Bonnie Brae Tavern**. Run by the same family since 1934, it wasn't always a pizza joint; while the menu fare has changed over the years, the traditional pub atmosphere has endured. No reservations; expect to wait for a table. Closed Monday. ~ 740 South University Boulevard; 303-777-2262. MODERATE.

HIDDEN ►

Vietnamese grocers, shops and small restaurants cluster west of downtown along Federal Boulevard. The longest-established eatery among them, the family **T-Wa Inn** offers a simple ambience and outstanding, affordably priced Asian dishes with an emphasis on seafood. Try the seafood egg rolls and the succulent soft-shell crab. 555 South Federal Boulevard; 303-922-4584. BUDGET TO MODERATE.

In the mood for something exotic? Try **India's**. A big tandoori oven forms the centerpiece in this casually elegant neighborhood restaurant. Tandoori cookery involves heating such an oven to more than 700°F and cooking the savory meat and fish entrées until precisely the right moment. Outstanding curry and vegetarian dishes are also available. Closed Sunday for lunch. ~ 3333 South Tamarack Drive; 303-755-4284. MODERATE.

Long one of Denver's favorite Italian restaurants, **Carmine's on Penn** is in an older but far from elegant former residence hidden away on a side street in a south Denver neighborhood. Though the decor may not be exceptional, the cuisine and presentation will knock your socks off. Besides a tantalizing range of pasta choices, meat, fowl and seafood specials change nightly; most dishes are prepared for two. ~ 92 South Pennsylvania Street; 303-777-6443. MODERATE TO DELUXE.

The **Denver Salad Company** has a 70-item salad bar plus soups, homemade muffins, pasta, baked potatoes, cakes and puddings. The no-nonsense ambience features touches of Eurotech decor. ~ 2700 South Colorado Boulevard; 303-691-2050. BUDGET.

Mataam Fez serves Moroccan food in a sumptuous Arabian Nights atmosphere with tented ceiling and decor from Morocco. Diners are seated on the floor on pillows and leather puffs. The five-course prix-fixe meal includes a choice of entrées such as Cornish game hen in a sauce of honey and almonds or shrimp *pel-pel*, plus soup, salad, appetizer and fresh-fruit dessert. ~ 4609 East Colfax Avenue; 303-399-9282. DELUXE.

A restaurant considered by many to be the best in the greater Denver area is **The Swan** in the Inverness Hotel and Golf Club near the Denver Tech Center on the southern outskirts of the city. The restaurant's ambience is light and airy, minimal and chic.

The serving staff is impeccably attentive. The bill of fare high-lights continental house specialties such as chateaubriand and leg of lamb. There's a seafood buffet on Friday and Saturday evenings. ~ 200 Inverness Drive West, Englewood; 303-799-5800. ULTRA-DELUXE.

Certainly the most prominent restaurant in Lakewood, **Casa Bonita** serves a tasty, though predictable, range of Mexican dishes in an all-you-can-eat buffet. Its size alone makes this place remark-able; the 52,000-square-foot restaurant seats 1100 people. The real draw here, though, is its nonstop family-oriented (that is, mainly for kids) entertainment—Old West shootouts, wandering mariachis, puppet shows, magicians, prizes and fire-juggling cliff divers who leap from the top of a 30-foot artificial waterfall. ~ 6715 West Colfax Avenue, Lakewood; 303-232-5115. BUDGET.

SHOPPING The reigning queen of metropolitan Denver shopping malls is the **Cherry Creek Shopping Center**, located at University Avenue southeast of downtown. This one-million-square-foot indoor mall features such upscale chain department stores as Saks Fifth Avenue, Neiman Marcus and Lord & Taylor, along with more than 130 specialty shops and restaurants. ~ 3000 East 1st Avenue; 303-388-3900. The adjoining **Cherry Creek North** area along 3rd Avenue features one of the city's highest concentrations of fine-art galleries. PISMO specializes in works made with natural materials such as shells, fossils and minerals. ~ 2727 East 3rd Avenue; 303-333-7724. **Show of Hands Gallery** showcases hand-dyed silks, stained glass and other creations by Colorado artisans. ~ 2610 East 3rd Avenue. **West South West** features arts, crafts and accessories from (southwest) Seattle to Santa Fe. ~ 257 Fillmore Street; 303-321-4139. But the *sine qua non* for browsing in the Cherry Creek area is the **Tattered Cover Book Store**, one of the largest independent bookstores in the United States. The shelves of the immense four-story store display an astonishing 400,000 volumes. ~ 2955 East 1st Avenue; 303-322-7727.

Most antique dealers in Colorado import their wares from the Midwest. To the extent that there are any authentic Colorado antiques to be found, the place to look for them is the **Antique Mall of Lakewood**, several miles west of downtown Denver. The mall provides showroom space for more than 100 antique deal-ers under one roof. ~ 9635 West Colfax Avenue, Lakewood; 303-238-6940. Another big antique shopping center is the **An-tique Guild**, where nearly 250 dealers show their wares. ~ 1298 South Broadway, Denver; 303-722-3359.

NIGHTLIFE On a Saturday night you may find more cowboys and ranch girls in Denver area bars than ever rode the range. You'll find country-and-western music nightly at the **Grizzly Rose Saloon & Dance**

Hall, the kind of place where Wednesday is known as "Strut-Your-Stuff-in-Jeans Night," meaning that women wearing jeans get free wine. There's a Family Night on Sunday, and free dance lessons are offered nightly. Cover. ~ 5450 North Valley Highway; 303-295-1330.

The city's longest-established gay club is a mellow restaurant/bar called The Den. ~ 5110 West Colfax Avenue; 303-534-9526. Cowgirls seeking same head for Ms. C's. ~ 7900 East Colfax Avenue; 303-322-4436.

Perhaps the most spectacular western dance club in the area, though, is the Stampede Mesquite Grill & Dance Emporium, a larger-than-life place with a huge racetrack-shaped dancefloor, an amazingly long antique saloon bar, double-sided video screens, state-of-the-art disco lighting, and a second-floor balcony dining area overlooking the action. Cover. ~ 2430 South Havana Street at Parker Road, Aurora; 303-337-6909.

Alternative dance music is featured on Wednesday evenings at the eclectic Jimmy's Grille, which also offers live blues on Monday and reggae on Thursday, Friday and Saturday nights. There's a cover on reggae nights. ~ 320 South Birch Street, Glendale; 303-322-5334. You'll find contemporary jazz at Bourbon Street, a sleek young professional hangout located at the Denver Tech Center. ~ 5139 South Yosemite Street, Englewood; 303-721-5117.

For a family-oriented evening on the town, try the Country Dinner Playhouse, the state's only year-round professional dinner theater. The entertainment fare consists of recent and classic Broadway musicals. The reasonable ticket charge includes a dinner buffet. Admission. ~ 6875 South Clinton Avenue, Englewood; 303-799-1410.

The world's largest dancefloor is the draw at the Cactus Moon, with live country-and-western Tuesday through Sunday. Cover. ~ 10001 Grant Street, Thornton; 303-451-5200.

PARKS

BARR LAKE STATE PARK 🚶 🚲 ⛵ 🛥️ 🎣 This artificial lake was once part of Denver's sewer drainage system. Abandoned after a flooding South Platte River washed it out in 1965, the lake became lush, exceptionally fertile wetlands. Thirty-three years later, it provides habitat for about 300 bird species and is the favorite birdwatching spot in the Denver area. A nine-mile hiking and biking trail encircles the lake, and boating is permitted (10-horsepower or less). Fishing is good for trout, walleye, wiper and catfish. Facilities include a nature center. Day-use fee, $4 per vehicle. ~ Take Route 76 for 23 miles northeast of downtown Denver, past the reservoir, to Bromley Lane (Brighton, Exit 23). Head east and follow Piccadilly Road South to the park entrance; 303-659-6005.

CHATFIELD STATE PARK

The Denver area's most popular recreational lake is shared by sailboats, windsurfers, waterskiers, fishermen, scuba divers and swimmers. It gets very crowded on sunny summer weekends. It also offers 24 miles of horseback and hiking trails through the surrounding foothills. It is the starting point for the Denver Greenways Trail, a paved biking and jogging trail that follows the South Platte River for more than 20 miles to downtown Denver. Great blue herons are abundant in the area, as are birders. Fishing is fair to good for perch, crappie, bass, bullhead, bluegill and catfish. Facilities include a picnic area, restrooms, nature trails, an arboretum, horse rentals, limited groceries, a boat ramp and a marina that rents boats from May through mid-September and sells bait and tackle. Day-use fee, $4 per vehicle. ~ Located 25 miles southwest of downtown Denver in suburban Littleton. Take Wadsworth Boulevard or Route 470 to Route 121, which goes south through the park; 303-791-7275.

▲ There are 153 RV/tent sites (52 with electric hookups); $9 to $12 per night.

ROXBOROUGH STATE PARK

This natural area is dominated by a series of hogback ridges thrust through the earth's crust by the same seismic upheavals that created Red Rocks west of Denver and the Garden of the Gods at Colorado Springs. Miles of hiking and biking trails wind through the canyons between the rock ridges. Cross-country skiers flock here after snowstorms. Facilities include a visitors center, restrooms and hiking, biking and cross-country ski trails. Day-use fee, $4 per vehicle. ~ Located seven miles south of Chatfield State Park on Roxborough Park Road; 303-973-3959.

CHERRY CREEK STATE PARK

The nearest large lake to Denver, now surrounded by suburbs on three sides, gets unbelievably crowded on weekends as tens of thousands of locals descend on Cherry Creek Reservoir for windsurfing, waterskiing, sailing, fishing, swimming and sunbathing at the small, sandy beach. Fishing is good for walleye, trout, perch, crappie, largemouth bass, catfish, pike and bluegill. Facilities include picnic areas, restrooms, hiking and horseback trails, a marina, boat rentals, and a swimming beach. Day-use fee, $5. ~ Located one mile south of Route 225 on Parker Road; 303-699-3860.

▲ There are 102 RV/tent sites (some with electric hookups); $9 to $12 per night. Call 303-470-1144 or 800-678-2267 for reservations.

CASTLEWOOD CANYON STATE PARK

About 20 miles upstream from Cherry Creek Reservoir is the site of an early reservoir that provided water for Denver until the dam was destroyed by a flood in 1933. Today, the canyon where the lakebed used to be is thickly wooded with pine, fir, aspen and scrub oak protected by sheer sandstone cliffs. Relatively few visitors come to this idyllic area. Hidden as it is in the midst of dry, featureless prairie, you don't see the creek and woodlands until you reach the canyon rim. Birdwatching and hiking are the main attractions. Facilities include a picnic area, restrooms, a visitors center and nature trails. Day-use fee, $4 per vehicle. ~ Located 27 miles southeast of downtown Denver off Route 83. From Franktown, take Route 86 west for a quarter-mile, then County Road 51 south for three miles; 303-688-5242.

▼▼▼▼▼▼▼▼▼▼▼▼▼▼

Outdoor Adventures

FISHING

The waters of Cherry Creek and Chatfield reservoirs are home to largemouth bass, trout, pike, channel catfish, bluegill, carp, bullhead, perch and crappie. **Cherry Creek Marina** has fishing boats for rent. ~ 303-779-6144. You can also rent fishing boats, along with bait and tackle, at **Chatfield Marina**. ~ 303-791-6104, 303-791-5555.

WATER SPORTS

Sailboats, power boats, paddleboats, pontoons, sailboards and kayaks can be rented at **Cherry Creek Marina** for use on Cherry Creek Reservoir south of Denver from April through mid-September. ~ 303-779-6144. **Chatfield Marina** on Chatfield Reservoir rents sailboats, pontoons, canoes, paddleboats and jet skis. ~ 303-791-6104, 303-791-5555.

BALLOON RIDES

For ballooning aficionados, **Life Cycle Balloon Adventures** offers daily champagne flights along the Front Range out of Denver. ~ 2540 South Steele Street, Denver; 303-759-3907

SKIING

Although there are no ski slopes in the immediate Denver area, some of the world's finest ski areas are within a couple of hours' drive (see Chapter Five for complete information). Downhill and cross-country ski rentals, as well as snowboard rentals, are available in Denver at many locations, including **Sports Rent**. ~ 560 South Holly Street; 303-320-0222. **Breeze Ski Rentals** has seven locations in the greater Denver area. ~ 405 Urban Street #205, Lakewood; central reservations: 303-980-1223.

GOLF

Denver has 40 golf courses. Most have club and cart rentals. The 18-hole **City Park Golf Course** has cart rentals and, like all Denver municipal courses, offers reduced rates for Colorado residents. ~ East 25th Avenue at York Street; 303-295-4420. **Overland Park Golf Course**, one of the first golf courses in the region, was built in 1895. This 18-hole course is now favored by senior players because of the relatively flat terrain. ~ South Santa Fe Drive at Jewell Street; 303-698-4975. **Harvard Gulch Golf Course** is a nine-hole, par-3 course. There are no cart rentals. ~ East Iliff and South Clarkson streets; 303-698-4078. **Kennedy Golf Course** also offers nine holes. ~ 10500 East Hampden Avenue; 303-751-0311. Other 18-hole courses open to the public include two long-established clubs, the **Wellshire Country Club** (3333 South Colorado Boulevard; 303-692-5636) and the spikeless **Park Hill Golf Course** (Colorado Boulevard at 35th Avenue; 303-333-5411). Robert Trent Jones, Jr., designed the beautiful—and pricey—**Arrowhead Golf Club** among the dramatic red sandstone rock formations in Roxborough State Park; carts are required and included in the fee. ~ 10850 West Sundown Trail, Littleton; 303-973-9614.

Denver has nine hard-surfaced, lighted courts at **City Park** (23rd and York streets) and eight more in **Washington Park** (East Louisiana Avenue at South Humboldt Street). For a complete listing, call Denver Parks and Recreation. ~ 303-964-2522.   **TENNIS**

Public pools in Denver are at **Glenarm Recreation Center** (2800 Glenarm Place; 295-4475), **Martin Luther King Recreation Center** (3880 Newport Street; 303-331-4034), **Washington Park Recreation Center** (701 South Franklin Street; 698-4962) and, in summer only, the outdoor pool at **Eisenhower Recreation Center** (4300 East Dartmouth Avenue; 303-692-5650).   **SWIMMING**

   The city's splashiest swimmin' hole is 60-acre **Water World**. It's the largest water park in America, with river rapids, wave pools and huge spiral water slides; senior citizens get in free. ~ 88th Avenue and Pecos Street; 303-427-7873.

Horse rentals are available for riding in tate Recreation Area at **McLain Farms**. ~ 6025 South Eaton Lane, Littleton; 303-730-3923. **Precious Ponies** is another option ~ 5990 West Bowles Ave-   **RIDING STABLES**

✔ **CHECK THESE OUT—UNIQUE OUTDOOR ADVENTURES**

• Take the plunge on a giant slide at Water World, America's largest water park. *page 69*

   • Tee off at the historic century-old Overland Park Golf Course, the first links in Colorado. *page 68*

      • Rent a bike and cruise more than 100 miles of urban cycling trails connecting downtown Denver to outlying recreation areas. *page 70*

         • Trek between and beneath tall sandstone ridges at Roxborough State Park. *page 70* nue, Littleton; 303-279-3049. At Cherry Creek State Park you can rent horses from **Paint Horse Stables.** ~ 4201 South Parker Road, Aurora; 303-690-8235.

BIKING

Denver has an extensive urban trail system. Though shared with hikers, joggers and equestrians, the more than 100 miles of trails that reach out from the city as far as Chatfield and Cherry Creek state parks are smooth, fairly level and perfect for cycling. Detailed bike route and urban trail maps are available from the **Colorado State Parks Division of Parks and Outdoor Recreation.** ~ 1313 Sherman Street #618; 303-866-3437.

Bike Rentals   Mountain and suspension bikes are available for rent at **Arvada Bicycle Company**, located in a Denver suburb northwest of downtown. ~ 6595 Wadsworth Boulevard, Arvada; 303-420-3854.

HIKING

Two parks in this chapter offer real hiking trails; however, they are interconnecting trail segments and not single long trails. Serious hikers should look for nearby trails in Chapter Three. All distances for hiking trails are one way unless otherwise noted.

Roxborough State Park near Littleton, a southwestern suburb of Denver, has a network of trails through the canyons formed between tall sandstone ridges. Although the longest trails run for only a mile or so one way, they interconnect to create hikes of up to eight miles. **Castlewood Canyon State Park** has a number of interconnected trails totaling about four miles through a green canyon carved into the prairie near Franktown, a southeastern suburb.

▼▼▼▼▼▼▼▼▼▼▼▼
Transportation

CAR

Route 25 is Denver's main north–south thoroughfare, leading south to Colorado Springs and north to Fort Collins. **Route 70** splits the city horizontally, running east–west, quickly bringing motorists to the mountain forests and rock cliffs of the Front Range. **Route 76** enters Denver from the northeast.

AIR

The state-of-the-art **Denver International Airport** (DIA), opened in February 1995, ranks as the world's largest airport, covering an area of 53 square miles—twice the size of Manhattan. At $5 billion, it is the most expensive airport ever built, yet it actually handles fewer flights than the old airport it replaced did.

Denver International Airport is served by America West, American Airlines, Continental Airlines, Delta Air Lines, Great Lakes Airlines, Mexicana, Trans World Airlines, United Airlines and USAir, as well as the commuter carriers Mesa Airlines, Continental Express and United Express.

Airport transportation from Denver International Airport is by taxi or shuttle. The **Airporter** (303-227-0000) runs shuttle vans from the airport to downtown hotels every 30 minutes and to southeast Denver hotels every 30 minutes. They can also schedule home pickups. The RTD (303-299-6000) regional bus system offers low-cost bus service to and from the airport.

TRAIN

Amtrak's "Zephyr" stops at Union Station on its run between Chicago and San Francisco. The portion of the route that crosses the Rockies between Denver and Glenwood Springs is one of the most spectacular rides on the Amtrak system. ~ 707 17th Street, Denver; 303-534-2812, 800-872-7245.

BUS

Greyhound Bus Lines (800-231-2222) serves Denver's large, modern downtown bus terminal, departing several times daily in all four compass directions on Routes 70 and 25. ~ 1055 19th Street; 303-293-6590.

CAR RENTALS

Among the many car-rental agencies at or near the Denver and Colorado Springs airports are **A-Courtesy Rent A Car** (800-441-1816), **Alamo Rent A Car** (800-327-9633), **Avis Rent A Car** (800-331-1212), **Budget Rent A Car** (800-527-0700), **Dollar Rent A Car** (800-800-4000), **Enterprise Rent A Car** (800-325-8007), **Hertz Rent A Car** (800-654-3131) and **National Interrent** (800-328-4567). Motor homes and RVs are for rent at **Cruise America**. ~ 8950 North Federal Boulevard, Denver; 800-327-7799.

PUBLIC TRANSIT

RTD (Regional Transportation District) provides bus service throughout the Denver metropolitan area. ~ 303-299-6000.

TAXIS

Major cab companies that serve the greater Denver area include **Metro Taxi** (303-333-3333), **Yellow Cab** (303-777-7777) and **Zone Cab** (303-444-8888).

THREE

The Front Range

Trace the Continental Divide on a map of Colorado and you'll notice that it veers due east from Steamboat Springs all the way to Rocky Mountain National Park. From there, the Divide extends southward for nearly a hundred miles as a 12,000-foot-high wall of solid granite before meandering westward again. The wall of mountains poses an obstacle so formidable that in pioneer days wagon trains journeyed hundreds of miles to the north or south to avoid it. As recently as the 1960s, the builders of the interstate highway system concluded that the only way to extend a four-lane freeway west from Denver was to forget about trying to cross over the Continental Divide and instead tunnel *through* it.

This mountain range, extending from Rocky Mountain National Park south to Hoosier Pass near Breckenridge, together with the lower mountains that step their way down the eastern slope from the Continental Divide to the plains, is officially known as the Front Range. It is the easternmost major mountain range in the Rockies—the first to be explored by mountain men, gold prospectors and early-day tourists, and the most populous mountain area in Colorado today. Besides accessibility, the lower elevations of the Front Range enjoy the mildest winter weather in the central Rockies thanks to the "rain shadow" cast by the higher mountains along the Continental Divide.

The Front Range has come to mean something different to most Coloradoans. "Front Range Corridor" has become the common term for the string of cities at the foot of the Front Range mountains, from the southern edge of the Denver metro area northward to Fort Collins, including Boulder, Longmont, Loveland and Greeley, as well as a number of increasingly suburban mountain towns such as Golden, Evergreen and Estes Park.

Nowhere else in Colorado will visitors find such diversity as along the Front Range. Even a cursory auto tour of this region, which could be accomplished in a single day, might include the state's richest farmland, its largest universities, its highest mountain roads, its oldest gold and silver boom towns, as well as high-tech industries, high-priced housing developments, tourist traps galore and vast expanses of alpine wilderness studded with peaks that present challenges to novice hikers and veteran mountain climber alike. All the towns and sights included in this chapter lie within an hour's drive west of Route 25.

▼▼▼▼▼▼▼▼▼▼▼▼

Denver Mountain Parks Area

The western suburbs of the greater Denver area collide with mountain forests and rock cliffs no more than 20 miles from the state capitol downtown. Thanks to this proximity, Denver's municipal government has been able to acquire areas outside the city over the years to create the Denver Mountain Parks System. As a result, today Denver has more municipal park acreage than any other city in the country, and the acquisition has been coordinated with county and state park departments and the national forest service to form a huge greenbelt including virtually all of the mountains visible from Denver on a smog-free day. Exploring these areas just west of Denver makes for memorable day trips—and a complete change of pace from the bustle of the city.

SIGHTS

Golden is set at the foot of Lookout Mountain, the low peak crowned by broadcast towers serving the Denver area. There are spectacular views of the city from the paved road that winds seven miles up the mountain to **Buffalo Bill's Grave and Memorial Museum**. William F. "Buffalo Bill" Cody began his career on the prairies of Kansas and Nebraska as a Pony Express rider, army scout, Indian fighter and bison hunter for construction crews laying the first railroad tracks to the West. Stretching the truth a little, dime novelist Ned Buntline made Cody famous as the hero of numerous best-selling tales of the American frontier. Cody cashed in on his reputation by producing a Wild West spectacular that featured a cast of hundreds including Annie Oakley, Chief Sitting Bull and several live bison. The hugely successful show toured the eastern United States and Europe for 30 years but finally collapsed into bankruptcy. Cody died a 70-year-old pauper in 1917 while staying with relatives in Denver. Exhibits in the museum at the gravesite show both sides of Cody's life—frontiersman and show-business promoter—including the flashy saddle and fringed buckskin suit he wore in his Wild West show. Admission. ~ Lookout Mountain Road, Golden; 303-526-0747.

Golden is best known for its largest employer, the **Adolph Coors Company**. Visitors can take a free tour of the brewery and see the huge vats where the beer is made. There is a tasting room. ~ 13th and Ford streets, Golden; 303-277-2337.

Adjacent to the Coors brewery is a completely different kind of brewery—**Hakushika Sake USA**, where much of the sake (Japanese rice wine) sold in the United States is made and bottled. An exhibition of Japanese art, a gift shop and a tasting room are open to the public, and tours of the brewery are available by reservation a day in advance. ~ 4414 Table Mountain Drive, Golden; 303-279-7253.

The **Colorado Railroad Museum** provides an overview of 19th-century railroad development with maps, memorabilia and more than 50 locomotives, carriages and trolley cars. There is also a large model-train collection on display. ~ 17155 West 44th Avenue, Golden; 303-279-4591.

The **Rocky Mountain Quilt Museum**, the only museum in Colorado devoted to the art of quilting, presents changing exhibits that range from historical retrospectives to shows highlighting the work of contemporary craftspeople. A guide explains the quilts and their history, and a gift shop offers not only locally handmade quilts but also patterns and publications for do-it-yourselfers. Closed Sunday and Monday. Admission. ~ 1111 Washington Avenue, Golden; 303-277-0377.

Two other local-history museums offer a look at Golden in the 1860s, when it was the first capital of the Colorado Territory. One is the small **Golden Pioneer Museum**, with its collections of guns, antique furnishings and territorial documents. Admission. ~ 923 10th Street, Golden; 303-278-7151. Nearby the **Astor House Hotel Museum** was the first stone masonry hotel west of the Mississippi when it was built in 1867, and it is the oldest hotel in Colorado that is still standing, though it no longer rents rooms. Instead, it has been restored as a museum of 19th-century furniture and decorative art, with room after room of brass beds and baroque wallpaper and a sumptuous sitting room. Admission. ~ 822 12th Street, Golden; 303-278-3557.

Since 1871, Golden has been the site of one of the nation's leading colleges for geologists, the Colorado School of Mines. For the largest exhibit of minerals, fossils, gems and ores to be found anywhere in the state, visit the **Colorado School of Mines Geology Museum**. The museum also exhibits mining drills and other equipment from the gold boom days. Of particular interest is the Thomas Allen Minelighting Collection, showing ingenious methods of underground lighting devised in the days before electricity. ~ 16th and Maple streets, Golden; 303-273-3823. Also on the campus is the **U.S. Geological Survey National Earthquake Information Center**, where seismographs monitor earthquake activity throughout the world. Free tours, which must be arranged in advance, are available on weekdays. Visitors see the banks of machines that track the earth's rumblings, while a guide explains how the scientists at work there collect and organize all those squiggly lines into a coherent picture of geological activity and

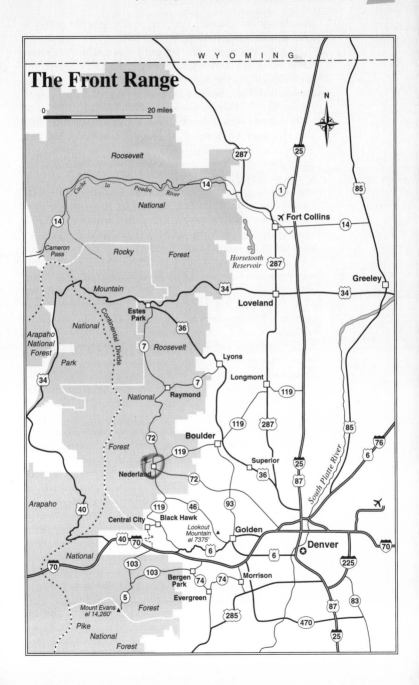

The Front Range

describes efforts to develop ways of predicting future quakes. ~ 1711 Illinois Street, Golden; 303-273-8500.

The visitors center of the **National Renewable Energy Laboratory** contains exhibits showing how technologies are being developed to transform the power of the sun and wind into electricity. Free tours of the laboratory facilities are offered daily. ~ 14869 Denver West Parkway, Golden; 303-384-6565.

Red Rocks Park is located along the sandstone escarpment above the town of Morrison. To get there, take Route 285 west from Route 25 through Englewood, the major suburb on the south side of downtown Denver. Turn north on Route 8. The park is best known as the site of **Red Rocks Amphitheater**, one of the most important concert venues in the Rockies. Bruce Springsteen, U2 and the Beatles (on their first U.S. tour!) are among the performers who have stood on the stage. You can stand there, too, unless preparations are being made for a concert that night. The acoustics of the natural amphitheater surrounded by sandstone cliffs are so perfect that a person standing at the back of the 8000 seats can hear a ping-pong ball drop on the concrete stage—without a microphone. Also in the 2700-acre park is **Dinosaur Ridge**, where visitors can see a working fossil dig and the actual footprints of a *Tyrannosaurus rex*. ~ Hogback Road, Morrison; 303-640-2637.

Generations of kids (and their parents) have marveled at **Tiny Town**, a unique array of more than a hundred miniature houses, stores, churches, and other structures covering nearly 20 acres, best viewed from the little coal-fired steam train that carries sightseers around the grounds. Admission. ~ Route 285, Morrison; 303-697-6829.

Ten miles up Bear Creek Canyon on serpentine Route 74 is **Evergreen**, a former ranching town next to an artificial lake at the foot of Mount Evans. The village is now the center of an exclusive bedroom community set among ponderosa pines and sandwiched between the Red Rocks Park backcountry on the east and the 4000-acre Mount Evans State Wildlife Area on the west.

The **Hiwan Homestead Museum** preserves a rustic mansion in a narrow valley. The antique furnishings and decor of the interior span a 50-year period from 1889 to 1930. Exhibits tell about Evergreen's early settlers. The neighborhood of custom homes on five-acre lots surrounding the museum were once part of the ranch. Afternoon tours are available by advance reservation. ~ 4208 South Timberville Drive, Evergreen; 303-674-6262.

Five miles north of Evergreen on Route 74, the town of **Bergen Park** is the starting point of the road up Mount Evans. Bergen Park is only three miles from busy Route 70 (Exit 252). At Exit 253, a mile east on the interstate, is **Genessee Park**, a Denver mountain park, where a city-owned bison herd has roamed since 1914.

From Bergen Park, Route 103 climbs laterally across the steep north face of the mountain for 19 miles among aspen groves and tall fir forests to picture-perfect **Echo Lake**, just below timberline, where the paved **Mount Evans Road** (Route 5) turns off for its ascent to the 14,264-foot summit. Open only during the summer months, the 14-mile-long road over alpine tundra is the highest auto route in the Rocky Mountains, reaching 164 feet higher than the summit of Pikes Peak. In fact, Mount Evans is only 169 feet shorter than Mount Elbert, the highest mountain in Colorado. Three miles up the road to the summit from Echo Lake is the trailhead for the **Mount Goliath Natural Area**, where an easy one-and-a-half-mile (one-way) nature trail leads through a rare forest of bristlecone pine, a small species of evergreen that grows only at timberline and is sculpted into strangely twisted forms by alpine winds. Some of the trees here are more than 1600 years old. Adventuresome visitors may wish to forgo the drive up the last steep, twisting mile to the summit, park at **Summit Lake** and climb the trail up the last 600 vertical feet of the mountain. Take your time, though. Strenuous exercise can bring on altitude sickness in the thin atmosphere, with symptoms of dizziness, fainting or nausea. Thunderstorms can also pose a hazard: more people are struck by lightning on Mount Evans than anyplace else in the state.

From Echo Lake, Route 103 continues for another 14 miles down Chicago Creek Canyon and returns to Route 70 at **Idaho Springs**. The springs for which the town was named feed a greenhouse swimming pool, individual tubs and a vapor pool at the **Indian Springs Spa**. The spa's unique feature is Club Mud, a pool where you can immerse your whole body in warm, earthy ooze. Admission. ~ 302 Soda Creek Road, Idaho Springs; 303-567-2191.

✔ CHECK THESE OUT—UNIQUE SIGHTS

- Play paleontologist for a day at Red Rocks Park's **Dinosaur Ridge**, where you can observe an actual fossil dig and touch the footprints of a *Tyrannosaurus rex.* page 76
- Tour the family-owned **Phoenix Gold Mine**, a working old-time gold mine in Idaho Springs. page 78
- Grin at artist José Perez's unflattering presidential portraits in the **Satirical World Art Museum**. page 95
- See one of the world's few antique steam-powered cars in the lobby of Estes Park's **Stanley Hotel**. page 95

Idaho Springs, founded as the site of the first important gold strike in the Colorado Rockies, grew up as the hub of the silver district that included Black Hawk and Central City. The downtown **historic district** along Miner Street between 13th and 17th avenues is lined with ornate Victorian buildings, some of them dating back to the 1850s.

Several sights recall the region's old mining days. The **Phoenix Gold Mine** offers tours of a family-owned gold mine that still operates on a small scale and utilizes traditional mining methods. You'll be escorted 600 feet underground and shown a three-foot-long vein of gold ore. Feeling lucky? Gold panning is possible for a small fee. Admission. ~ Trail Creek Road, Idaho Springs; 303-567-0422.

HIDDEN ►   For a different slant on mining, visit the **Edgar Mine**, an 1870s shaft that the Colorado School of Mines in Golden has revived as an underground research and instruction facility where visitors can take a peek at the latest mining technology. It's used for classes during the school year and offers tours during summer vacation. Admission. ~ Dry Gulch, Idaho Springs; 303-567-2911.

Most of the gold ore mined in the Central City–Black Hawk area was transported through a tunnel more than four miles long for refining in Idaho Springs at the **Argo Mill and Museum**, the state's largest ore mill. Guides show visitors the furnaces where gold concentrate was turned into ingots and the vaults where it was stored, providing a vivid demonstration of the huge quantities of precious metal that poured out of the Colorado Rockies in the 19th century. Thoroughly commercialized today, the mill offers gold panning, curios and staged shootouts. Admission. ~ 2317 Riverside Drive, Idaho Springs; 303-567-2421.

An old-time assay office has been restored at the **Underhill Museum**. It now serves as the headquarters for the Idaho Springs Historical Society and displays photographs, documents and equipment used for analyzing ore. ~ 1416 Miner Street, Idaho Springs; 303-567-4709.

HIDDEN ►   A mile west of town at Exit 238 from Route 70, the paved 12-mile Fall River Road leads to the ghost town of **Alice**, which dates back to the 1860s and was the site of the richest gold mine in the area. A 1915 schoolhouse and a scattering of old log cabins remain. Above the town site at the end of a half-mile walking trail, **St. Mary's Lake** shimmers at the foot of St. Mary's Glacier, one of the few true glaciers in Colorado, on the slope of Mount Kingston (12,136 feet).

HIDDEN ►   From the Idaho Springs vicinity, the nine-mile **Oh My God Road** winds up through Virginia Canyon to Central City. It is unpaved but well maintained and can easily be driven in a passenger car. Along the way are hundreds of old mines and the ghost town of **Russell Gulch,** which got its start in the 1860s and grew to a peak population of 2500, mostly immigrant miners from the Italian and Austrian Alps. For motorists who are timid about mountain driving, an easier, paved road—Route 119—goes through Clear Creek Canyon to Central City from Exit 244 on Route 70, three miles east of Idaho Springs.

While most visitors opt to stay in the Denver metro area while exploring the nearby mountains, Golden has several chain hotels and motor inns geared primarily toward business travelers that can make convenient havens beyond the reach of big-city traffic. For instance, the **Ramada Hotel–Denver West,** a modern 225-room hotel, is ideally located as a base for exploring areas west of Denver. The rooms are spacious and the furnishings are exactly what you'd expect from a first-class corporate motor inn—flawless and virtually identical—following a recent renovation. The indoor recreation center, including a swimming pool, whirl-

LODGING

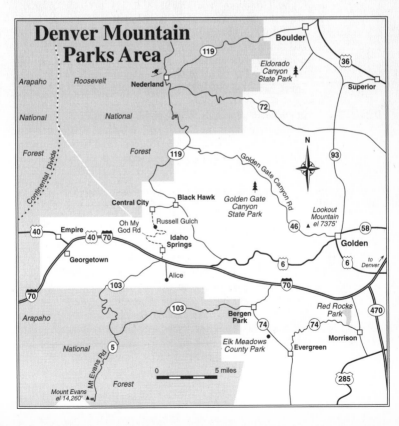

Denver Mountain Parks Area

pool spa, exercise room, miniature golf, ping-pong and video games, makes it a good choice for families. ~ 14707 West Colfax Avenue, Golden; 303-279-7611, 800-729-2830, fax 303-278-1651. MODERATE.

Originally built in the early 1900s as a private mansion, the **Table Mountain Inn** was so extensively remodeled in 1992 that its original character is concealed by a no-expense-spared coat of Santa Fe style. Most of the 32 rooms have balconies or patios with views of the foothills, and some suites have jacuzzis. ~ 1310 Washington Avenue, Golden; 303-277-9898, 800-762-9898, fax 303-271-0298. DELUXE.

Inexpensive accommodations can be found in Golden at the **Mountain View Motel**, a low-slung highway motel that offers 34 clean, recently carpeted motel rooms, each with two double beds. Some rooms have refrigerators and bathtubs, and a few have efficiency kitchens. ~ 14825 West Colfax Avenue, Golden; 303-279-2526. BUDGET.

Built from local sandstone in 1873, the **Cliff House Lodge** was originally the mansion of George Morrison, the founder of the town that bears his name. Today the mansion operates as a bed-and-breakfast establishment. Each of the guest rooms is individually decorated with period antiques. Two honeymoon suites feature private hot tubs and woodburning fireplaces. ~ 121 Stone Street, Morrison; 303-697-9732. DELUXE.

DINING

In the Golden foothills, **Briarwood Inn** is considered one of the finest restaurants in the Denver area. It features Continental dining, candlelight, polished silver, fine china and lavish European-country decor. The menu offers prime rib, lobster, Dover sole and

✔ CHECK THESE OUT—UNIQUE LODGING

- *Budget:* Be kind to your wallet by staying at the unpretentious **Mountain View Motel**, a rarity in these parts with rates under $50. *page 80*
- *Moderate to deluxe:* Visit the gambling capital of the West, without stepping onto a plane, at **Harvey's Wagon Wheel Casino Hotel and Resort**, Colorado's only big Vegas-style casino hotel. *page 86*
- *Deluxe:* Enjoy the Victorian luxury of the **Cliff House Lodge**, the sandstone mansion of Morrison's town founder. *page 80*
- *Deluxe to ultra-deluxe:* Horseback ride, swim, fish, hike or soak in a hot tub at **Aspen Lodge**, an Estes Park log lodge that sets the standard for Colorado dude ranches. *page 98*

Budget: under $50 Moderate: $50–$90 Deluxe: $90–$130 Ultra-deluxe: over $130

beef Wellington; all entrées include appetizers and dessert. ~ 1630 8th Street, Golden; 303-279-3121. ULTRA-DELUXE.

Another great dining option in Golden is the **Capital Grill**, a spin-off location of a perennially popular restaurant in Silverthorne. The food is all-American, featuring home-style ribs, chicken and fish. Guests get to grill some of the meat and fish entrées themselves on a stone slab. ~ 1122 Washington Street, Golden; 303-279-6390. MODERATE.

Historic El Rancho Village, a mountain lodge, has been a favorite special-occasion restaurant for generations of Front Range residents. Diners enjoy a spectacular Continental Divide view. Primarily a steakhouse, El Rancho also serves prime rib and trout. Ice-cream sundaes are included with all dinners. ~ 29260 Route 40, Golden; 303-526-0661. MODERATE TO DELUXE.

If you've never seen a buckskin-clad waitperson open a champagne bottle with a tomahawk, you'll have a chance to witness this spectacle at **The Fort**. Designed in Southwestern adobe style after Bent's Fort, the first trading post in Colorado, The Fort has a lovely setting near Red Rocks Park, an Indian teepee out front, a picturesque courtyard and round *horno*-style fireplaces. It serves more buffalo meat than any other restaurant, along with such other frontier delicacies as rattlesnake, roast buffalo marrow bone, and Rocky Mountain oysters (which, it should be mentioned, are not really oysters at all). ~ 19192 Route 8, Morrison; 303-697-4771. DELUXE.

Buffalo Bar and Restaurant has a bar that dates back to 1860, a museum-like assemblage of memorabilia, a retail smoke house and trading post, and great views of Bridal Veil Falls from the back dining rooms. The menu is eclectic, specializing in buffalo and also featuring salads, soups, pizza and Texas-style barbecue. ~ 1617 Miner Street, Idaho Springs; 303-567-2729. MODERATE.

SHOPPING

When it comes to shopping, the small towns west of Denver are in the shadow of the big city and offer less than you would find in similar-sized communities on the other side of the Continental Divide. An exception is Evergreen, which had a reputation as an artsy-crafty haven before the town evolved into a high-priced bedroom community in the 1980s. Artisans who make their homes here tend to sell elsewhere these days, but an hour spent strolling Evergreen's main-street "historic district" will turn up the occasional locally made item among the pricey decorative imports that make up most of the inventory in the galleries and shops.

In Golden, **Heritage Square** is a combination shopping center and theme park with an Old West motif. You can, if you wish, browse through gift shops with an ersatz old-fashioned flavor while the kids get their thrills on the alpine slide and go-cart racetrack or try bungee jumping. The amusement park is open daily in summer and weekends in April, May, September and October. ~ Colfax Avenue, Golden; 303-279-2789.

NIGHTLIFE   The **Little Bear Inn** in the center of Evergreen was the town's original saloon, a rowdy roadhouse that used to serve as a meeting place for bikers from all over the West. Though it retains a slightly disreputable look, the present-day clientele is more likely to be made up of lawyers and trust-fund kids than black-leather outlaws. There's live music nightly, featuring local and sometimes national rock and R&B bands. ~ 28075 Route 74, Evergreen; 303-674-9991.

PARKS   **ARAPAHO NATIONAL FOREST** 🚶 🏊 ⛵ This 1,025,000-acre forest covers both sides of the Continental Divide and reaches from the southwestern outskirts of the Denver metropolitan area northwest almost to Steamboat Springs, a distance of 90 miles as the crow flies, spanning some of the Colorado Rockies' most rugged terrain. The forest's principal feature in the Denver Mountain Parks area is the Mount Evans Wilderness, a 74,000-acre roadless area that extends into Pike National Forest to the south and encompasses all of the mountain except for a pie-shaped corridor through which the Mount Evans Highway zigzags to the summit. Fishing is good for rainbow and other trout species, particularly in Chicago Creek and Echo Lake along the Mount Evans Highway and in Chicago Lake near the summit. The forest is under the same administration as Roosevelt National Forest. Facilities include picnic areas, restrooms, hiking trails and jeep trails. ~ The main road through this area of the forest is paved Route 103, the Mount Evans Highway. West Chicago Creek Campground is 6 miles southwest of Idaho Springs on this highway, and Echo Lake Campground is 14 miles from Idaho Springs on the same road; 303-567-2901.

▲ There are two national forest campgrounds in this area. West Chicago Creek Campground has 11 RV/tent sites (no hookups), and Echo Lake Campground has 18 RV/tent sites (no hookups). Both are open through mid-September and sometimes later, depending on the snowfall. Fees at both are $8 per night.

RED ROCKS PARK 🚶 Seventy-million-year-old splinters of sandstone broke through the earth's surface in the upheavals that created the Front Range to form 400-foot-tall rock formations shaped like the prows of sinking ships. Two of them wrap around a 8000-seat natural amphitheater that serves as one of the nation's most unusual rock and country concert venues. Although the amphitheater is the main sightseeing highlight, the surrounding 600-acre Denver mountain park offers paved roads to picnic spots and hiking trails through foothills covered with scrub oak

and rock monoliths. Rock climbing is prohibited. There are picnic areas, restrooms and a store. ~ The park is near the town of
Morrison. From Route 70, take Exit 259 and follow Route 26
south to the well-marked park road. It can also be reached via
Route 74; 303-640-2637.

ELK MEADOWS COUNTY PARK AND DEDISSE PARK 🚶 🚲 Elk
Meadows, a Jefferson County Open Space Park, adjoins Bergen
Peak State Wildlife Area on one side and Dedisse Park, part of the
Denver Mountain Parks system, on the other to form one vast recreation area. An easy six-mile trail that loops through varied terrain—meadows, sunny mountain slopes and dark forest nooks—
is a favorite of joggers and mountain bikers. There are plenty of
benches at scenic overlooks, and longer trails climb into the wildlife area and wind south toward Dedisse Park, which has more
well-worn hiking trails as well as picnic sites with stone fireplaces
and shelters built in the 1930s by the WPA. There are picnic areas
and restrooms at Dedisse Park. ~ Parking area and trailhead located along the west side of Route 74 about three miles north of
Evergreen; 303-697-4545.

MOUNT FALCON PARK 🚶 🚲 This 1400-acre Jefferson County
Open Space Park has ten miles of hiking and mountain-biking
trails on the slopes of Mount Falcon, overlooking Denver and
Red Rocks Park to the northeast and Mount Evans to the west.
The park was once part of the estate of John Brisbane Walker,
publisher of *Cosmopolitan* magazine, who had a castlelike summer home here. In 1914, Walker began construction on a "Summer White House," which he planned to donate to the federal
government as a vacation home for U.S. presidents. The vacation
cabin was never completed, nor was it ever visited by any U.S.
president, and Walker's own castle burned in 1918, leaving only
stone walls. The ruins of both summer homes afford spectacular
views. ~ Take Route 285 for 14 miles southwest of Denver to
Indian Hills Road; turn north and go three and a half miles to
the sign marking the park entrance; 303-697-4545.

Central City, one of Colorado's preeminent historic
mining towns, has a population of 300 today but
was the largest city in the territory around the time

Central City Area

of the U.S. Civil War: in the early 1860s Central City had 15,000
residents, well over Denver's 6000. It became the cultural center
of the Colorado Rockies as well, with a theater district that included the grandest opera house in the West. When Colorado became a state in 1876, Central City was one of the top choices for
the state capital and lost the honor by a close vote. Black Hawk,
a tiny mining camp about a mile down canyon from Central City,
was transformed into a real town in 1877, when a railroad spur

made it that far but could not reach Central City. But the richest gold and silver ore ran out by 1880, and creeping unemployment brought about the city's agonizingly slow abandonment over a period of 50 years. The restoration of Central City's elegant hotel during the 1930s focused attention once more on the picturesque old town of Victorian brick buildings adorned with fluted columns and fanciful stonework that loom like wraiths out of a not-so-ancient past.

Although tourists have crowded the streets of Central City for decades, an economy based on seasonal curio shops and luncheon restaurants could not generate the kind of money needed to keep most of the old buildings from deteriorating. In 1990, Coloradoans voted to legalize $5-limit casino gambling in Central City and Black Hawk as well as Cripple Creek, with the provision that casinos could be operated only in existing historic buildings. Given Central City's location, half an hour's drive from a city of a million people, it's no wonder that the casino idea has succeeded enormously in bringing money to the town and fixing up every building in sight. The controversial change also has obscured much of Central City's unique historical character behind a veneer of glitz, clamor and greed, and it has driven most old-timers to sell out and leave town. Today, Central City and Black Hawk together have a total of 36 casinos offering 6609 slot machines and 174 blackjack and poker tables.

SIGHTS History still exists in Central City—if you look for it. The **Central City Opera House** has crystal chandeliers and elaborate wall murals. Although it was open for only about five years at the end of the mining boom, since its restoration in the 1930s it has been, and continues to be, the most popular place to see opera in Colorado. Some of America's leading opera singers appear in the annual July and August performance season. There are no winter performances because the opera house lacks a heating system. Admission. ~ 200 Eureka Street, Central City; 303-292-6500.

Next door to the opera, the **Teller House** was built in 1872 as a boardinghouse for miners, but when the sidewalk in front of the hotel was paved with silver ingots to welcome visiting

---

CENTRAL CITY'S SALOON LEGEND

The claim is often heard that the haunting "Face on the Barroom Floor" in the Teller House casino bar was the subject of H. Antoine D'Arcy's tragic 19th-century poem of the same name. But in fact it was the poem that inspired Colorado artist Herndon Davis, who restored the hotel's murals during the 1930s, to paint his wife's face on the floorboards.

President Ulysses S. Grant, it began to gain its reputation as the city's elegant hostelry. When silver baron and U.S. Senator Horace Tabor turned one floor of the hotel into a lavish suite for his mistress, Black Hawk divorcee Elizabeth "Baby Doe" (who would become his second wife and a legendary figure in Colorado history), he refurbished the hotel in a grand manner, redecorating in opulent French Provincial style and lining the walls with 12-foot-tall diamond-dust mirrors imported from Italy and brought from the East Coast by wagon. When University of Denver students began restoration efforts in 1932, they found the mirrors still in place and part of the abandoned hotel in use as a chicken coop. Today, the Teller House is owned by a Swiss investment group that has converted much of it into Central City's most lavish gambling casino, but visitors can still see the Baby Doe suite on guided tours and the famous "Face on the Barroom Floor" in the casino bar. Admission. ~ 120 Eureka Street, Central City; 303-582-3200.

Across from the Teller House, the **Thomas-Billings Home** was boarded up in 1917 and, like a huge time capsule, remained untouched until new owners reopened it 70 years later. Restored with original furnishings and period decor, the house operates as a museum. Since the original owners were local merchants, the exhibits emphasize 19th-century product packaging and advertisements. Admission. ~ 109 Eureka Street, Central City; 303-582-3435.

The **Gilpin County Historical Society Museum,** in the old high school building, displays artifacts and photographs from the mining era along with collections of Victorian clothing, dolls and toys. Admission. ~ 228 East High Street, Central City; 303-582-5283.

Less than a mile down the road from the eastern outskirts of Central City is the smaller town of **Black Hawk**, where the main sight to see is the **Lace House**, a restored 1863 Carpenter Gothic–style gabled home known locally as "the Gingerbread House." Its rooms are filled with household antiques from the mining-boom period. Admission. ~ 161 Main Street, Black Hawk; 303-582-5211.

Route 119/6, the Clear Creek Canyon Highway, parallels the newer interstate highway at a distance and goes downhill for 20 miles to the city of Golden. For a slower but more scenic and much less busy alternative, motorists may wish to try the Golden Gate Canyon Road (Route 46). It turns off from Route 119 at the Dory Hill campground, seven miles north of Black Hawk, and threads its way out of the mountains through a narrow canyon to the north side of Golden.

Until recently, the Central City–Black Hawk area has had practically nothing to offer in the way of accommodations. Lodging was limited to two guest suites, furnished in country southwest-

LODGING

ern pieces, at the **Winfield Scott Guest Quarters** on the hillside above Central City. Rates include breakfast. ~ 210 Hooper Street, Central City; 303-582-3433. DELUXE. There are also three small, rather plain rooms in the **Shamrock Inn**. ~ 351 Gregory Street, Central City; 303-582-5513. MODERATE.

The lodging situation changed in 1995 with the opening of **Harvey's Wagon Wheel Casino Hotel and Resort**. This large modern hotel built up a hillside on the road into town is the closest thing to a Las Vegas–style resort hotel you'll find anywhere in Colorado. The 118 rather spartan guest rooms and suites are decorated in soft earth tones, and some have good views overlooking the town. ~ 321 Gregory Street, Central City; 303-582-0800, fax 303-582-5860. MODERATE TO DELUXE.

DINING

Emily's Fine Dining Parlors, located in the Glory Hole Saloon & Gaming Hall, is one of the few restaurants in Central City that rises above fast-food quality and ambience. The restaurant's Victorian decor and antique furniture, including marble-top tables, create an intimate feeling. The menu includes prime rib, seafood, pasta and poultry dishes. Emily's takes special pride in its desserts, such as a scrumptious mud pie. ~ 13 Main Street, Central City; 303-582-0800. DELUXE.

The **Black Forest Inn** was a centerpiece of the Central City–Black Hawk District long before the first casino opened. In fact, Denverites have been driving out here since 1956 to enjoy the finest German food in Colorado. Though it now shares space with Otto's Casino, the atmosphere is still family-oriented and as Bavarian as cuckoo clocks and oompah bands, and so is the dinner menu, which includes beautiful presentations of *wienerschnitzel*, *sauerbraten* and other authentic German specialties along with wild game entrées. The lunch menu offers more usual American fare. ~ 260 Gregory Street, Black Hawk; 303-279-2333. MODERATE TO DELUXE.

NIGHTLIFE

Gambling casinos are the sole entertainment—indeed, the only industry of any kind—in Central City (15 casinos) and Black Hawk (20 casinos). The betting limit is $5 at all casinos; only blackjack and poker tables are permitted, along with mechanical "one-armed bandits" and video gaming including poker, blackjack and keno machines.

In Central City, the biggest casino (nine blackjack tables, four poker tables, 530 slot and video poker machines) is the multilevel **Glory Hole Saloon & Gaming Hall** at the east end of the three-block Main Street casino strip. ~ 13 Main Street, Central City; 303-582-1171. Other top casinos cluster around the corner of Lawrence and Main streets. Among them are the flashy **Golden Rose**, known for its dinner buffet and grab-all-you-can money

Colorado's Casino Comeback

One of the most familiar images of the Hollywood version of the Old West is the smoke-filled saloon where cowboys and cardsharks face off around the poker table as women of ill repute make eyes at the winners. There is a lot of truth to the image. Gambling played an important role in 19th-century frontier life for many of Colorado's ranch and mine workers, who were so poorly paid that gaming tables offered the only chance, however illusory, to get together enough cash to buy a piece of ranch land and start a better life. More often, of course, gambling merely perpetuated their poverty instead.

Most games of chance except horse and dog racing were declared illegal in Colorado early in the 20th century, partly due to the same nationwide moralistic fervor that led to Prohibition, but also partly because of the social ills—notably violent crime—associated with gambling.

Beginning in the mid-1970s, Colorado became one of the first states besides Nevada to relax its prohibitions against gambling. The state legislature passed the Colorado Lottery, and it unexpectedly generated more than $25 million in state revenues in its first 90 days of operation. Since then, the Colorado Lottery has expanded with a full range of colorful, sometimes bewildering games you can play at any convenience store. Thus gambling won renewed respectability.

So it sounded reasonable when, in 1990, state legislators proposed legalizing limited-stakes casino gambling in three great old mining towns—Central City, Black Hawk and Cripple Creek—in hopes of generating funds for historic preservation in these towns. The first casinos opened in 1993, sparking a controversy that has raged ever since.

Slot machines, video poker screens, and poker and blackjack tables suddenly packed every decrepit old building that was still standing and resulted in grand-scale refurbishment of the towns. The casinos also drove out the modest ma-and-pa cafés and small grocery stores that used to occupy the towns' storefronts and pushed old-time curio shops into bankruptcy. Crowd control needs and the threat of crime inspired Cripple Creek to quadruple the size of its police force. Traffic on the winding mountain routes to all three towns increased 20-fold. This, combined with drunk driving incidents, make them among the most dangerous roads in the state.

Critics have amassed substantial proof that allowing the casinos was a mistake; however, gambling has proved so financially successful that it is almost certain to continue. Leadville, whose mines have recently closed down, is busy lobbying the legislature to legalize casinos there, too.

chamber. ~ Main Street, Central City; 800-929-0255. The most historic of the Central City casinos is the **Teller House**, bedecked with antiques left over from the gold-mining days of the Victorian era, when this was one of Colorado's most elegant hotels; though it has no gaming tables, it boasts 400 slots and poker machines and sponsors nightly video poker tournaments. ~ Lawrence Street, Central City; 303-582-3200.

The largest casino in the area is Black Hawk's **Colorado Central Station**, with ten blackjack tables, six poker tables and 600 video poker and slot machines. ~ Main Street, Black Hawk; 303-279-3000. The **Gilpin Hotel Casino** offers not only gaming but also live entertainment—country, rock-and-roll, oldies, R&B or karaoke nightly in the Mine Shaft Bar. ~ Main Street, Black Hawk; 303-271-9327. Other casinos along Black Hawk's three-block Main Street include the British-motif **Pick-a-Dilly Casino**, which hosts a comedy club on Tuesday nights. ~ Main Street, Black Hawk; 303-582-1844. There's also the **Canyon Casino**. ~ Main Street, Black Hawk; 303-777-1111. At the lower end of Main Street, across from Colorado Central Station, **Jazz Alley** features live music on Friday and Saturday evenings, as well as a Cajun restaurant. ~ Main Street, Black Hawk. Casinos also line Black Hawk's Gregory Street (now locally nicknamed "The Strip") uphill toward Central City. Biggest among them is **Bronco Billy's**, which has expanded to include a sports bar with 37 TVs and seven big screens. ~ Gregory and Main streets, Black Hawk; 303-582-3311. Notable for its traditional Bavarian decor is **Otto's Casino at Black Forest Inn**. ~ Gregory Street, Black Hawk; 303-642-0415.

PARKS

ARAPAHO AND ROOSEVELT NATIONAL FORESTS 🚲 ⛵
Central City is situated near the boundary between these two contiguous national forests. Extensive past mining and logging have scarred hillsides in the area but left an extensive network of roads suitable for four-wheel-drive vehicles and mountain bikes. Columbine Campground offers the only camping in the Central City area. You can fish for rainbow trout in Pine Creek and Missouri Creek. ~ Main roads through this part of the forest include the Peak to Peak Highway (Route 119) and Oh My God Road (County Road 279). Columbine Campground is two miles northwest of Central City on County Road 279; 303-567-2901.

▲ Columbine Campground has 47 RV/tent sites (no hookups); open from late May through mid-October; $9 per night.

GOLDEN GATE CANYON STATE PARK 🚶🏇 🛶 ⛵ This 14,000-acre expanse of mountain meadows and canyons is the largest of the many state, county and municipal mountain parks along the Front Range. It has 35 miles of hiking and horseback trails, many of which are open for cross-country skiing in winter. Fishing is good for rainbow trout. Panorama Point offers a spectacular view of the Continental Divide. The visitors center has interpretive exhibits on plant and animal life, history and geology. Parking spaces can be hard to find on summer weekends. There are picnic areas and restrooms. Day-use fee, $4. ~ From Golden, take Route 93 north for one and a half miles; then turn west on Golden Gate Canyon Road. This paved road runs for about 15 miles through the park and comes out on Route 119 between Central City and Nederland; 303-582-3707.

▲ There are 164 RV/tent sites (some with electric hookups); $7 to $12 per night; reservations, 303-470-1144 or 800-678-2267.

From Denver, the most direct route to Estes Park and Rocky Mountain National Park is through Boulder, a prosperous university town. Although Boulder, like Denver, was founded by gold prospectors immediately after the first gold was discovered along the Front Range in 1858, Boulder emerged as an educational center practically from the start. Colorado's first schoolhouse was built there in 1860. The University of Colorado started in 1877 with a class of 64 freshmen, of which seven would receive diplomas four years later. Adult education also began here in 1898 with the Chautauqua, a lecture and symposium series held each summer in the state's first conference center and whose goal it was to expose Westerners to the thoughts of the era's leading intellectuals and moralists. Today, Boulder's unique character is a blend of high technology, humanism and youthful exuberance.

▼▼▼▼▼▼▼▼
Boulder

The main campus of the University of Colorado sprawls across the south side of town, bounded by Foothills Parkway on the east and Broadway on the west. The easiest access is from 26th Street (Route 36, the main highway from Denver). At the heart of the campus, broad green quadrangles are shaded by century-old fir trees and flanked by massive stone buildings with Mediterranean-style red-tile roofs. One main visitors' attraction on the campus is the **University of Colorado Museum**, which displays a full range of collections from dinosaur fossils to plant specimens, including a treasure trove of southwestern artifacts. ~ Henderson Building, 15th Street and Broadway; 303-492-6892. Also of interest on campus is **Fiske Planetarium**, whose Zeiss star projector, one of the largest in the world, accurately simulates more than 3000 celestial bodies. Public star shows are presented on weekend evenings and Sunday afternoons. Admission. ~ Regent Drive; 303-492-5001.

SIGHTS

The best show in Boulder is along **Pearl Street Mall**. In the 1970s, Boulder's main downtown street was the model for the kind of cute, café-lined, pedestrians-only historic district that has since sprung up in urban-renewal zones all over America. But the feel of Pearl Street remains unique thanks in large part to its street performers. Almost any day of the year finds folksingers playing for handouts beside the fountains and sculptures. On sunny summer weekends the mall is often completely lined with musicians, magicians, mimes and even acrobats performing in a dizzying impromptu circus. ~ Downtown between 11th and 15th streets.

The **Boulder Historical Society and Museum**, situated in the restored Harbeck Mansion (circa 1899), features both permanent and changing exhibits from the society's 35,000-item local-heritage collection. Outstanding displays include a pre-electric kitchen, fully equipped in the Victorian manner, and an extensive array of antique clothing. Admission. ~ 1206 Euclid Avenue; 303-449-3464.

Visitors are welcome to take a self-guided tour of the **National Center for Atmospheric Research**. The red sandstone building, set at the foot of the huge, slanted cliffs called the Flatirons on the southwest outskirts of the city, was designed by I. M. Pei, whom many consider to be America's finest living architect. Inside, exhibits cover everything from thunderstorms to global warming and offer a close-up look at the surface of the sun. Visitors can see two Cray supercomputers, whose speed of up to a billion calculations per second makes them the world's fastest computers at the time of this writing. ~ 1850 Table Mesa Drive; 303-497-1174.

Two of Boulder's most unusual manufacturing firms strive to attract visitors. **Celestial Seasonings**, which produces herb teas, offers weekday factory tours revealing how its teas are invented, blended and packaged. ~ 4600 Sleepytime Drive; 303-530-5300.

HIDDEN ► **Leanin' Tree**, the leading publisher of western greeting cards, has a free museum of Western art containing the originals of paintings reproduced on their cards as well as other cowboy paintings and sculptures. ~ 6055 Longbow Drive; 303-530-1442.

HIDDEN ► The **Women of the West Museum**, the first of its kind in the country, is slated to open in 2001. The 100,000-square-foot museum will include exhibits of clothing, artifacts and artwork, as well as an education center and a research archive containing diaries and letters written by women in the Old West. ~ Discovery Drive between Foothills Parkway and Colorado Avenue; 303-541-1000.

For the best view of the Boulder area, take the paved, serpentine **Flagstaff Mountain Road** about three miles to a 7000-foot summit overlooking the city. Before entering wild Boulder Mountain Park with its dramatic cliffs and canyons, the road goes through **Chautauqua Park**. At the center of this large, grassy foothills park is a big, whitewashed wood community center that was built in 1898 and, like its namesake at Lake Chautauqua, New York, has been used for summer conferences, lectures and concerts ever since. ~ 900 Baseline Road; 303-441-3410.

Another scenic mountain drive from Boulder is Route 119, which winds for 16 miles up **Boulder Canyon**. Midway up the canyon, the creek plunges over **Boulder Falls**, a pretty spot anytime and most spectacular during the spring runoff. At the upper end of the canyon is the lakeside community of **Nederland**. The silver ore mined around Nederland was considered low-grade because it contained tungsten, which was hard to remove in the refining process. But with World War I the tungsten, a rare metal used to harden steel alloys, became much more valuable than silver had ever been, and Nederland experienced a belated—and short-lived—mining boom. In the 1970s, the town experienced a new flurry of activity as the site of Caribou Ranch, a famed recording studio used by such pop music legends as the Rolling Stones and Elton John. In recent years, the block-long town has been engulfed by new custom-home development. At Nederland, motorists can join the **Peak to Peak Highway** and follow it 15 miles south to Central City or 42 miles north to Estes Park and the entrance to Rocky Mountain National Park. While this is not the most direct route from Boulder to the national park, much less the fastest, it is certainly the most scenic. ~ Route 72 North and Route 119 South.

> Sixty percent of Boulder's population is under the age of 21.

Built in 1908, the **Hotel Boulderado** has been painstakingly restored to the grandeur of earlier times, when such celebrities as Bat Masterson, Ethel Barrymore and Douglas Fairbanks Jr., stayed here. Rich woodwork and overstuffed antique armchairs and sofas grace the lobby under a two-story-high stained-glass canopy. The 160 rooms feature antique furnishings and flowery period decor as well as such amenities as fresh flowers daily. ~ 2115 13th Street; 303-442-4344, 800-433-4344, fax 303-442-4378. ULTRA-DELUXE.

LODGING

A few blocks east of the pedestrians-only part of downtown, the **Pearl Street Inn** offers eight antique-decorated rooms, all with private baths, fireplaces and private entrances, surrounding a peaceful central courtyard. Some rooms are in the historic main house; others are in a contemporary annex built in 1985. Rates include a full breakfast. ~ 1820 Pearl Street; 303-444-5584, fax 303-444-6494. DELUXE.

Another Victorian-era home turned B&B in the downtown area, the **Briar Rose** has nine rooms—five in the main 1890-vintage house and four in a separate guest house. Some rooms have fireplaces, others have balconies or patios, and all have queen-size beds with feather comforters. A gourmet continental breakfast is served sitdown-style. ~ 2151 Arapahoe Avenue; 303-442-3007. DELUXE TO ULTRA-DELUXE.

While lodging rates in Boulder tend to run higher than in most communities in the state, affordable accommodations can be found at the **Foot of the Mountain Motel**. The 18 rooms are in rustic cabins dating back to 1930. They have been nicely renovated and feature all the conveniences of a modern midrange motel. The location—at the mouth of Boulder Canyon and the start of the Boulder Creekpath—makes this motel special. ~ 200 Arapahoe Avenue; 303-442-5688. MODERATE.

DINING   Boulder's ultimate fine-dining establishment is the **Flagstaff House Restaurant** on Mount Flagstaff 1000 feet above town. Floor-to-ceiling walls of glass give diners an unparalleled view, especially after dark, when dinner is served by candlelight and the city's lights along the Front Range have full impact. Dining is formal (no T-shirts or shorts, please), and the menu changes frequently. A typical dinner might include an appetizer of ahi sushi, a main course of spicy elk dumplings and, for dessert, an edible milk-chocolate box filled with raspberry mousse. ~ 1138 Flagstaff Road; 303-442-4640. ULTRA-DELUXE.

Trios Grille & Wine Bar serves gourmet Southwestern cuisine in a New Mexico–style setting with Santa Fe–style decor. The menu, which focuses on unique dishes, changes monthly. A recent menu offered an appetizer of poached sea scallops, entrées like sesame salmon with jasmine rice and a tofu piccata, and a crushed pink-peppercorn lemon tart. The restaurant also serves pizzas and features live jazz six nights a week. ~ 1155 Canyon Road; 303-442-8400. DELUXE.

The menu is heart-healthy and totally organic at **Q's**, the new restaurant in what was the original dining room of the Hotel Boulderado. Teddy Roosevelt ate there. Centrally located on Pearl Street Mall, it has been the site of a long succession of Boulder's favorite fine restaurants, and Q's promises to continue the tradi-

▸▸

✔ **CHECK THESE OUT—UNIQUE DINING**

- *Budget:* Grab a Reuben or a burger at the **New York Delicatessen**, the local eatery that inspired the setting for the '70s TV series *Mork and Mindy*. page 93
- *Moderate to deluxe:* Indulge in *wienerschnitzel* and Bavarian ambience at the **Black Forest Inn**, which has served visitors since 1956. page 86
- *Deluxe:* Allow the buckskin-clad waiters and waitresses at **The Fort** to serve you heaping plates of buffalo, rattlesnake and Rocky Mountain oysters. page 81
- *Ultra-deluxe:* Feast on elk dumplings and sushi overlooking the lights of Boulder at the **Flagstaff House Restaurant**. page 92

Budget: under $8   Moderate: $8–$16   Deluxe: $16–$24   Ultra-deluxe: over $24

tion The fare ranges from elaborate salads to gourmet cuisine, with a good selection of vegetarian dishes. ~ Hotel Boulderado, 2115 13th Street; 303-442-4560. MODERATE TO DELUXE.

The **New York Delicatessen**, a long-time local favorite, inspired the setting for *Mork and Mindy*, the '70s TV show in which then-unknown young comedian Robin Williams got his start playing a space alien. Twenty-five years later, it looks pretty much the same—but more crowded. The menu features Reuben sandwiches and New York–style hot dogs, along with pizzas and 15 kinds of hamburgers. It's a perfect place for picnic purchases, too. ~ 1117 Pearl Street; 303-447-3354. BUDGET.

Boulder has a great selection of ethnic restaurants. One of the more unusual is **Narayan's Nepal Restaurant**, a storefront restaurant decorated with Nepalese artifacts at the west end of Pearl Street Mall. Lamb curry, the house specialty, shares the menu with unusual chicken and pork dishes as well as a variety of vegetarian choices. ~ 921 Pearl Street; 303-447-2816. MODERATE.

SHOPPING

Pearl Street Mall, Boulder's pedestrians-only downtown main street, is so full of life that shopping is almost incidental. Many of the small shops that line the street specialize in arts, crafts and unique gift items. **Art Mart** exhibits the works of more than 200 Boulder-area artisans in all media. ~ 1222 Pearl Street; 303-443-8248. Across the street, **Art Source International** is Colorado's largest dealer in historic photos and 19th-century prints and maps. ~ 1237 Pearl Street; 303-444-4080. Good selections of local arts and crafts can be found at the **Boulder Arts & Crafts Cooperative**. ~ 1421 Pearl Street; 303-443-3683. Also stop by **Handmade in Colorado** for crafts. ~ 1426 Pearl Street; 303-938-8394. For shoppers whose tastes run to the exotic, **Traders of the Lost Art** has clothing and one-of-a-kind imports from South America, Asia and Africa. ~ 1912 Pearl Street; 303-440-9664.

Antique dealers dominate the main street of tiny **Niwot**, midway between Boulder and Longmont on Route 119.

NIGHTLIFE

The University of Colorado sponsors a full range of events, most of them open to the public. Check the Boulder *Daily Camera*'s Friday edition or any of the many bulletin boards around town for current happenings.

University students dominate the Boulder bar scene. A popular, eclectic hangout is the **West End Tavern**, which features alternative music on Tuesday, jazz on Wednesday, comedy on Saturday and a deejay on other nights. Cover. ~ 926 Pearl Street; 303-444-3535. The **Walnut Brewery**, one of the town's many brewpubs, has live jazz and blues on Friday nights. ~ 1123 Walnut Street; 303-447-1345. **Tulagi**, a longtime favorite student beer joint, has local dance music four or five nights a week. ~ 1129 13th Street; 303-

442-1369. **The Sink** serves up pizza, burgers, beer and, on weekends, live reggae or rock. ~ 1165 13th Street; 303-444-7465.

The **Fox Theatre**, a 625-seat showcase concert club, features a variety of local and national acts, from jazz and folk to contemporary and alternative music nightly. Cover. ~ 1135 13th Street; 303-447-0095.

The **Brillig Works Cafe and Bakery** offers a nonalcoholic, caffeine-infused socializing environment with vegetarian munchies and Wednesday-night poetry readings. ~ 1322 College Avenue; 303-444-0814.

PARKS

BOULDER MOUNTAIN PARK 🏃 Little by little, Boulder taxpayers' dollars have purchased the mountains that flank the west side of the city in order to protect this dramatic stretch of the Front Range from development. The park includes the huge slanted expanse of granite cliffs known as the Flatirons as well as Flagstaff Mountain, where a three-mile switchback winds to the 1600-foot summit—a great spot for watching stars, the lights of Boulder or the breaking dawn. Several hiking trails start from Sunrise Circle Amphitheater. There are picnic areas and restrooms. Day-use fee, $5. ~ Follow Baseline Road west from Boulder; it becomes Flagstaff Mountain Road as it winds its way up to the trailhead and the summit; 303-441-3410.

ROOSEVELT NATIONAL FOREST 🏃🚲🛶 The mountains west of Boulder are a checkerboard of national forest and state, county and municipal parks, many of them undeveloped. Numerous forest roads and jeep trails radiate into park and from the town of Nederland at the upper end of Boulder Canyon. Among the noteworthy is the Moffat Road, a four-wheel-drive and mountain bike road that starts at Rollinsville south of Nederland and follows a former railroad route over Rollins Pass. The Indian Peaks Wilderness, a 70,000-acre area of alpine tundra with nearly 50 lakes, lies west of Nederland and adjoins the south boundary of Rocky Mountain National Park. It is the most popular wilderness area in Roosevelt National Forest; more hikers use its extensive trail network than all other trails in the national forest combined. Fishing is good for lake trout and kokanee salmon at Gross Reservoir, located southwest of Boulder, just beyond Boulder Mountain Park. ~ Forest access is provided by Routes 72 and 119 as well as the roads through Golden Gate State Park and Boulder Mountain Park. Kelly Dahl Campground is three miles south of Nederland on Route 119; 303-444-6001.

▲ Kelly Dahl Campground has 48 lakeside RV/tent sites (no hookups), with a small campers store and coin laundromat; open mid-May through October; $9 per night.

ELDORADO CANYON STATE PARK 🏃🚲🐎⛵🛶 Rock climbers come from as far away as Europe to challenge the sheer, vertical 850-foot sandstone cliffs that enclose Eldorado Canyon. There are picnic areas along the creek at the canyon's bottom and ten miles of trails for hiking and mountain biking. Rainbow trout is the main catch here. Day-use fee, $4. ~ Located eight miles southwest of Boulder on Route 170, above the village of Eldorado Springs; 303-494-3943.

Estes Park is a world apart from the rest of the Front Range, though it's on a direct route to Rocky Mountain National Park and just 30 miles from Boulder, Longmont or Loveland. The sole point of interest along the way is the town of Lyons, at the intersection of Routes 7 and 36. The town has a spread-out historic district made up of 15 buildings dating back to the turn of the century, all constructed from locally quarried red sandstone.

Estes Park Area

The starting point for a historic district tour in Lyons is the **Lyons Redstone Museum**, where artifacts and photos from the town's early days are displayed in an old sandstone schoolhouse. ~ 340 High Street, Lyons; 303-823-5271.

SIGHTS

Estes Park has thrived as a tourist town since the park opened in 1915, and today it feels a little quaint with its old-fashioned curio shops full of ersatz Indian items, Asian-made Colorado ashtrays and souvenir rocks. Since there is no food or lodging within the national park, Estes Park is the place for noncampers who wish to spend more than a single day there. Visitors can ride the **Aerial Tramway** up 1200 feet from the middle of town to the top of Prospect Mountain for an overview of Estes Park, Lake Estes and the Big Thompson River. Admission. ~ 420 East Riverside Drive, Estes Park; 970-586-3675.

Don't miss the **Satirical World Art Museum**, probably the most politically incorrect museum you're ever likely to visit and certainly the funniest. It contains more than 150 oil paintings and drawings by José Perez, the Will Rogers of American art, including caustic portrayals of dozens of government agencies as well as other targets, ranging from the medical profession to skiers. Admission. ~ 170 Moraine Avenue; 970-586-3141.

◄ *HIDDEN*

Perhaps the most interesting sight in Estes Park is the grand old **Stanley Hotel**. Even if you're not planning to stay there, stroll the lobby and grounds of this elegant, historic resort hotel. It was built in 1909, six years before the national park opened, by the man who invented the steam-powered automobile, the Stanley Steamer. The hotel is said to have inspired Stephen King's breakthrough novel, *The Shining*. ~ 333 Wonderview Avenue, Estes Park; 970-586-3371.

An original Stanley Steamer is on display in the **Estes Park Area Historical Museum**, along with a 19th-century settler's log cabin, the original Rocky Mountain National Park headquarters building and exhibits on the town's history, including kitsch from the early years of tourism. Admission. ~ 200 4th Street, Estes Park; 970-586-6256.

The free **MacGregor Ranch Museum** preserves the homestead of one of the Estes Park region's first settlers, Alexander Mac-Gregor, who led the legal battle against a British earl who claimed all the area's land in the 1870s. Besides a complete documentary record of the land dispute, the museum has antique furnishings, ranch implements and a sizable collection of Western paintings. Open in summer only. ~ Devil's Gulch Road, Estes Park; 970-586-3749.

A best-selling mystery novel of the 1920s, *Seven Keys to Baldpate*, inspired another historic Estes Park hotel. Gordon and Charles Mace, who built it in 1917, named it the Baldpate Inn after the novel. Later, attorney Clarence Darrow started a tradition by declaring that each guest should contribute a key to the hotel. Over the years the collection grew to become the world's

HIDDEN ▶

largest. The more than 20,000 keys in the free **Baldpate Inn Key Room** include keys to Mozart's wine cellar, Jack Benny's dressing room and the Pentagon. ~ Route 7, eight miles south of Estes Park; 970-586-6151.

Close by on the same highway, the free **Enos Mills Cabin and Nature Study Area** was the 1885 homestead of the naturalist who persuaded Congress to create Rocky Mountain National Park. The old cabin, where Mills' writings and photographs are on display, sits within a 200-acre preserve laced with nature trails. ~ Route 7, Estes Park; 970-586-4706.

The 19 miles of Route 7 from Estes Park south to Raymond are part of the **Peak to Peak Highway**, which continues as Route 72 for another 37 miles through Nederland, at the upper end of Boulder Canyon, to Central City. The Route 7 portion skirts the Rocky Mountain National Park boundary, passing between two of the area's highest mountains, Mount Meeker (13,911 feet) and Longs Peak (14,256 feet). The latter marks the southeast corner of Rocky Mountain National Park.

While all the mountains that flank Colorado's busy Route 25 corridor are commonly referred to as the Front Range, the actual mountain range of that name runs through **Rocky Mountain National Park**. The most popular tourist spot in Colorado, the national park is where the Continental Divide reaches closest to the eastern Colorado plains. The park encompasses some of the highest, most rugged terrain in the Rockies. During the summer months, expect long lines of cars at the main park entrance on Route 36 just west of Estes Park. Every place that is accessible by car in the east side of the park is crowded at all times in tourist season and on weekends all year. Relatively few visitors wander far from the roadways, however, and with 76 mountain summits above 12,000 feet in elevation, the possibilities for exploring the wilderness on foot or horseback are practically endless.

As soon as you enter the park, you find yourself facing a fork in the road. A left turn takes you to **Moraine Park**, where the Big Thompson River meanders through a broad, grassy valley gouged by ancient glaciers and surrounded by mountain crags. The rustic **Moraine Park Museum** has exhibits that explain the natural history of Rocky Mountain National Park. The road climbs for ten miles, following Glacier Creek and passing numerous marked trailheads, to **Bear Lake**, a classic mountain lake surrounded by a paved nature trail and, most of the time, hundreds or even thousands of sightseers. It is typical of dozens of other fair-size natural lakes in the park, most of them accessible only by hiking or horseback trails. While motorists can drive their cars to Bear Lake and join others in a desperate search for parking spaces, an easier and more scenic option is to take one of the shuttle buses that run frequently from the Moraine Park Museum and stop at each trailhead on the way to the lake.

Take the right-hand fork inside the park entrance to drive up **Trail Ridge Road**, the highest continuous automobile road in North America. Completed in 1932, the 45-mile-long paved road traces an old Ute Indian migration route along a ridge high above timberline, paralleling the jagged, impassable rock-and-ice wall of the Continental Divide. Just beyond the highest point on the road (12,183 feet), the **Alpine Visitors Center** stands on the windswept brink of rocky cliffs where snowdrifts remain year-round. It has snacks, souvenirs and an observation deck. While most peo-

WILDLIFE UP CLOSE

Because they have enjoyed protection from hunters for more than 75 years in Rocky Mountain National Park, wildlife both large and small is abundant and not too shy. You are more likely to see elk here than anywhere else in Colorado. Watch for them in high, distant meadows in the summer and in the lowlands of Moraine Park during the cold months. Bighorn sheep and mountain goats sometimes graze within sight of Trail Ridge Road; bald eagles and peregrine falcons ride updrafts where the wind meets the mountains; marmots whistle signals across the high tundra; and black bears roam deep in the forests. Chipmunks swarm around every scenic turnout, greedily stuffing their cheeks with tourist handouts, as camp-robber jays swoop down to grab their share. Be sure to bring binoculars and a loaded camera.

ple turn around at the visitors center and return the way they came, the road continues over the Continental Divide to the town of Grand Lake at the park's west entrance (see "Winter Park–Grand Lake Area" in Chapter Four). Oddly enough, Milner Pass, where Trail Ridge Road crosses the Great Divide, is about 1200 feet *lower* than the Alpine Visitors Center.

A less-used (and less-spectacular) road to the heart of the park is the Old Fall River Road, which was the main park road from 1915, when Rocky Mountain National Park opened its gates to the public, to 1932, when Trail Ridge Road was completed. The unpaved one-way (uphill) road branches off just inside the east entrance and follows Fall River for 12 miles through ancient forests of Douglas fir and blue spruce, nearing the river's source at Iceberg Lake, then scrambles up over Fall River Pass (11,796 feet) to join Trail Ridge Road at the Alpine Visitors Center. Admission. ~ Estes Park; 970-586-1333.

LODGING   Right in town and as romantic as they come is the **Black Canyon Inn**. Accommodations are in a two-story 1929 lodge and separate one- to three-bedroom cabins, some with porches, kitchen facilities and fireplaces. Amenities include a heated pool, hot tub, fishing pond and barbecue area. ~ 800 MacGregor Avenue, Estes Park; 970-586-8113. MODERATE.

The **Stanley Hotel** was built as a resort in 1909 by inventor F. O. Stanley (one of his Stanley Steamers, a steam-powered touring automobile, is on display in the lobby). Most of the 92 guest rooms in this hillside hotel have views of the Continental Divide or Lake Estes. A recent $4 million renovation has left the stately old hotel gleaming like new inside and out. Amenities include a swimming pool, hot tub and volleyball court. The hotel has hosted guests as diverse as the Emperor of Japan and Bob Dylan. ~ 333 Wonderview Avenue, Estes Park; 970-586-3371, 800-762-5437. ULTRA-DELUXE.

Built in 1917, the **Baldpate Inn** took its name from a best-selling mystery novel of the time called *Seven Keys to Baldpate*, which inspired its huge, world-famous key collection. Autographed photos of celebrities who have been guests there are also on display. The 12 guest rooms and three individual cabins are rather small but nicely furnished with antiques and handmade quilts. Set at an elevation of 9000 feet, the inn commands a grand view of the valley below. ~ 4900 South Route 7, Estes Park; 970-586-6151. MODERATE TO DELUXE.

Colorado's largest log lodge is the **Aspen Lodge**. Set on 3000 acres of ranchland with a spectacular view of Longs Peak, the lodge offers a full range of sports activities for guests, including horseback riding, hayrides, barbecues, swimming, fishing, tennis, racquetball, hiking and sleigh rides (in season). Facilities also include hot tubs and saunas. Some of the 59 guest rooms are in the main lodge, while others are in luxurious individual log cabins. There is a three-night minimum stay in summer. Rates include all three meals in summer, breakfast the rest of the year. ~ Route 7, Estes Park; 970-586-8133, 800-332-6867, fax 970-586-8133. DELUXE TO ULTRA-DELUXE.

Built on land that formerly belonged to the Irish Earl of Dunraven, **Tiny Town Cottages** has 20 cozy cottages set on the banks of a river stocked for trout fishing. The cottages feature queen- or king-size beds, kitchens and fireplaces. Rates include a continental breakfast. ~ 830 Moraine Road, Estes Park; phone/fax 970-586-4249. MODERATE.

Perhaps the most unabashedly romantic lodging in the Estes Park area is the **Antlers Pointe**, a couples-only hideaway nestled in a grove of spruce and pine on the banks of the Fall River near the entrance to Rocky Mountain National Park. Each luxury one-bedroom cabin has a king-size bed, a jacuzzi, a cozy parlor with a fireplace and loveseat, and a deck at the water's edge. Southwestern-style furnishings emphasize logs, leather and polished oak. ~ 1515 Fish Hatchery Road, Estes Park; 970-586-8881. DELUXE.

DINING

The **Fawn Brook Inn**, four miles south of Estes Park, has a reputation for the finest dining in the vicinity. Open Friday, Saturday and Sunday only, this mountain lodge offers a changing selection of wild-game dishes, veal, duck and seafood traditionally prepared in Continental style. The contrast of the rugged setting and rustic old lodge with the elegant presentation and service makes the Fawn Brook Inn extra-special. Closed Monday through Thursday from October to mid-May. ~ Route 7, Allenspark; 303-747-2556. ULTRA-DELUXE.

For a more affordable feast, try **Nicky's**, an eclectic American-Greek-Italian restaurant specializing in prime-rib dinners in a clean, contemporary family-dining atmosphere. The new open-air dining deck overlooks the river. Entrées range from spinach pie to lasagna, with ice cream, fruit pie or cheesecake for dessert. ~ 1350 Fall River Road, Estes Park; 970-586-5376. MODERATE TO DELUXE.

Even more eclectic is the **Gazebo Restaurant**, next to Bond Park in downtown Estes Park. The international menu features specialties from Italy, Afghanistan, the Caribbean and Mexico among its 48 entrées. The environment is formal, with white-linen service for both lunch and dinner, and the decor is bursting with silk flowers and floral prints. ~ 225 Park Lane, Estes Park; 970-586-9564. DELUXE.

Giant breakfast burritos are the claim to fame at **Ed's Cantina & Grill**, which also serves burgers and Mexican favorites for lunch and dinner among baseball memorabilia and beer signs. ~ 362 East Elkhorn Avenue, Estes Park; 970-586-2919. BUDGET.

You'll find big, hearty Western meals served on a riverside patio at the **Cowpoke Café**. Though most meals are built around beef, this is also just about the only place in town where you can order rattlesnake. For the squeamish, there's also a good salad bar. ~ 165 Virginia Drive, Estes Park; 970-586-0234. MODERATE.

SHOPPING   Estes Park, where the tourism industry has thrived for more than a century, has every kind of gift and curio shop you can imagine. Venerable tourist traps selling authentic reproduction turquoise-and-silver Indian-design jewelry and "Colorful Colorado" ash-trays from Taiwan stand alongside sleek modern-art galleries and outdoor fashion boutiques. There are also clusters of arts and crafts retailers such as the **Old Church Shops**, which feature works by more than 75 Colorado craftspersons. ~ 157 West Elkhorn Avenue, Estes Park. There are also more sophisticated galleries such as the **Art Center of Estes Park**, which offers not only local and out-of-state artists' paintings and sculptures for sale but also art classes and painting trips. ~ Wonderview Avenue and Route 134, Estes Park; 970-586-5882.

The world's largest pewter casting studio is the **Michael Ricker Studio and Museum**, located at the base of Lake Estes Dam. With the help of 70 employees, artist Michael Ricker casts more than 25,000 sculptures a month. His work is on display in the White House, Walt Disney World and the Vatican, as well as in the museum adjacent to the studio. ~ Route 34, Estes Park; 970-586-2030.

One of the oldest and most beloved stores in the Estes Park area—and still one of the best—is the **Eagle Plume Gallery** of Native American Arts ten miles south of town. Started in the 1930s by Charles Perkins (a native Coloradoan who was so proud to be one-fourth Blackfoot Indian that he changed his name to Charlie Eagle Plume to reflect his heritage), it was one of the first stores in America to deal exclusively in American Indian collect-ibles. The store continues to uphold Eagle Plume's reverence for Indian arts and traditions: it contains one of the world's finest private collections of Plains Indian artifacts and offers high-quality tourist-trade goods and collectibles for sale. Open daily in summer, weekends only in winter. ~ Route 7, Estes Park; 970-586-4710.

NIGHTLIFE   The name tells you everything you need to know about the **Barleen Family Country Music Dinner Theater**, one of the town's favorite entertainment spots. ~ 1110 Woodstock Drive, Estes Park; 970-586-5749. For a rowdier scene, check out **Lonigan's Saloon**, with live acoustic music on Tuesday and loud rock for dancing on Friday and Saturday. ~ 110 West Elkhorn Avenue, Estes Park; 970-586-4346.

The **Stanley Concert Hall** adjoining the Stanley Hotel offers a summer concert series and stage plays. ~ 333 Wonderview Avenue, Estes Park; 970-586-3371.

ROCKY MOUNTAIN NATIONAL PARK 🏃 🐎 ⛵ One of the premier areas in the U.S. National Park System, this 266,957-acre mountain recreation area reaches from meadows at 8000-foot elevation into the high mountains, containing 107 peaks over 12,000 feet. Major features include Bear Lake, a natural lake surrounded by a half-mile paved trail that connects to other, more ambitious hiking trails into the high country; Trail Ridge Road, one of Colorado's most scenic high-altitude routes; and Longs Peak, a legendary weekend climb that requires no special equipment in summer. Easy access from Denver and other Front Range cities makes this one of the most crowded summertime destinations in Colorado. Fishing is permitted for trout in backcountry lakes and streams. There are picnic areas, restrooms, visitors centers, campfire programs, a cafeteria, horse stables, shuttle buses and hiking trails (355 miles of them). Day-use fee $10, good for seven days. ~ The main east entrance is three miles west of Estes Park on Route 34/36. The west entrance is about two miles north of Grand Lake on Route 34; 970-586-1206.

▲ Camping is permitted in five public campgrounds totaling 586 sites (no hookups); $14 per night. In July and August, reservations are required for the two largest campgrounds, Glacier Basin and Moraine Park (800-365-2267; credit card required). A limited number of backcountry campsites are available by permit.

ROOSEVELT NATIONAL FOREST 🏃 ⛵ This 788,000-acre forest spans the eastern slope of the Rockies from Central City to the Wyoming state line and wraps around three sides of Rocky Mountain National Park. Its most distinctive feature is a series of deep gorges, including Big Thompson Canyon below Estes Park. Two national forest wilderness areas—Indian Peaks Wilderness and Comanche Peak Wilderness—adjoin Rocky Mountain National Park. Fishing is good for native cutthroat, rainbow and brown trout species in Big Thompson Canyon. Facilities include picnic areas, hiking trails and jeep trails. ~ There is extensive forest access along Route 34 East (Big Thompson Canyon), Route 36 East, Route 7 South (Peak to Peak Highway) and Route 72. Trailheads for the Comanche Peaks Wilderness are off Devil's Gulch Road, which runs northeast from Estes Park. The Brainard Lake Road off Route 72 at Ward provides trailhead access to the Indian Peaks Wilderness. Olive Ridge Campground is 15 miles south of Estes Park on Route 7; 303-444-6001.

▲ The only national forest campground in the area, Olive Ridge Campground has 56 RV/tent sites (no hookups); open May through October; $12 per night.

PARKS

▼▼▼▼▼▼▼▼▼▼▼▼
Fort Collins Area

Along the northern part of the Front Range Corridor, agriculture is king. The major towns in the area—Loveland, Greeley and Fort Collins—were founded by farmers rather than gold prospectors. Fort Collins, for example, sprang up in 1873 when the army abandoned a small frontier outpost called Camp Collins and auctioned the land to a utopian agricultural colony, which offered memberships to persons "of good moral character." Today, Fort Collins is the largest town in the area and the site of the state's "Aggie" school, Colorado State University. Traditionally, the major crop in this part of Colorado has been sugar beets. The juice of the beets was refined into white granulated sugar, and the pulp that remained was used to fatten cattle in vast feed lots. Declining demand for beet sugar has forced area farmers to diversify in recent years, and the region now produces everything from herbs and organic vegetables to experimental "beefalo," a cross between cattle and bison.

SIGHTS

The most direct route from Route 25 to Estes Park and Rocky Mountain National Park is through Loveland. The site of Colorado's first beet sugar mill in 1901, Loveland still has the look of a typical farm town, with its silos, cattle feedlots and railroad yards. But looks can be deceiving. Loveland has developed into the main artists' community on the Front Range. Visitors can watch bronze sculptures being poured at **Art Castings**. ~ 511 8th Street Southeast, Loveland; 970-667-1114. Another one of Loveland's art foundries is **Loveland Sculpture Works**. ~ 205 12th Street Southwest, Loveland; 970-667-0991. See some of the locally-made sculptures on exhibit in the city-owned **Benson Park Sculpture Garden**. ~ 29th Street at Aspen Drive, Loveland; 970-663-2940.

Much of the **Loveland Museum and Gallery** is given over to showing the works of local artists. The museum also features a 2000-square-foot relief map of Big Thompson Canyon. You can see the lower portion of the canyon for yourself by taking Route 34 west toward Estes Park, a distance of 30 miles. If the name rings a bell, it is probably because the long, narrow canyon gained national notoriety in 1977 as the scene of one of Colorado's most terrible disasters, a huge flash flood in which scores of campers drowned. ~ 5th Street at Lincoln Avenue, Loveland; 970-962-2410.

Before heading into the mountains, travelers may wish to take a detour from Loveland 13 miles east to **Greeley** for a dose of history straight out of Colorado's richest farm country. The city was named for *New York Tribune* publisher Horace Greeley. Horace Greeley used his newspaper to recruit members for a Utopian farming cooperative, the Union Colony, which, under the leadership of the *Tribune*'s agriculture editor, Nathan Meeker, founded the town in 1870 and developed the first large-scale irrigation system in Colorado to serve the community's farms. In an era when most Colorado communities seemed to exist primarily to provide booze, gambling and prostitution for area cowboys and miners, liquor and the other forms of entertainment that went with it were prohibited in Greeley, giving the town a reputation for clean living that it has yet to live down.

Horace Greeley is often credited with coining the slogan, "Go West, young man, go West." (Actually, the words were written by journalist John Babson Lane, but Greeley printed them.)

For a look at the early years of the Union Colony, visit the **1870 Meeker House Museum**, the original two-story adobe house built by the colony's leader and furnished with articles belonging to him and his family. Admission. ~ 1324 9th Avenue, Greeley; 970-350-9220. More about the colony, including lots of documents and photographs, can be found nearby at the **Greeley Municipal Museum**. Admission. ~ 919 7th Street, Greeley; 970-350-9220.

While **Centennial Village** officially got its name because it was opened in 1976 on the 100th anniversary of Colorado statehood, it also recalls James A. Michener's fictionalized history of the region, *Centennial*. Michener, who lived here while researching and writing the book, used Greeley as the model for his fictitious town of Centennial. The village is actually a large, grassy park where historic buildings have been collected from throughout the northeastern plains and arranged in a chronology of 60 years of settlement. Included, among other structures, are an Indian teepee, a homesteader's house, a whitewashed one-room schoolhouse, a Victorian residence, a firehouse and a blacksmith's shop. Admission. ~ 1475 A Street, Greeley; 970-350-9224.

Also in Greeley is **Houston Gardens**, where typical flora from four of the five life zones found in Colorado—all except alpine tundra—makes up a pleasant botanical garden. Admission. ~ 23rd Avenue at 4th Street, Greeley; 970-353-1262.

Twenty miles east of Greeley off Route 34, **Riverside Reservoir White Pelican Nesting Colony** draws birding enthusiasts from around the state during the nesting season. The reservoir is not open to recreational use, but a trail provides access to the shore. Bring binoculars, which will allow you to view the island in the middle of the lake, where about 500 pairs of white pelicans nest each spring.

◄ HIDDEN

Twelve miles north of Loveland via Route 25, **Fort Collins** is the site of **Colorado State University**, which includes the state's agricultural, forestry and veterinary schools. The town's original commercial district, which dates back to the 1870s, has been refurbished as the **Historic Old Town District**, a pretty town square lined with galleries, specialty shops and cafés, on Mountain Avenue between Remington Street and North College Avenue.

The **Fort Collins Museum** displays artifacts from the city's early years as a fur trappers' outpost and a U.S. cavalry fort protecting pioneers on the Overland Trail. Outside the main museum are two cabins and a one-room schoolhouse, all relocated from elsewhere in the county. Closed Monday. ~ 200 Matthews Street, Fort Collins; 970-221-6738.

The oldest log cabin in the state is located at the Fort Collins Museum.

Nearby, the 1879 Victorian **Avery House**, one of the city's grandest mansions, has been restored and furnished with antiques of the period. Public tours are offered twice weekly, on Wednesday and Sunday afternoons. ~ 328 West Mountain Avenue, Fort Collins; 970-221-0533.

The **Fort Collins Municipal Railway**, the last of the old-time streetcars that provided public transportation in most Colorado cities from the 1930s through the 1950s, operates only on weekends and holidays from May through September. It travels a route between Historic Old Town and the **City Park** at Roosevelt Avenue and Oak Street. Admission. ~ 970-482-5821.

Free tours are offered at the **Anheuser-Busch Brewery**. More modern and high-tech than the Coors brewery in Golden but lacking Coors' ties to Colorado tradition, the Anheuser Busch facility is worth a visit primarily because of its mascot Clydesdale team. The horses perform once a day (except Tuesdays and Wednesdays off-season), and all tours include a walk through their barn. The first Saturday of each month is Clydesdale Camera Day, when visitors can take photos of each other with the horses. ~ 2351 Busch Drive, Fort Collins; 970-490-4691.

East of town on the other side of the interstate is Fort Collins' most unusual sight, the **Swetsville Zoo**. The more than 70 "animals" in the park are actually life-size sculptures made from junkyard pieces of cars and farm machinery. ~ 4801 Harmony Road, Fort Collins; 970-484-9509.

Of the cities along the northern Colorado Front Range, Fort Collins is the only one not on a direct route to Rocky Mountain National Park. Instead, motorists who head west into the mountains from Fort Collins on Route 14 discover a less-traveled highway that runs north of the national park through the **Poudre River Canyon**, snaking along the Cache La Poudre River past campgrounds, picnic areas and fishing spots and through a long tunnel on its way up to the summit of **Cameron Pass** (10,276 feet). Turnouts on both sides of the pass afford dramatic views of the 2000-foot cliff faces of the **Nokhu Crags**, which mark the northwest corner of Rocky Mountain National Park. The area is mountain wilderness so rugged that even though the park boundary is less than five miles away from Cameron Pass, it is impossible to reach by road. The distance from Fort Collins to Cameron Pass is 68 miles.

You won't find more unique lodging anywhere than at the **Heritage Inn**, located near Greeley in the small town of Evans. The 14 individually decorated rooms feature fantasy motifs that include a space capsule, a rainforest, an igloo and even a genuine '59 Cadillac. ~ 3301 West Service Road, Evans; 970-339-5900, 800-759-7829. MODERATE TO DELUXE.

The **Lovelander Bed and Breakfast** has 11 individually decorated guest rooms in a majestic 1902 Victorian a few blocks from downtown. Most of the rooms are decorated in true Victorian style with antiques and floral wallpaper, but a few are contemporary additions and feature themes such as the Southwest or an African safari. A couple have jacuzzis and private balconies. The full gourmet breakfast is served on the wraparound porch or in the garden during warm weather. ~ 217 West 4th Street, Loveland; 970-669-0798, 800-459-6694, fax 970-669-0797. DELUXE.

Lodgings in Fort Collins generally can't compare with those in Boulder for history or charm but are much less expensive. Try the **Mulberry Inn**, which has 120 motel-style rooms, all with queen-size beds and standard amenities. In addition, some rooms have jacuzzis, and suites have private sundecks. Rooms are in the budget range, suites in the moderate range. ~ 4333 East Mulberry Street, Fort Collins; 970-493-9000, 800-234-5548. BUDGET TO MODERATE.

The **Edwards House Bed & Breakfast** offers six attractively furnished guest rooms with shared baths in a three-story 1904 mansion. The inn doubles as a small conference center and features such high-tech conveniences as computer data ports in the rooms. ~ 402 West Mountain Avenue, Fort Collins; 970-493-9191, fax 970-484-0706. MODERATE TO DELUXE.

Affordable and convenient to the CSU campus, the **University Inn** has 74 clean though plain motel rooms, cable TV and a heated pool. Guests have privileges at a nearby health club. Bland? Well, maybe so; welcome to Fort Collins. ~ 914 South College Avenue, Fort Collins; 970-484-1984, fax 970-484-1987. BUDGET.

In Fort Collins, a good place for dinner is **Cuisine! Cuisine!**, a cozy Continental restaurant with candles, lace curtains and turn-of-the-century decor. The menu presents a tempting array of choices, with appetizers such as mussels, smoked salmon and veal sweetbreads; a roasted red-pepper salad; entrées including lamb chops with rosemary sauce and several seafood choices; plus homemade desserts and a long wine list. ~ 130 South Mason Street, Fort Collins; 970-221-0399. MODERATE.

The **Silver Grill Cafe** has been a fixture in Fort Collins' Old Town Historic District for more than 60 years. The café serves no-nonsense breakfasts from biscuits and gravy to steak and eggs. The lunch menu features daily grill specials and a choice of sandwiches. Refurbished in the recent gentrification of Old Town, the café still makes you feel as if you've stepped into an earlier era. ~ 218 Walnut Street, Fort Collins; 970-484-4656. BUDGET.

Another local favorite is **Bisetti's**, located a block south of Old Town. This cozy family-style Italian restaurant emphasizes Sicilian cuisine, with a menu that offers (on the one hand) heart-healthy selections and (on the other hand) homemade cheesecake so rich it's downright sinful. ~ 120 South College Avenue, Fort Collins; 970-493-0086. BUDGET TO MODERATE.

SHOPPING In Fort Collins, the triangular **Old Town Square** has a handful of galleries. ~ Mountain and College avenues, Fort Collins. **Walnut Street Gallery** offers fine art. ~ 21 Old Town Square, Fort Collins; 970-221-2383. Also stop by **Trimble Court Artisans**, featuring local arts and crafts. ~ 118 Trimble Court, Fort Collins; 970-221-0051.

NIGHTLIFE Fort Collins, the cultural hub of Colorado's northern farmlands, has its own symphony orchestra, which performs in a new arts complex called **Lincoln Center**. The center, which has an art gallery, an auditorium, and several other performance spaces, including an intimate little theater and an outdoor courtyard stage surrounded by gardens, also provides a venue for local theater and dance companies from several smaller communities in the area. Call for the current schedule and you'll usually find something going on here in the evening—unlike most other northern Colorado farm towns, which roll up the sidewalks when the sun goes down. Closed Saturdays in summer and Sundays year-round. ~ 417 West Magnolia Street, Fort Collins; 970-221-6735.

With its large college-student population, Fort Collins supports a beer-and-burgers sort of nightlife scene, though no place tries very hard to compete with the live music clubs of Boulder.

PARKS **BOYD LAKE STATE PARK** Just outside the Loveland city limits, this reservoir is used for swimming, waterskiing, sailing and windsurfing. Its soft sand beaches are perfect for sunbathing. Surrounded by prairie and numerous smaller lakes, Boyd Lake has a view of Rocky Mountain National Park on the distant western horizon. Facilities include picnic areas, restrooms and a marina with rentals. There's fishing for walleye, perch, crappie, catfish, bass, bluegill, pike, carp and bullhead. Day-use fee, $4. ~ Located one mile east of Loveland. From Eisenhower Boulevard, take Madison Avenue north and follow the signs; 970-669-1739.

▲ There are 148 RV/tent sites (no hookups); $9 per night.

HORSETOOTH RESERVOIR AND HORSETOOTH MOUNTAIN PARK Long, narrow Horsetooth Reservoir hugs the foothills due west of Fort Collins. The lake is a popular, often crowded water-sports area used for waterskiing, boating, windsurfing and swimming. A paved county road runs along the eastern shore, which is often lined with anglers. There are walleye, bass, bluegill and rainbow trout here. The lake is flanked on the west by the Lory State Park and Horsetooth Mountain Park. Facilities include picnic areas, restrooms, a marina and hiking trails. Day-use fee, $5. ~ From Bellvue, ten miles west of Fort Collins, County Road 23 heads south along the eastern shore of the lake; 970-679-4570.

▲ There are 115 RV sites (20 with water and electric hookups) and 100 tent sites around the lake. The tent camping cost is included in the day-use fee (additional $5 for hookups).

LORY STATE PARK 🚶 🚲 🐎 An unpaved road and 30 miles of hiking trails wind among Lory State Park's arid foothills, grasslands and upthrust rock formations. Deer are abundant. A gravel trail, ideal for mountain biking, runs from the park boundary across the east face of nearby Horsetooth Mountain, named for its crowning rock formation, which some say resembles a horse's bicuspid. There are picnic areas and restrooms. Day-use fee, $4. ~ Shortly before reaching Horsetooth Reservoir, County Road 25G branches off westward to Lory State Park; 970-493-1623.

▲ There are six hike-in backcountry tent sites; $3 per night.

ROOSEVELT NATIONAL FOREST 🚶 🛶 🚣 The northern section of Roosevelt National Forest includes the Poudre River Canyon west of Fort Collins. While most of the canyon is accessible by paved highway, one of the most spectacular sections of the canyon runs through the relatively small Cache La Poudre Wilderness and can only be reached on foot. A much larger wilderness area, the Rawah Wilderness, covers the eastern slope of the Medicine Bow Mountains on the west edge of the national forest. An abundance of lakes, especially in the Red Feather Lakes area, is a key feature of this part of Roosevelt National Forest. Two areas of the Cache La Poudre River in Poudre River Canyon are designated wild trout waters with native (not stocked) cutthroat, rainbow, brown and brook trout. Dowdy, Parvin and West lakes in the Red Feather Lakes area offer excellent kokanee salmon and cutthroat and rainbow trout fishing, as do Chambers and Barnes Meadow lakes at the headwaters of the Cache La Poudre River. There are picnic areas, restrooms, boat ramps, hiking trails and jeep trails. ~ The main recreational access is up the Poudre River Canyon on Route 14. Kelly Flats and Tom Bennett campgrounds are 26 miles west of Fort Collins on this highway. The Red Feather Lakes area is reached from the town of Livermore via paved Red Feather Lakes Road (County Road 74E); 970-498-2770.

▲ Among the nine small national forest campgrounds along the Cache La Poudre River are the 23-site Kelly Flats Campground and 12-site Tom Bennett Campground. Both are open from mid-May through October; $7 per night. In the Red Feather Lakes area, Dowdy Lake Campground has 66 RV/tent sites; open mid-May to mid-October; $7 per night.

▼▼▼▼▼▼▼▼▼▼▼▼▼▼

Outdoor Adventures

FISHING

Most fishing along the Front Range is in warm-water reservoirs such as Horsetooth Reservoir near Fort Collins. The catch in these lakes includes walleye, largemouth bass, channel catfish, pike, bluegill, carp, bullhead, perch and crappie. **Inlet Bay Marina**, located at Horsetooth Reservoir, rents fishing boats and can provide bait and tackle. ~ 970-223-0140. **Boyd Lake Marina** also offers boat rentals, bait and tackle for angling on Boyd Lake. ~ 970-663-2662.

BALLOON RIDES

For nearly 30 years, **Air Boulder** has been conducting one- to one-and-a-half-hour sunrise balloon flights followed by a champagne picnic brunch. ~ 3345 15th Street, Boulder; 303-442-5253. **Life Cycle Balloon Adventures** offers daily champagne flights along the Front Range. ~ 2540 South Steele Street, Denver; 303-759-3907.

SKIING

Eldora Mountain Resort, near the upper end of Boulder Canyon, may be modest in size as Colorado ski areas go, but with five chairlifts and a vertical drop of 1400 feet, it is the largest ski area in the Front Range. The slopes are often packed with students from the University of Colorado, a short drive away. Open December through March. ~ Nederland; 303-440-8700.

The region's best cross-country skiing trails are found within **Rocky Mountain National Park**.

Ski Rentals   Cross-country skis and guided tours within Rocky Mountain National Park are available at **Colorado Wilderness Sports**. ~ 358 East Elkhorn Avenue, Estes Park; 970-586-6548.

ICE SKATING

Evergreen Lake, just west of the town of Evergreen, is one of the most popular outdoor ice-skating spots in the state from the beginning of December until the ice gets too thin in the spring. Skate rentals are available at the lake. ~ 303-674-2677. Fort Collins has a fine indoor ice rink, open year-round, at the **Edora Pool Ice Center**. ~ 1801 Riverside Drive; 970-221-6679.

GOLF

In the mountains within an hour's drive west of Denver is Evergreen's 18-hole **Evergreen Golf Course** has narrow fairways, rock obstacles and cart and club rentals. ~ 29614 Upper Bear Creek

Road; 303-674-4128. There's also the **Hiwan Golf Club,** one of the region's finest golf courses. ~ 303-674-3366; prior arrangements necessary.

In Boulder, there is the challenging 18-hole semiprivate **Lake Valley Golf Course.** ~ Route 36 at Neva Road; 303-442-7851. You can also tee off at the beautiful **Flatirons Golf Course,** which dates back to the 1930s and has mature shade trees, with creeks, streams or ponds on 14 of the 18 holes. ~ 5706 Arapahoe Avenue; 303-442-7851. Fort Collins has the **Collindale Golf Course,** an easy, flat 18-hole walking course. ~ 1441 East Horsetooth Road; 970-221-6651. In Estes Park there's the **Estes Park Golf Club,** a traditional 18-hole mountain course that is cited by golf magazines as one of Colorado's best. ~ 1080 South Saint Vrain Avenue; 970-586-8146. Also try the nine-hole par-three **Lake Estes Executive Course.** ~ 690 Big Thompson Avenue; 970-586-8176. All these courses offer club rentals.

TENNIS

In Boulder, look for free hard-surface, lighted courts at **Chautauqua Park.** ~ 9th Street at Baseline Road. There are also asphalt courts lighted for night play at the **North Boulder Recreation Center;** fee for court reservations. ~ 3170 North Broadway; 303-441-3444. Estes Park has hard-surface municipal courts at **Stanley Park.** ~ Community Drive. In Fort Collins, try **Warren Park.** ~ Lemay Street at Horsetooth Road.

RIDING STABLES

In Fort Collins, hour-long guided rides around Avery State Park are available at **Double Diamond Stables** for riding on trails in the park. ~ Lory State Park; 970-224-4200. In the Estes Park area, the **Cowpoke Corner Corral** offers guided rides ranging from one to four hours on Grant Track Mountain, ~ YMCA Road, Estes Park; 970-586-5890. There's also **Elkhorn Stables.** ~ 650

✔ **CHECK THESE OUT—UNIQUE OUTDOOR ADVENTURES**

• Soar high above Boulder's spectacular Flatirons on a hot-air balloon adventure with Air Boulder, starting at dawn and finishing with a champagne brunch. *page 108*

• Let the cowboy guides at National Park Village Stables take you on a trail ride among the towering granite peaks of Rocky Mountain National Park. *page 110*

• Rent a mountain bike at and explore the Boulder Creekpath, the main artery of a 50-mile town-and-country trail system. *page 110*

• Scale the summit of 14,255-foot Longs Peak, one of the tallest mountains in the Front Range, a 16- to 18-mile roundtrip hike. *page 111*

West Elkhorn Avenue, Estes Park; 970-586-5525. **National Park Village Stables** leads small guided tours, limited to seven riders, including trips along Fall River and all-day rides to the top of Deer Mountain in Rocky Mountain National Park. ~ Fall River Road, Rocky Mountain National Park; 970-586-5269.

BIKING   **Elk Meadows County Park** north of Evergreen has six miles of trails through varied terrain that are used by hundreds of mountain bikers daily (mostly local residents).

The **Boulder Creekpath** forms the main artery of a 50-mile bicycle trail system throughout the Boulder area.

Bike Rentals   **University Bicycles** rents mountain bikes, hybrids and three-speed town bikes. ~ 839 Pearl Street; 303-444-4196. **Estes Park Marina** at Lake Estes rents mountain bikes, four-wheel surreys and tandems. ~ Estes Park; 970-586-2011.

HIKING   All distances listed for hiking trails are one way unless otherwise noted.

DENVER MOUNTAIN PARKS AREA   Nearly ten miles of trails meander among the eroded sandstone formations of Morrison's **Red Rocks State Park**. In the Evergreen area, **Elk Meadows County Park** has an easy six-mile loop trail through mountain meadows and ponderosa-covered mountainsides shared by hikers, joggers and bikers. **Golden Gate Canyon State Park**, which lies between Golden and Central City, offers 35 miles of hiking trails through dramatic canyon country. **Arapaho National Forest** in the vicinity of Idaho Springs and Georgetown has a truly vast trail network. Among the best trails are the four-mile **Chicago Lakes Trail** from Echo Lake on the Mount Evans Highway and the 12-mile climb from the Echo Lake trailhead to the summit of Mount Evans.

BOULDER AREA   The mountains on Boulder's western edge, including Boulder Mountain Park, offer some of the most accessible hiking trails in the Front Range. Major trailheads at Chautauqua Park and at Sunrise Amphitheater on Flagstaff Mountain provide access to such backcountry routes as the **Enchanted Mesa Trail** (3 miles) and longer trails leading to the Flatirons. There is also good hiking just outside the city in **Sunshine Canyon**, at the west end of Mapleton Street.

ESTES PARK AREA   Rangers estimate that only 15 percent of visitors to Rocky Mountain National Park venture more than a quarter-mile from their cars. Considering how many people visit the park on a typical summer day, this still means that the main trails see heavy use. You may never find solitude, but you will find hundreds of miles of alpine trails through mountain scenery as spectacular as any you can imagine. Among the great trails in the national park are the fairly easy **Bridal Veil Falls Trail** (3 miles), near the north boundary of the park; the hike from the **Flattop Trail** starting at Bear Lake on the **Fern Lake Trail** (3 miles); and the climb to the summit of Longs Peak by either the more popular **East Longs Peak Trail** (4 miles) or the longer, less crowded **North Longs Peak Trail** (4.5 miles), which merges with the East Longs Peak Trail about three miles below the summit.

FORT COLLINS AREA   In the Poudre River Canyon west of Fort Collins, the **Greyrock Trail** (3 miles) makes a steep climb to a spectacular viewpoint overlooking the canyon and the lofty mountain ranges to the west.

▼▼▼▼▼▼▼▼▼▼▼
Transportation

CAR

Every place described in this chapter is within about an hour's drive from **Route 25**, which traces the edge of the Rockies northward to Fort Collins and Cheyenne, Wyoming, and southward to Colorado Springs, Pueblo and Trinidad. Route 25 intersects east–west **Route 70** in Denver. Following Route 70W will take you to Idaho Springs and Central City.

Boulder is reached via **Route 36**, which runs northwest from Denver. This highway continues into the mountains, ending in Estes Park.

AIR

Denver International Airport is the primary commercial airport serving the Front Range communities north and west of Denver.

Boulder has no commercial air service; the **Airporter** runs hourly shuttle vans between Boulder and the Denver airport. ~ 303-227-0000, 303-444-0808. RTD buses also go to the Denver airport from Boulder. ~ 303-299-6000. **Charles Tour and Travel Services** operates shuttle vans to the Denver airport. ~ 970-586-5151, 800-950-3274. Continental Express flies to the **Fort Collins–Loveland Municipal Airport**. Area residents take one of these commercial flights to Denver and then make connections with interstate or international flights.

BUS

RTD buses connect Denver with Boulder, Nederland and Longmont. ~ Regional Transportation District; 303-299-6000.

Greyhound Bus Lines (800-231-2222) serves Fort Collins. ~ Route 501 at Riverside Avenue; 970-221-1327.

CAR RENTALS

Most air travelers visiting this region rent cars upon arrival at Denver International Airport. Among the many rental agencies at or near DIA are **A Courtesy Rent A Car** (800-441-1816), **Alamo Rent A Car** (800-327-9633), **Avis Rent A Car** (800-331-1212), **Budget Rent A Car** (800-527-0700), **Dollar Rent A Car** (800-800-4000), **Enterprise Rent A Car** (800-325-8007), **Hertz Rent A Car** (800-654-3131) and **National Interrent** (800-328-4567).

PUBLIC TRANSIT   RTD (Regional Transportation District) provides bus service in the Denver, Evergreen, Boulder and Longmont areas. ~ 303-299-6000. Public buses in Fort Collins are operated by **Transfort**. ~ 970-221-6620. Greeley also has public bus service, called simply **The Bus**. ~ 970-353-2812.

TAXIS   In Boulder, **Boulder Yellow Cab** provides taxi service. ~ 303-442-2277. In Fort Collins, it's **Shamrock Yellow Cab**. ~ 970-224-2222.

FOUR

North Central Colorado

From the last splash of gold October aspen leaves until the May thaw, a layer of snow up to 25 feet deep covers the mountain ridges along the Continental Divide. Half-burying the steep-slope forests of Douglas fir, gleaming unmarred and unreachable in the cold winter sunlight, it is this combination of phenomenal snowfall and mountain slopes of vast size that accounts for Colorado's unrivaled reputation as a winter resort destination. Whether any of the state's ski areas can legitimately lay claim to being the world's best is a topic of endless debate, but one thing's for sure: the northern Colorado Rockies contain more major ski slopes than any other region of the United States—among them local favorites such as Arapaho, Loveland, Keystone, Cooper, and Copper Mountain, as well as the internationally renowned Winter Park, Breckenridge, Steamboat Springs and, above all, Aspen and Vail. All clustered within an area less than 80 miles in diameter, these sporty winter fantasylands boast a winter season so big and busy that the snowless summer months—peak tourist season in most of Colorado and the West—are considered the off-season here.

The huge scale of the hospitality industry that has grown up around Colorado's ski resorts means that visitors who come during the summer for high-country hiking, mountain biking, fishing or cultural events can enjoy a wide choice of luxury lodgings and exceptional restaurants at bargain prices with no waiting. The ski resort towns devote huge amounts of energy to promoting off-season events, from golf tournaments to theatrical performances and concert series, all with an eye toward filling some of the thousands of vacant hotel rooms and restaurant tables. They have devised ingenious ways of using ski lifts when the snow is gone (from alpine slides to mountaintop biking) and have developed other warm-weather thrill sports, such as hang-gliding and bungie jumping, that are well suited to mountainsides and sheer cliffs. Yet a hike across boundless alpine tundra sparkling with wildflowers in hues of scarlet, lavender, yellow and snow white surrounded by views that reach for a hundred miles is still perhaps the biggest thrill of all.

History, too, is all around. Long before the first ski lift was built, the northern Colorado Rockies were already booming, enjoying economic prosperity and attracting people from all over America with the promise of gold and silver there for the finding. From the first gold strikes in the Georgetown area in 1859 through the discovery in the 1870s of fabulous silver lodes that transformed grubby mining camps like Leadville and Aspen overnight into sizeable cities with opera houses and elegant Victorian mansions, the history of the area was a fantastic rags-to-riches tale. You can't go far without learning about the glamourous but doomed romance of prospector-turned-senator Horace Tabor and his lover, Baby Doe, or the dizzying climb of the Unsinkable Molly Brown from the miner's shack of her childhood to the pinnacle of Denver high society and international notoriety. The mining boom ended abruptly in 1893 because of a collapse in silver prices, and most towns in the northern Colorado Rockies were almost completely abandoned for more than 50 years. Although much of the gingerbread architecture and elegant decor have been preserved in mountain towns throughout the area, backroad excursions into more remote areas reveal the remains of camps where less fortunate miners and prospectors lived and died in far harsher conditions.

The destinations covered in this chapter lie along Route 70 or within an hour's drive on highways that exit from Route 70. They are presented from east to west in the order that motorists would exit Route 70 to reach them. The Continental Divide meanders through north central Colorado in a haphazard manner, so that although all the major ski resorts are west of the Divide, paradoxically, many of them actually lie to the east of nonskiing historic towns such as Georgetown and Leadville. In fact, if you visit all the major towns covered in this chapter in east-to-west sequence, you will cross the Continental Divide at least five times.

▼▼▼▼▼▼▼▼▼▼▼▼▼
Winter Park–
Grand Lake Area

Leaving Route 70 at Empire (Exit 233), Route 40 will take you up a sweeping series of switchbacks to the top of 11,315-foot Berthoud Pass and then twist down the other side of the Continental Divide into Winter Park, one of Colorado's most popular ski areas and one of the closest to Denver, just 67 miles away.

SIGHTS

If you're looking for a unique ski weekend and want to avoid the heavy ski-season traffic on Berthoud Pass, make reservations early for the **Winter Park Ski Train**. Running from Denver's Union Station only on ski-season weekends, the train carries passengers on a scenic two-hour trip through areas that are inaccessible by road in winter. ~ 303-296-4754. In the summer, the ski slopes at Winter Park offer chairlift rides and an **alpine slide**. ~ 970-726-5514.

With no old town to serve as a nucleus for the community, **Winter Park** has sprawled into a characterless agglomeration of condominiums and shopping centers where sporting-goods stores are the specialty. Once virtually deserted outside of ski season, Winter Park has recently gained renown as a mountain-bike mecca thanks to its 500-mile bike trail network, one of the largest in the

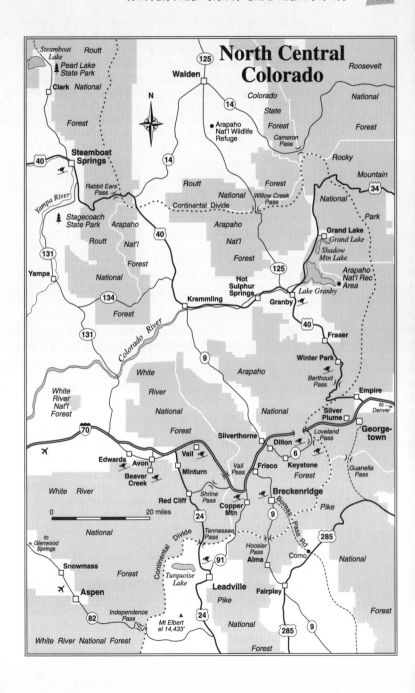

North Central Colorado

Steamboat Lake
Pearl Lake State Park
Routt
Clark National
Forest
Walden
125
Roosevelt
Colorado
14
State
National
Forest
Arapaho Nat'l Wildlife Refuge
Cameron Pass
Forest
N
Rocky
40
Steamboat Springs
14
Mountain
Rabbit Ears Pass
Routt
Forest
National
Willow Creek Pass
National
34
Yampa River
Continental Divide
Park
Stagecoach State Park
Arapaho
Arapaho
Grand Lake
Grand Lake
131
Nat'l
Nat'l
Shadow Mtn Lake
Yampa
Routt
Forest
Forest
125
Arapaho Nat'l Rec Area
National
134
Hot Sulphur Springs
Lake Granby
131
Kremmling
Granby
40
Colorado River
Fraser
9
Winter Park
White
Arapaho
Berthoud Pass
White River Nat'l Forest
River
National
National
Empire
to Denver
Silver Plume
70
Forest
Silverthorne
Dillon
6
Loveland Pass
George-town
Vail
Frisco
Keystone
Edwards   Avon
Keystone
Guanella Pass
Beaver Creek
Minturn
Vail Pass
Forest
White   River
Red Cliff
Shrine Pass
Breckenridge
Pike
0   20 miles
National
24
Copper Mtn
9
Boreas Pass Rd
285
to Glenwood Springs
Continental Divide
Tennessee Pass
Hoosier Pass
Como
National
Snowmass
91
Alma
82   Aspen
Turquoise Lake
Leadville   Fairplay
Independence Pass
Pike
285   9
Mt Elbert el 14,433'
24
National
White River National Forest
Forest

state. Music festivals and Saturday-night rodeos also enliven the summer season.

The area's early days are recalled at the **Cozens Ranch House Museum**, located between Winter Park and Fraser. Started by a retired Central City sheriff in the late 1870s, the ranch also served as the stage stop and store for the Winter Park area for decades and had the only hotel in the valley. Today, the ranch buildings have been refurnished with simple frontier-style antiques of the period. Admission. ~ Route 40, Winter Park; no phone.

North of Winter Park, the highway becomes straight and level as it crosses **Middle Park**, one of the Colorado Rockies' three broad natural "parks"—high, grassy plains that form bowls in the surrounding mountains. North Park lies straight ahead, while South Park is described in Chapter Six. The idea of a huge mountain park sounds more idyllic than the reality. Middle Park, like North and South Parks, is windswept ranchland where the main industry is growing hay for sale as feed to other ranches all over the state. Haystacks, hay rolls, hay bales in heaps taller than a barn—the sheer quantity of hay visible from the highway is impressive. The park's ranch towns, Fraser, Granby and Kremmling, are not.

Granby, however, is an important crossroads in this rarely visited part of the state. If you continue on Route 40 as it veers westward in the direction of distant Steamboat Springs, you soon come to Hot Sulphur Springs, site of a spa of the same name that was popular in the 1920s, when trainloads of people arrived daily to take the waters. After decades of decrepitude, **Hot Sulphur Springs** has been completely renovated. It now has seven outdoor pools and four private indoor pools fed by 104°F water. The spa also offers massages, facial and body wraps, and snacks. ~ Route 40, Hot Sulphur Springs; 970-725-3306.

Located in a historic old schoolhouse, the **Grand County Museum** displays local history exhibits that range from prehistoric Indian artifacts to memorabilia from the early days of Hot Sulphur Springs, Fraser, Granby and Kremmling. The most noteworthy exhibit reveals the early history of recreational skiing in Colorado, reminding visitors that Hot Sulphur Springs was the site of the state's first ski area back in the 1920s, long before any skier made tracks down Aspen Mountain. ~ Route 40, Hot Sulphur Springs; 970-725-3939.

If you continue north from Granby on Route 125, you'll cross the Rabbit Ears Range back to the eastern slope of the Continental Divide over gentle, pine-clad 9621-foot Willow Creek Pass. Beyond the pass, the highway descends into **North Park**, bigger and broader than Middle Park, with even more hay. The only town in North Park large enough to have a café or gas station is

Walden, which is not on the direct route to any tourist destination and may be the least-visited town in the Colorado Rockies.

The only place in any of the parks where you can experience what North Park, Middle Park and South Park were like before the arrival of ranching is **Arapaho National Wildlife Refuge,** oc-   ◀ HIDDEN
cupying a broad area on both sides of the road for about 15 miles south of Walden. Many ponds throughout the refuge attract large numbers of migrating ducks and geese, which in turn attract quite a few hunters in the fall; in summer, though, the knee-high grass-lands of the refuge are home to nearly 300 species of birds, includ-ing songbirds darting wherever you look as well as grouse and quail trotting through the underbrush. East across the plains rises the **Colorado State Forest,** most of it virtually inaccessible except on horseback, against the sheer, impassable ridge that forms the southern part of the Medicine Bow Mountains. To the west tower the dramatic peaks of the **Mount Zirkel Wilderness** in the Park Range.

Upon reaching the highway intersection at Granby, most trav-elers take Route 34 northeast to the town of **Grand Lake,** a small resort town at the western entrance to Rocky Mountain National Park. The town is set on the north shores of 12-mile-long, 400-foot-deep, glacier-carved **Grand Lake,** Colorado's largest natural lake, and the larger, manmade **Shadow Mountain Lake** nearby.

In town, during the summer months the chamber of commerce gives free guided tours of the **Kauffman House,** a two-story lodge that was the area's finest resort hotel from the 1890s to the 1920s. ~ Grand Lake; 970-627-3402. Most visitors to Rocky Mountain National Park enter from the Estes Park side and turn around after reaching the summit of Trail Ridge Road; you'll be surprised at how few people enter the park from the west side near Grand

◆◆

✔ CHECK THESE OUT—UNIQUE SIGHTS

- Browse the collection of tomes at the **Hotel de Paris,** converted from a bakery into a grand hotel that now stands as a museum. *page 121*
- Pass through sheer rock under the Continental Divide via the **Eisen-hower Memorial Tunnel,** which lets Interstate 70 avoid a 12,000-foot pass. *page 124*
- Contemplate the **Matchless Mine,** which made Leadville merchant Horace Tabor both the richest and poorest man in Colorado. *page 132*
- Get a bird's-eye view of the Roaring Fork Valley by riding the **Silver Queen Gondola** to the summit of 11,212-foot Aspen Mountain. *page 138*

Lake, even at the peak of the summer season. For information on Rocky Mountain National Park, see Chapter Three.

LODGING   The Viking consists of six humbly furnished mobile homes. Each trailer has two dormitory rooms with two to four bunks each. Occupants of each trailer share bathroom and kitchen facilities. ~ P.O. Box 3323, Winter Park, CO 80482; 970-726-5356. BUDGET.

Winter Park offers a vast array of accommodations in all price ranges. The town is packed to capacity on winter weekends but has an abundance of lodging at other times. As at many ski resorts, room rates tend to be expensive in winter but drop by as much as 50 percent in summer. Among the several luxury ski lodges there, the **Iron Horse Resort** stands out because of its easy access to the main trail between the Winter Park and Mary Jane ski areas, affording from-your-doorstep skiing in winter and boundless biking or jogging possibilities in summer. It also has an indoor-outdoor pool and four open-air hot tubs. The 120 rooms and suites in this modern lodge have fireplaces, balconies and kitchenettes with microwave ovens. Rooms are done in cheerfully contemporary Southwestern decor. ~ P.O. Box 1286, Winter Park, CO 80482; 970-726-8851, 800-621-8190. MODERATE TO ULTRA-DELUXE.

Affordability and Old World ambience combine at **Gasthaus Eichler**, an exact replica of a charming little alpine inn in Germany. The 15 cozy rooms have down comforters on the beds, lace curtains on the windows and a host of other homey touches. Breakfast and dinner are included in the rate ~ 78786 Route 40, Winter Park; 970-726-5133, 800-543-3899, fax 970-726-5175. MODERATE TO DELUXE.

Winter Park also has many rental condominiums. For information and reservations, call **Winter Park Central Reservations**. ~ 970-726-5587, 303-447-0588, 800-453-2525.

Although Granby itself is a cattle-shipping town with little to interest visitors aside from a sprinkling of budget-priced independent motels, a number of ranches in the area have evolved into first-class dude ranches. Located seven miles west of Granby, **Drowsy Water Ranch** specializes in horseback riding, with services running the gamut from beginners' lessons to all-day pack trips. The ranch also has a swimming pool, a hot tub and fishing ponds. Accommodations are in nine cabins and eight guest rooms in the main lodge, originally built as a ranch house in the 1920s and recently renovated. While this is by no means the most expensive guest ranch in the Granby area, rates are in the ultra-deluxe range, and minimum-stay requirements apply in midsummer. ~ Route 40, Granby; 970-725-3456, 800-845-2292. ULTRA-DELUXE.

Hot Sulphur Springs—the spa, not the town—operates a 16-unit motel adjacent to the springs. The plain-vanilla guest rooms themselves have the usual amenities (cable TV and phones). It's the hot-springs spa that makes staying here special. Use of the hot pools is included, and some packages include massages and wraps. ~ Route 40, Hot Sulphur Springs; 970-725-3306. BUDGET TO MODERATE.

The **Grand Lake Lodge**, a historic mountain lodge built in 1925, offers fabulous views of Grand Lake and Shadow Mountain Lake from its hillside vantage point. Amenities include an outdoor swimming pool overlooking the valley below and a huge lobby fireplace to chase away the evening chill. Accommodations are in 66 rustic two-room cabins, some with kitchenettes. ~ 15500 Route 34, Grand Lake; 970-627-3967 or 303-759-5848. MODERATE.

Built from rough-hewn logs and local stone, **Shadowcliff Lodge** overlooks Grand Lake from an even more spectacular location at the top of a cliff. While there are three individual cabins with kitchenettes and fireplaces (bring your own sheets; six-night minimum stay), most accommodations are in the 19 lodge rooms containing four to eight bunk beds each and in youth hostel–style dorms. Closed October through May. ~ P.O. Box 658, Grand Lake, CO 80447; 970-627-9220. BUDGET TO MODERATE.

Winter Park specializes in food with a German accent. For one of the finest dinners in town, make reservations at the **Gasthaus Eichler**. Situated on the ground floor of the small inn of the same name, the dining room has a distinctly Old World feeling and serves the most authentic *rindsrouladen*, *jägerschnitzel* and *kassler rippchen* in the Colorado ski country. ~ Route 40, Winter Park; 970-726-5133. MODERATE TO DELUXE.

DINING

The café-style **Carver Brothers Bakery** serves pastries, gourmet coffee, full breakfasts and, for lunch, soups, salads and submarine sandwiches. For dinner, served during ski season only, you can choose from a menu including steaks, chicken and veal prepared in a variety of ways, as well as pastas. ~ Behind Cooper Creek Square, Winter Park; 970-726-8202. MODERATE.

The **Grand Lake Lodge Restaurant** lets you enjoy a fantastic view of Grand Lake and Shadow Mountain Lake along with your breakfast buffet, pasta luncheon special or elegant dinner. Nightly chef's specials include fish, lamb, wild-game entrées and steaks. ~ Route 34, Grand Lake; 970-627-3967. MODERATE.

In a restored 90-year-old historic lodge with a whitewater view of the Blue River, **The Rapids Restaurant** features gourmet Italian cuisine such as fettuccine Alfredo and scampi. All meals are served with an appetizer tray of boiled shrimp, beef pâté and salmon mousse, a caesar salad, and sorbet for dessert. ~ 209 Rapids Lane, Grand Lake; 970-627-3707. MODERATE TO DELUXE.

A long-established local favorite in Grand Lake, the **Mountain Inn** is in a cozy old knotty-pine log inn warmed by a big woodburning stove. Choose from a charbroiled New York strip steak, a beef kebab, trout amandine or barbecued chicken. All dinners are served with soup, salad, biscuits and ice cream. Dinner only. ~ 612 Grand Avenue, Grand Lake; 970-627-3385. MODERATE.

Fine dining is surprisingly affordable at **Caroline's Cuisine**. This casually elegant restaurant in the round alongside the headwaters of the Colorado River, north of Grand Lake, is worth the drive for its imaginative presentations of shellfish, duck and veal as well as roast beef, filet mignon and pasta dishes. ~ 9921 Route 34, Grand Lake; 970-627-9404. MODERATE TO DELUXE.

SHOPPING   This is not an area for recreational shopping, unless you're interested in sporting goods, available in abundance at Winter Park's shopping centers. For souvenirs, the **West Portal Galleria** has T-shirts and inexpensive curios. ~ Base of Winter Park Mountain, Winter Park.

In Grand Lake, an attractive shop on the lakefront boardwalk is the long-established **Gallery of Western Art**, featuring American Indian art, designer jewelry and Southwestern fashions. ~ 1114 Grand Avenue, Grand Lake; 970-627-3339.

NIGHTLIFE   In ski season you'll find live music most evenings at a number of lively après-ski bars. In Winter Park these include **The Slope** (Route 40; 970-726-5727), **The Derailer** (Winter Park Resort; 970-726-5514) and **Stampede** (Cooper Creek Square; 970-726-9433).

The most popular partying bar in the valley is the **Crooked Creek Saloon**, a rock-and-roll roadhouse in nearby Fraser where mountain bikers meet the local cowboys, get rowdy and remain so until 2 a.m. ~ Route 40, Fraser; 970-726-9250.

The **Rocky Mountain Repertory Theatre** presents light, contemporary plays in Grand Lake nightly throughout the summer. ~ Grand Avenue, Grand Lake; 970-627-3421. Otherwise, when it comes to nightlife, Grand Lake is on the slow side. But you'll find a Western atmosphere and live country bands on weekends at the **Lariat Saloon**. ~ 1121 Grand Avenue, Grand Lake; 970-627-9965. Down the street at the historic **Stagecoach Inn** is more of the same. ~ 920 Grand Avenue, Grand Lake; 970-627-9932.

PARKS   **ARAPAHO NATIONAL FOREST** 🚶‍♂️🚲🐎 ⟍ The part of the forest around Winter Park includes the Vasquez Mountains, where a major system of horse pack trails connects several 12,000-foot peaks surrounding the scenic St. Louis Creek area. The forest just west of Winter Park has an extensive system of roads and trails that are good for mountain biking. Fishing is fair for trout in St. Louis Creek. Facilities include hiking trails, pack trails and jeep roads. ~ The main forest access in this area is on St. Louis Creek

Road (Forest Road 1602), off Route 40, one mile south of Winter Park; 970-887-4100.

▲ Idlewild Campground on St. Louis Creek has 26 RV/tent sites (no hookups); open mid-July through early September; $8 per night.

Georgetown began as a short-lived gold boom town in 1859. Although the gold ran out within two years and miners and prospectors began to drift away to

▼▼▼▼▼▼▼▼▼▼▼▼▼▼
Georgetown Area

richer digs, the first large silver strike in Colorado catapulted Georgetown and neighboring Silver Plume, two miles away, into prosperity that lasted for more than 30 years.

Today, the **Georgetown–Silver Plume Historic District** stands out because of the sheer number of Victorian buildings remaining there—thanks, it is said, to the town's well-organized volunteer fire brigade, which repeatedly saved Georgetown from the kind of fires that devastated many other early-day mining towns. The historic district has more than 200 19th-century residences and commercial buildings.

SIGHTS

Among the several elegant old structures that now serve as museums within the historic district, one of the most impressive is the **Hotel de Paris**. Much of the period decor and furnishings survives from the 1870s, when this posh hotel was ranked among the most luxurious lodgings in the West. Besides showing off some of the finest examples of Victorian decorative arts to be found anywhere in Colorado, the museum displays mementos of the hotel's founder, Louis Dupuy, a French philosopher and chef who came to Colorado hoping to strike gold. After he was crippled in a mine accident, the townspeople took up a collection to help him out, which financed his plan to convert a former bakery into a grand hotel. Exhibits include much of Dupuy's 3000-volume private library, in its day one of the largest collections of books in the Rocky Mountain West. Admission. ~ 6th and Taos streets, Georgetown; 303-569-2311.

Nearby, the Gothic Revival **Hamill House** offers a look at a mining tycoon's ostentatious lifestyle in the silver boom days. It was one of the first homes in the state with central heating and gas lighting, and the deluxe outhouse must surely have been a legend in its day. The two-story, 19-room mansion was originally a modest little residence, but as owner William A. Hamill's mine-camp fortune grew, he not only redecorated the interior (with such touches as a ten-foot-tall handcarved walnut fireplace mantle, camel-hair wallpaper and gold-plated doorknobs) but also added rooms, towers and a solarium to create one of the most impressive mansions in the state. The hand-milled hardwood and marble interiors have been polished to their original rich gleam. Open daily

June through September, weekends only October through December; closed January through May. Admission. ~ 305 Argentine Street, Georgetown; 303-569-2840.

The **Georgetown Loop Railroad** carries passengers between Georgetown and Silver Plume on a 1920s-era narrow-gauge train pulled by a steam locomotive. The scenic highlight of the trip is the Devil's Gate Bridge, which curves around to loop over itself 95 feet above Clear Creek. The six-mile round-trip excursion takes an hour; visitors may also wish to tour the Colorado Historical Society's **Lebanon Mine** (separate admission), which is accessible only by the train. The railroad and mine tour operate daily in the summer months, and the train continues to run on weekends through September. Admission. ~ P.O. Box 217, Georgetown, CO 80444; 303-569-2403.

The Hotel de Paris' restaurant was the first to bring French gourmet cuisine to the mining camps of Colorado, and the kitchen is one of the high points of the hotel tour today.

The history of Silver Plume is recounted with old photos and Victorian memorabilia in the **George Rowe Museum**, housed in the town's old schoolhouse. Closed October through May. Admission. ~ 95 Main Street, Silver Plume; 303-569-2562.

A large population of Rocky Mountain bighorn sheep—about 175 at last count—grazes among the rugged crags above Georgetown, providing highway travelers with their best chance to glimpse Colorado's official state animal. The **Georgetown Watchable Wildlife Viewing Station**, located by Georgetown Lake just north of town and just off the freeway, has telescopes to spot the sheep. Viewing is best in the early morning and late afternoon. ~ Route 6, Georgetown.

One of Colorado's finest scenic routes starts from downtown Georgetown. The **Guanella Pass Road** climbs by switchbacks up the near-vertical mountain slope that looms over the town. Though easier than it looks, the dramatic ascent is not for sightseers who suffer from a fear of heights. After the first two miles of steep grades and sharp turns, the road grows gentle and takes motorists on a wonderful trip through wild mountains that feel as if they couldn't possibly be just a few miles off the interstate. It's a 12-mile drive from Georgetown to the 11,669-foot Guanella Pass summit, the most spectacular viewpoint on the road, above timberline on the west side of Mount Evans. From there, you can either return to Georgetown or drive down the south side of the pass for 15 miles to join Route 285, a main highway linking the Denver area with South Park.

LODGING Located in the very small town of Empire, about five miles north of Georgetown on the other side of Route 70, **The Peck House** originally opened its doors as a stagecoach stop in 1862 and has been in continuous operation longer than any other hotel in Colorado. The parlor and all 11 guest rooms are so sumptuously decorated in Victorian-era antiques that the Peck House won the Governor's Award for Historic Restoration in 1993. The rates include a continental breakfast. ~ 83 Sunny Avenue, Empire; 303-569-9870, fax 303-569-2743. MODERATE.

A red-and-white Victorian Cape Cod home in the Georgetown Historic District, **The Hardy House B&B Inn** was built in 1880 by the local blacksmith. Today, the inn offers five guest rooms with private baths and period decor. There is a fireplace in the sitting room and a hot tub on the sundeck out back. Rates include an elegant candlelight breakfast. ~ 605 Brownell Street, Georgetown; 303-569-3388, 800-490-4802. MODERATE TO DELUXE.

Built by the founder of the Coors brewery in 1928, **Alpendorf on the Lake** consists of a two-bedroom chalet, a three-bedroom chalet and two rustic cabins without plumbing, all on the shore of a private lake on Guanella Pass, 13 miles above Georgetown. All lodgings have fireplaces and are furnished with an eclectic assortment of well-used furniture. The secluded lake is ideal for sailboating, canoeing and trout fishing, and the surrounding national forest has an abundance of hiking trails and possibilities for cross-country skiing. Rates are deluxe for the chalets and moderate for the cabins. ~ P.O. Box 819, Georgetown, CO 80444; 303-569-2681. MODERATE TO DELUXE.

The Peck House, Colorado's oldest hotel, is also one of the finest restaurants in the area. The intimate dining room with its rustic antique decor, hardwood furnishings and red-brick fireplace features a traditional beef and seafood menu with a few touches of continental flair. Sunday brunch is extra-special here—a gourmet fantasy featuring such exotica as roast quail, assorted pâtés, raspberry duck, venison medallions and beef-and-oyster pie. ~ 83 Sunny Avenue, Empire; 303-569-9870. DELUXE.

DINING

In Georgetown, you'll find fine dining at reasonable prices at **The Happy Cooker**. A Victorian-era home freshly decorated with rattan furnishings and a garden motif provides contemporary Continental luncheon fare such as chicken Marsala, steak Diane and changing pasta and seafood specials. The imaginative menu features such options as a waffle topped with shrimp marinated in sherry and a chipped beef and artichoke crêpe. Breakfast and lunch only. ~ 412 6th Street, Georgetown; 303-569-3166. MODERATE.

The place locals go for good, affordable food in Georgetown is the **Pretzel Kaffee Haus**, an unpretentious little café with decor that hints at a Bavarian lineage. The Old World motif carries over into the menu, where among the standard chili and cheeseburger selection you'll find such fare as bratwurst and Polish sausage. ~ 511 Rose Street, Georgetown; 303-569-3404. BUDGET.

SHOPPING   Georgetown's historic district is home to a growing number of galleries of varying quality. The works of a number of local artists and crafters are shown at the cooperative **Georgetown Gallery**. ~ 612 6th Street, Georgetown; 303-569-2218.

PARKS   **ARAPAHO NATIONAL FOREST** 🚶🏇 ⛴ The part of this large national forest that lies south of Georgetown includes the scenic Guanella Pass area along the western boundary of the Mount Evans Wilderness and a series of picturesque lakes around Square Top Mountain. Fishing is good for rainbow trout in Murray, Silver Dollar and Flat Top lakes. Facilities include picnic areas, restrooms, hiking trails, pack trails and jeep trails. ~ The main national forest access from Georgetown is Guanella Pass Road (Forest Road 381); 303-567-2801.

▲ Guanella Pass Campground has eight RV/tent sites (no hookups); closed mid-November to late May; $8 per night.

▼▼▼▼▼▼▼▼▼▼▼▼▼▼
Breckenridge Area

Summit County, a long, narrow mountain region set apart from the outside world by the Continental Divide on the east and Vail Pass on the west, contains more ski slopes and winter resorts than any other Colorado county. The charmingly European-flavored ski town of Breckenridge is the county seat and was also the main population center until recently, but while steep mountain slopes and historic preservation concerns have limited Breckenridge's growth, development has been explosive in the communities of Dillon, Frisco and Silverthorne just off Route 70.

SIGHTS   Heading west on Route 70, about 60 miles from Denver, you cross the Great Divide and enter Summit County through the **Eisenhower Memorial Tunnel**, a 9000-foot tunnel carved through a formerly impassable ridgeline on the Continental Divide. When it was opened in 1973, the tunnel streamlined travel on Route 70, which had previously been routed over 11,992-foot **Loveland Pass** to the south. You can still take paved Route 6 over the old pass, now a relatively traffic-free scenic route. Along the old route, three ski areas—**Loveland Basin–Loveland Valley** (303-569-3203), on the east side of the Continental Divide; **Arapahoe Basin** (970-468-0718), on the west side; and **Keystone Resort** (970-468-4300), midway between the pass and Dillon Reservoir—rank as the busiest slopes in Colorado.

The highest-altitude inhabited town in the United States, the isolated former silver camp of **Montezuma** (elevation 10,268 feet) can be reached by turning off Route 6 just east of Keystone onto Montezuma Road, which backtracks east for about seven miles to the mostly ghostly old town. Though the town may not look like much, the setting, in the shadow of Santa Fe Peak's 13,180-foot summit, is spectacular. The history of Montezuma and other mining camps along this part of the Continental Divide is the subject of exhibits at the **Montezuma Schoolhouse Museum**, operated by the Summit County Historical Society. ~ Montezuma; 970-453-9022.

The Keystone Resort operates a chairlift for hikers and sightseers during the summer.

Route 70 and the Loveland Pass Road merge again at the foot of the pass beside **Dillon Reservoir**. The west shore of the reservoir has grown into a rather bland, conformist sprawl of townhouses and shopping centers making up the communities of **Dillon**, **Silverthorne** and **Frisco**. These towns are older than they look, and the curious can still find vestiges of the days when they were logging and mining camps.

Many outgrown old schoolhouses in Colorado mountain towns have been resurrected as local history museums. Dillon's is unusual in that it actually focuses on schooling. The Summit County Historical Society's **Dillon Schoolhouse Museum**, furnished with all the trappings of a typical one-room schoolhouse in the late 1800s, is an eye-opener for modern schoolkids. ~ 403 La Bonte Street, Dillon; 970-453-9022.

Near the southwest shore of Dillon Reservoir, seven rustic buildings dating back to the 1880s make up **Frisco Historic Park**. The structures, including a schoolhouse, a small church and a jail, contain photos and memorabilia from the town's early days. ~ Main and 2nd streets, Frisco; 970-668-3428.

From Frisco, take Route 9 south for ten miles to reach the town and ski area of **Breckenridge**. If ever a mountain town was at risk of becoming "another Aspen," in both the best and worst senses of the term, it is Breckenridge. It is the closest major ski resort to the fast-growing Colorado Springs area, less than two hours' drive away. It is even closer to Denver—not quite as close as Winter Park, Arapahoe Basin, Loveland Basin, Copper Mountain or Keystone—but the town's personality makes the longer drive worth it for many Denverites. As a result, it sometimes gets very crowded. From Thanksgiving through the end of March, skiers descend on Breckenridge in astonishing numbers every weekend, packing the miles of parking lots that lie between the streets of town and the ski slopes, creating long lift lines and bumper-to-bumper traffic up and down Main Street.

If possible, plan your ski trip to Breckenridge during the week, when overcrowding is not a problem, in order to really enjoy your stay. This former gold- and silver-mining town of stately old Victorian homes painted in wild color combinations, often refurbished with Tyrolean-style decorative trim, seems to be the community of choice for ski instructors, restauranteurs, innkeepers and others who choose to relocate from the Alps to the Rockies.

At any time of year German and the Scandinavian languages are commonly heard on the streets and in the coffee shops.

Breckenridge has a kind of theme-park quality in the summer months, when the ski mountains are transformed into thrill rides. The **SuperChair** (970-453-5000; admission) chairlift runs to the top of the Peak 8 ski slope May through August, providing easy access to trails through 11,000-foot-high alpine meadows for hiking, mountain biking and horseback riding (there is a rental stable on Peak 8). When you're ready to head back down the mountain, consider the **Super Slide** (admission). Adults and kids alike plunge down the mountainside on wheeled sleds via a fiberglass chute, at speeds of up to 40 miles per hour—it's like riding a roller coaster that's entirely downhill. And if that's not enough family fun for one day, at the foot of Peak 8 is **Amaze'n Breckenridge** (970-726-0214; admission), Colorado's largest human maze, covering 10,000 square feet and containing more than a mile of passageways; an observation deck above gives you the chance to giggle at family members as they get themselves hopelessly lost.

As you continue south from Breckenridge on Route 9, you face a series of sudden, tight switchback curves that makes its way up a steep mountain slope to the summit of 11,541-foot Hoosier Pass on the Continental Divide.

HIDDEN ► A scenic unpaved alternative to the highway over Hoosier Pass is the **Boreas Pass Road**, a wide and well-maintained gravel road that follows an old narrow-gauge railroad route as it gradually climbs above timberline to cross the Continental Divide at an elevation of 11,482 feet. Remains of old ranches and railroad buildings dot the roadside on this spectacular drive, which brings you out at the ghost town of **Como**, northeast of Fairplay on Route 285.

LODGING   The lowest-cost accommodations in the area are at **Alpen Hütte**, an unaffiliated hostel with 66 beds in nine spartan dormitory rooms with shared baths. The lounge area has a fireplace, and there are a reading room and a game room. Though the town of Silverthorne lacks character, a free shuttle bus runs to Breckenridge and several ski areas. ~ 471 Rainbow Drive, Silverthorne; 970-468-6336. BUDGET.

Among the upscale ski lodges in Breckenridge, it's hard to beat **The Lodge & Spa at Breckenridge**, located high on a mountainside. The lodge's guest-room balconies and picture windows offer some of the most majestic mountain views you're ever likely to experience from the comfort of a luxury suite. The 45 suites, each with a kitchen and sitting room, are individually decorated in contemporary Western, Southwestern and European themes. The lodge has landscaped gardens and a spa complete with jacuzzis, hot tubs, saunas, indoor and outdoor swimming pools, exercise room and racquetball courts. Massages and beauty wraps are available. ~ 112 Overlook Drive, Breckenridge; 970-453-9300, 800-736-1607, fax 970-453-0625. ULTRA-DELUXE.

A wide range of modern accommodations can be found in **The Village at Breckenridge**, a huge, 11-building complex with heated walkways that sprawls around the Peak 9 chairlift. A single reservation desk offers rooms in what is virtually a hotel shopping mall consisting of the Village Hotel (standard rooms), the Liftside Inn (studio suites), the Hotel Breckenridge (full suites), the Plaza Condominiums (standard condos) and the Châteaux (deluxe condos). Besides lodging, The Village at Breckenridge complex contains ten restaurants, a full range of shops and two health clubs with swimming pools, hot tubs, saunas, exercise rooms and racquetball courts. ~ 655 South Park Street, Breckenridge; 970-453-2000, 800-800-7829, fax 970-453-3116. DELUXE TO ULTRA-DELUXE.

A perennial favorite among Breckenridge's many bed and breakfasts is the **Fireside Inn**, a historic 1879 home where lodgings include four deluxe-priced private rooms decorated with antiques, including a lavish Victorian-style suite, as well as five budget-priced youth-hostel dorm rooms. You meet a fascinating assortment of people around the fireplace and the hot tub. Continental breakfast in summer. ~ 114 North French Street, Breckenridge; 970-453-6456. BUDGET TO DELUXE.

The **Evans House** offers three guest rooms and a newly added suite, individually decorated in Victorian, Old West and Southwestern styles, in a restored 1886 home complete with hot tub, two blocks from the restaurants and shops of Main Street. A full breakfast is included in the room rate. ~ 102 South French Street, Breckenridge; 970-453-5509. DELUXE TO ULTRA-DELUXE.

✔ CHECK THESE OUT—UNIQUE LODGING

- *Budget:* Sleep cheap in Winter Park at **The Viking**, a ski-country youth hostel made up entirely of mobile homes. *page 118*
- *Moderate:* Settle into Victorian luxury at the **Delaware Hotel**, built in 1886 and newly restored to gold-boom opulence. *page 133*
- *Deluxe:* Soak up the serenity on the lake shore at **The Country Inn at Steamboat Lake**, a classic B&B 20 miles from the nearest town. *page 153*
- *Ultra-deluxe:* Burst into song and you'll feel like a star in *The Sound of Music* at Vail's very European **Gasthof Gramshammer**. *page 147*

Budget: under $50 Moderate: $50–$90 Deluxe: $90–$130 Ultra-deluxe: over $130

DINING

Breckenridge has more than 50 restaurants, each one apparently trying to be as different as possible from the others. Northern Italian cuisine is featured at the **St. Bernard Inn**, housed in a warmly restored Victorian-era building with its original tin roof. The restaurant serves its own pasta daily as well as fresh seafood in creamy sauces. ~ 103 South Main Street, Breckenridge; 970-453-2572. MODERATE.

In an 1893 building decorated with authentic photos of Breckenridge during the mining era, **The Prospector** serves good old-fashioned home-style cooking. Menu choices include meat loaf, homemade soups, pork roast and fried chicken. Breakfast specialties include *huevos rancheros* made with the hottest chili in town. ~ 130 South Main Street, Breckenridge; 970-453-6858. BUDGET TO MODERATE.

History also helps create the romantic mood at the **Briar Rose**. The finest restaurant in Summit County when it was built in the early 1960s, soon after the ski slopes were opened, the Briar Rose provided a new home for many antiques from old-time Breckenridge. The taxidermy that lines the walls may unnerve sensitive diners, but the Victorian-era saloon bar—originally a fixture in the Breckenridge Opera House—is an atmospheric gem that dominates the restaurant's decor. Specials featuring buffalo and wild game often supplement a fairly predictable beef and seafood menu. ~ 109 East Lincoln Street, Breckenridge; 970-453-9948. DELUXE.

Down the street, **Poirrier's Cajun Café** serves Cajun and Creole cuisine in an atmosphere of southern hospitality. The menu includes blackened catfish, grilled shrimp, crawfish in gravy and the chef's award-winning bread pudding. ~ 224 South Main Street, Breckenridge; 970-453-1877. MODERATE.

The Blue Moose, specializing in salads and vegetarian dishes, also offers burgers, fish and steaks. Dine inside or on the open deck with a great view of the Ten Mile Range. ~ 540 South Main Street, Breckenridge; 970-453-4859. BUDGET.

SHOPPING

While sporting goods shops dominate the historic main street and adjacent modern shopping centers of Breckenridge, there is also a small but stylish collection of art galleries. Established for more than 25 years, **Breckenridge Galleries** features original artwork from the Rocky Mountain region with an emphasis on landscapes and Western-theme paintings and sculptures. ~ 124 South Main Street, Breckenridge; 970-453-2592. **Images of Colorado** offers beautiful mounted Colorado landscape photographs. ~ Four Seasons Plaza, 411 South Main Street, Breckenridge; 970-453-2219. Jewelry, pottery, wooden toys, antler art and gourmet food are among the affordably priced handmade gift items at **Homegrown Creations**. ~ 109 North Main Street, Breckenridge; 970-453-1025.

The **Breckenridge Brewery & Pub,** a lively, youth-oriented après-ski brewpub, is one of the most happening places in Breckenridge these days. ~ 600 South Main Street, Breckenridge; 970-453-1550. **Tiffany's** is a disco dance club at the base of Peak 9. ~ Beaver Run Resort, Breckenridge; 970-453-6000 ext. 8754. **Downstairs at Eric's** features live rock music. ~ 111 South Main Street, Breckenridge; 970-453-1401.

NIGHTLIFE

The **Backstage Theater** presents plays several nights a week during the summer and ski seasons. ~ Bell Tower Mall, 605 South Park Street, Breckenridge; 970-453-0199.

Many of the hottest nightspots in Summit County are not in Breckenridge but in Keystone. The rowdy **Snake River Saloon,** has live rock-and-roll nightly in ski season and Thursday through Saturday year-round. ~ 23074 Route 6, Keystone; 970-468-2788. For something a little more mellow, enjoy a game of bridge, chess or backgammon in front of the 15-foot fireplace in the **Tenderfoot Lounge.** ~ Keystone Lodge, Keystone; 970-468-2316.

DILLON RESERVOIR Proximity to Route 70 and explosive real estate development in the Silverthorne and Frisco areas have made this large, scenic reservoir surrounded by wooded mountain slopes one of the most popular recreational lakes in the state. Most of the north shore is developed, while the south shore is a series of wooded peninsulas offering secluded campgrounds. Fishing is good for rainbow trout, brown trout, cutthroat and kokanee salmon. Facilities include restrooms and marinas. ~ Located just off Route 70 at Exits 203 (Frisco) and 205 (Silverthorne/Dillon). Paved roads encircle the lake, providing access to campgrounds and boat ramps; 970-468-5400.

PARKS

▲ Four campgrounds operated by the U.S. Forest Service on Dillon Reservoir offer 380 RV/tent sites (no hookups); $8 to $10 per night.

ARAPAHO NATIONAL FOREST Breckenridge is at the southernmost tip of this large national forest. Here the forest encompasses seven mountain peaks over 13,000 feet high, rising steeply on all sides of the town. Unpaved roads left by past mining operations are suitable for mountain biking and cross-country skiing. The forest also lines the south and east shores of Dillon Reservoir. Swimming is permitted (though cold) in Dillon kanee salmon in Dillon Reservoir. Facilities include picnic areas and restrooms. ~ The best forest access from Breckenridge is on unpaved Boreas Pass Road (Forest Road 404). Dillon Reservoir is just off Route 70; Routes 6 and 9 run along the lakeshore; 970-468-5400.

▲ There are five campgrounds on the shores of Dillon Reservoir, including Elliott Creek Campground, with 64 RV/tent sites (no hookups); open late May through October; free; and Prairie Point Campground, with 34 RV/tent sites; open late May to late September; $8 per night.

▼▼▼▼▼▼▼▼▼▼
Leadville Area

Located on top of one of the world's largest concentrations of precious ores—not only the gold and silver that gave rise to so many strike-it-rich stories in the late 19th century but also even rarer metals like molybdenum, manganese and zinc—Leadville was Colorado's second-largest city during the mining boom days. Today, with the mines closed and lacking the ski slopes or casinos that have revived the economies of other historic mining towns, Leadville's population has slid to one-eighth of what it was a century ago. The town's main claim to fame now is a well-preserved historic district that's a must-see for anyone intrigued by Colorado's gold and silver boom years.

SIGHTS

There was a time when all roads in the Colorado Rockies led to Leadville, and although bypassed by the present-day interstate, the town is still easily accessible from every direction. Route 24 puts the town on the direct approach to most major ski areas from the Colorado Springs region and southern Colorado. It is also a reasonably short drive from the Vail Valley; in fact, many Leadville residents today work in Vail hotels and restaurants, commuting 45 minutes each way on special shuttle buses. For motorists coming from Denver on Route 70, the most direct route to Leadville is Route 91, exiting the interstate at **Copper Mountain Ski Area**. ~ Route 70, Copper Mountain; 970-968-2882, 800-458-8386. The most curious spot on this 25-mile shortcut is the **Climax Molybdenum Mine**, a massive operation that produced most of the world's supply of molybdenum, a metal used in stainless-steel alloys. The mine shut down in 1980 because of the decline in American steel production and the development of synthetic substitutes. Climax, the company town for the mine workers, has joined the new generation of ghost towns.

Whichever route you take to **Leadville**, the trip is bound to be easier than it was for the people who started a mining camp on this site in 1860 during the Pikes Peak gold rush. Early prospectors followed a narrow track around Pikes Peak and across wind-blasted South Park to reach this inhospitable place at an elevation of more than 10,000 feet, surrounded by the Gore, Mosquito and Sawatch mountain ranges. Many came on foot, transporting their worldly possessions in wheelbarrows. Within 20 years, Leadville grew to be the second-ranking city in Colorado, with a population nine times as large as it is today.

The greatest mining-camp legends of Colorado history came out of these silver fields. There was Leadville Johnny Brown, who found a rich gold vein and built a Denver mansion for his "un-

Colorado's Painted Ladies

In older residential neighborhoods in Denver and Colorado Springs, in historic towns like Aspen and Leadville, even on the open prairie where houses stand solitary, Colorado boasts an abundance of "painted ladies"—Victorian houses that have been given fresh, multihued color schemes to emphasize their ornate architectural elements. Many of these mini-mansions have become bed-and-breakfast inns; others serve as small local museums; many others are private residences.

Colorado's favorite historical style got its start in England during the reign of Queen Victoria (1837–1901). Faced with the challenge of designing new kinds of buildings for the increasingly urbanized society of the newborn Industrial Age, innovative British architects borrowed ornamental elements from a wide range of traditions, including Greek, Roman, Gothic, Elizabethan, Italianate, Queen Anne and French Empire buildings, and combined them in fresh new ways. A house might feature Greek columns, a medieval turret and windows etched with designs from the court of Marie Antoinette. At the time, critics dismissed the Victorian look as superficial and inauthentic, but it caught the public's fancy as no other school of architecture ever had, for the first time offering to the middle class stylistic touches copied from the great palaces of Europe.

This "every man a king" architecture captured America's imagination about the same time the settlement of Colorado began. Its principal building materials—wood and red brick—were readily available in Colorado. As businessmen grew wealthy in the mining districts of the Rockies, rough-and-ready gold and silver boom towns began to sprout the kind of houses originally designed for London's nicer neighborhoods. These homes, often built by tradesmen with little or no formal architectural training, tended to exaggerate eccentric ornamentation known as "gingerbread," giving rise to "frontier Victorian" style buildings.

Victorian homes went out of fashion in the early 20th century. In the cities, they were broken up into apartments as older neighborhoods became slums. As populations declined in the mining towns, big old abandoned houses were torn down for firewood. By the 1970s, these high-ceilinged, energy-inefficient white elephants could be bought very cheaply. When a 1976 change in the law gave special tax breaks for fixing up historic buildings, old Victorian homes suddenly came back into vogue, transforming old-fashioned fixer-uppers into sought-after property. Happily, the trend has lasted, and today Colorado's unique "painted ladies" are the kind of status symbol a ski resort condominium just can't match.

sinkable" wife, Molly. There was David May, who turned his Leadville general store into the largest department-store chain in the Rockies, May D & F. Others who started from the streets of Leadville on their way to wealth and power include Marshall Field and Meyer Guggenheim.

Above all, there were Horace Tabor and Baby Doe, whose story epitomizes the euphoria and tragedy of Colorado's mining past. A shopkeeper by trade, Tabor set up a small general store in Leadville and grubstaked a pair of down-and-out miners for one-third of their claim. A month later, the pair struck a rich silver vein. A confidence man bilked Tabor out of his share of the profits by selling him a "worthless" mine that had been salted with a few ounces of gold buckshot. Tabor dug just a few feet and struck the richest silver lode in Colorado history. Tabor renamed his mine The Matchless. After he was elected to the U.S. Senate, Tabor divorced the wife who had come to Colorado with him in favor of his young Washington mistress, Elizabeth "Baby Doe" McCourt. Together they proceeded to spend Tabor's money lavishly but found it virtually impossible to squander it as fast as it poured in. But then. . . .

Despite Tabor's vigorous representation of the silver interests in Washington, in 1893 Congress repealed the law requiring the government to buy silver for minting $1 coins, and the price of silver collapsed—along with Horace and Baby Doe Tabor's fortunes. Tabor was working for the post office when he died six years later. Penniless, Baby Doe clung to the Matchless Mine for 36 years, hoping the price of silver would recover, living in an adjacent one-room cabin where she was discovered one winter morning during the worst days of the Great Depression, wrapped in newspapers for warmth, frozen. You can visit Baby Doe's cabin and the **Matchless Mine** located one mile east of town on a well-marked road. Admission. ~ East 7th Street, Leadville.

With its red velvet seats and ornately hand-painted stage backdrops, the **Tabor Opera House** was the most elegant theater between St. Louis and San Francisco when Horace Tabor built it in 1879. Miners paid large sums to see world-class operas, theatrical presentations and vaudeville shows on this stage. Today, visitors can wander through the opera house on a self-guided tour. Admission. ~ 308 Harrison Street, Leadville; 719-486-3900.

For more on Leadville's history, visit the **Healy House and Dexter Cabin**. Run by the Colorado Historical Society, the two very different homes—one an early prospector's cabin, the other an ornate Victorian mansion—house a museum of gold-rush and boom-town memorabilia. The most surprising part is the cabin, which an early-day mining millionaire converted into a private poker club. It still looks rustic on the outside but was luxuriously

appointed inside with richly polished woodwork. Admission. ~
912 Harrison Avenue, Leadville; 719-486-0487.

Housed in Leadville's historic 1904 Carnegie Library building,
the **Heritage Museum**, re-creates the town's early days in a series
of dioramas and exhibits that include everything from Victorian-
era furnishings to memorabilia of the 10th Mountain Division and
contemporary paintings by local artists. Closed November to mid-
May. Admission. ~ 9th Street at Harrison Avenue, Leadville; 719-
486-1878.

The most unusual of Leadville's several historical museums is
the **National Mining Hall of Fame and Museum**. The museum is
chartered by the federal government, and much of what is on display is on permanent loan from the Smithsonian Institution. There
is an amazingly realistic full-size reconstruction of a hard-rock
mine, as well as a collection of gold nuggets and an exhibit that
details the roles mining has played in shaping America's history
and economy. Admission. ~ 120 West 9th Street, Leadville; 719-
486-1229.

The **Leadville, Colorado & Southern Railroad** offers three-
hour round trips between Leadville and Climax twice daily in
summer and on weekends during fall colors. Though the trains
are of '30s to '50s vintage, the guide's narration focuses on the
early boom days of the Leadville area, pointing out abandoned
gold and silver mines. ~ 326 East 7th Street, Leadville; 719-486-
3936.

Fifteen miles south of Leadville on Route 24, the Twin Lakes
turnoff (Route 82) offers a shortcut from the Front Range cities
to Aspen—over 12,095-foot Independence Pass, the highest Rocky
Mountain pass that can be reached on a paved road.

LODGING

En route to Leadville, **Copper Mountain Resort** offers a range of
hotel- and condominium-style accommodations in several buildings clustered around the foot of the ski slopes. While lodgings
vary in size and amenities (higher-priced units have kitchens, fireplaces and balconies), the mildly Southwestern decor is fairly uni-
form throughout. Guests have complimentary privileges at the
Copper Mountain Athletic Club, where facilities include an indoor
swimming pool, hot tubs, saunas, exercise rooms and tennis and
racquetball courts. Ski package rates are available. ~ P.O. Box
3001, Copper Mountain, CO 80443; 970-968-2318, 800-458-
8386, fax 970-968-2308. ULTRA-DELUXE.

The historic **Delaware Hotel**, dating back to 1886, was reopened on its 100th birthday after a beautiful restoration to its
original gold-boom opulence. The 36 guest rooms feature brass
beds with cozy down quilts and lace curtains. Crystal chandeliers
and Victorian antique furniture grace the lobby. Rates include

breakfast. ~ 700 Harrison Avenue, Leadville; 719-486-1418, 800-748-2004. MODERATE.

The **Leadville Country Inn,** a Queen Anne–style Victorian mansion built in 1893, has nine guest rooms, some in the main house and others out back in the carriage house, with restored polished wood trim, brass beds and claw-foot tubs. A full gourmet breakfast is included in the room rate. ~ 127 East 8th Street, Leadville; 719-486-2354, 800-748-2354; fax 719-486-0300. BUDGET TO ULTRA-DELUXE.

Club Lead is an unaffiliated youth hostel with five six-bunk dorm rooms as well as five private rooms with queen-size beds. There is a hot tub. ~ 500 East 7th Street, Leadville; 719-486-2202. BUDGET.

DINING   In contrast to the highly competitive haute cuisine scene in nearby ski resorts, Leadville eateries seem to have trouble keeping their doors open for more than a single season. The old standby for fine dining in the area, **The Prospector,** is three miles north of town in a rustic-looking lodge with rust-coated mining equipment strewn in the yard. The menu has a standard selection of steak, seafood and chicken entrées along with a salad bar and homemade soup. Portions are huge and the cooking is just like Mom's. ~ Route 91, Leadville; 719-486-3955. MODERATE TO DELUXE.

Callaway's serves gourmet pizzas, roast beef and rainbow trout in the dark wood and floral Victorian atmosphere of the renovated dining room at the historic 1886 Delaware Hotel. The restaurant serves breakfast, lunch and dinner but is closed for several hours between mealtimes. ~ 700 Harrison Avenue, Leadville; 719-486-1418. MODERATE.

Leadville has had a large Hispanic population throughout its history as a mining town, but until recently most Spanish-speaking residents lived in a separate municipality called Stringtown, adjacent to Leadville's southern city limit. Annexed to Leadville in the late '70s, Stringtown still retains its own ethnic identity—and some of the tastiest and most atmospheric no-frills Mexican restaurants in the Rockies.

A long-time favorite is **La Cantina.** Seating is in big wooden booths scarred by time. Mexican jukebox music plays in the background. Enchiladas, tamales and Mexican beer are among the specialties of the house. ~ 1942 Route 24 South, Leadville; 719-486-9021. BUDGET.

Another of Leadville's best Mexican restaurants is the recently remodeled **Casa Blanca.** Located right in the center of town, Casa Blanca enjoys a statewide reputation for its Mexican and Southwestern food, featuring excellent New Mexico–style green chili as well as *chiles rellenos* and stuffed *sopapillas*. ~ 118 East 2nd Avenue, Leadville; 719-486-9969. BUDGET.

Leadville has a handful of unpretentious galleries featuring the **SHOPPING**
work of local artists, such as the **Little Cottage Gallery**. ~ 108 West
8th Street, Leadville; 719-486-2411. A number of antique shops
specialize in mining-era memorabilia, notably **Sweet Betsy's from
Pike**. ~ 122 East 7th Street, Leadville; 719-486-2116. The most
unusual gift items to be found around Leadville are mineral specimens and mining artifacts, found at a number of shops including
The Mining Gallery in the Tabor Grand Hotel. ~ 711 Harrison
Street, Leadville; 719-486-0622.

Leadville's historic old saloons tend to be a tad less sophisticated **NIGHTLIFE**
than the chic nightspots of Breckenridge, Aspen and Vail, but at
least a beer costs a lot less. Saturday night on the town means bars
with pool tables, country-and-western on the jukebox, and sometimes barroom brawls straight out of the cowboy movies. If this
sounds like your idea of a good time, head for the **Silver Dollar
Saloon**, a historic gin joint that dates back to the height of the
1879 silver boom and never bothered to close down for Prohibition. The current owners have reinvented it as an Irish Pub. ~ 315
Harrison Street, Leadville; 719-486-9914. Across the street, the
Scarlet Tavern is the kind of place where hard-rock miners used
to start barroom brawls a few years ago before the mines shut
down.Once in a while, old-timers still do—if only for nostalgia's
sake. ~ 326 Harrison Street, Leadville; 719-486-9928.

SAN ISABEL NATIONAL FOREST 🏃 This portion **PARKS**
of the narrow national forest that extends all the way from Leadville to the New Mexico state line includes one of the most beautifully situated recreational lakes in Colorado, Turquoise Lake, just
west of town. A hilly, paved 19-mile loop road encircles the lake
at a distance, while more than a dozen access roads lead to secluded
campgrounds, picnic areas and fishing spots along the shore. A foot
trail meanders among the pines all the way around the lake, hug-
ging the shoreline out of sight of the main road. A popular segment of the Colorado Trail runs from Turquoise Lake to Twin
Lakes through the Mount Massive Wilderness. This area of the
national forest also encompasses Mount Elbert (elevation 14,433
feet), the highest mountain in Colorado. Fishing is good for cutthroat, rainbow and lake trout and kokanee salmon. Facilities include picnic areas, restrooms and hiking trails. ~ Turquoise Lake is
located five miles west of Leadville via Turquoise Lake Road (6th
Street). There is also access to alpine tundra in the national forest from the Independence Pass Road (Route 82); 719-486-0752.
   ▲ Eight lakeside campgrounds have a total of 269 RV/tent
sites (no hookups). Among them are Baby Doe Campground,
with 50 sites, and Molly Brown Campground, with 49 sites; closed
mid-September to late May; $10 per night.

TWIN LAKES RECREATION AREA 🚶 ⛵ 🚤 ⛺ Two small natural lakes alongside the road up Independence Pass have been augmented by dams to create a pair of reservoirs that merge into a single large lake when the water is high. Although the lakeshore is barren, rocky and unappealing, the spectacular views of Mount Elbert and La Plata Peak more than make up for it. The Colorado Trail skirts the lakeshore. Fishing is good for trout. Facilities include a picnic area, restrooms and hiking trail. ~ Located 15 miles south of Leadville via Route 24, then six miles west on Route 82; 719-486-0752.

▲ Permitted in a large lakeside parking area with a few tent sites nearby (no hookups); $8 to $10 per night.

▼▼▼▼▼▼▼▼▼▼▼
Aspen Area

From Twin Lakes south of Leadville, Route 82 follows the North Fork of Lake Creek around the south slope of 14,433-foot Mount Elbert, the highest mountain in Colorado, and then climbs by switchbacks up the granite spine of the Sawatch Range to cross the Continental Divide over 12,095-foot Independence Pass. At the pass summit, where tiny flowers spangle the permafrost tundra in midsummer, you get an incomparable panoramic view of the vast, high mountain wilderness that forms the heart of the central Rockies. A Y-shaped chain of mountains extends 30 miles northward to Vail, 30 miles southward to Salida and 50 miles westward to Redstone, dominated by 20 peaks over 14,000 feet high. Aspen nestles in the notch of the Y, sheltered by a natural fortress of alpine pinnacles that protect it from everyday reality.

Snow banks up to 16 feet deep close Independence Pass in the winter, so the only way to drive to Aspen then is via the fast four-lane segment of Route 82 that links the town with Glenwood Springs and Route 70. This approach creates a much different impression of Aspen, taking you past the suburban rows of custom and tract homes that have all but swallowed the town of Carbondale, where many Aspen locals actually live, and from which they daily commute 30 miles to work through a landscape thick with recently constructed homes and condominiums. By the time you pass the sprawling industrial and warehouse district and big, busy airport and reach the town of Aspen itself, you may feel as if you've reached the downtown area of a fair-sized city.

SIGHTS

Aspen! In every small town in the Rockies preservationists worry that their corner of the world will become another one, while developers fantasize about being the next one. **Aspen** has served as the prototype for redevelopment of old mountain villages for a half-century, yet there's still only one Aspen—the ultimate ski resort and one of the most expensive places on earth.

Aspen sprang up in 1879 as a silver boom town. It grew slowly and steadily to a population of 12,000 in 1892, when its mines produced $12 million in silver, inspiring one journalist to proclaim it "the greatest silver mining camp in the world today." That same year, the federal government stopped buying silver to mint $1 coins, causing the price of silver to collapse. The mines shut down, the railroad stopped running and, by the following summer, three-quarters of the townspeople had moved away.

Aspen's population had dwindled to a few hundred by 1936, when locals opened the tiny Highlands Bavarian ski resort near Ashcroft. The ski run had a 16-bed dormitory lodge and a boat-tow-style ski lift that cost a dime a ride. It was the first downhill ski area in Colorado and one of the first in the United States. Austrian-born ski instructor Friedl Pfeifer, who moved to Aspen after World War II, persuaded Chicago cardboard-box tycoon Walter Paepke to invest the kind of money it took to develop a European-style resort, creating the Aspen Skiing Company and the beginning of the present ski slopes on Aspen Mountain.

The new ski slopes drew worldwide attention in 1950, when Aspen hosted the World Alpine Ski Championships. Walter Paepke, the Chicago cardboard-box tycoon who was the original investor in Aspen's ski slopes, recognized early that it takes more than snow to make a world-class resort. In fact, he envisioned Aspen primarily as a conference center and secondarily as a ski resort. Paepke restored and reopened the Hotel Jerome and Wheeler Opera House, gave local residents free paint to spruce up their homes, then sponsored Aspen's first major cultural event— a celebration of the bicentennial of Goethe's birth—and brought in an all-star cast of great minds and talents including Albert Schweitzer, Thornton Wilder, Arthur Rubinstein and the Minneapolis Symphony Orchestra. The event became the forerunner of the Aspen Music Festival and School as well as the Aspen Institute of Humanistic Studies.

The town's reputation picked up momentum during the Kennedy administration, when the president and his family and all their friends began coming here for ski weekends. Soon celebrities were everywhere, including a few whose very names evoked fantasies of the Aspen lifestyle, notably John Denver, Hunter Thompson and Claudine Longet. The police grew long hair and drove Japanese compact cars, people smoked marijuana openly on the streets, and Aspen became known as a place where anything went—if you could afford the rent. (But don't even think about lighting up a doobie on main street today. Times change.)

Other rundown old mining towns throughout Colorado have blossomed into winter megaresorts, but none has ever matched Aspen's image for glamour. A vacation home in Aspen has become

an ultimate status symbol. The Aspen Skiing Company has been
bought by Twentieth Century Fox. Aspen now has more movie
stars than Yellowstone has bears, and the police
have come to take their job—keeping the riffraff
out—very seriously. The wild Aspen lifestyle probably still exists, but it's in the hot tubs of huge houses
up private lanes protected by armed guards. The closest most visitors are likely to get to it is a glimpse of a
celebrity in a restaurant or supermarket.

The Wheeler Opera
House, which opened
in 1888, is still the
tallest building in
Aspen.

As for the town's Victorian past, most historic buildings of
downtown Aspen have been preserved, though they have
been engulfed by more contemporary structures and renovated
beyond recognition. The most impressive older building is the
Wheeler Opera House, one of Colorado's finest opera houses
when it opened in 1888. The opera house was in use for barely
five years before the silver market's collapse shut down the nightly
performances. Abandoned, it was gutted by fire a few years later.
It was restored in 1947 and again in 1989, and today it serves as
Aspen's principal indoor stage, hosting concerts, theater performances, opera, ballet, big bands and classical artists almost every
night of the year. Guided tours are available by request during the
day. Aspen's **visitors information center** is located in the opera
house, which was named for Jerome B. Wheeler, who made his
fortune as a partner in Macy's department store in New York City
and moved to the dismal little mining camp of Aspen in 1883,
bringing with him so much investment capital that he is generally
remembered as the town's founding father. ~ 320 East Hyman
Avenue, Aspen; 970-920-5770.

Jerome B. Wheeler lived in the beautiful 1888 Queen Anne–
style mansion that now houses the **Wheeler-Stallard House Museum**. Open afternoons only, the museum traces Aspen's history
from silver boom to bust and back to its current status as one of
the world's premier resorts. Also in the Wheeler-Stallard House
is the **Aspen County Historical Archives**, a treasure trove of historical photos, century-old newspapers and historical documents.
Admission. ~ 620 West Bleeker Street, Aspen; 970-925-3721.

Oddly enough, the **Aspen Art Museum** has no permanent collection. Instead, this large brick Victorian-era building, originally
the town's power plant, provides public visual arts space for rotat-
ing painting, sculpture, architecture and design exhibitions. The
museum hosts lectures, lunchtime art-history programs, monthly
benefit dinners and Thursday-evening cocktail receptions. Admission. ~ 590 North Mill Street, Aspen; 970-925-8050.

The essence of downtown Aspen is its array of expensive galleries, sportswear shops and restaurants; yet less than a mile away
from downtown lies roadless wilderness. One way to reach the
high mountains is to take the **Silver Queen Gondola** to the 11,212-

foot summit of Aspen Mountain. It operates in both winter and summer. In summer, the gondola provides easy access to high-country trails, as well as to the mountaintop Sundeck Restaurant, where Aspen Music School students perform regularly. ~ 970-925-1220.

A very popular spot nearby is **Maroon Lake,** a beautiful mountain lake set at the foot of North and South Maroon Peaks and Pyramid Peak, all over 14,000 feet in elevation. Defoliated by too many visitors, the lake is closed to motor-vehicle traffic during the summer (mid-June through Labor Day) except for overnight campers with hard-to-get U.S. Forest Service permits. Maroon Lake is the trailhead for a vast network of foot and horse trails in the **Maroon Bells–Snowmass Wilderness**. There are also easy, scenic trails around the lake and along the creek.

Shuttle buses operated by **Roaring Fork Transit Agency** run frequently from the T-Lazy-7 Ranch, partway up Maroon Creek Road. The last bus leaves the lake in late afternoon. ~ Aspen; 970-925-8484; fee.

Today only nine abandoned and tumbled buildings remain of the town of **Ashcroft**, which in the 1880s boasted a population larger than Aspen's. To reach the picturesque old townsite, drive 12 miles south of town on Castle Creek Road. Midway between Aspen and Ashcroft is the turnoff for the Conundrum Creek trailhead. From there it is a long but gentle nine-mile walk from the trailhead to **Conundrum Hot Springs**, a pair of idyllic hot-spring pools, three feet and four feet deep, with water temperatures that fluctuate from 99° to 103°F. Camping is permitted in designated backcountry campsites.

◀ *HIDDEN*

If you have to ask about room rates, overnighting in Aspen is probably a bad idea. Just about every private room in the area is priced in the ultra-deluxe range during ski season, though a few plummet into the deluxe range off-season.

LODGING

The original class act in town is the **Hotel Jerome**. Originally built by local silver tycoon Jerome B. Wheeler in 1889 with the intention of surpassing even the finest New York hotels, the Jerome was restored in 1950 as the centerpiece of the newly opened ski resort. Since then, the management has added to the decor year by year with museum-like care. Fine Victorian antiques grace not only the common areas but also the 89 guest rooms and suites, each of which is uniquely furnished and decorated. The spacious bathrooms are done in white marble and feature jacuzzi tubs large enough for two. ~ 330 East Main Street, Aspen; 970-920-1000, 800-331-7213, fax 970-925-2789. ULTRA-DELUXE.

While the Jerome vied with the best New York hotels of the late 19th century, the **Luxury Collection Hotel of Aspen** is designed to rival the great hotels of today. Opened in 1991, the

Luxury Collection Hotel is presently the darling of top-tier jet setters, so if you plan to stay here, make reservations far in advance. Despite its size, the red-brick exterior of this 257-room hotel merges gently into downtown's remaining Victorian-era architecture. The lobby, a wonderland of fine art and classic luxury, makes an ideal place to loiter and watch for movie stars. The guest rooms, like everything else in the hotel, feel larger than life, with rich carpeting, flowery upholstery and giant marble-clad bathrooms as well as all the little niceties like fresh flowers, terrycloth robes, three phones (one in the bathroom) and Godiva chocolates on the pillows. ~ 315 East Dean Street, Aspen; 970-920-3300. ULTRA-DELUXE.

For well-heeled travelers who shudder at the term resort hotel, there's the wonderful **Hotel Lenado** a small, elegant European-style luxury hotel situated in the heart of downtown Aspen. The 19 guest rooms are done entirely in various kinds of wood (*lenado* means "wooded" in Spanish), from the polished wood floors, ceilings and wall paneling to the bentwood beds and sofas. Wood-burning stoves and down comforters add to your comfort on chilly winter evenings. The lobby area features a vaulted ceiling, a two-story-high fireplace and a profusion of windows that lets you view the town streets from the stairway. The common areas also have a library, a bar and a hot tub. A gourmet breakfast is included in the room rate. ~ 200 South Aspen Street, Aspen; 970-925-6246, 800-321-3457, fax 970-925-3840. ULTRA-DELUXE.

Among Aspen's many bed and breakfasts, **Sardy House** boasts the most historic building. Originally built as a private residence in 1892, this red-brick mansion was one of the first Victorian-style homes in Aspen. Now a 20-unit inn, the Sardy House was expanded with renovation of its carriage house and the addition of a new wing that was carefully designed to mirror the mansion's interior architecture. Exceptional care is evident in the decor and furnishings, which seamlessly blend period antiques with modern items to create a distinctive feel of opulence that transcends time. The lofty, century-old blue spruces in the front yard conceal the additions, creating the illusion that the inn is smaller than it actually is. Guest rooms in both the old and new sections have jacuzzis; a hot tub, sauna and swimming pool are behind the main house. Rates include a full menu breakfast. ~ 128 East Main Street, Aspen; 970-920-2525, 800-321-3457, fax 970-920-4478. ULTRA-DELUXE.

The closest thing in Aspen to low-cost lodging is the **St. Moritz Lodge**—part unaffiliated youth hostel and part hotel, with 12 small dorm rooms sharing communal bathroom facilities and 13 small, deluxe-priced standard rooms including private baths. There's a fireplace in the lobby and a jacuzzi, a sauna and an outdoor swimming pool. Dormitory beds are in the budget range all year. ~ 334 West Hyman Avenue, Aspen; 970-925-3220. BUDGET TO DELUXE.

The **Alpine Lodge,** a Bavarian-style house that dates back to the turn of the century and has operated as a ski lodge since the 1950s, is reputed to be the best lodging bargain in Aspen. The main lodge contains seven compact guest rooms, some with private bath, and there are four rustic cabins. ~ 1240 East Cooper Street, Aspen; 970-925-7351. MODERATE TO DELUXE.

Room rates in nearby Snowmass run slightly lower than in Aspen. Representative of these somewhat affordable lodgings is the 44-room **Snowmass Inn,** a modern four-story ski lodge with crazily compact rooms: each has a wall bed that is stored during the day and pulled out at night, and there's a sofa bed, too, so four people can share a room, albeit in cramped quarters. The lodge has a lobby fireplace, heated swimming pool, jacuzzi and sauna. ~ Daly Lane, Snowmass Village; 970-923-4202. DELUXE TO ULTRA-DELUXE.

"Aspen Nouveau" may best describe the cuisine at **Piñons,** which is widely considered the best restaurant in town. It is certainly one of the most innovative restaurants anywhere. The constantly evolving menu features such specialties as an appetizer of lobster with morel and chanterelle mushrooms and an entrée of sautéed ahi crusted with sesame seeds. The decor is a light, airy takeoff on western ranch-house style, with log pillars, leather-wrapped banisters and window shutters fashioned from willow twigs. ~ 105 South Mill Street, Aspen; 970-920-2021. ULTRA-DELUXE.

DINING

The **Restaurant at the Little Nell,** located in a stylish luxury ski lodge near the foot of the Aspen Mountain gondola, characterizes its food as "American alpine cuisine," which apparently

✔ CHECK THESE OUT—UNIQUE DINING

- *Budget:* Savor some of the most authentic Mexican food in Colorado in the equally authentic, no-frills surroundings of **La Cantina.** *page 134*
- *Moderate:* Heat up your tastebuds with award-winning Cajun cuisine in the heart of the Rockies at **Poirrier's Cajun Café.** *page 128*
- *Deluxe:* Enjoy a Sunday brunch of quail, duck and venison at **The Peck House,** Colorado's oldest hotel. *page 123*
- *Ultra-deluxe:* Whet your appetite with a cross-country ski trek or sleigh ride before dining at the **Pine Creek Cookhouse,** a rustic log cabin 12 miles from Aspen. *page 142*

Budget: under $8 Moderate: $8–$16 Deluxe: $16–$24 Ultra-deluxe: over $24

means originality and innovation: highly improbable combinations of many fresh ingredients that result in surprisingly delicious dishes. For example, there's elk with caramelized onions, apples, sweet-potato crisps and sun-dried cherries. If that doesn't suit, try the roast rack of lamb served with peanut-vegetable rice, tortilla salad and a sauce of roasted tomatoes and ancho peppers. Desserts include warm apple-blackberry tarts with cinnamon Calvados ice cream. ~ 675 East Durant Avenue, Aspen; 970-920-4600. ULTRA-DELUXE.

For a more affordable full dinner, try **The Grove**, also near the gondola. This casual spot offers fairly conventional meals such as pasta, chicken and steak. The most popular entrée is Rocky Mountain trout. They also offer a wide selection of breakfast dishes and lunch sandwiches and salads. ~ 525 East Cooper Avenue, Aspen; 970-925-6162. BUDGET TO MODERATE.

Cache Cache brings Aspen-style culinary innovation to French-country cooking in a casual bistro setting that glows with pastel hues and art deco touches. Try the osso buco on risotto cake or the free-range chicken Provençal. ~ 205 South Mill Street, Aspen; 970-925-3835. MODERATE TO DELUXE.

Bentley's at the Wheeler, an old-fashioned English pub located in the Wheeler Opera House and decorated with Victorian antiques (including a handcrafted hardwood bar that was originally a British bank counter), features traditional fish-and-chips as well as other fresh fish dishes, pasta and homemade cheesecake. ~ 328 East Hyman Avenue, Aspen; 970-920-2240. MODERATE.

Out of town, a fine dining favorite is the **Pine Creek Cookhouse**, an elegantly rustic log cabin decorated in old-fashioned ski-lodge style 12 miles from Aspen near Ashcroft. You can drive there in summer, but in winter the trip itself is a wonderful part of this exceptional dining experience: starting at the Nordic ski center on Castle Creek Road, you can either follow a guide on a 20-minute cross-country ski trek in the moonlight or ride to the restaurant in a horse-drawn sleigh. The menu is limited to three entrées, which are different every night. ~ 11399 Castle Creek Road, Ashcroft; 970-925-1044. ULTRA-DELUXE.

No survey of Aspen dining would dare omit the legendary **Woody Creek Tavern**, located on Woody Creek Road, six miles down-valley from Aspen. Made famous in the '70s by *Rolling Stone* journalist Hunter Thompson, still a regular here, it attracts resident celebrities like musician Don Henley of the Eagles and "Miami Vice" veteran Don Johnson. Its pool tables, burgers 'n' beer and self-consciously funky ambience offer a welcome change of pace when Aspen chic starts to cloy. The fare includes locally grown ground-beef burgers, tamales, enchiladas, barbecued ribs and chicken, a different homemade soup each day and an array of bar appetizers such as Buffalo hot wings, nachos and bison

sausage. ~ 2 Woody Creek Plaza, Woody Creek; 970-923-4585.
MODERATE.

Shopping, of course, is a big part of what Aspen is all about. The **SHOPPING**
array of beautiful clothing, jewelry, art and gift items is staggering,
and the price tags are mind numbing. If you like to window-shop,
you could easily spend your whole vacation right here. If you like
to shop for keeps, you could spend your life savings.

Solidly in the realm of fine contemporary visual arts is the
Barney Wyckoff Gallery. ~ 312 East Hyman Avenue, Aspen; 970-
925-8274. The **Aspen Grove Fine Arts** is one of the area's few galleries that show work by Pitkin County's local artists. ~ 525 East
Cooper Avenue, upstairs, Aspen; 970-925-5151. For something
a bit more traditional, visit **Galerie Du Bois**, an ornate salon showing gilt-framed works by French post-Impressionist painters. ~ 407
East Hyman Avenue, upstairs, Aspen; 970-925-5525. The **Hunts-
man Gallery of Fine Art**, showing a full range of nationally known
traditional painters, is Aspen's largest gallery. ~ 521 East Hyman
Avenue, Aspen; 970-920-1910. Contemporary Western art is featured at the **Spotted Horse Gallery**. ~ 525 East Cooper Avenue,
upstairs, Aspen; 970-920-6755. International art is the focus at
E. S. Lawrence Gallery. ~ 516 East Hyman Avenue, Aspen; 970-
920-2922.

Highline Art Gallery offers imaginative, high-priced glass and
crystal art by American and European artisans. ~ 213 South Mill
Street, Aspen; 970-920-9098. **Chepita** carries jewelry by several
designers as well as paintings, folk art and "toys for adults." ~
525 East Cooper Avenue, Aspen; 970-925-2871.

Just for fun, poke your head into **Angels Can Fly**, a gallery cele-
brating humor in comical arts and crafts and zany jewelry. ~ 301
East Hopkins Avenue, Aspen; 970-925-8660. Humor also meets
art at the **Art Tee Gallery**, where original "wearable art" T-shirts
are displayed on the walls like paintings. ~ 401 East Hyman Avenue, Aspen; 970-920-2648.

For a completely different concept in wearable art, check out
Cheeks (420 Hyman Avenue, Aspen; 970-925-3634) and **The
Freudian Slip** (416 South Hunter Street, Aspen; 970-925-4427),
both of which deal in lingerie as elegant as it is naughty. The **Mar-
gaux Baum Gallery** specializes in erotic art. ~ 610 East Hyman
Avenue, Aspen; 970-925-6068.

Last, perhaps, but far from least, you'll find end-of-the-season
leftovers from many of Aspen's finest boutiques, along with celebrity cast-off clothing, at the oldest secondhand store in town,
Gracy's. ~ 202 East Main Street, Aspen; 970-925-5131.

Summer brings a full schedule of cultural events to Aspen. Draw- **NIGHTLIFE**
ing some of the country's most talented musicians and enthusi-

astic audiences, the two-month-long **Aspen Music Festival** offers daily performances in its tent theater on Gillespie Street at the northwest edge of town. Held every summer since the early 1950s, the festival attracts the world's top students and leading virtuosos in a broad range of musical styles, from classical to jazz and avant-garde. ~ 970-925-3254. More very lively arts: **Theatre in the Park** (Art Park, Aspen; 970-925-9313), a two-month series of contemporary plays; the six-week **DanceAspen** (970-925-7718) festival; and the week-long **Aspen Filmfest** (610 East Bleeker Street, Aspen; 970-925-6882). The **Wheeler Opera House** presents live concerts, plays and dance programs almost every night year-round. ~ 320 East Hyman Avenue, Aspen; 970-920-5770.

Aspen's nightclub scene is built to accommodate elbow-to-elbow après-ski crowds during the winter season. In summer, most clubs continue to present live music at least on Friday and Saturday evenings. The **Flying Dog Brew Pub** has contemporary rock music and a young crowd. ~ 424 East Cooper Avenue, Aspen; 970-925-7464. **Legends of Aspen**, another young, loud bar, features live rock music on some nights and sports on big-screen TV on other nights. ~ 325 East Main Street, Aspen; 970-925-5860. **Shooters Saloon**, Aspen's only country-and-western dance club, features nationally known live bands on weekends. ~ 220 South Galena Street, Aspen; 970-925-4567.

For a more sophisticated scene, there is **Mezzaluna**, which has a reputation as the best club in town for celebrity-gawking. ~ 600 East Cooper Avenue, Aspen; 970-925-5882. The ITT **Luxury Collection Lobby Lounge** offers live jazz. ~ 315 East Dean Street, Aspen; 970-920-3300. Live jazz can also be heard at the **Bar at the Little Nell**. ~ 675 East Durant Avenue, Aspen; 970-920-4600.

Bartenders entertain customers with magic acts at **The Tower**, where photographs by John Denver hang on the walls. ~ Snowmass Village Mall, Snowmass Village; 970-923-4650.

PARKS   **WHITE RIVER NATIONAL FOREST** 🏃 🐎 🛶 This 2.25-million-acre forest is Colorado's largest. Of its eight designated wilderness areas, two—the Maroon Bells–Snowmass Wilderness and the Hunter-Fryingpan Wilderness—flank the town of Aspen. The main trailheads that provide access into the wilderness areas are at Maroon Lake, Ashcroft and near the summit of Independence Pass. The Maroon Bells–Snowmass Wilderness is one of the most heavily used wilderness areas in Colorado, and human impact on the delicate alpine ecosystem has become a serious problem. By contrast, the Hunter-Fryingpan Wilderness offers plenty of pristine solitude. Fishing is good for trout, particularly in mountain lakes in the Hunter-Fryingpan Wilderness. Facilities include jeep, hiking and horse trails. ~ Forest access from Aspen is via Independence Pass Road (Route 82 East), Castle Creek Road (Forest Road 102) and Maroon Creek Road (Forest Road 125). Maroon Lake Campground is at the end of Maroon Creek Road; Difficult Campground is just off Independence Pass Road.

▲ Permitted in designated areas. Eight campgrounds totaling 183 RV/tent sites (no hookups); maximum-stay requirements in summer. Among them are Maroon Lake Campground with 44 sites, closed November through May, three-night maximum; $10 per night; and Difficult Campground with 47 sites, closed October through mid-May, five-night maximum; $8 per night.

▼▼▼▼▼▼▼▼▼
Vail Area

Vail, site of America's largest ski resort, is still a young town. Taking its name from the pass to the east (which had unglamorously been named for a Depression-era state highway engineer), the resort was built in secrecy within a single year and unveiled to the public in 1962. Lacking the historic patina of towns like Aspen, Crested Butte and Breckenridge, Vail gained a reputation as a snow-swept, artificially Swiss, theme-park sort of place that mocked the "real" Colorado. But Vail's image has mellowed with age as the saplings planted in 1962 have grown into a forest of shade trees enfolding each street and pathway. The windowboxes of Vail Village still contain plastic flowers in ski season, but real ones are substituted in summer.

SIGHTS

Beyond the busy pseudosuburban zone of Silverthorne and Frisco on the shore of Dillon Reservoir, Route 70 West passes Copper Mountain Ski Area and climbs in a few miles to **Vail Pass** (10,666 feet). The summit is not a lofty ridge but rather an expanse of mountain meadows that's not much to look at. If you're seeking alpine majesty, take **Shrine Pass Road**, just west of the Vail Pass

◀ HIDDEN

summit. Open in summer only and normally suitable for passenger cars, the unpaved road crests the 11,089-foot pass to the west in about four miles, then descends through a scenic canyon to the tiny mining town of Redcliff on Route 24 between Leadville and Vail. From Vail Pass, the interstate descends into the **Vail Valley**.

Vail Village is a shimmering neverland of chic galleries, boutiques, offices and luxury hotels, condominiums and private townhouses flowing along the banks of Gore Creek. Motor vehicles are not allowed in the main part of the village. Unless you have hotel reservations, park at the huge lot near the visitors center just off Route 70. Walk from there and luxuriate in the traffic-free environment.

During summer, gondolas and chairlifts carry picnickers, hikers and mountain bikers to the tops of the ski mountains from several points. The **Vista Bahn Express Lift** (970-476-5601; admission) runs from Vail Village up to Mid-Vail, below the summit of Vail Mountain, while about a mile to the west, **Lionshead Gondola** (970-476-5601; admission) runs up to Eagle's Nest Ridge.

Several miles west in Beaver Creek, the free **Centennial Express Chairlift** (970-949-5750) runs to Spruce Saddle, high on Beaver Creek Mountain.

The **Colorado Ski Museum and Ski Hall of Fame** traces the history of Colorado skiing with videos and exhibits, including one that demonstrates the evolution of ski equipment from the improbably long, heavy wooden skis of a century ago to the latest in fast, nimble fiberglass skis and high-tech boots. A new exhibit traces the evolution of snowboarding, featuring a snowboard used in a James Bond movie. ~ Route 70, Exit 176, Vail; 970-476-1876.

The **Betty Ford Alpine Gardens**, adjacent to the Gerald R. Ford Amphitheater just east of town, sparkle in summer with tiny bright blossoms unique to the fragile alpine environment. There is also a children's playground and a broad park lawn for picnicking. Open from snowmelt to snowfall; tours on Monday and Thursday in summer. ~ South Frontage Road, Vail; 970-476-0103.

The Betty Ford Alpine Gardens are the world's highest public gardens.

Nearby, the **Vail Nature Center** preserves an unspoiled seven-acre sample of the Vail Valley's natural environment and has a visitors center in a restored farmhouse, one of the oldest remaining buildings in the Vail Valley. The nature trails are groomed in winter for cross-country skiing, and in summer the river that runs through it is great for fly fishing and kayaking. Admission. ~ 75 South Frontage Road, Vail; 970-479-2291.

Development has kept expanding westward down the valley to include **Avon** and the newest resort, **Beaver Creek**, below the gleaming slopes of a ski megaresort covering 15 square miles with 25 chairlifts and gondolas and 182 named trails. Although winter visitors may marvel at the astonishing lattice of trails that spans Vail Mountain, the real appeal of this ski area lies hidden behind the mountain's top ridge. The Back Bowls of Vail are every deep-powder skier's fantasy—the most remote and expansive mountain skiing that can be reached by ski lift anywhere in the world.

As you begin to appreciate the scope of this place, you might pause for a moment to imagine how many housekeepers, waitpersons, bartenders, security guards and other service personnel it takes to keep Vail running. If you're curious about where they live, head south from town on Route 24. Just two miles down this highway lies the old, low-rent railroad town of **Minturn**. Nine miles farther along, you come to even smaller, nearly abandoned **Redcliff**, the county seat until 1921. From here a road winds through scenic Turkey Creek Canyon and climbs to the summit of Shrine Pass.

Only a neat grid of abandoned streets and the concrete foundations of a few buildings mark the site of **Camp Hale** (Route 24), a World War II U.S. Army training camp where soldiers of the 10th Mountain Division trained on skis for combat missions in the Alps of wartime Europe. Many graduates of Camp Hale returned after the war to play various roles in the early development of Colorado's ski resorts.

Virtually all accommodations in Vail Village are very expensive, so you might as well go for the best, right? The reigning lodge in the village is **Sonnenalp**, actually three inns—the Bavaria Haus, Austria Haus and Swiss Chalet—under unified management, separated by other lodges in a two-block span along Gore Creek near the center of Vail Village. Though Sonnenalp has 180 guest rooms and suites, the decentralized arrangement preserves the feel of a small European-style country inn. Rooms feature furnishings imported from Germany. ~ 20 Vail Road, Vail; 970-476-5081, 800-654-8312, fax 970-476-1639. ULTRA-DELUXE.

LODGING

Gasthof Gramshammer is another European-style lodge that radiates that *Sound of Music* charm distinctive to Vail. This 27-room inn, one of the first lodges in Vail, set the style for much of the architecture and decor in Vail Village. Rooms range from standard hotel rooms to two-bedroom suites with full kitchens, and all have fireplaces. There's a one-week minimum stay in the winter. ~ 231 East Gore Creek Drive, Vail; 970-476-5626, fax 970-476-8816. ULTRA-DELUXE.

The Lodge at Vail is the longest-established American-style luxury resort hotel in Vail Village. Guest rooms, each with a private balcony, are richly appointed in gleaming mahogany and marble. Facilities include a heated swimming pool, jacuzzis, a sauna, a workout room and tennis courts. Rates include breakfast and lift tickets. Closed October and November. ~ 174 East Gore Creek Drive, Vail; 970-476-5011, 800-331-5634, fax 970-476-7425. ULTRA-DELUXE.

Low-cost lodging—in Vail? Actually, **The Roost Lodge** is in West Vail, on the other side of the interstate from Vail Village and the ski slopes; shuttle buses run hourly. This 72-unit, family-run A-frame lodge offers newly remodeled rooms plus swimming pool, jacuzzi, sauna and continental breakfast. ~ 1783 North Frontage Road, West Vail; 970-476-5451, 800-873-3065. DELUXE.

Other relatively affordable accommodations are farther west in the Avon–Beaver Creek area. The four-story **Comfort Inn** offers 147 big, comfortable, though otherwise unexceptional guest rooms with two queen-size beds each. There's a giant fireplace in the Santa Fe–style lobby. Other facilities include a heated outdoor pool and a jacuzzi. ~ P.O. Box 5510, Avon, CO 81620; 970-949-5511, 800-423-4374, fax 970-949-7762. DELUXE.

The finest hotel in the Vail Valley may be **The Lodge at Cordillera**, a European-style mountain lodge secluded in 3200 acres of private forest about three miles from Beaver Creek Resort. Designed by Belgian architects, the lodge is as eclectic as it is elegant, featuring Chinese slate roofs, Spanish wrought-iron filigree, handmade French furnishings and natural wood and stonework from the Colorado Rockies. The 56 rooms feature balconies and queen- or king-size beds with down quilts, and many have fireplaces. The European-style spa has hydrotherapy tubs, a full range of exercise machines, two swimming pools, jacuzzis, a sauna and a steam room. On the grounds are an 18-hole golf course, tennis courts and miles of mountain-bike trails. ~ P.O. Box 1110, Edwards, CO 81632; 970-926-2200, 800-877-3529, fax 970-926-2486. ULTRA-DELUXE.

DINING   Candlelight dining and French cuisine make **The Left Bank** an excellent choice for fine dining in Vail. Established in 1970 by a top French chef, the restaurant is decorated with family heirlooms and paintings enhanced by a pretty view of Gore Creek. Bouillabaisse is a house specialty, along with rack of lamb, homemade pâté de foie gras, and duck à l'orange, and the wine list offers more than 400 selections. Dinner only. Closed Wednesday. ~ Sitzmark, Vail Village; 970-476-3696. DELUXE.

Michael's American Bistro, on the second floor of Vail's largest enclosed mall, under an atrium overlooking the shops below, doubles as a gallery for international photographers and painters. House specialties include a European-style pizza baked in a wood-fired oven and a gingery tuna pepper steak served with garlic mashed potatoes. The menu also features grilled seafood and wild game; the wine list is one of the largest in Vail. Closed Sunday. ~ Vail Gateway Plaza, 12 South Frontage Road, Vail; 970-476-5353. DELUXE.

For cheap eats, Vail-style, the place to go is **DJ's Classic Diner**, open 24 hours a day during ski season, shorter hours off-season. As the name promises, this is an improbably down-home little counter-service restaurant where your waitperson is likely to also be the cook and dishwasher. The menu includes pasta, burritos, blintzes, omelettes and dessert crêpes, as well as wine and beer. Portions are big, prices are small. ~ 616 West Lionshead Circle, Vail; 970-476-2336. BUDGET.

Sweet Basil, a cozy bistro with a pretty, shady creekside view, offers a creative, wonderfully eclectic menu with such items as apple and jicama salad; a portabello mushroom goat-cheese tart with two vinaigrettes; a five-onion appetizer pizza with a port and balsamic vinegar glaze; and seared rare tuna served with leek and parsnip purée and red and yellow peppers. For dessert try the crème brulée. ~ 193 East Gore Creek Drive, Vail; 970-476-0125. MODERATE TO DELUXE.

Don't be fooled by the funky name: **Beano's Cabin** is the most exclusive restaurant in the Vail Valley. Guests arrive by Sno-Cat–drawn sleigh in winter (horseback or horse-drawn wagon in summer) at this elegantly rustic hunting lodge decorated with pioneer paraphernalia, secluded in the Larkspur Bowl on Beaver Creek Mountain. The prix-fixe menu, which changes daily, features a six-course dinner with a choice of eight entrées, including lamb, beef, poultry and seafood dishes as well as special gourmet pizzas. Dinner only; reservations essential. Closed October through mid-December. ~ Larkspur Bowl, Beaver Creek; 970-949-9090. ULTRA-DELUXE.

Also in the Beaver Creek area, the family-oriented **Cassidy's Hole in the Wall** started as a barbecue place. It still offers a full rack of barbecued baby back ribs but has expanded its menu to include more than 80 items, including burgers, Mexican food and Rocky Mountain oysters. The decor is Old West-saloon style (later in the evening it turns into a cowboy dance club). ~ 82 East Beaver Creek Boulevard, Avon; 970-949-9449. BUDGET TO DELUXE.

Many of Colorado's most exclusive art galleries are located in Vail. The place to start browsing is **Knox Galleries** (970-476-5171), located in the Village Inn Plaza, which is remarkable for its life-size bronze sculptures of people, ranging from kids at play to Indian warriors and historical figures like Benjamin Franklin, placed around the plaza in front of the gallery. Also here is **Claggett/Rey Gallery** (970-476-9350), featuring traditional and Western paintings and bronze sculptures. For 19th-century American folk art and contemporary art by local painters with national reputations visit **Olla Podrida** (970-476-6919). ~ Village Inn Plaza, 100 East Meadow Drive, Vail.

SHOPPING

Vail Fine Art Gallery exhibits an array of regional and international paintings and prints including works by Renoir, Picasso, Warhol, Dali and Chagall. ~ 141 East Meadow Drive; 970-476-2900. **Bader-Melnick Gallery** shows paintings and sculpture by emerging and established American artists. ~ 141 East Meadow Drive; 970-476-0600. **Aboriginal Art, Inc.** has indigenous art from North and South America, Australia, the South Pacific and Africa. ~ 143 East Meadow Drive; 970-476-7715. You'll find Southwestern and international paintings and graphics at **Gateway Gallery**. ~ Gateway Plaza, Vail and Gateway roads; 970-476-1661. In summer and ski seasons, the **Vail Valley Gallery Association** offers Saturday art walks on which you can tour these and other fine art galleries. Call 970-949-1626 for current information.

Fine jewelry is another Vail specialty. For fun pieces in sterling and semiprecious stones stop by **Karats by the Fountain**. ~ 201 East Gore Creek Drive; 970-476-4766. **Currents** offers imaginative variations on traditional designs in gold and diamonds. ~ 285 Bridge Street; 970-476-3322. Unusual, eye-catching inlaid stone jewelry are featured at **Gotthelf's**. ~ 196 Gore Creek Drive; 970-

476-1778. Authentic Western collectibles are highlighted at the **Battle Mountain Trading Post.** ~ Vail Gateway; 970-479-0288.

NIGHTLIFE The Vail Valley supports a nightclub scene that runs the gamut from sedate to rowdy. In Vail, **The Club** features rock music live and loud Tuesday through Saturday. ~ 304 Bridge Street, Vail; 970-479-0556. **Garton's** offers rock music on Thursday, Friday and Saturday nights. ~ Crossroads Center, Vail; 970-479-0607. **Mickey's** features a mellow atmosphere and stylings from the Piano Man, a local fixture for more than 20 years. ~ The Lodge at Vail, 174 East Gore Creek Road, Vail; 970-476-5011. You'll find a hot disco environment at **Sheika's.** ~ Gasthof Gramshammer, 231 East Gore Creek Drive, Vail; 970-476-1515. Pool tables and country music—sometimes live, more often recorded—are found at the **Sundance Saloon** (675 Lionshead Place, Vail; 970-476-3453) and the **Jackalope Cantina** (2161 North Frontage Road, West Vail; 970-476-4314).

PARKS **WHITE RIVER NATIONAL FOREST** 🏃 ⛵ Two large wilderness areas, part of White River National Forest, surround the Vail area. The Eagle's Nest Wilderness, a spectacular area of serrated mountain ridges and glacial valleys, lies just north of Vail Pass. Lakes, waterfalls and wetlands characterize the lofty Holy Cross Wilderness south of Vail. Fishing is good for native and stocked trout in many lakes and streams, particularly in the Holy Cross Wilderness. The Colorado Wildlife Commission has designated Gore Creek east of Vail as a Gold Medal Stream offering exceptional opportunities to catch large trout; special restrictions apply. Facilities are limited to hiking trails. ~ Access to the Eagle's Nest Wilderness is from a trailhead east of the summit of Vail Pass as well as several dead-end hikes lower in the Vail Valley. The main trailheads for the Holy Cross Wilderness are on Forest Roads 707 and 703, which turn off Route 24 between Minturn and Redcliff. Gore Creek Campground is located just off Route 70, four miles east of Vail; 970-827-5715.

▲ Gore Creek Campground has 25 RV/tent sites (no hookups); closed mid-September through May; ten-night maximum stay; $10 per night.

▼▼▼▼▼▼▼▼▼▼▼▼▼▼▼▼
Steamboat Springs Area

As you follow the long, sweeping curve of Route 40's steep descent from the summit of 9426-foot Rabbit Ears Pass, the first thing you see when you approach Steamboat Springs is a hillside completely covered with condominiums that fill up on winter weekends. Thriving on the recreation industry, Steamboat Springs has a hip, sporty subculture. It often seems as if everyone in town rides a mountain bike—at the same time. Yet unlike other famous-name ski resorts like Aspen, Breckenridge or Telluride, Steamboat was not a boom-and-bust mining town, and it was never abandoned. Instead, this former rough-and-ready ranching center still retains a bit of its original character.

The downtown area is preserved as the **Steamboat Springs Historic District**. Its storefronts have a look of western small-town Americana with a fresh coat of paint. Unlike almost all other ski towns mentioned in this chapter, Steamboat Springs is low enough (6000 feet) in elevation so that its streets are usually free of snow and ice. The commercial area known as Steamboat Village, around the base of the ski area, is 900 feet higher and stays snowpacked most of the winter.

The **Tread of Pioneers Museum** is home to the local history exhibit. Along with typical assortments of Indian artifacts and ranch relics, the museum contains a fascinating collection of ski memorabilia that shows how far skiing has come since the beginning of the 20th century. Admission. ~ 800 Oak Street, Steamboat Springs; 970-879-2214.

North of town, the lower slope of **Steamboat Ski Area** rises from the jumble of condominiums and ski lodges. Viewing it from below, you can't see a hint of the ski area's true extent. Above the midpoint, a long ridgeline leads back to a maze of slopes and trails spanning the faces of four mountains. The Thunderhead Chairlift and more expensive Silver Bullet Gondola run all summer, carrying mountain bikers to the ski area's mountain-bike trail network, which joins longer trails in adjoining Routt National Forest. ~ 2305 Mt. Werner Circle, Steamboat Springs; 970-879-6111.

Steamboat Spring, for which the town was named, is located alongside two other small springs on the bank of the Yampa River at the 13th Street Bridge. The spring used to spew water and steam 15 feet into the air with a steamboatlike chugging noise that could be heard for miles, but it slowed to a trickle in 1909, the same year the railroad reached the town; local historians speculate that railroad construction "broke" the spring. On the other side of the river, the paved **Yampa River Trail** provides a two-mile scenic route through town.

Many of the 150 other hot springs in the area still work fine. The venerable **Steamboat Springs Health and Recreation Association** has been a spa since 1887, when the first bathhouse was built there. Today, a modern recreational center stands on the site, with several 100°F swimming and soaking pools, a water slide and new sun decks, as well as tennis courts and a snack bar. A small, heart-shaped stone pool is an artifact of the spa's earlier days. Admission. ~ 136 Lincoln Avenue, Steamboat Springs; 970-879-1828.

HIDDEN ►   Seven miles north of town, **Strawberry Park Hot Springs** is one of the most idyllic hot springs in Colorado. Water from several scalding hot springs mixes with chilly creek water in a series of six hot-tub–depth rock pools. This site used to be a closely guarded secret spot where locals went to bathe nude, but so many people have discovered it over the years that now bathing suits are required during daylight hours, though they are still optional after dark. There are a few rustic cabins and campsites available for rent, plus a newly finished private pool and a sauna that was under construction as this book went to press. Admission. ~ 44200 Country Road 36, seven miles north of Steamboat Springs; 970-879-0342.

Another picture-perfect spot just beyond the edge of Steamboat Springs is **Fish Creek Falls**, a popular picnic spot four miles east of town on the road of the same name. The falls plunge 200 feet into a canyon. A short trail leads down to a picnic area in the canyon, and a bridge provides a great view of the falls. Another short, steep trail leads to an overlook above the falls.

LODGING   The **Rabbit Ears Motel** has 65 standard motel rooms recently refurbished in bright colors and an array of thoughtful little appliances such as coffeemakers and clock radios. The prices are among the lowest in town, and if that's not enough, guests receive a discount at the Steamboat Springs Health and Recreation hot-springs spa across the street. ~ 201 Lincoln Avenue, Steamboat Springs; 970-879-1150, 800-828-7702, fax 970-870-0483. MODERATE.

Even more than in most other Colorado ski-resort towns, the lodging scene in Steamboat Springs is dominated by condominiums, from spartan "efficiency condos" (which look suspiciously like motel rooms with kitchenettes) to luxury townhouses with up to five bedrooms. Typical prices are moderate in summer and deluxe to ultra-deluxe during ski season. To learn more, contact **Big Country Management** (1445 South Lincoln Avenue; 970-879-0763, 800-872-0763) or **Steamboat Marketing and Management** (2350 Ski Trail Lane; 970-879-4477 ext. 101, 800-879-4477 ext. 103).

Homey and historic, the little **Harbor Hotel** has been in operation for more than 50 years. Of the 113 guest rooms, only 15 are in the old hotel, and these feature Victorian-period furnishings and decor. Two recent annexes contain everything from standard motel rooms to two-bedroom condominiums with full kitchens. Facilities include jacuzzis and a sauna. ~ 703 Lincoln Avenue, Steamboat Springs; 970-879-1522, 800-543-8888, fax 970-879-1737. MODERATE TO DELUXE.

Located downtown, a short shuttle bus trip from the ski slopes, the **Steamboat Bed & Breakfast** was originally built in 1891 as the town's first church. Partly gutted by fire, it was completely renovated into a comfortable little inn. The six guest rooms are furnished with antiques and period reproductions. Facilities include fireplaces, a large hot tub and an outdoor deck overlooking meticulously landscaped gardens. Rates include a full breakfast. ~ 442 Pine Street, Steamboat Springs; 970-879-5724, fax 970-870-8787. DELUXE.

Set on a hillside between downtown and the ski area, the **Ramada Vacation Suites Hilltop** was Steamboat's premier luxury ski lodge until new owners recently converted it to time-share condos. Units are available for rent when not in use by the co-owners. Besides the 117 uniformly pleasant suites, the complex offers a full complement of facilities including a heated indoor pool, saunas, jacuzzis, tennis courts and a miniature golf course. ~ 1000 High Point Drive, Steamboat Springs; 970-879-2900, 800-752-5666. ULTRA-DELUXE.

Among the many guest ranches in the Steamboat Springs area, **The Home Ranch**, located 19 miles up the road to Steamboat Lake, stands out as the most luxurious. Some of the 13 guest units are in the main ranch house, while others are in modern, beautifully appointed cabins a short walk away. Each cabin has its own jacuzzi. Riding and flyfishing lessons are offered, as are treks into the Mount Zirkel Wilderness, and there are a swimming pool and a sauna. The ranch is open from June through September and December through March and offers 25 miles of groomed cross-country ski trails in winter. ~ 54880 County Road 129, Clark; 970-879-1780, 800-223-7094, fax 970-879-1795. ULTRA-DELUXE.

A number of resorts dot the area around Steamboat Lake and Hahn Peak. The one with the most atmosphere is **The Country Inn at Steamboat Lake**. Newly built in 1990 in classic style, this eight-room bed-and-breakfast inn has a huge porch and wraparound balcony complete with hot tub overlooking the lake. Rooms are wood-paneled and spacious with contemporary furnishings. ~ 61276 County Road 129, Clark; 970-879-3906, 800-934-7829. MODERATE TO DELUXE.

DINING

For the ultimate in Steamboat Springs dining, take a gondola ride to the top of Thunderbird Peak and **Hazie's**, where china, sterling silver and crystal catch the soft glow of candlelight in a spectacular setting overlooking the town. Fixed-price four-course dinners offer a choice of seafood, chicken, beef and veal entrées plus appetizers, soup, salad and a dessert cart. The gondola ride and live music are included in the dinner price. Closed in fall and spring. ~ Thunderhead Terminal, Silver Bullet Gondola, Steamboat Springs; 970-879-6111. ULTRA-DELUXE.

La Montaña, an exceptional Southwestern restaurant located in a shopping center at the foot of the ski slopes near the gondola, serves intriguing variations on traditional New Mexico and Tex-

Mex cuisine. Elk meat, a specialty here, turns up in a variety of forms—elk loin with pecans, elk fajitas and braided elk sausage—but you'll also find mesquite-grilled lamb and chorizo sausages as well as *chiles rellenos* and other favorites. The thoroughly modern decor features art photographs, murals, stained-glass windows and abundant greenery in a sunny atrium. ~ 2500 Village Drive, Steamboat Springs; 970-879-5800. MODERATE TO DELUXE.

A very popular Mexican restaurant at the slopes, **Dos Amigos** is known for such house specialties as *chiles rellenos* stuffed with Monterey jack cheese and a wide range of enchilada choices, including spinach and mushroom enchiladas, *vegetarino del cocinero* (fresh vegetable enchiladas) and enchiladas *pescador* (seafood enchiladas) with blue-corn tortillas. Adobe-style stucco walls, old-time photos and lots of plants enhance the casual ambience. ~ Ski Time Square, Steamboat Springs; 970-879-4270. MODERATE.

Antare's, located in a 1906 building, cultivates an air of casual elegance with polished hardwood floors, parquet tables and an antique bar in the lounge. Its New American cuisine highlights eclectic blends of regional and ethnic recipes adapted to contemporary tastes. Appetizers include prawns sautéed in Thai chili and served on jasmine rice, and ahi encrusted with sesame seeds and herbs. Among the entrées are Maine lobster in mushroom sauce on a bed of chili-pepper linguine; lamb chops with a chutney of melon, mint and chili; and tender veal with a chardonnay and watercress sauce. Closed Sunday and Monday. ~ 57-H 8th Street, Steamboat Springs; 970-879-9939. MODERATE TO DELUXE.

A local downtown favorite for breakfast or lunch, **Winona's** serves traditional American food for breakfast, lunch and dinner as well as specialty coffees. This casual café doubles as a bakery, so house specialties include homemade muffins, cinnamon rolls and scones. Other breakfast choices include Belgian waffles, eggs Benedict and huevos rancheros. Lunch features design-your-own hoagie sandwiches, homemade soups and salads. ~ 617 South Lincoln Avenue, Steamboat Springs; 970-879-2483. BUDGET.

SHOPPING　In Steamboat Springs you'll find Western crafts and collectibles at **Art Quest**. ~ 511 Lincoln Avenue, Steamboat Springs; 970-879-1989. **Southwest Design** features Indian jewelry. ~ 729 Lincoln Avenue, Steamboat Springs; 970-879-6332. **Bunkhouse Interiors** specializes in Western-style interior decor. ~ 908 Lincoln Avenue, Steamboat Springs; 970-879-6802. For Western-style leather goods there's **Old Town Leather, Etc.** ~ 929 Lincoln Avenue, Steamboat Springs; 970-879-3558. An intriguing place to browse is the **Fair Exchange Company**, a long-established secondhand store that carries everything from used skis and military surplus camping gear to natural-fiber consignment clothing, as well as ranch country antiques. ~ 54 9th Street, Steamboat Springs; 970-879-3511.

In ski season, live rock and reggae are featured at **Heavenly Daze,** a vast, 4000-square-foot brewpub at the foot of the ski mountain. ~ Ski Time Square, Steamboat Springs; 970-879-8080. In the same shopping center, **The Tugboat** has been serving up televised sports on weekdays and live rock and blues on weekends since 1973. ~ 970-879-7070.

Live rock music by the ski slopes can also be found at **The Inferno,** the most notorious singles bar in town, where happy-hour drink prices change constantly, determined by the spin of a "shot wheel." ~ 2305 Mt. Werner Circle, Steamboat Springs; 970-879-5111.

STAGECOACH STATE PARK

Stagecoach Reservoir on the Yampa River is the closest recreational lake to Steamboat Springs and provides the most convenient public camping for visitors to the area. The lake is surrounded by hilly native grasslands with distant views of the mountains around Steamboat Springs. Waterskiing and fishing are the main activities, and a hiking trail traces the entire undeveloped south shoreline. Fishing is good for rainbow and Snake River cutthroat trout. Facilities include picnic areas, restrooms, a marina with boat rentals, phones and groceries. Day-use fee, $4. ~ Located 16 miles south of Steamboat Springs via Route 131 and County Road 14; 970-736-2436.

▲ Permitted in 92 RV/tent sites (62 sites have electrical hookups); $10 per night.

STEAMBOAT LAKE AND PEARL LAKE STATE PARKS

Located on the pine-clad slopes of Hahn Peak near the Continental Divide, Steamboat Lake State Park is a popular recreational area for fishing, boating, windsurfing and waterskiing. Smaller, older Pearl Lake State Park, five miles away, is also administered by the Steamboat Lake State Park office. Pearl Lake is set aside for wakeless boating and flyfishing and lure fishing. Fishing is good for rainbow trout in Steamboat Lake and cutthroat in Pearl Lake. Facilities include picnic areas, restrooms, a marina with rentals and a nature trail. Day-use fee, $4. ~ Both parks are located 24 miles north of Steamboat Springs on paved County Road 129; 970-879-3922.

▲ There are 198 RV/tent sites (50 with electric hookups) at Steamboat Lake and 39 RV/tent sites (no hookups) at Pearl Lake; $9 to $12 per night. Reservations, 800-678-2267.

ROUTT NATIONAL FOREST This 1,127,000-acre expanse of forest and high grasslands virtually surrounds Steamboat Springs. It includes the Mount Zirkel Wilderness, one of the first wilderness areas created in Colorado, with its steep, rugged bare granite pinnacles and lush valleys along the Elk and Encampment rivers. Also within the Routt National Forest boundaries are parts of the Flattop Wilderness and the Never Summer Wilderness. Fishing is good for several trout species in streams and alpine lakes. Facilities include picnic areas, restrooms and hiking trails. ~ Main forest access is from the Rabbit Ears Pass area on Route 40 southeast of Steamboat Springs, and from Forest Road 400, which follows the Elk River east from the main road to Steamboat Lake, ending in the main trailhead for the Mount Zirkel Wilderness. Walton Creek Campground is near Rabbit Ears Pass, 18 miles from Steamboat Springs on Route 40. Summit Lake Campground is four miles north of town on County Road 36 and then 13 miles northeast on Forest Road 60; 970-879-1722.

▲ Seven national forest campgrounds in the area include Walton Creek Campground, with 16 RV/tent sites $8 per night, closed October through June; and Summit Lake Campground, with 8 RV/tent sites and 8 tent-only sites, no drinking water; closed November through June, $5 per night.

▼▼▼▼▼▼▼▼▼▼▼▼▼▼
Outdoor Adventures

**RIVER
RUNNING**

ASPEN AREA   In Aspen, whitewater enthusiasts run the Roaring Fork river, an exhilarating half-day or all-day trip from sheer-walled red rock canyons to lush evergreen forests. Raft and inflatable kayak trips on the Roaring Fork River are operated by **Aspen Whitewater Rafters**, also known as **Colorado Riff Raft**. ~ 555 East Durant Street; 970-925-5405, 800-759-3939. **Blazing Paddles** offers a similar selection of rafting trips, but no kayaks. ~ 407 East Hyman Avenue; 970-925-5651. The **Aspen Kayak School** offers classes for all skill levels on the Roaring Fork River, from one-day and weekend classes to full week-long courses. ~ P.O. Box 1520, Aspen, CO 81611; 970-925-4433. Guided canoe trips on the Roaring Fork River are available from **Snowmass Whitewater**. ~ Snowmass; 970-925-7238.

VAIL AREA   In the Vail area, there is whitewater rafting during the spring runoff (May to mid-July) on the **Eagle River**, which runs among forests of cottonwoods and through the farmlands of the Vail Valley. Half-day and all-day trips are offered by **Timberline Tours** (Vail; 970-476-1414) and **Lakota River Guides** (Lionshead Circle, Vail; 970-476-7238). Both companies also run wetter, wilder raft trips on the rapids of the Colorado River above Glenwood Springs.

STEAMBOAT SPRINGS AREA   Raft trips on the Yampa around Steamboat Springs can be mild or wild depending on the season. Make arrangements through **Buggywhip's Fish & Float Service**. ~ 435 Lincoln Avenue, Steamboat Springs; 970-879-8033. **High Adventures** runs trips on the Yampa and other rivers around the state using rafts and "duckies"—small two-person inflatable boats. ~ P.O. Box 774832, Steamboat Springs, CO 80477; 970-879-8747.

ASPEN AREA   Adventures Aloft II (970-925-9497) and Unicorn **BALLOON**
Balloon Company (970-925-5752) offer hot-air balloon flights **RIDES &**
over the Aspen area and alpine elk range, while **Gliders of Aspen,** **GLIDING**
Inc. (Aspen Airport; 970-925-3694) offers glider lessons and in-
troductory flights above some of the most spectacular terrain in
the Rockies. Aspen is also the only place in Colorado where you
can experience paragliding, a hybrid between skydiving and hang-
gliding that involves leaping off a mountaintop with a steerable
rectangular parachute. Call the **Aspen Paragliding School.** ~ 417
South Spring Street, Aspen; 970-925-7625.

VAIL AREA   In Vail, **Camelot Balloons** (970-476-4743) and
Mountain Balloon Adventures (970-476-7622) offer daily sunrise hot-air balloon rides complete with champagne.

STEAMBOAT SPRINGS AREA   In Steamboat Springs, balloon trips
offered by **Balloons over Steamboat** (970-879-3298) and **Pegasus
Balloon Tours** (970-879-9191) afford panoramic views of the area
from the Flattop Wilderness to Wyoming's Snowy Range.

WINTER PARK–GRAND LAKE AREA   Winter Park Resort is a **DOWNHILL**
large ski area covering four mountains with a vertical drop of **SKIING**
3060 feet. Even though Winter Park has 20 chairlifts with a total
capacity of 30,600 skiers an hour, it is often crowded, especially
on weekends, because of its nearness to Denver. The majority of
the ski trails are rated intermediate. There are no snowboarding
restrictions, and a new half pipe run is for snowboarders only. ~
Winter Park; 970-726-5514. An alternative is the new, smaller
SilverCreek Ski Area near Granby, north of Winter Park. With a
vertical drop of 1000 feet and three chairlifts, SilverCreek offers
five miles of trails from beginner to advanced, and welcomes snowboarders, snow bikers and tubers. ~ Route 40, SilverCreek; 970-
887-3384. Both ski areas are open Thanksgiving through March.
    North of Winter Park near the small ranching center of Fraser,
you can rent a giant inner tube and bounce down steep, powdery
slopes at the **Fraser Valley Tubing Hill.** ~ Route 40, Fraser; 970-
726-5954.

BRECKENRIDGE AREA   Several major downhill ski areas are located along the Loveland Pass Road (Route 6), which diverges
from Route 70 just east of the Eisenhower Memorial Tunnel and
rejoins the interstate at Silverthorne. **Loveland Basin and Loveland Ski Valley,** just off Route 70 and 12 miles from Georgetown,
receive the second-highest snowfall in the Colorado Rockies—375
inches in an average year. With eight chairlifts and a vertical drop
of 1520 feet, this moderate-size ski area offers 25 percent beginner, 48 percent intermediate and 27 percent advanced slopes, as
well as a new snowboarding park. Its proximity to Denver, plus
an absence of lodging at the slopes, means Loveland Basin and
Valley is used mainly by Denverites; it is very crowded on week-

ends but nearly empty on weekdays. The slopes are open from mid-November to early April. ~ Route 6; 303-569-3203.

On the other side of 11,992-foot Loveland Pass, **Arapahoe Basin** is America's highest ski area and one of Colorado's first, built in 1947. The highest lift reaches an elevation of 12,450 feet above sea level. With five chairlifts and a vertical drop of 1670 feet, "A-Basin" (as Coloradoans have nicknamed it) may not be among the region's largest ski areas, but it is certainly one of the most dramatic. The slope is so steep it looks almost like a sheer, snowpacked cliff, and 90 percent of the terrain is rated intermediate to advanced. Snowboarding is allowed. The mogul fields at Arapahoe Basin are legendary. A-Basin is open from mid-November to early April. ~ Route 6; 970-468-0718.

Keystone Resort doesn't look like much from the road; steep, tree-covered slopes conceal most of the ski trails higher up the mountain and on its back side, accessible on two gondolas and four chairlifts. The vertical drop is 2580 feet. Only 8 percent of the ski area is suitable for beginners, while 55 percent is rated intermediate and 37 percent expert. There is a snowboarding park, and a large ski school offers downhill and cross-country lessons for kids and adults of all skill levels. Operated by the same management as Arapahoe Basin, Keystone is open from mid-November to late April. ~ Route 6; 970-468-2316.

The most impressive ski slopes in these parts are at **Breckenridge Ski Area**. Breckenridge covers three mountains with an interconnected trail network that offers a vertical drop of 3400 feet. About 20 percent of the trails are rated for beginners, 30 percent intermediate and 50 percent advanced and expert. The back bowl of Peak 8 offers the highest-altitude in-bounds skiing in the world. The season runs from Thanksgiving to mid-March. ~ Breckenridge; 970-453-5000.

LEADVILLE AREA   Leadville's little-known downhill ski area, located ten miles north of town on Tennessee Pass, is **Ski Cooper**. It has two chairlifts and a vertical drop of 1200 feet. Trails are 30 percent beginner, 40 percent intermediate and 30 percent advanced, and there's a backcountry ski bown plus a new snowboard park. Open Thanksgiving through early April. ~ Route 24; 719-486-2277.

ASPEN AREA   Aspen has four ski mountains in a row, all under the same management—Aspen Mountain, Aspen Highlands, Tiehack and Snowmass. You can buy a lift ticket for any of the mountains or a comprehensive ticket for all four. The most expensive ski areas in the United States, in 1996 Aspen's slopes became the first to break the $50 mark for one-day lift tickets. **Aspen Mountain**, the original Aspen ski area, sprawls in plain view just a few blocks from the center of town. It has a vertical drop of 3267 feet with a challenging array of ski trails—35 percent intermediate, 35 percent advanced and 30 percent expert—and is served by a gondola and seven chairlifts. Snowboarding is prohibited on Aspen Mountain, though it is allowed on all other Aspen-Snowmass area ski slopes. **Aspen Highlands** is about the same size as Aspen Mountain, and taller, with a vertical drop of 3800 feet. Although most of the ski area is not visible from below, nine chairlifts carry skiers up to the higher reaches of the ski area and a number of challenging ski trails. The area is 23 percent beginner, 48 percent intermediate and 29 percent advanced and expert. **Tiehack/Buttermilk**, the smallest of the Aspen ski mountains, is a good midsize ski area in its own right, with six chairlifts and a vertical drop of 2030 feet. Its trails are balanced for all skill levels—35 percent beginner, 39 percent intermediate and 26 percent advanced. **Snowmass** is the largest of the Aspen ski areas, nearly as large in area and lift capacity as all the other three combined. Its vertical drop is 3615 feet. It has 15 chairlifts. Its trails are 9 percent beginner, 51 percent intermediate, 18 percent advanced and 22 percent expert. The season for all Aspen ski areas runs from Thanksgiving through the end of March. ~ 970-925-1220 for all four ski areas.

VAIL AREA The Vail Valley reigns as the world's largest ski development, with a total lift capacity of more than 61,000 skiers per hour. There are three separate base areas. **Vail Ski Area** alone spans seven miles of mountainside, served by one gondola and 18 chairlifts. The vertical drop is 3250 feet. The front side of the mountain is well balanced for all skill levels, with about 33 percent beginner trails, 33 percent intermediate and 33 percent advanced. The much larger bowl area on the back side of the mountain is 36 percent intermediate, 64 percent advanced. Snowboarding is permitted. ~ Vail; 970-476-3239. Just west of Vail, the **Beaver Creek Ski Area** surpasses Vail in height, with a vertical drop of 3340 feet. Its ten chairlifts have about half the capacity of the larger ski area next door. Its trails are challenging,

✔ **CHECK THESE OUT—UNIQUE OUTDOOR ADVENTURES**

- Ski one of the most famous slopes on earth—your choice of Vail, the world's largest ski area, or Aspen, the most expensive. *page 159*
- Go "skinny-skiing" on the vast 60-mile groomed trail network of Devil's Thumb Ranch near Winter Park. *page 161*
- Bike over Pearl Pass Road, the backcountry Aspen-to-Crested Butte route where mountain biking was invented. *page 165*
- Jump off a mountaintop with a steerable parachute and a few tips from the Aspen Paragliding School. *page 157*

with 43 percent of them rated advanced or expert. ~ Avon; 970-949-5750. Finally, there's **Arrowhead Ski Area**, a small area just west of Beaver Creek on the lower slope of the same mountain. The vertical drop is 1714 feet. There are two chairlifts, and the trails are well balanced for all ski levels—30 percent beginner, 50 percent intermediate and 20 percent advanced. ~ 676 Sawatch Drive, Edwards; 970-926-3029. The season at all three Vail Valley ski areas runs from Thanksgiving through March.

STEAMBOAT SPRINGS AREA Steamboat Ski Area ranks third among Colorado ski areas, after Vail and Aspen. From its deceptively compact base, the big 18-passenger gondola and 17 chairlifts carry skiers up a long ridgeline to trails that cover four mountainsides. The vertical drop is 3488 feet. The trails are 15 percent beginners, 54 percent intermediate and 31 percent advanced. There is a half-pipe run for snowboarders only. ~ 2305 Mount Werner Circle, Steamboat Springs; 970-879-6111.

Ski Rentals Among the many ski-rental shops in Winter Park are **Sport Stalker** (Cooper Creek Square; 970-726-8873) and **Flanagan's/Black Dog Mountaineering Ski Rentals** (Route 40; 970-726-4412); both rent cross-country and downhill skis as well as snowboards. In Grand Lake, **Never Summer Mountain Products** rents cross-country skis. ~ 919 Grand Avenue; 970-627-3642.

The Breckenridge area has an overwhelming number of ski-rental shops. For downhill skis, snowboards and cross-country skis, check out **Wilderness Sports** (171 Route 9, Silverthorne; 970-468-8519), **Virgin Islands Ski Rental** (Summit Place Shopping Center, Silverthorne; 970-468-6655), **Mountain View Sports** (22869 Route 6, Keystone; 970-468-0396) and **Rebel Sports** (111 Ski Hill Road, Breckenridge; 970-453-2565). You'll find Nordic equipment at **Mountain Outfitters**. ~ 112 South Ridge Street, Breckenridge; 970-453-2201.

Downhill skis and snowboards are for rent at many Vail area shops, including **Base Mountain Sports** (492 East Lionshead Circle, Vail; 970-476-3689) and **American Ski Exchange** (225 Wall Street, Vail; 970-476-1477). For both Nordic and alpine equipment, visit **Christy Sports, Ltd.** ~ 293 Bridge Street, Vail, 970-476-2244; and 182 Avon Road, Avon, 970-949-0241.

In Steamboat Springs, downhill skis are for rent at **Sport Stalker**. ~ Ski Time Square; 970-879-2445. Both alpine and Nordic equipment are available at **Ski Haus International**. ~ Pine Grove Road; 970-879-0385. Alpine and Nordic equipment can also be found at **Straightline Sports**. ~ 744 Lincoln Avenue; 970-879-7568.

CROSS-COUNTRY SKIING

WINTER PARK–GRAND LAKE AREA You'll find more than 60 miles of groomed cross-country ski trails through deep evergreen forest and along ridgelines with spectacular mountain views north of Winter Park at **Thumb Ranch**. ~ County Road 83, Fraser; 970-726-8231. In Granby, the **SilverCreek Nordic Center** has three miles of easy, scenic groomed and tracked ski trails and a telemarking slope. ~ Route 40, SilverCreek; 970-887-3384. At Grand Lake, cross-country skiing trails are found at the **Grand Lake Ski Touring Center**. ~ Grand Lake Golf Course; 970-627-8008. They can also be found throughout Rocky Mountain National Park.

BRECKENRIDGE AREA There are 20 miles of challenging groomed trail designed by Olympic silver medalist Bill Koch at the **Frisco Nordic Center**, which also offers lessons and rentals. ~ Frisco; 303-668-0866. **Keystone Cross-Country Center**'s 18 miles of groomed trails include the expert-rated Mountain Top Trail, reached via the ski slope gondola for an additional charge. The center also offers telemarking lessons. ~ Keystone; 970-468-4275. There are also 20 miles of groomed, tracked trails through the pine forest at **Breckenridge Nordic Ski Center**, Colorado's oldest public cross-country ski area. ~ 1200 Ski Hill Road, Breckenridge; 970-453-6855.

LEADVILLE AREA **Piney Creek Nordic Center** has 24 miles of groomed trails and a 300-acre telemarking slope. ~ Route 24, Leadville; 719-486-1750.

The **Tenth Mountain Trail Association Hut System** provides a network of more than 250 miles of trails, with mountain huts (reservations required), linking Vail, Leadville and Aspen. For maps, organized tour information and hut reservations, contact Tenth Mountain Trail Association. ~ 1280 Ute Avenue, Aspen; 970-925-5775.

ASPEN AREA Groomed cross-country trails are found at the **Aspen Cross-Country Ski Center**. ~ 39551 West Route 82; 970-544-9246. Another **Ashcroft Ski Touring Center**. ~ Castle Creek Road; 970-925-1971.

VAIL AREA Groomed cross-country ski trail networks include the nine-mile course at **Vail Nordic Center**, which is perfect for snow skating. ~ 1778 Vail Valley Drive, Vail; 970-476-8366. Or ski naked at **Vail Nature Center**'s eight miles of groomed trails. ~ 75 South Frontage Road, Vail; 970-479-2291. With 12 miles of trails, Vail's **Golden Peak Center** offers a gourmet cross-country ski tour with hot drinks, appetizers, entrées and desserts served along the route. ~ Vail Golf Course, Vail; 970-476-3239 ext. 4390. Another option is the **Cordillera Nordic Ski Trail System**, which has more than a dozen loops for varying ski levels off a main ski trail surrounding an exclusive subdivision-in-progress. ~ The Lodge at Cordillera, Edwards; 970-926-2200. The 11-mile **Shrine Pass Road**, which starts at Vail Pass and winds up in Redcliff (arrange to have a vehicle waiting at the end), is among the area's best cross-country ski trails.

STEAMBOAT SPRINGS AREA   For cross-country skiers, the favorite area near Steamboat Springs is the maze of roads and trails from the vicinity of **Rabbit Ears Pass** in Routt National Forest. **Hahn Peak** is another popular cross-country area. There are groomed Nordic trails at **Steamboat Ski Touring Center**. ~ Mount Werner Road, Steamboat Springs; 970-879-8180. Or try the small **Howelsen Hill Ski Area**. ~ Steamboat Springs; 970-879-8499.

For information on renting equipment, see the ski-rental section in "Downhill Skiing" above.

GOLF

WINTER PARK–GRAND LAKE AREA   Near Winter Park, the public 18-hole **Pole Creek Golf Club** is the only golf course in Middle Park. Club rentals are available, and the views of the Continental Divide from every hole are impressive. ~ Route 140; 970-726-8847. Built by local golf enthusiasts in the '60s, the 18-hole championship **Grand Lake Golf Course** features challenging narrow fairways nearly 8500 feet above sea level. It is not uncommon to see elk, moose and bears ambling across the course. ~ Grand Lake; 970-627-8008.

BRECKENRIDGE AREA   The **Eagle's Nest Golf Club** presents a particularly challenging golf experience. Designed by Richard Phelps, the course has over 1000 feet of elevation change and an abundance of wildlife. There are carts and clubs for rent. ~ 305 Golden Eagle Road, Silverthorne; 970-468-0681. The **Keystone Ranch Golf Club**, designed by Robert Trent Jones, Jr., is open to nonguests who reserve tee times at least four days ahead. It features a front nine flanked by evergreen forest and a back nine in open meadows with many water hazards. Carts are required, and included in the greens fee. ~ 1437 County Road 150, Keystone; 970-468-4250. Not to be outdone, the **Breckenridge Golf Club** had its course designed by Jack Nicklaus. The terrain of the mountainous 18-hole course is exceptionally varied, and it may be the only place where golfers have to watch out for beaver-pond water hazards. Cart and club rentals are available. ~ 200 Clubhouse Drive, Breckenridge; 970-453-9104.

LEADVILLE AREA   The semiprivate 18-hole **Copper Creek Golf Club** is very mountainous and shorter than most, with a par of 70, many water hazards and abundant wildlife. Carts are mandatory, and clubs are available for rent. ~ 104 Wheeler Place, Copper Mountain; 970-968-2339. At 10,200 feet, the nine-hole **Mount Massive Golf Course** is the world's highest and has views of the two highest mountains in Colorado, Mount Massive and Mount Elbert. Club and cart rentals are available. ~ 259 County Road 5, Leadville; 719-486-2176.

ASPEN AREA   In Aspen, the 18-hole municipal **Aspen Golf Course** is designed as an environmentally sensitive, wildlife-friendly course.

Carts and clubs are available for rent, along with just about everything else including golf shoes. There are also putting and chipping greens and a driving range. ~ 22475 West Route 82; 970-925-2145. The more expensive, privately owned golf course at the **Snowmass Lodge and Club**, designed by Arnold Palmer, is open to the public on a limited basis. ~ 239 Snowmass Club Circle, Snowmass Village; 970-923-3148.

VAIL AREA A creek meanders the length of the 18-hole **Vail Golf Course,** one of the longest-established courses in the Vail area. The public course has cart and club rentals. ~ 1778 Vail Valley Drive, Vail; 970-479-2260. Flanked by White River National Forest and the Eagle River, the 18-hole **Eagle-Vail Golf Course** and adjacent nine-hole par-three **Willow Creek Golf Course** offer the best in mountain golfing. Carts are mandatory; players must provide their own clubs; lessons and clinics are available. ~ 646 Eagle Road, Avon; 970-949-5267, 800-341-8051. Designed by Robert Trent Jones, Jr., the 18-hole, semiprivate **Beaver Creek Golf Course** is particularly challenging—some say brutal—on the first three holes. The course has cart and club rentals and exceptionally high green fees. ~ 75 Offerson Road, Beaver Creek; 970-845-5775.

STEAMBOAT SPRINGS AREA Steamboat Springs has a nine-hole course with stands of trees and running water throughout at the **Steamboat Golf Club.** Carts and clubs are for rent. ~ Route 40; 970-879-4295. The very expensive **Sheraton Steamboat Golf Club** offers an 18-hole course designed by Robert Trent Jones, Jr., in a mountain setting with abundant deer and other wildlife. ~ Clubhouse Drive; 970-879-2220.

In Grand Lake, there are two free public asphalt-surfaced tennis courts at the **Grand Lake Golf Course.** ~ 970-627-8328. In Breckenridge, there are seven hard-surfaced outdoor public tennis courts at the **Breckenridge Recreation Center** (880 Airport Road; 970-453-1734; fee) and two more in municipal **Carter Park** on High Street. There are also four clay municipal courts in Dillon's **Town Park.** ~ reservations, 970-468-2403. In the Aspen area, two indoor and 11 outdoor asphalt tennis courts are open to the public for a steep fee at **Snowmass Lodge and Tennis Garden.** ~ Snowmass Village; 970-923-5600 ext. 122. Vail has 24 hard-surfaced public tennis courts, located in **Ford Park** on South Frontage Road and in the **Gold Peak, Lionshead** and **Booth Creek** town parks. Steamboat Springs has three outdoor asphalt tennis courts, open in summer only, at the **Steamboat Springs Health and Recreation Association.** ~ 136 Lincoln Avenue; 970-879-1828. None of the courts mentioned above is lit for after-dark play because the cold night air tends to break the lights, which cool too quickly when they are turned off.

TENNIS

RIDING STABLES

WINTER PARK–GRAND LAKE AREA   In the Grand Lake area, you can rent horses for guided or solo trail rides in Rocky Mountain National Park at **Sombrero Stables**. ~ 304 West Portal Road, Grand Lake; 970-627-3514.

BRECKENRIDGE AREA   In Breckenridge, guided trail rides and dinner rides are offered at **Breckenridge Stables** above the Alpine Slide parking area on Peak 8. ~ 970-453-4438. Organized trail rides through the pine and aspen woods of Arapaho National Forest are available in nearby Silverthorne at **Eagle's Nest Equestrian Center**. ~ Route 9; 970-468-0677.

LEADVILLE AREA   **Leadville Stables** rents horses for individual riding and offer guided trail rides into the high country. Many of the organized rides climb above timberline for magnificent views. ~ 181 North Route 91, Leadville; 719-486-1497. Group rides can also be arranged at **Pa and Ma's Guest Ranch**. ~ East Tennessee Road, Leadville; 719-486-3900.

ASPEN AREA   In Aspen, **T-Lazy-7: The Ranch** offers guided rides, pack trips, hay rides, sleigh rides, stagecoach rides, and special Tennessee Walker day rides. Four-hour lunch rides to Maroon Lake are limited to nine people, and full-day rides into the Maroon Bells mountains are limited to five. ~ 970-925-4614, 970-925-7140. **Snowmass Stables** offers riding lessons, guided trail rides, wilderness pack trips and backcountry fishing expeditions, as well as hay-wagon dinner rides and weekly rodeos. ~ P.O. Box 6088, Snowmass Village, CO 81615; 970-923-3075. **Brush Creek Stables** also has trail rides and pack trips. ~ P.O. Box 5621, Snowmass Village, CO 81615; 970-923-4252. **The Rocky Mountain Cattle Moo-vers, Inc.** takes city slickers on day-long cattle drives in the foothills of Mount Sopris, including a steak lunch; they also rent horses for independent riding. ~ P.O. Box 457, Carbondale, CO 81623; 970-963-9666.

VAIL AREA   In Vail, most horseback riding is in the form of guided rides and pack trips. **Beaver Creek Stables** outfits trail rides for groups of up to 60, ranging from an hour to all day, following the east ridge above Beaver Creek, and offers sleigh rides in winter. ~ Beaver Creek Resort, Avon; 970-845-7770. At **Spraddle Creek Ranch**, too, horses are available for trail rides only. Rides range from one to three hours, with destinations like Bald Mountain, Elk Springs and Bear Hollow. ~ 100 North Frontage Road East, Vail; 970-476-6941.

STEAMBOAT SPRINGS AREA   A number of stables and guest ranches that rent horses to the public are located along the road from Steamboat Springs to Steamboat Lake. **Glen Eden Stables** has horses to rent for independent rides and offers guided one-hour to half-day trips through high country where elk are often seen. ~ 61276 County Road 129, Steamboat Springs; 970-879-

3864. There are also guided rides at **Sunset Ranch**. ~ 42850 County Road 129, Steamboat Springs; 970-879-0954. **Steamboat Lake Outfitters** offers a full range of guided horseback tours of the mountains surrounding Steamboat Lake, from an hour to overnight and longer. ~ Steamboat Lake; 970-879-4404.

WINTER PARK–GRAND LAKE AREA   The **Winter Park Mountain Bike Trail System** includes 500 miles of designated trails, eight major loop trips and access to hundreds of miles of logging roads in Arapaho National Forest north of Winter Park. The Grand Lake area has an extensive network of multiple-use trails that are ideal for mountain biking in surrounding areas of Arapaho National Forest.

BIKING

BRECKENRIDGE AREA   The favorite mountain-bike trail in the Breckenridge area is the **Peaks Trail** (9 miles), which runs between Breckenridge and Frisco along the Ten Mile Range. Breckenridge and Keystone chairlifts carry mountain bikers to summer trails high on the ski mountains.

LEADVILLE AREA   In recent years a growing number of mountain bikers have been discovering the old mining roads that surround Leadville. A number of four-wheel-drive roads, including the spectacular climb over **Mosquito Pass**, also offer mountain-biking challenges.

ASPEN AREA   Around Aspen, you'll find the rugged trail where mountain biking got its start in the early 1980s—the **Pearl Pass Road**, which climbs from Ashcroft over the 12,700-foot pass and descends to Crested Butte. Easier trails are also found throughout the area. For steep road touring, try the **Maroon Lake Road**, closed to private motor vehicles in the summer months but open to cyclists.

VAIL AREA   In the Vail area mountain bikes can be rented at Eagle's Nest above the **Lionshead Gondola** for riding on the upper ski trails. For road-bike touring, the **Vail Pass Bikeway** parallels the interstate over Vail Pass. The first half of the 40-mile trip is a grueling climb to the pass summit; from there, it's an unforgettable coast down the mountain in either direction—to Frisco or to Vail.

STEAMBOAT SPRINGS AREA   The most popular backcountry mountain-biking area around Steamboat Springs is the extensive national forest trail network accessed from trailheads at **Rabbit Ears Pass** on Route 40 southeast of town. For an easier ride, take the paved five-mile **Yampa River Trail** from Steamboat Village to downtown Steamboat Springs; you can continue on a good dirt road that follows the Yampa River for nine miles south of town.

Bike Rentals   In Winter Park, you can rent a mountain bike at **Winter Park Sports Shop**. ~ King's Crossing Shopping Center; 970-726-5554. Or visit **Ski Depot Sports**. ~ Park Plaza Shopping

Center; 970-726-8055. In Grand Lake, rent them at **Rocky Mountain Sports**. ~ 711 Grand Avenue; 970-627-8124.

Rent a mountain bike in Breckenridge at **Kodi Rafting & Bikes**. ~ Bell Tower Shops; 970-453-2194. The equipment-rental shop at the base of Peak 8 at **Breckenridge Ski Resort** also rents mountain bikes during the summer months and on September weekends. ~ 970-453-5000.

In Leadville, mountain bikes are for rent at **10th Mountain Sports**, which also distributes great bike trail maps of the area. ~ 500 East 7th Street; 719-486-2202. **Bill's Sport Shop** rents mountain bikes and also organizes half-day and all-day group tours to the Twin Lakes area and Mosquito Pass. ~ 225 Harrison Avenue; 719-486-0739.

In Aspen, you can rent mountain bikes by the hour, day, week or month at **Ajax Bike & Sports**; they also rent kids' bikes, trailers and trailer bikes, baby joggers and rollerblades and provide maps of Aspen area bike trails. ~ 635 East Hyman Street; 970-925-7662. Mountain-bike rentals are also available at **Aspen Velo Bike Shop**. ~ 465 North Mill; 970-925-1465. Aspen's oldest bicycle tour outfitters, **Timberline Bicycle Tours**, rents mountain bikes and organizes guided day trips to Ashcroft, Woody Creek and Hunter Creek, including transportation, equipment and food. They also offer three- and five-day hut-to-hut tours between Aspen and Vail. ~ Silver Queen Gondola; 970-920-3217. **Aspen Bike Tours** not only rents bikes but also offers a shuttle service to transport you to trailheads or to the top of the pass for a once-in-a-lifetime downhill coast. ~ 434 East Cooper Street; 970-920-4059.

Mountain bikes, as well as kids' bikes and inline skates, can be rented in Vail at **Wheel Base Mountain Bikes**, which also provides maps of area bike trails. ~ Sonnenalp Hotel; 970-479-0913. **Christy Sports** rents blades and bikes, too, and can put customers in touch with area mountain bike tour guides. ~ 293 Bridge Street, 970-476-2244; and 182 Avon Road, Avon, 970-949-0241.

In Steamboat Springs, mountain bikes and kids' bikes are for rent at **Sore Saddle Cyclery**, where the shop's staff delights in helping customers plan individually customized rides. ~ 1136 Yampa Avenue; 970-879-1675. **Ski Haus International** can also meet your rental needs for mountain bikes, cross bikes, kids' bikes and tandems, along with maps and information on where to ride. ~ 1450 South Lincoln Avenue; 970-879-0385.

HIKING   All distances listed for hiking trails are one way unless otherwise noted.

WINTER PARK–GRAND LAKE AREA   In the Grand Lake area you'll find trailheads for several spectacular, uncrowded trails on the west side of Rocky Mountain National Park. Among the prettiest is the **Cascade Falls Trail** (3.5 miles), which starts near the park visitors center just north of Grand Lake and makes an easy 300-foot ascent to the waterfalls. Farther north in the park, the **Lulu City Trail** (3 miles) leads to old mines and the ghost town of Lulu City. Nearby, the challenging **Timber Lake Trail** (5 miles) climbs more than 2000 feet from marshy meadows to alpine lakes and tundra.

GEORGETOWN AREA   You can climb to the twin summits of **Grays Peak and Torreys Peak** on a five-mile trail starting from a marked trailhead on Stevens Gulch Road west of Georgetown. One of the easiest ways to climb to the summit of a 14,000-foot mountain is to hike the **Mount Bierstadt Trail** (2.5 miles) from Guanella Pass above Georgetown.

BRECKENRIDGE AREA   Above Breckenridge, Blue Lakes Road near the summit of Hoosier Pass leads to the 2.5-mile hiking trail that leads to the summit of 14,264-foot **Quandary Peak**.

LEADVILLE AREA   The challenging six-mile hike from the Elbert Creek campground near Turquoise Lake west of Leadville takes you to the 14,421-foot summit of **Mount Massive**, following the Colorado Trail for the first part of the way.

ASPEN AREA   In the Aspen area, the popular **East Maroon Creek Trail** (8.5 miles) from Maroon Lake goes to the top of 11,280-foot East Maroon Pass; you can walk as far as you like and return to the lake by the same route. You may wish to plan an expedition with **Town Taxi** (Aspen; 970-349-5543), on which you take the 13-mile, seven- to ten-hour hike from Maroon Lake over East Maroon Pass to the ghost town of Gothic; then a shuttle picks you up, takes you to Crested Butte for the night and returns you to Aspen the next day. You can arrange for your lodging, or they can help you make arrangements as part of the package. Another classic Aspen-area hike is the **Conundrum Creek Trail** (9 miles) to Conundrum Hot Springs, starting from Castle Creek Road.

VAIL AREA   Near Vail, the **Booth Lake Trail** climbs from a trailhead parking lot beside Route 70 for two miles to 60-foot-high Booth Creek Falls and then climbs for four more miles to Booth Lake in the Eagle's Nest Wilderness. A six-mile trail from the end of Forest Road 707 near Minturn climbs to the 14,003-foot summit of **Mount of the Holy Cross** in the heart of the Holy Cross Wilderness.

STEAMBOAT SPRINGS AREA   One of the first wilderness areas in Colorado, the Mount Zirkel Wilderness northeast of Steamboat Springs has an extensive trail network that can be accessed from the Slavonia trailhead at the end of Forest Road 400, which turns off County Road 129 south of Steamboat Lake. A magnificent day hike from this trailhead is the **Gilpin Lake Trail** (4 miles), a moderate hike to a 10,000-foot alpine lake.

▼▼▼▼▼▼▼▼▼▼▼▼

Transportation

CAR

All major areas described in this chapter lie within an hour's drive of **Route 70**. To reach Winter Park, take **Route 40** north from the Empire exit; turn off on **Route 34** at Granby to reach Grand Lake. For Breckenridge, turn off south on **Route 9** at Frisco. Leadville can be reached either from the Copper Mountain exit via **Route 91** or from Vail via **Route 24**. Aspen can be reached via **Route 82** either from the east over Independence Pass from Leadville (closed in winter) or from Glenwood Springs to the west. Three highways—Route 40 from Winter Park; Route 9 north from Silverthorne; or **Route 131** north from Wolcott, at the west end of the Vail Valley—lead to Steamboat Springs.

AIR

United Express and Continental Express both have frequent flights from Denver International Airport to Aspen's **Pitkin County Airport**, and both airlines offer a few flights from other U.S. cities. American Airlines and America West Airlines offer direct flights to the **Vail–Beaver Creek Jet Center**. Located about 25 miles west of Steamboat Springs in the town of Hayden, the **Yampa Valley Regional Airport** has commuter service from Denver on Continental Express.

TRAIN

The **Rio Grande Ski Train** (303-296-4754) runs directly from Denver to Winter Park on winter weekends. **Amtrak** (800-872-7245) offers passenger service to Winter Park and Granby on the "California Zephyr" or the "Desert Wind." Following the most scenic route on the Amtrak system, the trains run through the Vail Valley but don't stop until they reach Glenwood Springs.

BUS

Greyhound (800-231-2222) offers bus service to Winter Park (Vasquez Road; no local phone), Aspen (Rubey Park Transportation Center; 970-625-3980), Vail (Vail Transportation Center; 970-476-5137) and Steamboat Springs (30060 West Route 40; 970-879-0866).

CAR RENTALS

In Aspen, you'll find **Alamo Rent A Car** (800-327-9633), **Eagle Rent A Car** (800-282-2128), **Thrifty Car Rental** (800-367-2277), **National Interrent** (800-328-4567) and other car-rental desks at the Pitkin County Airport. Four-wheel-drive vehicles are available at **Rocky Mountain Rent A Car**. ~ Aspen; 800-525-2880.

Car rentals are available from **Hertz Rent A Car** (800-654-3131) at the Vail–Beaver Creek Jet Center in Eagle.

Avis Rent A Car (800-331-1212), **Budget Rent A Car** (800-527-0700) and **Hertz Rent A Car** (800-654-3131) are located at the Yampa Valley Regional Airport near Steamboat Springs.

PUBLIC TRANSIT

The **Lift Bus Service** provides summer and winter shuttle service among the hotels, shopping areas and ski slopes of Winter Park. ~ 970-726-4118.

The **Town Trolley** provides shuttle service around Brecken-ridge. ~ 970-453-2251. The free **Summit Stage** carries passengers throughout the area of Frisco, Dillon, Silverthorne/Keystone, Copper Mountain and Breckenridge. ~ 970-668-0999.

The **Leadville Transit Department** runs morning and evening shuttle service to Vail and Breckenridge, where many Leadville residents work. ~ 800 Harrison Avenue, Leadville; 719-486-2044.

Aspen's **Roaring Fork Transit Authority** offers free shuttle service in Aspen and runs commuter buses to Snowmass, Basalt, Carbondale and Glenwood Springs. ~ 20101 West Route 82; 970-920-1905.

Free municipal shuttle service operates constantly throughout Vail Village, Lionshead and West Vail about once every five minutes. **Shuttle service** (970-949-1938) is also available, but not free, to the Avon–Beaver Creek area.

Steamboat Springs Transit operates regularly scheduled shuttle service between downtown Steamboat Springs and the ski area. ~ 970-879-3717.

Home James Taxi Service provides taxi service in the Winter Park area. ~ 970-726-5060. In Breckenridge, call **Around Town Taxi**. ~ 970-453-8294. Local transportation in Aspen is provided by **Town Taxi**. ~ 970-349-5543. **Aspen Limo** offers scheduled shuttle service to Aspen's Pitkin County Airport, the Glenwood Springs Amtrak station and Denver International Airport, all twice daily in the winter and summer seasons and once daily in the off-seasons. ~ 970-925-1234, 800-222-2112. **Vail Valley Taxi** serves the Vail area. ~ 970-476-8294. **Steamboat Taxi** (970-879-3335) and **Alpine Taxi** (970-879-8294) serve Steamboat Springs.

TAXIS

FIVE

Northwestern Colorado

An unpaved road winds through ancient forests, past jumbles of fractured lava rock, among pristine lakes dancing with rainbow trout. It is a broad, nearly level landscape, high enough to be chilly even in midsummer, and except for a few roads like this one, seemingly untouched by civilization. The road ends at the rim of the mesa, and from there you can look off across the farmlands of the Colorado River Valley a mile below and the sandstone and slickrock desert that stretches from there far into Utah. It's like standing on a rocky headland along the coast of a very large yet uninhabited island overlooking an ocean that, a few million years ago, somehow drained away.

Hot springs, secret waterfalls, dinosaur bones, majestic mesa tops and redrock canyonlands—these are a few of the hidden pleasures that await the adventurous traveler who takes time to explore the northwestern corner of Colorado, one of the state's least-visited regions. Tell the folks back home (even if home is as close as the Denver metro area) that you're planning a trip to Grand Mesa, the Flat Tops Wilderness, Browns Park and the Gates of Lodore, and they'll most likely respond with blank stares. Most of northwestern Colorado is far enough removed from both major population centers and popular tourist areas so that if you visit the region at any time of year except the autumn hunting season (which is considered peak season in these parts), you're likely to find yourself completely alone with nature.

The two main towns in the region are Glenwood Springs, a long-established spa resort that has grown in popularity thanks to its proximity to both the trendy Aspen scene and the spectacular scenery of Glenwood Canyon, and Grand Junction, the nontouristy commercial center for the fruit-growing communities that line the banks of the Colorado River. Located 90 miles apart on Route 70, they are the only towns of any size in an area larger than Connecticut, Massachusetts and New Hampshire combined.

In fact, a look at a road map would lead most people to believe that the northwestern quadrant of Colorado is completely empty and featureless. It is the purpose of this chapter to show that this impression is not exactly accurate. This is a landscape full of natural wonders concealed by canyons and mesas as wild and remote as they are beautiful—all in all, the most hidden part of "Hidden Colorado."

Glenwood Springs has had a roller-coaster career as a resort town since the 1880s, when Aspen silver tycoon Jerome B.

▼▼▼▼▼▼▼▼▼▼▼▼▼▼▼▼
Glenwood Springs Area

Wheeler built a hot-springs spa there. He hoped to attract wealthy easterners and Europeans, but the resort soon became a rough-edged playground for the wealthier denizens of nearby mining towns like Aspen and Leadville. Alongside the grand Colorado Hotel, the elegant bathhouse and the polo field stood some of the finest gambling casinos in the West and no fewer than 22 saloons.

Glenwood Springs' popularity waned by the 1920s, though in the '30s it gained notoriety as a mountain hideaway for Al Capone and other gangsters. Until as recently as the 1970s it remained a low-budget party town where college students flocked on weekends. The recreation boom that transformed other nearby towns pretty much bypassed Glenwood Springs until the past few years, when the wave of big-money tourism that poured out of Aspen to create such upscale bedroom communities as Carbondale finally washed over Glenwood Springs like a fresh coat of paint. Now a popular weekend destination for Denverites as well as an easy day trip from Vail, Glenwood Springs is once again one of Colorado's liveliest mountain towns.

The center of the action is **Glenwood Hot Springs**, with the world's largest hot-spring pool: it's 92° to 94°F, two blocks long, holds 1000 bathers and has a water slide. There is also a smaller, hot tub–temperature (104°) therapeutic pool. Lockers and towels are provided, and a shop beside the locker rooms sells bathing suits. Although the pools are outdoors, they are open until 10 p.m. year-round. Admission. ~ 401 North River Street, Glenwood Springs; 970-945-7131.

SIGHTS

A short distance from the hot springs is **Yampah Vapor Caves**, geothermally heated steam baths in three natural caves—two for men and one, the largest, for women. The Ute Indians are said to have revered the caves for their healing powers. The recently renovated vapor caves now feature soft, spacey music; additional amenities include massages and individual hot tubs. Admission. ~ 709 East 6th Street, Glenwood Springs; 970-945-0667.

One memento of Glenwood Springs' colorful past is **Doc Holliday's Grave** in Linwood Cemetery, reached by foot trail from Cemetery Road, two blocks east of the Chamber of Commerce, which is located along Route 82. Holliday, a dentist from Virginia, had moved west to seek a cure for tuberculosis. Making his way as a professional gambler, he gained national notoriety as the subject of a best-selling paperback book, *My Friend, Doc Holliday*, written by lawman Wyatt Earp. Following the legendary gunfight at the OK Corral in Tombstone, Arizona, Holliday moved to Glenwood Springs, where he spent the last year of his life and then succumbed to tuberculosis. Buried in the same cemetery is Kid Curry (a.k.a. Harvey Logan), a member of Butch Cassidy's gang.

More recollections of the town's early days can be found at the **Frontier Historical Museum**, where you can see a generous sampling of Victorian-era mine-camp elegance, including the marriage bed shared by silver tycoon and scandal-ridden senator Horace Tabor and his mistress-turned-wife, Baby Doe. There are also American Indian artifacts and a walk-through replica of a coal mine. Closed Tuesday and Wednesday in winter and Sunday year-round. Admission. ~ 1001 Colorado Avenue, Glenwood Springs; 970-945-4448.

In 1993 construction was completed on the formerly narrow winding 12-mile stretch of Route 70 through **Glenwood Canyon**, the last portion of the road to become a four-lane divided highway. Thanks to imaginative engineering, half a billion taxpayer dollars and Colorado's tough, controversial environmental laws, Glenwood Canyon is today the most beautiful scenic area on any U.S. interstate highway. The roadways, terraced up the canyon walls with eastbound and westbound lanes at different levels, stand on concrete pillars up to 80 feet tall to minimize impact on the environment. In the few places where rock cuts or blasting were necessary, the rock was resculpted to make the surface look natural. Contractors were fined for *any* shrubs or trees they destroyed while building the road, the amounts ranging from $35 for a raspberry bush to more than $22,000 for a Douglas fir. A 4000-foot tunnel conceals the freeway from sight of hikers on the Hanging Lake Trail, the most popular recreational spot in the canyon.

At the bottom of the 1800-foot-deep gorge, well below the din of the interstate, the paved **Glenwood Canyon Trail** takes walkers, joggers, cyclists and even rollerbladers along the bank of the Colorado River. Hiking trails start at three rest areas along the way. The most spectacular is the steep 1.2-mile trail that climbs to **Hanging Lake**, where waterfalls feed a gem-blue pool on a narrow terrace 930 feet up the canyon's sheer granite wall. Formerly one of the "hidden" wonders of the Rockies, Hanging Lake Trail has become the single most popular hiking trail in Colorado since completion of the Glenwood Canyon Project. The trail starts from Sixth Street on the east side of Glenwood Springs, near the Yampah Vapor Caves. The Hanging Lake trailhead is ten miles from town. The entire Glenwood Canyon Trail is 20 miles long, paved all the way.

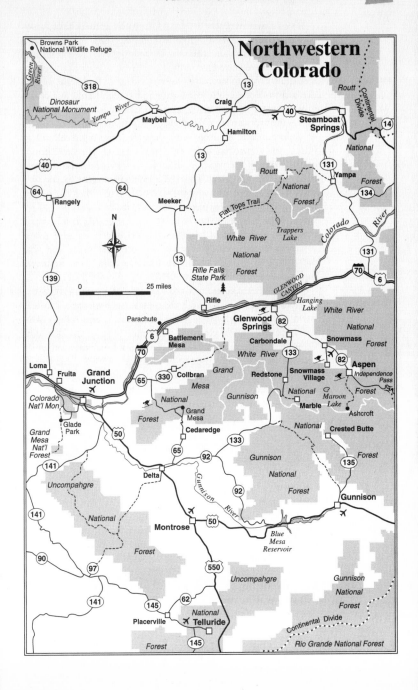

Northwestern Colorado

Browns Park
National Wildlife Refuge

Green River

318

Dinosaur
National Monument

Yampa River

Maybell

Craig

40

Steamboat
Springs

Routt

Continental Divide

14

13

Hamilton

131

Yampa

National

134

64

Rangely

64

Meeker

Routt

National

Forest

40

13

Flat Tops Trail

Trappers
Lake

White River

Colorado River

131

139

National

Forest

70

6

Rifle Falls
State Park

GLENWOOD CANYON

Parachute

Rifle

Hanging
Lake

White River

6

Glenwood
Springs

82

70

Battlement
Mesa

Carbondale

133

Snowmass

National

Forest

Loma

Fruita

Grand
Junction

65

330

Colbran

Grand

Mesa

White River

Redstone

Snowmass
Village

82

Aspen

Independence
Pass

Colorado
Nat'l Mon.

Glade
Park

National

Forest

Grand
Mesa

Gunnison

National

Marble

Maroon
Lake

Ashcroft

Forest

Grand
Mesa
Nat'l
Forest

50

Cedaredge

Crested Butte

141

65

133

92

Uncompahgre

National

Gunnison

National

135

141

Delta

Gunnison River

92

Forest

National

Forest

Gunnison

90

97

Montrose

50

Blue
Mesa
Reservoir

Uncompahgre

Gunnison

National

141

550

National

Forest

145

62

Placerville

Telluride

National

Continental Divide

Forest

145

Rio Grande National Forest

0   25 miles

HIDDEN ►

For a fascinating day trip from Glenwood Springs, take Route 82 south for 12 miles to Carbondale and then fork right on Route 133, which goes around the twin 14,000-foot red-hued mountain peaks known as the Maroon Bells on the non-Aspen side. Seventeen miles down this road lies the tiny village of **Redstone**, originally a turn-of-the-century coal-mining town and now one of the most secluded luxury resort areas in Colorado. The sight that makes the trip worthwhile is **Redstone Castle**. Built by the founder of Colorado Fuel & Iron, which operated the big steel mill at Pueblo and controlled most of the state's coal mines, the 42-room castle is one of the most remarkable architectural achievements of Colorado's early days. The massive red sandstone mansion was abandoned after only a few years of occupancy when the owner lost everything in a corporate takeover. It has recently been restored in lavishly authentic fashion. Now operated as a bed and breakfast, the castle welcomes sightseers. Redstone also has a small art center featuring marble sculptures and a tiny historical museum with exhibits on the coal-mining days. ~ 58 Redstone Boulevard, Redstone; 970-963-3463.

HIDDEN ►

About five miles southeast of Redstone on a well-marked, exceptionally scenic back road is the even smaller village of **Marble**, site of a huge abandoned marble mill, still surrounded by broken slabs and columns of gleaming white marble scattered all about. Continue up the mountain on a dirt road for four miles and you'll find the quarry, which used to produce up to 3000 cubic feet of marble a day. The marble from the quarries and mill here was used to build many federal government buildings and monuments, among them the Lincoln Memorial and the Tomb of the Unknown Soldier.

LODGING

The AYH-affiliated **Glenwood Springs Youth Hostel** offers 24 dormitory beds and several private rooms, along with kitchen and laundry facilities and shared baths, as well as a photographers' darkroom and book and record library. ~ 1021 Grand Avenue, Glenwood Springs; 970-945-8545. BUDGET.

One of the first grand hotels in the Rocky Mountains, the **Hotel Colorado** celebrated its 100th birthday in 1993. Modeled after the Villa de Medici and built of native sandstone and Roman brick, the formerly opulent Italianate-style hotel once welcomed President William Taft and was a favorite haunt of Theodore Roosevelt during his presidency. Though it has also served intermittently as a youth hostel, the venerable hotel never closed its doors, and in the 1970s a top-to-bottom renovation transformed it with modern fixtures and period decor. The landscaped courtyard is inviting, the lobby is truly vast, and each of the 126 rooms and suites is individually decorated in restful, muted hues. It also has a jacuzzi, a sauna and an exercise room, and the hot springs are just a short walk away. ~ 526 Pine Street, Glenwood Springs; 970-945-6511, 800-544-3998, fax 970-945-7030. MODERATE.

Hot Springs Lodge is right across the street from Glenwood Hot Springs; guests get a discount at the hot-spring pool. The decor is contemporary western, the lobby recently and cheerily re-modeled, and 107 guest rooms are bright and exceptionally spacious, offering a choice of two queen-size beds or one king-size, and most have balconies. ~ 415 6th Street, Glenwood Springs; 970-945-6571, 800-537-7946, fax 970-945-6683. MODERATE.

The classiest accommodations in town today are at the **Hotel Denver**, across the street from the Amtrak station and a short walk from the hot springs. Built in 1906, the hotel has been completely renovated in art deco–revival style. The rooms are spacious and modern. ~ 402 7th Street, Glenwood Springs; 970-945-6565, 800-826-8820; fax 970-945-2204. MODERATE TO DELUXE.

Adducci's Inn Bed & Breakfast is an antique-decorated B&B in an older downtown residence, this one built in 1900. More budget-oriented than the Kaiser House, Adducci's Inn offers five simple, pleasant rooms. Each room has a private WC, but bathtub and showers are down the hall. There's a private hot tub. ~ 1023 Grand Avenue, Glenwood Springs; 970-945-9341. MODERATE TO DELUXE.

You don't have to drive far from Glenwood Springs to get away from it all. Twelve miles out of town, the **Sunlight Inn** has 23 rustic rooms—most with private baths—in a ranch setting with horses for rent and hiking and fishing close by. ~ 10252 County Road 117; 970-945-5225. BUDGET TO MODERATE.

In the hideaway community of Redstone, the **Redstone Castle** (also known as the Cleveholm Manor) was the turn-of-the-century home of Colorado's leading coal and steel baron. Today the castle has been restored to the opulence of that era with museum-quality antiques including chandeliers and velvet-upholstered furnishings.

✔ **CHECK THESE OUT—UNIQUE SIGHTS**

- Bask in the soothing waters of **Glenwood Hot Springs**, the world's largest geothermal bathing pool. *page 171*
- Watch paleontologists in action at the fossil quarry in **Dinosaur National Monument**. *page 180*
- Take a stroll through history at Grand Junction's **Cross Orchards Historic Site**, a working farm dating from the early 1900s. *page 186*
- Venture by four-wheel-drive vehicle into Colorado's forgotten ex-national monument, **Rattlesnake Canyon**. *page 187*

It operates as a bed and breakfast with eight rooms and suites as well as eight more modest rooms, once servants' quarters, which share bathrooms. ~ 58 Redstone Boulevard, Redstone; 970-963-3463, 800-643-4837. DELUXE TO ULTRA-DELUXE.

DINING

In contrast to the high cost of eating in Aspen, Glenwood Springs presents an array of good restaurants for every culinary preference at surprisingly low prices.

Centrally located downtown, **Mi Restaurante** is a long-time local favorite. The big, brick-walled restaurant is on the second floor, and the nonsmoking section has picture windows overlooking the main street of town. The menu features home-style American and Mexican food. ~ 720 Grand Avenue, Glenwood Springs; 970-947-0888. BUDGET.

Across the street, the **Italian Underground** is located in the basement of the historic Silver Club Building, originally a turn-of-the-century gambling hall. Northern Italian food, pizzas and ice cream are all homemade. ~ 715 Grand Avenue, Glenwood Springs; 970-945-6422. MODERATE.

The **19th Street Diner** is an authentic '50s-style local hangout decorated entirely in black and white. The large menu features a little of everything, from hamburgers with fries, chicken-fried steak with mashed potatoes and gravy, to fajitas, *huevos rancheros* and fettuccine. ~ 1908 Grand Avenue, Glenwood Springs; 970-945-9133. BUDGET.

Big, crackling fireplaces in each of two separate dining areas set the tone for **The Fireside**, a quiet, friendly, family-style restaurant that serves some of the best home-style food in the area. While the menu features a full selection of steak, seafood and chicken entrées, the house specialty is baby back pork ribs smoked over apple wood. Dinner is served daily. The restaurant also offers a good salad bar, homemade soups and a luncheon buffet every day except Saturday. ~ 51701 Route 6, Glenwood Springs; 970-945-6613. MODERATE.

The elegant Victorian-style **Sopris Restaurant** is widely considered the best in the Glenwood Springs area. Fresh flowers and candlelight set the mood. For starters, there are salads topped with raspberry vinaigrette and appetizers like escargot and snow crab claws. Entrées include veal, rack of lamb, fresh Miami stone crab and vegetarian dishes. ~ 7215 Route 82, Glenwood Springs; 970-945-7771. MODERATE TO DELUXE.

Buffalo Valley, located in a building that used to be a local historical museum, has a saloonlike atmosphere and a bar inlaid with 1000 silver dollars. Beef dominates the menu in the form of steak, prime rib and barbecued ribs, and there is a large, elaborate salad bar. ~ 3637 Route 82, Glenwood Springs; 970-945-5297. BUDGET TO DELUXE.

A standout among the galleries and gift shops lining Grand Avenue in Glenwood Springs, **The Watersweeper and The Dwarf** has been in business in the same location for over 20 years. It exhibits a whimsical array of fine one-of-a-kind handicrafts. ~ 717 Grand Avenue, Glenwood Springs; 970-945-2000. Other intriguing little shops have sprung up nearby, including the fanciful **Treasures Under the Stairs**. ~ 812 Grand Avenue, Glenwood Springs; 970-945-2168. The work of local craftspeople is exhibited at **Mountain Valley Weavers**. ~209 8th Street, Glenwood Springs; 970-928-0774.

SHOPPING

The Redstone area is well on the way to becoming a full-fledged artists' colony, and several local galleries have opened there, including one at **Redstone Art Center**, showing works by more than 80 local and regional artists and artisans. ~ 173 Redstone Boulevard, Redstone; 970-963-3790. The nearby Wild Horse Enterprises, with Western art, jewelry and antiques. ~ 306 Redstone Boulevard, Redstone; 970-963-8100. Up the road in Marble, the **Lost Trail Gallery & Coffee Bar** specializes in wildlife and nature art. ~ Raspberry Ridge, Marble; 970-963-4084. The **Gold Pan Gallery** exhibits sculptures carved from local marble. Open in winter by appointment only. ~ Marble; 970-963-3316.

It's a good thing the hot springs stay open until 10 p.m., because Glenwood Springs does not have an overabundance of other nightlife. **Buffalo Valley** has live music on weekend nights, tending toward country-western, with dance lessons on Tuesday evening. Its dance floor is said to be the largest in the state. ~ 3637 Route 82, Glenwood Springs; 970-945-5297.

NIGHTLIFE

WHITE RIVER NATIONAL FOREST 🚶 🚲 ⛵ Glenwood Springs is surrounded by White River National Forest, one of the oldest and largest national forests in the Rocky Mountains, which also includes the forest around Aspen and Vail (see Chapter Four). The forest is split into two separate units by Glenwood Canyon, a strip of Bureau of Land Management land that follows the Colorado River. With the exception of Glenwood Canyon, most of which lies within a corner of the national forest boundary, direct access to the national forest from the Glenwood Springs area is mainly limited to jeep trails. Many miles of such trails follow creeks among the ridgelines and plateaus north of town. A good road, suitable for passenger cars, leads from the upper end of Glenwood Canyon to the Heart Lake area, a cluster of lakes at the 10,500-foot elevation on the White River Plateau north of Glenwood Springs. Fish for rainbow and brown trout in Heart Lake, Deep Lake and other lakes on the White River Plateau, as well as in many streams in the area. There are parking areas, picnic

PARKS

areas, restrooms, bike trails, hiking trails and jeep trails. ~ To reach the Heart Lake area, take Route 70 Exit 133 17 miles east of Glenwood Springs at the upper end of Glenwood Canyon and follow Forest Road 600 (Coffee Pot Road) for 27 miles; 970-328-6388.

▲ There are no national forest campgrounds in the Glenwood Springs vicinity. The remote Heart Lake area has Supply Basin Campground, with 8 RV/tent sites and the Deep Lake Campground, with 21 RV/tent sites. There are no hookups, drinking water or camping fees at either campground. Both are closed from November through June.

▼▼▼▼▼▼▼▼▼▼▼▼
Rifle/Craig Area

Continuing west on Route 70 from Glenwood Springs, motorists leave the mountains behind and enter a rugged land of dry hills and high mesas. Northwestern Colorado is part of the vast expanse of small mountain ranges and rocky desert basins that reaches from here across Utah and Nevada to the foot of California's High Sierras. Little-known and far from major population centers, northwestern Colorado is largely undeveloped as a tourist destination; the busiest time of year is the fall hunting season. This is one of the least populated and most pristine areas in the lower 48 United States, and its beauty lies hidden in some of the least likely places.

SIGHTS

HIDDEN ▶

From the interstate, the most direct gateway to northwestern Colorado is the small town of Rifle, 27 fast miles west of Glenwood Springs. To realize that there's more to this area than first impressions would suggest, all you have to do is take a 20-minute detour to **Rifle Falls** (for directions, see "Parks" below). Suddenly you find yourself in a lush creekside forest. A short walk takes you to the falls themselves, three separate cascades that arc outward from a limestone canyon rim. A short but strenuous and precarious trail climbs to the top of the falls and continues along the rim to loop back to the parking area and campground.

Sixteen miles west of Rifle, the odd little town of **Parachute** boomed during the energy crisis of the 1970s, when the Union Oil Company of California opened large-scale oil shale operations in the canyons north of town. The cream-colored shale rock there is so permeated with petroleum that you can actually light it with a match; unlike coal, the rock remains after the fire burns out. The oil company believed that skyrocketing world petroleum prices would make it profitable to mine the shale and extract the oil from it. Unfortunately, prices soon declined, operations were halted at the multimillion-dollar facility, and Parachute was virtually abandoned. You can see several units of the oil shale plant as you drive about 12 miles up Parachute Creek Canyon as it slices its way through the center of the mesa into a labyrinth of smaller canyons, still owned by the oil company and off-limits to the public.

If you take Route 13 north from Rifle, a 39-mile drive will bring you to the little town of **Meeker**, which is remembered in Colorado history as the site of the "Meeker Massacre." In 1879, recently appointed Indian agent Nathan C. Meeker and ten employees were killed by a Ute war party—with justification, according to most accounts. The government responded by banishing the Northern Ute people from Colorado to a reservation south of Vernal, Utah. They were the last Indian tribe to be driven out of Colorado and, ironically, almost all the land that was taken from them remains uninhabited to this day. Meeker's history is recounted in photos, antiques and artifacts—including items belonging to President Theodore Roosevelt, who used to go elk hunting in the Flat Tops—in the free **White River Museum**, housed in a log army barracks built after the massacre. ~ Meeker; 970-878-9982.

Although Dinosaur National Monument encompasses a vast area of desert canyon wilderness, the Dinosaur Quarry is the only spot where dinosaur bones can be seen.

The best reason for going to Meeker is that it is the starting point for the **Flat Tops Trail Scenic Byway**. The road heads east   ◀ HIDDEN
for 82 miles to the equally out-of-the-way town of Yampa, on Route 131 midway between Vail Valley and Steamboat Springs. The middle 40 miles, within the White River National Forest boundary, are unpaved but wide and well graded. The scenic byway climbs to the broad mesa top and continues through gently rolling hills covered with aspen, fir and spruce. Frequent overlooks provide views of the Flat Tops themselves, sheer stone buttes formed in geological antiquity as gigantic volcano plugs, rising to elevations over 11,000 feet, accessible only on foot or horseback. A detour from the main route takes you to **Trappers Lake**, the largest of many lakes that dot the mesa. The lake and the road leading in to it are completely surrounded by the untamed Flat Tops Wilderness.

Continuing north from Meeker on Route 3 will bring you to **Craig**, a crossroads community on the Yampa River. The major industries here are three large coal mines and a coal-fired power plant that supplies electricity to several states. The **Museum of Northwestern Colorado** displays not only local history and railroad exhibits, rare 19th-century wildlife photographs by A. G. Wallihan, cowboy and Indian artifacts and geological specimens, but also one of the West's largest collections of old-time gunfighter memorabilia. Closed Sunday. ~ 590 Yampa Street, Craig; 970-824-6360.

"Marcia," a private railroad car built in 1906 for Denver railroad magnate David H. Moffat, stands alongside Victory Street near Craig's city park. Tours of the ultra-luxurious coach's restored interior—a real eye-opener for modern RV travelers—can be arranged by calling the Craig Visitors Center (970-824-5689).

West of Craig lies the emptiest part of Colorado, an arid stretch of shale badlands. The main point of interest in this part of the state is **Dinosaur National Monument**, which straddles the Colorado–Utah state line. The main entrance to Dinosaur National Monument, where some of the first complete dinosaur skeletons ever assembled for museums were unearthed as early as 1909, is 12 miles east of Vernal, Utah, via Route 149, 20 miles west of the Colorado state line. Admission. ~ Route 149; 801-789-2115.

Sixty-five million years ago, a sandy barrier island at the mouth of a river delta lush with tropical forest became the final resting place for dinosaurs that drowned when the river flooded. Over the eons, thousands of them were entombed in sandy sediments that later hardened into sandstone. The fossil remains of prehistoric giants such as the vegetarian aptosaurus, diplodocus and stegosaurus as well as the meat-eating allosaurus have been shipped to museums around the world. Today paleontologists continue to expose dinosaur bones at the quarry, but do not remove them. The sandstone face with its still-emerging jigsaw puzzle of fossil skeletons forms one wall of the **Dinosaur Quarry**, the main sightseeing attraction at this national monument.

Just inside the monument boundary is a huge parking lot at the Dinosaur Quarry Visitors Center. During the busy summer months, visitors must park here and take a shuttle bus to the quarry; exhibits and a short slide show at the visitors center are designed to keep people occupied as they wait as much as half an hour for their shuttle. In the off-season, you can drive directly to the quarry. Past the visitors center, the Cub Creek Road leads along the Green River to campgrounds, hiking trails, Indian petroglyphs and an early settler's cabin. The two-hour **Harper's Corner Scenic Drive** rounds out an all-day visit with a spectacular expedition into the center of the park. ~ Located 25 miles east via Route 40 on the Colorado side of the state line.

This side of the park is wild canyon country that includes 44 miles of the Green River, 48 miles of the Yampa and the two rivers' confluence. There are no roads and only a few two-track jeep trails through the northern backcountry of the park; the main access is by river raft. Taking a marked turnoff from Route 318, motorists can reach the launch point for trips down the Green River. From there it's an easy hike to an overlook view of the **Gates of Lodore**, dramatic quartzite cliffs that rise suddenly to an elevation of 2300 feet above the river. Plunging through the Canyon of Lodore, the water pounds over Disaster Falls and gushes through Hell's Half Mile before slowing to mirrorlike serenity as it makes its way through python bends that shelter sandy beaches nearing the raft pullout point at **Echo Park**, close to the south side of the national monument. A paved scenic road that starts just east of the town

HIDDEN ►

HIDDEN ►

Dinosaur Hunting in Colorado

More dinosaur fossils have been found in Colorado than anywhere else on earth. This is due in large part to the Morrison Formation, a 400-foot-thick layer of red sandstone that extends from Utah and northern Arizona to Colorado's Front Range, which formed as sandy muck in the wetland marshes and shallow shoals of a long-forgotten sea about 140 million years ago. It was the last geological stratum to form during the Jurassic era, the time when dinosaurs grew the largest and were the most numerous.

So why are more dinosaur fossils found in Colorado than in neighboring states that also have the Morrison sandstone layer beneath them? For two reasons: For millions of years, most of the formation was under the surface of the sea, while only its eastern edge (what is now Colorado) was shoreline. Here land-dwelling dinosaurs could wade and graze, the swampy wetlands offering slow, herbivores some measure of protection from fast-moving predators. Then, too, the uplifting of the Rocky Mountains some 80 million years later fragmented the Morrison Formation, pushing it up through the earth's surface like splinters along both sides of the mountain range, leaving more of this particular geological layer exposed in Colorado than in other regions.

All it takes is a visit to the Denver Museum of Natural History, where some of the best Colorado fossil finds are on permanent exhibit, to visualize these giant creatures roaming the lush, green world of Colorado's Jurassic era. In fact, fragmentary fossilized dinosaur skeletons are displayed in glass cases in the local history museums of more than a dozen towns in all parts of the state. But for the truly spectacular, nothing can compete with the far northwestern part of Colorado and the rugged, colorful tangle of sandstone canyons that extends from the Grand Junction area to Dinosaur National Monument.

You might expect that the best dinosaur sight around would be the national monument, where the world's largest dinosaur quarry is located. You'd be half-right, especially if you included the dinosaur museum and Jurassic sculpture garden in Vernal, Utah, west of the monument's main entrance. Grand Junction, however, is quickly emerging as Colorado's dinosaur capital. The downtown Dinosaur Valley museum is also a working paleontology lab where visitors can watch fossil experts at work. The active fossil digs at Riggs Hill, Dinosaur Hill and Rabbit Valley also offer a close-up look at the painstaking work involved in searching for hints about the nature of these amazing beings that inhabited Earth long before the Rocky Mountains were born.

of Dinosaur, three miles from the state line, runs 25 miles through slickrock country to an overlook that offers an awe-inspiring view of Echo Park. From this paved park road, a 14-mile unpaved side road bounces its way to the riverbank tent campground at Echo Park itself.

Continuing west from the turnoff to the Gates of Lodore, Route 318 passes through a remote desert valley known as **HIDDEN ►** **Browns Park** (or sometimes "Browns Hole"). In earlier times, mild winters and abundant grass made Browns Park a favorite wintering place for nomadic Indians, mountain men and outlaws. Today the area attracts mostly birdwatchers, who come to visit **Browns Park National Wildlife Refuge**, a major stopover and nesting area for migratory waterfowl on the Green River. ~ Route 318, 55 miles west of Maybell; 970-365-3613. Other points of interest in the Browns Park area include **Vermillion Falls**, a pretty canyon cascade a short distance south of the highway, and **Irish Canyon**, a colorful canyon that offers picnicking and hiking areas, rock climbing and Indian petroglyphs, reached by taking unpaved County Road 10N north from Route 318. A few miles farther on, another unpaved road turns south to the remains of the handhewn log buildings of the **Two Bar Ranch**, which was one of the largest cattle ranches in Colorado in the early 1900s. Nearby, a meeting hall and well-preserved old cemetery mark the location of **Lodore**, which formerly served area ranches, but is now a ghost town. Just before you reach the state line on Route 318, unpaved County Road 83 veers off to the south; along the way to scenic Crouse Canyon on the Utah side, the road offers a cheap thrill as it crosses the Green River on a one-lane swinging wooden bridge.

LODGING   Just off Route 70, Rifle offers a fair selection of low-priced independent motels. The two-story, 89-unit **Rusty Cannon Motel**

✔ CHECK THESE OUT—UNIQUE LODGING

- *Budget:* Sleep cheap within walking distance of the hot springs at the **Glenwood Springs Youth Hostel**. *page 174*
- *Budget to moderate:* Get acquainted with South America's miniature camels as you spend the night at the **Cedar's Edge Llama Ranch**. *page 190*
- *Moderate:* Bed down as Presidents Taft and Roosevelt did at Glenwood Springs' elegant **Hotel Colorado**. *page 174*
- *Deluxe to ultra-deluxe:* Escape to one of Colorado's most secluded luxury resorts, the magnificent **Redstone Castle**. *page 175*

Budget: under $50   Moderate: $50–$90   Deluxe: $90–$130   Ultra-deluxe: over $130

scores slightly above the competition because it has a heated swimming pool and sauna. The guest rooms themselves are about as conventional as motel rooms can be, simply decorated in brown and blue hues. The owners are Rifle natives who also operate a backcountry guide service and are full of suggestions for touring the area. ~ 701 Taughenbaugh Street, Rifle; 970-625-4004. MODERATE.

Battlement Mesa, across the highway from the oil shale ghost town of Parachute, got its start in the 1970s as a bedroom community for oil company executives, complete with its own golf course, indoor swimming pool and racquetball courts. Today, Battlement Mesa is primarily a retirement community but also serves as a resort for vacationers who don't mind that the location is not very convenient to any tourist destination. One- and two-bedroom condominium-style suites with kitchenettes rent by the night or week. For rental information and reservations, call **Battlement Mesa Guest Suites**. ~ 800-275-5687. MODERATE.

In Meeker, the **Meeker Hotel** is a handsome red-brick historic hotel dating back to 1896. The 27 refurbished guest rooms, some with shared baths, are modern and modest, and the lobby features a mural of the Meeker Massacre along with more than a dozen big-game trophy heads. Teddy Roosevelt slept here. ~ 560 Main Street, Meeker; 970-878-5255. MODERATE.

Great wilderness lodging is available at **Trappers Lake Lodge**, on the shore of a beautiful lake off the Flat Tops Trail Scenic Byway. Guest accommodations are in 14 simple cabins with cooking stoves; guests share central restrooms. Canoes, fishing skiffs and saddle horses are for rent, and the main lodge has a dining room and store. ~ P.O. Box 1230, Meeker, CO 81641; 970-878-4288. MODERATE.

Craig has more than a dozen unexceptional, budget-priced motels. For something a bit more special, try the **Williams Fork Bed & Breakfast**, 13 miles south of Craig in the small community of Hamilton. The four-unit contemporary log home sits on the bank of Williams Creek. The rates include a continental breakfast. ~ 17559 South Route 13, Hamilton; 970-824-3322. MODERATE.

DINING

In Rifle, an attractive alternative to the array of famous-name fast-food joints is the Asian atmosphere and succulent stir-fry fare at **Shanghai Gardens**. ~ 702 Taughenbaugh Boulevard, Rifle; 970-625-4430. BUDGET TO MODERATE.

Fresh homemade breads and pastries enhance breakfast, lunch or dinner at **The Bakery**, a cozy little restaurant that would be downright plain were it not for the exquisite olfactory ambience of bread baking. The menu features a range of sandwiches and Mexican food. ~ 265 6th Street, Meeker; 970-878-5500. BUDGET TO MODERATE.

Craig has dozens of fast-food joints and family restaurants. Among the most attractive of them, the **Golden Cavvy Restaurant & Lounge** serves steaks, seafood, soup, sandwiches and salads in a casual, friendly atmosphere. ~ 538 Yampa Avenue, Craig; 970-824-6038. BUDGET.

The best Mexican food in northwestern Colorado is found at the modest **La Plazuela Restaurant**. ~ 994 Yampa Avenue, Craig; 970-824-7345. BUDGET.

PARKS

RIFLE GAP STATE PARK This reservoir flanked by limestone cliffs on the way to Rifle Falls is popular among western Colorado water-sports enthusiasts because of its easy access from Route 70. Besides boating, waterskiing, windsurfing and fishing, the lake is a popular spot for scuba diving because of its unusually clear water. Fish here for walleye and largemouth and smallmouth bass, as well as some rainbow trout. There are restrooms, picnic areas, a swimming area and a winter play area. Day-use fee, $4. ~ Located on Route 325, five miles north of Rifle, which is 27 miles west of Glenwood Springs on Route 70; 970-625-1607.

▲ There are 47 RV/tent sites (no hookups) in four campgrounds; $7 per night.

RIFLE FALLS STATE PARK A 45-minute drive from Glenwood Springs, Rifle Falls is hidden in a shale canyon in northwestern Colorado's dry plateau country. Rifle Creek splits into several cascades that spill side by side into the canyon, creating an oasis lush with ferns, mosses and wildflowers. Among the falls and along the canyon wall are marked entrances to several small caves that are easy to explore with a flashlight. Facilities include picnic areas, restrooms and a nature trail. Day-use fee, $4. ~ Located on Route 325, 12 miles north of Rifle; 970-625-1607.

▲ There are 7 tent sites and 12 RV sites with electric hookups; $7 to $10 per night.

RIFLE MOUNTAIN PARK Recently established by the town of Rifle, this municipal park is actually an extension of Rifle Falls State Park, continuing up the canyon to the national forest boundary. Picnic spots and campsites lie along the banks of a tree-lined creek. Several caves, some of them extending for more than a mile, open along the base of the limestone cliffs, including at least two perpetually frozen ice caves. The park also has several rock-climbing practice walls. There are picnic areas, restrooms and hiking trails. Day-use fee, $4 per vehicle. ~ Located on Route 325, 13 miles north of Rifle.

▲ There are 19 RV/tent sites (no hookups); $7 per night.

WHITE RIVER NATIONAL FOREST The northern unit of White River National Forest encompasses the wild mesa area called the Flat Tops, where rolling hills dotted with small natural lakes surround the steep cliffs of truncated mountains—mesas upon the mesa top—that give the area its name. More than half of this section of the forest lies within the Flat Tops Wilderness, and is laced with hiking trails and full of wildlife. This wilderness area is accessible from several trailheads along the Flat Tops Trail Scenic Byway. Swimming is permitted at Trappers Lake. Fishing is good for rainbow trout and Snake River cutthroat in Lake Avery; exceptional for native cutthroat in Trappers Lake. There are parking areas, a grocery store and trailheads. ~ The principle access to the Blanco Unit is the Flat Tops Trail Scenic Byway, an 82-mile road (40 miles unpaved) between Meeker and Yampa. The forest road that continues beyond Rifle Falls State Park and Rifle Mountain Park provides unpaved access to the southwestern part of the forest. Trappers Lake is located 41 miles east of Meeker on the Flat Tops Trail and then 10 miles south on Forest Road 15205; 970-927-4079.

▲ There are eight national forest campgrounds along the Flat Tops Trail Scenic Byway, including four at Trappers Lake. Among them, Trappers Lake–Shepard's Rim Campground has 20 RV/tent sites (no hookups), closed mid-November to mid-June; and nearby Trappers Lake–Cutthroat Campground has 14 RV/tent sites (no hookups), closed October to mid-June. Fees are $7 per night at all Trappers Lake area campgrounds.

▼▼▼▼▼▼▼▼▼▼▼▼▼

Grand Junction Area

The Colorado River pours from a mountain canyon into the Grand Valley, where fruit orchards line its banks and fill the air with the scent of blossoms in the spring. Route 70 follows the river through Grand Junction, named for its location—where the Colorado River (once known as the Grand River) and the Gunnison River meet—and the largest city in Colorado west of the Continental Divide.

SIGHTS

Grand Junction is a long, narrow city, bounded by Route 70 on the north and the Colorado River on the south. Venturing off the main thoroughfares into the downtown area, you will find a graceful neighborhood of older homes harking back to the more prosperous era when Grand Junction was a major railroad center. Follow Main Street as it meanders from 2nd Street to 7th Street through the **Downtown Shopping Park**. This city center, imaginatively redeveloped back in 1963, combines the amenities of a pedestrian mall with a single traffic lane that curves between too few parking spaces.

The Grand Valley is one of the major dinosaur fossil areas on earth, and the centerpiece of downtown Grand Junction is **Dinosaur Valley**, a division of the Museum of Western Colorado. This unique museum, which features dinosaur skeletons and realistic, half-sized animated models, is housed in a former department store. One of the display windows contains a casting of the huge legbone of what was the world's largest dinosaur skeleton when it was discovered near Grand Junction in 1900. Through another display window passersby can watch paleontologists at work in the museum's fossil laboratory. Admission. ~ 4th and Main streets, Grand Junction; 970-243-3466.

Though it's hard to compete with Dinosaur Valley, school-age kids will find plenty of hands-on learning play at the **Doo Zoo Children's Museum**, where top attractions include a cage full of plastic balls and a working model post office. Closed Sunday. Admission. ~ 635 Main Street, Grand Junction; 970-241-5225.

The main location of the **Museum of Western Colorado**, the largest museum between Denver and Salt Lake City, features a timeline exhibit that traces regional history from 1880 to the present. Two blocks from Dinosaur Valley, the museum also displays American Indian artifacts, flora and fauna and historical documents and photographs. Closed Monday in winter. Admission. ~ 4th Street and Ute Avenue, Grand Junction; 970-242-0971.

A third unit of the Museum of Western Colorado is **Cross Orchards Historic Site**. Traditional farm life of the early 1900s is re-created at this open-air museum, originally the headquarters of one of Colorado's largest apple orchards. A portion of the orchard, along with the summer house, workers' bunkhouse, blacksmith shop, barn and packing house, is open to the public. Other exhibits include a collection of road-building machinery and railroad memorabilia. Living-history demonstrations are held daily from mid-April through October; special events include workshops where students learn traditional farming methods using teams of draft horses, antique appraisal sessions and classes on making cornhusk dolls. Closed November through April. Admission. ~ 3073 F (Patterson) Road, Grand Junction; 970-434-9814.

The Museum of Western Colorado also operates **Little Park Desert Preserve**, on Grand Junction's southern city limits. The 1200-acre wilderness area has trails for hiking and mountain bik-

SCULPTORS TAKE IT TO THE STREETS

Grand Junction's **Art on the Corner** program, initiated in 1989, has transformed the five-block Downtown Shopping Park into an outdoor sculpture gallery. Under the program, artists from all over Colorado loan their sculptures to the city for one year. At any given time more than 30 works of art wait along the downtown sidewalks to be seen, touched and admired. All are for sale.

ing. The museum also conducts ongoing fossil digs at **Riggs Hill** and **Dinosaur Hill**, situated near the west and east entrances of Colorado National Monument, as well as at **Rabbit Valley**, 24 miles west of town. All three digs have self-guided walking trails that are open to visitors.

The Grand Valley is wider than the Grand Canyon and nearly half as deep. Orange sandstone cliffs form a wall 2000 feet high along its south side, and from the top rim of the cliffs above Grand Junction you can see that they form one side of a canyon carved by the Colorado River. On its far side, 14 miles away, stands its other wall—the inaccessible, purple-gray Book Cliffs. **Colorado National Monument** encompasses 32 square miles of the south rim between Grand Junction and the smaller town of Fruita nearby, providing a small sample of the cliffs and side canyons that enclose the Grand Valley. What makes this particular segment of the rim special is that you can reach it in a passenger car. **Rim Rock Drive**, built by the Civilian Conservation Corps during the 1930s, climbs by switchbacks to the upper rim from either the east park entrance on the outskirts of Grand Junction or the west entrance near Fruita. The 23-mile drive offers more than a dozen scenic view points, some overlooking the orchards, towns and farmlands of the valley, others affording glimpses of secluded side canyons. For most travelers, the dramatic one-hour drive through the national monument alone is worth the price of admission. Admission. ~ Fruita; 970-858-3617.

Above the cliffs and canyons of Colorado National Monument stretches the broad expanse of Piñon Mesa. You can easily see part of the mesa top by following either of the two paved roads that lead from the back entrances of Colorado National Monument up into **Glade Park**. The roads pass through cool, ◄ *HIDDEN* dreamlike ranchlands to intersect at the Glade Park General Store, the pastoral setting providing a dramatic contrast to the desert-like landscapes below. About eight miles west of the store on a well-marked, unpaved road is the mesa's top sightseeing highlight, **Miracle Rock**, a balanced rock teetering on the edge of a cliff and said by some to be the largest of its kind on earth. Nearby **Little Dolores Falls** has a little-known campground. There is another Glade Park campground and recreational site at **Mud Springs**.

Rattlesnake Canyon may be one of the best-kept secrets in ◄ *HIDDEN* "Hidden Colorado." Huge natural arches of beige and red sandstone, some with spans of more than 100 feet, line the eastern rim of the canyon. A century ago, visitors arriving in Grand Junction by train rode horseback to Rattlesnake Canyon in such numbers that President Theodore Roosevelt declared it a national monument. A generation later, when the age of motorcars began, tourism dropped off so much that the National Park Service abandoned Rattlesnake Canyon National Monument, turning the canyon over to the Bureau of Land Management.

Caution: The clay surface of the road to Rattlesnake Canyon gets so slippery when wet that even four-wheel-drive vehicles can't travel on it.

By the time four-wheel-drive vehicles made the canyon accessible again, it was long forgotten. The turnoff for the canyon is just outside the back entrance to Colorado National Monument, off West Glade Park Road. You need a four-wheel-drive vehicle to reach the trailhead in the Black Ridge Wilderness.

There is plenty of spectacular canyon scenery to be found in the uninhabited public lands along the cliffs at the base of the Uncompahgre Plateau for 65 miles south and east of Grand Junction. Little-known canyons can be reached on unpaved ranch roads off Route 50 between Grand Junction and Montrose.

HIDDEN ► For instance, **Dominguez Canyon**, on the Gunnison River, offers 20 miles of hidden canyonlands with a marvelous range of environments—from desert to riverbank beaches, from cottonwood forests to waterfalls that plummet down sheer sandstone cliffs. A campground and wilderness trailhead are accessible by car.

For more information on Rattlesnake Canyon or Dominguez Canyon, as well as other scenic canyons on BLM land, contact the Bureau of Land Management, Grand Junction District Office. ~ 2815 H Road, Grand Junction, CO 81506; 970-244-3000.

First-time visitors to **Grand Mesa**, east of Grand Junction, often expect to find dry, scrubby terrain like that of Mesa Verde and other northwestern Colorado mesas. They are surprised to discover instead a cool mountain landscape of Douglas-fir trees studded with lakes like blue sapphires at elevations of more than 10,000 feet above sea level and a mile above the Grand Valley. Motorists who take the paved, 55-mile **Grand Mesa Scenic Byway** (Route 65) over the mesa top between Routes 50 and 70 feel as if they are climbing the steep, aspen-covered slopes of a mountain the size of Pikes Peak or Mount Evans—except that Grand Mesa's summit looks as if it had been neatly sliced off at timberline to create the world's largest flat-topped mountain. Grand Mesa's unique landscape was formed by an ancient lava flow that protected the softer layers of sandstone and shale beneath as the surrounding terrain eroded away. The mesa top, with its gently rolling, low hills, more than 300 lakes and innumerable streams, is a favorite destination for anglers in summer and cross-country skiers in winter. Despite a handful of rustic resort lodges, most of the mesa seems practically untouched by humankind. Two graded, unpaved roads, Land's End Road and Trickle Park Road, branch off the Grand Mesa Scenic Byway and lead deep into the forest. Land's End Road runs west along the rim of the mesa to offer spectacular views of the Grand Valley and the small crater of the volcano that created the mesa. Trickle Park Road runs east, providing access to the area's largest concentration of lakes as well as a number of four-wheel-drive roads and hiking trailheads. Because of the altitude, deep snowdrifts remain until the Fourth of July.

LODGING

Grand Junction, the only major town on an otherwise-empty 200-mile stretch of Route 70, has about 30 motels with a total of more than 2000 guest rooms. For exceptional accommodations in town, reserve one of the six individually decorated rooms—some with wrought-iron beds and Shaker armoires—at **Los Altos Bed & Breakfast**. Each window offers spectacular views of the Colorado National Monument and Grand Mesa, while French doors open onto a wraparound deck. Bonuses include afternoon tea, a rec room with an antique pool table, and a living room with a fireplace. ~ 375 Hillview Drive, Grand Junction; phone/fax 970-256-0964, 888-774-0982; e-mail losaltos@wic.net. MODERATE TO ULTRA-DELUXE.

Most national motor-inn chains are represented in Grand Junction. Room rates at these places are some of the lowest in the state. One option is the **Value Lodge**. ~ 104 White Avenue, Grand Junction; 970-242-0651. BUDGET. There's also the reasonably priced **Grand Junction Hilton**. ~ 743 Horizon Drive, Grand Junction; 970-241-8888, 800-445-8667, fax 970-242-7266. MODERATE TO DELUXE.

For more unique lodging, a good prospect is the **Historic Hotel Melrose** in downtown Grand Junction. This turn-of-the-century railroad hotel operates as an IYH hostel and has 12 individual guest rooms with private baths as well as even more affordable dormitory accommodations. It's modestly furnished with antiques and bursting with youthful energy. ~ 337 Colorado Avenue, Grand Junction; 970-242-9636. BUDGET.

There are several forest lodges atop Grand Mesa, all of them small and secluded. **Alexander Lake Lodge** has seven rustic cabins, some with kitchens, and a main lodge with a dining room and a huge fireplace built from 200 tons of stone. The lodge fills up with snowmobilers and cross-country skiers in winter. Due to the "range war" between the two groups, the forest service working with the lodges on Grand Mesa has set aside one vast forest area for cross-country skiing and a separate, equally extensive area for snowmobiling. ~ Grand Mesa; 970-856-6700. MODERATE.

Another popular year-round forest lodge on Grand Mesa is **Spruce Lodge**. There are 14 cabins, some with kitchens, and a restaurant and bar. ~ Grand Mesa; 970-856-3210. MODERATE.

Grand Mesa Lodge has 16 units including both housekeeping cabins and motel-style duplex units on Island Lake, the largest lake on Grand Mesa. There is a grocery store on the premises but no restaurant. Boat rentals are available. ~ Grand Mesa; 970-856-3250. MODERATE.

For a unique alternative to Colorado's conventional dude ranches, book a stay at the **Cedar's Edge Llama Ranch**, near the little town of Cedaredge at the south end of Grand Mesa. There are just four guest rooms—two with private baths in the main ranchhouse and two others that share a separate guesthouse. The owner-operators love to introduce their llamas to guests—especially kids. ~ 2169 Route 65, Cedaredge; 970-856-6836. BUDGET TO MODERATE.

DINING   Grand Junction's only Japanese restaurant and sushi bar, **Suehiro Japanese Restaurant**, serves authentic, traditional dishes including tempura, sukiyaki and beef or chicken teriyaki, accompanied by sake, plum wine or Asian beer. ~ 541 Main Street, Grand Junction; 970-245-9548. MODERATE.

There is an abundance of Chinese restaurants along North Avenue, including the long-established **Far East Restaurant**, a spacious tri-level place that specializes in Szechuan and Cantonese cuisine. An array of seafood entrées include Australian lobster tail and Alaskan king crab. ~ 1530 North Avenue, Grand Junction; 970-242-8131. MODERATE.

Creative twists on New Mexican food are featured at **W. W. Peppers**. Specialties include chimichangas and crabmeat enchiladas. Steaks and more conventional seafood dishes are also served. The decor strives for the look of contemporary Santa Fe. ~ 753 Horizon Court, Grand Junction; 970-245-9251. BUDGET TO MODERATE.

For just plain good food at the lowest prices in town, try **Starvin' Arvin's**. Particularly known as a breakfast spot—the hotcake stacks are formidable and the biscuits and gravy are legendary among Route 70 truckers—the restaurant also serves sandwiches and dinner specials. The decor focuses on the owner's snapshots of people rafting, biking and generally enjoying the out-

✔ CHECK THESE OUT—UNIQUE DINING

- *Budget:* Start the day off with hearty biscuits and gravy at **Starvin' Arvin's**, just like Route 70 truckers do. *page 190*
- *Budget to deluxe:* Hit the great salad bar and an Old West saloon atmosphere at **Buffalo Valley** in Glenwood Springs. *page 176*
- *Moderate:* Savor the sushi and sake at **Suehiro Japanese Restaurant**, one of Grand Junction's numerous Asian eateries. *page 190*
- *Moderate to deluxe:* Head out of town to the romantic **Sopris Restaurant** for escargot and stone crab. *page 176*

Budget: under $8   Moderate: $8–$16   Deluxe: $16–$24   Ultra-deluxe: over $24

doors in the Grand Junction area. ~ 752 Horizon Drive, Grand
Junction; 970-241-0430. BUDGET.

As Grand Junction's more-practical stores have abandoned the **SHOPPING**
downtown area for the North Avenue commercial strip just a few
blocks away, the smaller storefronts of Main Street Mall have reopened as modest galleries, boutiques and antique shops.

For the largest selection of dinosaur-motif gift items you're
likely to find anywhere, check out the gift shop at **Dinosaur Valley**.
~ 362 Main Street; 970-243-3466. **Sunspinner Hand Crafts** has
jewelry and assorted works in glass, pottery and wood handmade
by local artisans. ~ 454 Main Street, Grand Junction; 970-434-
4600. The best antique shopping in town is at **Haggle of Vendors
Emporium**. ~ 510 Main Street, Grand Junction; 970-245-1404

A country-and-western atmosphere pervades Grand Junction's **NIGHTLIFE**
after-dark entertainment scene. The top dance club in town is **The
Rose**. Spacious and neo-Victorian, it offers live country music
nightly. ~ 2993 North Avenue, Grand Junction; 970-245-0606.

Cahoots has live rock-and-roll and lively weekend dance
crowds, except Sundays, when televised football takes center stage.
~ 490 28¼ Road, Grand Junction; 970-241-2282.

GRAND MESA NATIONAL FOREST 🏃 🐎 🛶 This 360,000-acre **PARKS**
reserve encompasses the world's largest flat-topped mountain, a
vast expanse of lakes, lava fields and Douglas-fir forest ranging
between 10,000 and 11,000 feet above sea level. Although this
forest has no federally designated wilderness area, roads into the
central part are for four-wheel-drive vehicles, and much of the
eastern half of the mesa is accessible only by hiking and horse
trails. The Land O Lakes area, on the western part of the mesa,
has more than 300 lakes, many of them connected by a maze of
streams and creeks that are legendary among trout fishermen.
There's excellent fishing here for rainbow, cutthroat and brook
trout. At the western tip of the mesa, Land's End overlooks the
Grand Valley a mile below. There are five picnic areas, all with
tables, drinking water and restrooms. ~ The main access to Grand
Mesa National Forest is via the Grand Mesa Scenic Byway (Route
65). The 55-mile scenic road runs between Cedaredge, a small
town 15 miles off Route 50 near Delta, and the Island Acres/Mesa
exit from Route 70, about 15 miles east of Grand Junction. (For
the adventurous, the Land's End Road starts from Route 50 about
12 miles east of Grand Junction and climbs to the mesa top by a
series of 18 tight, unpaved switchbacks. It is usually passable by
passenger cars but not by trailers or motor homes; inquire at the
ranger station for current road conditions; 970-242-8211.

▲ Grand Mesa has 18 national forest campgrounds for tents and RVs (no hookups). Those along or near the paved Grand Mesa Scenic Byway include *Jumbo* (27 sites), *Spruce Grove* (16 sites), *Island Lake* (42 sites), *Valley View* (8 sites), *Little Bear* (40 sites), *Carp Lake* (20 sites) and *Ward Lake* (26 sites). All are open from late May through Labor Day; $6 to $10 per night. More campgrounds can be reached via the unpaved Trickle Park Road, which starts near Valley View campground and runs east from the scenic byway for about 14 miles.

UNCOMPAHGRE NATIONAL FOREST 🏃 Two separate areas make up Uncompahgre National Forest. The rolling juniper-and-pine-forest terrain of the Uncompahgre Plateau, a vast, uninhabited island in the sky 9000 feet above sea level, extends south of the Grand and Gunnison valleys for 65 miles, from the Grand Junction area to the Montrose area. The Plateau Unit, which has neither high mountains nor significant bodies of water, is not widely used for recreation. If it's solitude you want, this is a good place to look for it. Deer are abundant on the plateau; so are mountain lions and bobcats, though these nocturnal predators usually avoid human contact. Uncompahgre National Forest also includes the northern part of the San Juan Mountains around Telluride, Ouray and Lake City, described in Chapters Seven and Eight. ~ There is no paved road access. Divide Road, a wide, graded forest road, climbs to the north end of the plateau from Route 141 south of Grand Junction, runs its length and descends to Montrose. The Delta-Nucla Road, another graded dirt road, climbs southwest from Delta to join Divide Road; 970-874-6600.

▲ The Uncompahgre Plateau has four small campgrounds for RVs and tents (no hookups). The only one with water is *Divide Fork Campground* (11 sites; $7.50 per night), on Divide Road south of Grand Junction. *Columbine Campground* (6 sites; no fee) is located southwest of Delta. *Antone Spring Campground* (8 sites; $7.50 per night) and *Iron Spring Campground* (7 sites; $7.50 per night) are southwest of Montrose. All are open from June through October, weather permitting.

ISLAND ACRES STATE PARK 🚤 🛥 🛶 Originally a large island in the Colorado River used as a landmark and encampment site by Ute Indians and mountain men, Island Acres was later planted with peach orchards. In 1967, the State of Colorado converted the island into a recreation area by building a dike to link it with the riverbank, leaving four lakes for swimming, fishing and nonmotorized boating. There is rainbow trout in spring and fall and catfish, bluegill and carp year-round; ice fishing in winter. Facilities include picnic areas with tables, drinking water and restrooms, and a nature trail (.75 mile). Day-use fee, $3. ~ Located 15 miles east of Grand Junction on Route 70 at the exit for the Grand Mesa Scenic Byway; 970-464-0548.

▲ There are 32 RV/tent sites (no hookups); $9 per night; dump station for RVs.

VEGA STATE PARK 🚶🚴🏊⛺️🚣⛴️🛥️🚐 The largest body of water in the Grand Valley area, two-mile-long Vega Reservoir is a local favorite for waterskiing, windsurfing and jet skiing. Abundant wildflowers and the subalpine beauty of its mountain setting attract nature lovers to the lake's shore. Visitors sometimes spot deer, elk, beaver, blue grouse and wild turkeys here. The park affords access to Grand Mesa trails for hikers, mountain bikers and four-wheel-drive vehicles. The lake has trout in the spring and fall; a very popular ice-fishing spot in winter. There are picnic areas with tables, drinking water, restrooms and a nature trail. Day-use fee, $4. ~ Exit Route 70 at Island Acres State Park and follow Route 330 east through the town of Collbran to the park, a distance of about 35 miles; 970-487-3407.

▲ There are 109 RV/tent sites (no hookups); $6 per night; dump station for RVs.

HIGHLINE LAKE STATE PARK 🏊⛺️🚣⛴️🛥️🚐 Surrounding two lakes amid Grand Valley farmland near Fruita, this park provides a full range of water recreation. Highline Lake, a 160-acre manmade reservoir, is used for waterskiing, jet skiing and windsurfing; it also offers an overlook where birders watch the many species of migratory birds that use the lake as a rest stop. Boating on the smaller Mack Mesa Lake is limited to electric and hand-propelled craft, and there is a wheelchair-accessible fishing pier. Highline Lake has good warm-water fishing for catfish and crappie. Mack Mesa Lake offers excellent early-season trout fishing. Facilities include picnic areas with tables, drinking water, restrooms and a phone. Day-use fee, $4. ~ Located seven miles northwest of Loma near Route 139; 970-858-7208.

▲ There are 28 RV/tent sites (no hookups); $9 per night; showers.

▼▼▼▼▼▼▼▼▼▼▼▼▼
Outdoor Adventures

RIVER RUNNING

GLENWOOD SPRINGS AREA In Glenwood Springs, raft trips both through Glenwood Canyon on the Colorado River and down the Roaring Fork River are offered by **Rock Garden Rafting**. ~ 1308 County Road 129; 970-945-6737. Also contact **Whitewater Rafting** for rafting accommodations. ~ 51100 Route 6/24; 970-945-8477.

RIFLE/CRAIG AREA Multiday raft trips through the wild reaches of the Snake and Yampa rivers in Dinosaur National Monument can be arranged through **Buggywhip's Fish & Float Service**. ~ 435

Lincoln Avenue, Steamboat Springs; 970-879-8033. Also try **Adventures Wild Rafting** for rafting information. ~ P.O. Box 774832, Steamboat Springs, CO 80477; 970-879-8747. There are also outfitters in Vernal, Utah that serve this area.

GRAND JUNCTION AREA Near Fruita, the favorite stretch of the Colorado River for rafting runs through Ruby and Horse Thief canyons, where you may see ducks, beaver, coyote, mule deer and even eagles. **Rimrock Adventures** offers full-day raft trips through the canyons, as well as shorter guided trips and raft, canoe and tube rentals. The trips range from one hour to a half-day. Rimrock also has all-day combination horseback and river-rafting trips. ~ P.O. Box 608, Fruita, CO 81521; 970-858-9555.

BALLOON RIDES Grand Junction Balloon Port organizes balloon flights over the Grand Valley. ~ 2210 One Road, Grand Junction; 970-243-8553.

DOWNHILL SKIING **GLENWOOD SPRINGS AREA** Downhill skiing in the Glenwood Springs area is at the relatively small **Ski Sunlight**. Although this ski area has only three chairlifts, its trails—20 percent beginner, 58 percent intermediate and 22 percent advanced—offer a fairly impressive vertical drop of 2020 feet. The season is from Thanksgiving through mid-March. ~ 10901 Four Mile Road, Glenwood Springs; 970-945-7491.

GRAND JUNCTION AREA Powderhorn Ski Area is a small intermediate-level ski area with one chairlift and a 1650-foot vertical drop on the north slope of Grand Mesa. Located 40 miles east of Gunnison, the ski area has rentals and a ski school. Open December through March. ~ Route 65, Grand Mesa National Forest; 970-268-5700 or 800-241-6997.

Ski Rentals For downhill and cross-country skis, telemarking equipment and snowboards, visit **Sunlight Ski and Bike Shop**. ~ 309 9th Street, Glenwood Springs; 970-945-9425. **BSR Sports** rents snowboards. ~ 210 7th Street, Glenwood Springs; 970-945-7317.

CROSS-COUNTRY SKIING **GLENWOOD SPRINGS AREA** Ski Sunlight Nordic Center has miles of groomed cross-country trails, including several that are accessed by chairlifts. ~ 10901 Four Mile Road, Glenwood Springs; 970-945-7491.

GRAND JUNCTION AREA Cross-country skiing is an incomparable experience among the lakes, Douglas-fir forests and lava hills atop Grand Mesa. The **Grand Mesa Nordic Council**, a local nonprofit group of skinny-ski enthusiasts, grooms nearly 70 kilometers of trails each winter. ~ P.O. Box 3077, Grand Junction, CO 81501; 970-434-9753. The **Powderhorn Nordic Center** grooms six miles of gently sloping cross-country trails, particularly suited

for telemarking, within Powderhorn Ski Area. ~ Route 65, Grand
Mesa National Forest; 970-268-5700 or 800-241-6997.

GLENWOOD SPRINGS AREA   Glenwood Springs has only a nine-
hole executive golf course—the **Glenwood Springs Golf Club**. ~
193 Sunny Acres Road; 970-945-7086. Local duffers head down
the interstate to the **Rifle Creek Golf Course**—see below.

GOLF

RIFLE/CRAIG AREA   Public golf courses include the 18-hole **Rifle
Creek Golf Course**, adjacent to Rifle Gap Reservoir. This beautiful course offers a dramatic contrast between the front and back
nines: golfers on the front nine holes make their way through canyons between sandstone cliffs, while the back nine run through
mountain meadows along the banks of Rifle Creek. Cart and club
rentals are available. ~ 3004 Route 325, Rifle; 970-625-1093. At
Battlement Mesa Golf Course, the 18-hole course with views of
the Colorado River was designed by Joe Finger and Ken Dye. ~
Battlement Mesa; 970-285-7274. In Meeker, there's the modest
(but hardly ever crowded) nine-hole **Meeker Golf Course**. ~ 903
County Road 13, Meeker; 970-878-5624.

GRAND JUNCTION AREA   Grand Junction's main public golf
course, the 18-hole **Tiara Rado Golf Course** is located near the
entrance to Colorado National Monument. ~ 2063 South Broadway; 970-245-8085. In the nearby community of Fruita is the 18-
hole **Adobe Creek National Golf Course**. ~ 876 18 1/2 Road; 970-
858-0521.

RIFLE/CRAIG AREA   Horseback riding is one of the best ways to
explore the vast Flat Tops Wilderness. Horses can be rented by the
hour or day at **Trappers Lake Lodge**. ~ P.O. Box 1230, Meeker,
CO 81641; 970-878-4288.

**RIDING
STABLES**

GRAND JUNCTION AREA   **Rimrock Adventures**, near the Route
340 entrance to Colorado National Monument, offers guided
horseback trips into the back canyons of the national monument
and the nearby Black Ridge Wilderness. ~ P.O. Box 608, Fruita,
CO 81521; 970-858-9555.

For a true once-in-a-lifetime experience, join the **Uncompahgre
Wagon Train** on its journey across the remote, timeless expanse of
Grand Mesa. The wagon train, which operates continuously from
April until mid-September, can accommodate 40 passengers at a
time. A remuda of riding horses accompanies the wagon train, so
guests have their choice of traveling horseback or in the wagon.
You can join the wagon train for as many or as few days as you
wish—it's sort of like a horse-drawn bed and breakfast, except you
sleep in tents with cots and sleeping bags. Reservations should be
made far in advance by contacting Uncompahgre Wagon Train.
~ 21375 Route 550 South, Montrose, CO 81402; 970-249-3807.

**PACK TRIPS
& LLAMA
TREKS**

BIKING

GLENWOOD SPRINGS AREA   The *sine qua non* bike ride in the Glenwood Springs area is the paved **Glenwood Canyon Trail**, suitable for both mountain bikes and ten-speed touring bikes.

GRAND JUNCTION AREA   One of the most ambitious and memorable mountain-biking trips anywhere is **Kokopelli's Trail**, a route established in 1989 by the Colorado Plateau Mountain-Bike Trail Association in cooperation with the Bureau of Land Management. The trail begins at the Loma Boat Launch, off Route 70 near Fruita, and runs 128 miles along back roads and trails generally following the course of the Colorado River, all the way to Moab, Utah. ~ Grand Junction; 970-241-9561. Another ultimate mountain-bike route is the **Tabeguache Trail**, which goes south from Grand Junction for 142 miles along the Uncompahgre Plateau, climbing to 10,000-foot altitudes. For detailed information on both trails, contact the Bureau of Land Management. ~ 2815 H Road, Grand Junction; 970-244-3000. Or you may call the Colorado Plateau Mountain-Bike Trail Association. ~ P.O. Box 4602, Grand Junction, CO 81501; 970-241-9561.

Bike Rentals   Bicycles are for rent in Glenwood Springs at **Sunlight Ski and Bike Shop**. ~ 309 9th Street; 970-945-9425. Also try BSR **Sports** for rentals. ~ 210 7th Street, Glenwood Springs; 970-945-7317. In Grand Junction, mountain bikes can be rented at **The Bike Peddler**. ~ 710 North 1st Street; 970-243-5602.

HIKING

All distances listed for hiking trails are one way unless otherwise noted.

GLENWOOD SPRINGS AREA   Besides the **Hanging Lake Trail**, the most popular hiking trail in Colorado, a number of lesser-known trails start from the paved Glenwood Canyon Trail and climb to the upper reaches of the canyon. Among them are **No Name Trail** and **Grizzly Creek Trail**, each about two miles long. From the end of 8th Street in town, the well-marked 1.5-mile trail up Lookout Mountain offers spectacular views of the town and the Roaring Fork Valley.

RIFLE/CRAIG AREA   The fairly steep **Battlement Mesa Trail** (3 miles) runs through varied terrain of scrub oak, spruce, fir and aspen forests and offers views of the Colorado River Valley as it makes its way up to Battlement Reservoirs. To reach the trailhead, take County Road 320 from Rifle for three and a half miles, then turn left on Beaver Creek Road and continue for seven miles to the trailhead.

The four-mile shoreline trail around **Trappers Lake**, off the Flat Tops Trail Scenic Byway east of Meeker, serves as a hub for trails that head off in every direction into the Flat Tops Wilderness, providing access to more than 400 miles of maintained trails. Good day hikes include the trails to **Little Trappers Lake** (2 miles), **Wall Lake** (5 miles), and the **Fraser Creek Trail** to **Parvin Lake** (4 miles).

The **Sandrocks Nature Trail** (1 mile), just north of Craig on Alta Vista Drive, follows the base of a sandstone cliff where visitors can see hundreds of petroglyphs carved by Indians over a period of at least a thousand years.

GRAND JUNCTION AREA   Colorado National Monument has about 44 miles of trails. The most remote and challenging hike in the park is **No Thoroughfare Canyon** (8.5 miles) studded with juniper and enclosed by sheer cliffs 400 feet high. Midway up the canyon, the intermittent stream at the bottom plunges over two waterfalls about three-quarters of a mile apart whenever the water is flowing—usually in late spring. Another great hike in Colorado National Monument is the **Liberty Cap Trail** (5.5 miles), a fairly level trail that follows a ridge to an "island in the sky" overlooking the Grand Valley. The park also has a number of shorter trails suited to hikes of a half-hour to four hours.

One of the best hikes in the Grand Junction area is **Rattlesnake Canyon**, where rock formations include a dozen large natural arches. Take Black Ridge Road, which exits from West Glade Park Road just outside the back entrance to Colorado National Monument. The 11-mile drive to Rattlesnake Canyon takes about an hour. Passenger cars can negotiate the first nine miles, but visitors without four-wheel drive must walk the last two miles. From the road's end, a steep foot trail descends through the first arch, and you reach eight others on a two-mile loop hike.

On Grand Mesa, the main hiking trail is the **Crag Crest Trail** (10 miles). The trail keeps to the high ground as it winds among the lakes and through the fir-and-aspen forests, commanding sweeping views of the mesa, the valley below and the San Juan Mountains in the distance.

✔ CHECK THESE OUT—UNIQUE OUTDOOR ADVENTURES

- Explore the backcountry of Dinosaur National Monument on a week-long raft trip down the Snake and Yampa Rivers. *page 193*
- Ski cross-country on a vast network of gentle groomed trails that wind among hundreds of frozen lakes on Grand Mesa. *page 194*
- Join a hardy band of modern-day pioneers on the Uncompahgre Wagon Train through the high-country wilderness. *page 195*
- Ride a bike as far as you want up the wide, paved Glenwood Canyon Trail; then coast back down. *page 196*

▼▼▼▼▼▼▼▼▼▼▼▼
Transportation

CAR

Glenwood Springs, Rifle and Grand Junction are on Route 70. Meeker, and Craig are on **Route 13** north of Rifle. From Craig, **Routes 40 and 318** head west to the Dinosaur National Monument and Browns Park area.

AIR

Walker Field Public Airport, located in Grand Junction, has flights to and from Denver on Continental Airlines, Mesa Airlines/ United Express and Sky West/Delta Connection. **Blondie's Limousine Service** (970-523-5614) operates ground transportation.

BUS

Greyhound (800-231-2222) offers bus service to Glenwood Springs. ~ West 6th and Laurel streets; 970-945-8501. There's also a station in Grand Junction. ~ 230 South 5th Street; 970-242-6012.

TRAIN

Amtrak offers passenger service to Glenwood Springs and Grand Junction on the "California Zephyr" or the "Desert Wind." Both trains follow the same route through the Rockies between Denver and Salt Lake City. ~ 800-872-7245.

CAR RENTALS

Grand Junction has a full complement of name-brand car-rental agencies. Most are located at Walker Field Airport, including **Avis Rent A Car** (800-331-1212), **Budget Rent A Car** (800-527-0700), **Hertz Rent A Car** (800-654-3131) and **National Interrent** (800-328-4567).

TAXIS

Cab service in Glenwood Springs is provided by **Yellow Cab**. ~ 970-945-2225. In Grand Junction, call **Sunshine Taxi**. ~ 1331 Ute Avenue; 970-245-8294.

SIX

The Pikes Peak Region

From the summit of Pikes Peak, theoretically you can see parts of Wyoming, Nebraska, Kansas, Oklahoma, Texas and New Mexico—in addition to more than half of Colorado. Of course, the visible parts of these six states are merely indistinguishable segments of the flat, featureless horizon 200 miles away, blurring toward the north into the murky atmosphere that conceals both Denver and the horizon beyond, but the panoramic view of the immediate surrounding area is worth the drive, train ride or hike to the top of the mountain.

Jutting up out of the prairie like an 8000-foot pyramid, Pikes Peak offers a study in contrasts. Though it reaches to within five miles of downtown Colorado Springs, the mountain's 450 square miles of alpine tundra and evergreen forest is wilderness so slightly touched by humans that black bears, mountain lions, elk and bighorn sheep make it their home. To the north, the gentle, low mountains of the Rampart Range cradle the Garden of the Gods and the U.S. Air Force Academy. Looking west, the casino glitter and forgotten gold mines of Cripple Creek mark the gateway to South Park and the neat row of 14,000-foot peaks in the Collegiate Range. Cheyenne Mountain, which reaches southward toward the Arkansas River, the Royal Gorge and its namesake, Cañon City, appears to be a pristine wilderness of steep slopes and deep canyons, but in fact the mountain conceals a huge, bizarre underground military complex, a remnant of the Cold War era.

It's easy to see why "Pikes Peak or Bust!" was the rallying cry that carried more than 100,000 pioneers west in 1859, pursuing dreams of gold strikes deep in the unexplored wilderness of the Colorado Rockies. As they crossed the Great Plains in wagons or on foot with handcarts, Pikes Peak was the first mountain peak to break the skyline, announcing the end of the two-month journey. The huge mountain marked the gateway to the land where veins of gold and silver lay waiting to be claimed. Colorado City, at the foot of Pikes Peak, marked the start of a road many gold seekers took on their way to South Park and Leadville, and formed the nucleus of modern Colorado Springs.

The Pikes Peak region boasted Colorado's first major tourist resorts as early as the 1870s, when travelers came by train from the East Coast and Europe to hike to the top of Pikes Peak or bask in the soothing waters of world-famous Manitou Springs at the foot of the mountain.

More than thirty years after the "Pikes Peak or Bust" gold rush put the area on the map and made the mountain a household word, a new and even larger gold find on the west side of Pikes Peak brought a tidal wave of population and prosperity to the region. At the turn of the 20th century, Colorado Springs emerged as the financial center of the gold boom, setting the stage for an era of Roaring '20s elegance that added to the town's tourist appeal.

Gold mines come and gold mines go. Although many locals believe the rich gold veins that still remain in the earth beneath Cripple Creek to be merely an off-shoot of a fabulous mother lode in the center of Pikes Peak, the mines were abandoned in the 1930s as changes in federal law made gold mining unprofitable. Summer tourism, however, has sustained the region through bad times and good. Since the 1960s, Colorado Springs' beautiful setting and dry, sunny climate have also helped attract many high-tech industries to the area, swelling the population and making tourism relatively less important to the city's economy; yet the economy of every other town in the Pikes Peak region—including the Colorado Springs suburbs of Old Colorado City and Manitou Springs—still depends almost totally on tourist dollars.

▼▼▼▼▼▼▼▼▼▼▼▼▼▼▼▼

Colorado Springs Area

In 1872, railroad builder William Jackson Palmer ran 60 miles of track south from Denver, then founded Colorado Springs so people would have someplace to go on his railroad. The city's name is a synthesis of Colorado City and Manitou Springs, already a famous spa. There never were any springs in Colorado Springs.

As it grew into an exclusive resort, Colorado Springs was nicknamed "Little London" for its popularity with British nobility. Later still, it came to be known as "Newport in the Rockies" for its elegant mansions. From the 1890s to the 1960s, Colorado Springs was one of the wealthiest communities per capita in the country, the Aspen of another era.

SIGHTS

Today, **Colorado Springs** is by far the largest community in the Pikes Peak area—in fact, the second-largest city in Colorado and the third largest in the Rocky Mountain West. The population of Colorado Springs quadrupled between 1969 and 1972 as military personnel returning from Vietnam were discharged from the army at Fort Carson south of town. Electronics firms built plants on the north side. Suburbs and shopping malls sprawled farther and farther out across the eastern plains. But the old-time tourist towns in the hills and canyons along the west edge of the city, seemingly oblivious to the metropolis bustling along on the other side of the freeway, have changed hardly at all in two generations.

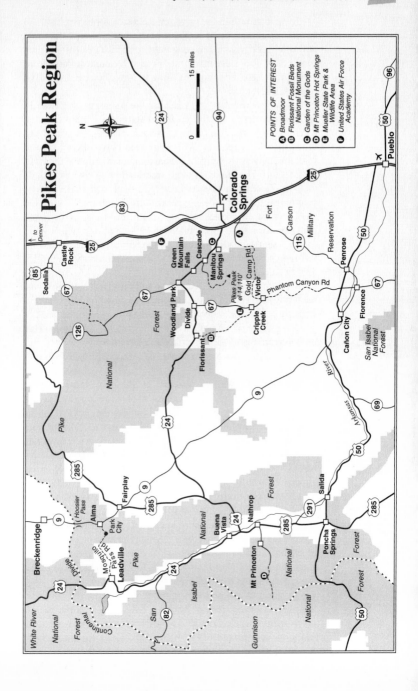

Pikes Peak Region

POINTS OF INTEREST
A Broadmoor
B Florissant Fossil Beds
National Monument
C Garden of the Gods
D Mt Princeton Hot Springs
E Mueller State Park &
Wildlife Area
F United States Air Force
Academy

N

0   15 miles

Colorado Springs

Pueblo

Castle Rock

Sedalia

to Denver

Green Mountain Falls

Cascade

Manitou Springs

Pikes Peak
el 14,110

Gold Camp Rd

Victor

Phantom Canyon Rd

Woodland Park

Divide

Cripple Creek

Florissant

Florence

Cañon City

Fort

Carson

Military

Reservation

Penrose

Arkansas   River

San Isabel

National

Forest

Pike

National

Forest

Fairplay

Alma

Hoosier
Pass

Park City

Breckenridge

Mosquito
Pass
Rd

Leadville

Continental   Divide

White River

National

Forest

San

Isabel

National

Pike

Forest

Buena
Vista

Nathrop

Mt Princeton

Gunnison

National

Forest

Salida

Poncha
Springs

Traveling south from Denver on Route 25, motorists leave the farthest reaches of Front Range suburbia upon passing the town of **Castle Rock** and the towering butte for which it is named, then crest a 9000-foot ridge inaccurately called **Monument Pass**. From here, the highway begins a long, slow 100-mile descent toward the Arkansas River.

About ten miles before reaching the outskirts of Colorado Springs, travelers come to the **United States Air Force Academy**, where college-age cadets train to become career officers in a rigorous four-year program. With more than one million visitors a year, the academy is the most-visited tourist attraction in the Pikes Peak region. The buildings of greatest interest to visitors include the Barry Goldwater Visitors Center, the planetarium, the athletic field house, and the cadet chapel with its 17 futuristic spires. On weekdays during the school year, visitors are welcome to watch the noon formation (it's actually at 12:30 p.m.), in which 4400 cadets assemble in rank and file on the central parade ground before marching to lunch. ~ Route 25 North, Colorado Springs; 719-333-1110.

Between the Air Force Academy and the Garden of the Gods, the **Pro Rodeo Hall of Fame and American Cowboy Museum** presents short films on rodeo riding and the more mundane work of punching cattle. The highlight of the museum, the Pro Rodeo Hall of Fame commemorates legendary bronco and Brahma riders. Admission. ~ 101 Pro Rodeo Drive, Colorado Springs; 719-528-4764.

A visit to the **Western Museum of Mining & Industry**, near the Air Force Academy's north gate, can enhance travelers' understanding and appreciation of the gold mines they will see in the Cripple Creek area and other parts of Colorado. Exhibits demonstrate the complete process of gold mining, from prospecting through drilling and blasting to refining the ore. Closed Sunday from October through May. Admission. ~ 125 Gleneagle Drive, Colorado Springs; 719-488-0880.

On the city's northwestern outskirts lies the **Garden of the Gods**. The 1350-acre city park is filled with orange sandstone spires and monoliths and bordered by an escarpment of pink alabaster. Take a hike or just drive through the park on paved roads to see Balanced Rock, Steamboat Rock and the Kissing Camels, some of the most photographed rock formations in the West. Although climbing without a permit is prohibited, on weekends you're sure to see expert rock climbers challenging the 200-foot-high faces of the Gateway Rocks. ~ One route into the park is north from Old Colorado City on 31st Street; others are from Manitou Springs and the Garden of the Gods Road exit from Route 25 north of Colorado Springs.

Near the north entrance to the Garden of the Gods is **White House Ranch Living History Site**. This city-operated living museum re-creates early-day farms of the Pikes Peak area. Buildings include a 1868 homestead, a 1895 ranch house, and a bigger 1907 home. Guides in period costume enact old-time lifestyles, and the fields and pastures of the ranch are worked by means of traditional 19th-century farming methods. Admission. ~ Gateway Road, Colorado Springs; 719-578-6777.

Nearby, **Glen Eyrie** was the mansion of Colorado Springs' ◄ *HIDDEN* founder, Denver & Rio Grande Railroad tycoon William Jackson Palmer. When it was built in 1904, the 67-room Tudor-style castle with its 700 acres of grounds was the largest and most expensive home west of the Mississippi. It had its own steam-powered electrical generator and a four-story elevator. A mile-long chimney tunnel that carried smoke from the mansion's 24 fireplaces far up the canyon reveals the dislike of smoke and soot that Palmer developed during his years as a railroad builder. The same aversion prompted him to include the nation's first air-pollution laws in the original Colorado Springs city charter. Glen Eyrie is now the headquarters of a Christian youth group called the Navigators. Call for current information on tours of the estate. Admission. ~ 3820 North 30th Street, Colorado Springs; 719-598-1212.

If you continue through the Garden of the Gods to one of its several west entrances, you will join Route 24 in Old Colorado City or Manitou Springs, both historic, visitor-oriented suburbs of Colorado Springs; Manitou Springs is outside the city limits, and Old Colorado City is inside. (Manitou Springs is covered separately in the "Pikes Peak Area" section later in this chapter.)

Colorado City, founded in 1859 during the Pikes Peak gold rush, was the first town in the area. Now part of Colorado Springs' west side, the old wooden storefronts and red-brick Victorian office buildings along the main street of **Old Colorado City** were

✔ **CHECK THESE OUT—UNIQUE SIGHTS**

- Tour the **U.S. Olympic Training Center** in Colorado Springs, where each year 15,000 young athletes strive toward the ultimate challenge. *page 205*
  - Ride an elevator a thousand feet beneath the earth in **Molly Kathleen Gold Mine** in the Cripple Creek District. *page 218*
    - Stroll among the stony stumps of a giant, ancient forest at **Florrisant Fossil Beds**. *page 219*
      - Take a thrill ride on Cañon City's **Skyline Drive**, built on a knife-edge ridge just to prove it could be done. *page 226*

refurbished in the 1970s and 1980s and reborn as a historic district of cafés and cute shops. Located on West Colorado Avenue between 24th and 31st streets (take Cimarron Street/Route 24 west from Route 24 and turn left on 26th Street), Old Colorado City is a centrally located starting point for touring the major tourist attractions of the Colorado Springs area.

It is possible to see all the major sights of the Pikes Peak area without going into the downtown or east-side areas of Colorado Springs. Visitors who take the time to explore these parts of town, however, can find a few unique places. The **Colorado Springs Pioneers Museum,** in the old county courthouse across the street from the present courthouse and jail at the south end of downtown, has two floors of exhibits ranging from antique Van Briggle pottery to firearms. The restored courtroom upstairs dates back to 1903 and has been used as a set for motion pictures and the *Perry Mason* television series. Closed Sunday off-season and Monday year-round. ~ 215 South Tejon Street, Colorado Springs; 719-578-6650.

North of downtown, the **McAllister House Museum** preserves the one-and-a-half-story brick home of Major Henry McAllister, one of the city's founding fathers. His enduring contribution was to plant 5000 trees along the now-shady streets north of downtown. Built in 1873, the McAllister House was the first brick residence in Colorado Springs. The exhibits consist entirely of the home's original furnishings, which offer a look at the lifestyle of one of the city's wealthiest residents in the late 19th century. Admission. ~ 423 North Cascade Avenue, Colorado Springs; 719-635-7925.

One mile north of downtown, adjacent to the Colorado College campus, is the **Colorado Springs Fine Arts Center**. The building is said to be the finest example of an odd architectural style called "Pueblo Deco"—a 1930s art deco variation inspired by the Indian architecture of New Mexico. The permanent exhibits also have a Southwestern flavor, with Pueblo and Navajo Indian collections and a replica of a *penitente* chapel. Three of the museum's five exhibition halls are used for traveling exhibits of folk art and contemporary art, many of them on tour from the Smithsonian Institution. The museum also houses one of the largest theaters in town, used by several community organizations for plays, concerts and dance performances. Closed Monday. Admission. ~ 30 West Dale Street, Colorado Springs; 719-634-5581.

HIDDEN ► Next to the Fine Arts Center is the **Museum of the American Numismatic Association**. Although the museum space appears small, it contains one of the world's largest exhibits of antique and exotic money; in the United States, only the Smithsonian's collection is larger. Displays include early American coins and currency, medals, privately minted coins of the gold rush era, and a world history of money from 600 B.C. to the present. Admission. ~ 818 North Cascade Avenue, Colorado Springs; 719-635-7925.

East of downtown, the **U.S. Olympic Training Center** occupies a former U.S. Air Force base that was abandoned as the city grew to surround it. Each year, more than 15,000 Olympic hopefuls attend training camps at the 37-acre complex. Regularly scheduled tours take visitors through the athletic facilities. ~ 1750 East Boulder Street, Colorado Springs; 719-578-4644.

Of the numerous special-interest museums in Colorado Springs, none is more offbeat than the **Tesla Museum**. Nikolai Tesla, inventor of alternating current, the electric motor and the Tesla coil, saw his reputation destroyed in a vicious publicity war with his rival, Thomas Edison. He moved to Colorado Springs to conduct experiments with lightning in search of a way to transmit electricity without wires. Although his original laboratory is long gone, some of his sensational scientific demonstrations, such as how one million volts of electricity can flow through the human body harm-

◄ HIDDEN

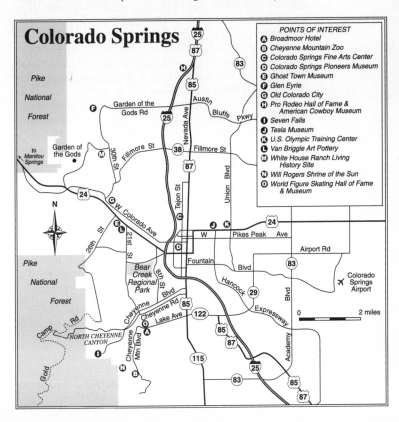

Colorado Springs

POINTS OF INTEREST
Ⓐ Broadmoor Hotel
Ⓑ Cheyenne Mountain Zoo
Ⓒ Colorado Springs Fine Arts Center
Ⓓ Colorado Springs Pioneers Museum
Ⓔ Ghost Town Museum
Ⓕ Glen Eyrie
Ⓖ Old Colorado City
Ⓗ Pro Rodeo Hall of Fame & American Cowboy Museum
Ⓘ Seven Falls
Ⓙ Tesla Museum
Ⓚ U.S. Olympic Training Center
Ⓛ Van Briggle Art Pottery
Ⓜ White House Ranch Living History Site
Ⓝ Will Rogers Shrine of the Sun
Ⓞ World Figure Skating Hall of Fame & Museum

lessly, are re-created daily by the museum staff. Admission. ~ 2220 East Bijou Street, Colorado Springs; 719-475-0918.

To tour the sights of the Broadmoor area on the southwest edge of Colorado Springs, start from Old Colorado City or Route 24 west and take 21st Street south. Near the intersection of 21st Street and Route 24 is a cluster of commercial tourist attractions, including **Ghost Town Museum**, which contains Old West antiques and re-creations of frontier buildings. Admission. ~ 400 South 21st Street, Colorado Springs; 719-634-0696.

Across the parking lot from Ghost Town Museum is **Van Briggle Art Pottery**. The legacy of famed ceramic artist Artus Van Briggle, the sculptural and free-form pottery is made in various styles, including some art-deco designs from the '30s. The free tour shows how artisans throw clay on potters' wheels, shape it, glaze it and fire it. Visitors can buy the pottery at the showroom. Van Briggle's is in the old railroad roundhouse where ore trains from Cripple Creek turned around. Across the street, a tall smokestack is all that's left of the old mill where gold was refined and cast into bars. Closed Sunday. ~ 600 South 21st Street, Colorado Springs; 719-633-4080.

Continue south on 21st Street for about two miles, past Cheyenne Boulevard and Cheyenne Road, to reach the extensive resort complex of the **Broadmoor Hotel**. Even if the ultra-deluxe rates discourage you from staying there, stop in to see this magnificent hotel, ranked as the finest resort west of the Mississippi during the 1920s. In 1918, Cripple Creek refinery tycoon Spencer Penrose, who made a fortune establishing gold refineries in the Cripple Creek district, built the original hotel on the site of an earlier gambling casino and dairy farm. In the era between the World Wars, the Broadmoor was the place where the crowned heads of Europe and Asia stayed when they visited the American West. The pink Italian Renaissance hotel, with its Mediterranean tile roof and multilevel lobby a fantasy of polished Colorado marble, is located on the shore of its own idyllic private lake. It has its own zoo and boasts two of the state's finest golf courses. ~ 1 Lake Avenue, Colorado Springs; 719-634-7711. At the south end of the lake is a building that houses two indoor ice-skating rinks—one open to the public year-round, the other reserved for the use of Olympic hopefuls. The **World Figure Skating Hall of Fame & Museum**, memorializes champion skaters who trained at the Broadmoor, including Peggy Fleming and Sonja Henie. Admission. ~ 20 1st Street, Colorado Springs; 719-635-5200. The hotel complex also houses the **El Pomar Carriage House Museum**, which exhibits antique horse-drawn vehicles from buckboards and a stagecoach to presidential carriages and a fire engine, as well as two covered wagons used by pioneers on the Oregon and Cherokee trails. ~ Broadmoor Hotel, Colorado Springs; 719-634-7711 ext. 5353.

The tennis club, spa and other facilities that surround the hotel itself are just the tip of the iceberg. Past the golf course and up the side of Cheyenne Mountain, the Broadmoor has not only its own ski slopes but also its own zoo. The **Cheyenne Mountain Zoo**, perched midway up the mountainside, has the most spectacular location of any zoo we've seen. Today the zoo has more than 500 animals, including an impressive herd of giraffes. Admission. ~ 4250 Cheyenne Mountain Zoo Road, Colorado Springs; 719-475-9555.

In peak tourist season, when South Cheyenne Creek often slows to a trickle, recirculating pumps supplement Mother Nature to keep the Seven Falls in operation.

The paved road through the zoo continues in a series of steep switchbacks up the mountain to the **Will Rogers Shrine of the Sun**. The four-story stone tower, which commands perhaps the finest possible view of the Colorado Springs area, was originally conceived as Cripple Creek gold tycoon and Broadmoor founder Spencer Penrose's monumental tomb. Before it was completed, humorist Will Rogers, a friend of Penrose's, died in a plane crash, and the tower was dedicated to him. Penrose and his wife (but not Will Rogers) are buried under the floor of the small room in the base of the shrine, making him perhaps the only man in history to successfully promote his own grave as a tourist attraction.

From the Broadmoor area, head west on either Cheyenne Boulevard or Cheyenne Road; they merge and less than a mile later divide again at the mouth of Cheyenne Canyon. **Seven Falls**, in the south fork of the canyon, is one of the region's oldest commercial tourist attractions. South Cheyenne Creek tumbles into this box canyon down a near-vertical granite cliff in a stairstep series of waterfalls—count 'em, seven—for a total drop of about 300 feet. In winter, when the falls are frozen, and in spring, when snowmelt swells the creek into a torrent, the falls are truly spectacular. It is not possible to see all the falls from the bottom of the canyon. A series of stairways goes up the cliff beside the falls, and another goes to a lookout point from which all can be seen. An incline elevator also goes up to the lookout. Near the foot of the falls are a small pavilion where American Indian dancers perform. At night, colored floodlights illuminate the cliffs for a mile down the canyon, all the way to the tollgate. Admission. ~ 2850 South Cheyenne Canyon Road, Colorado Springs; 719-632-0765.

Drivers who turn right instead of left at the Seven Falls turnoff find themselves in **North Cheyenne Canyon**, which is quite different from South Cheyenne Canyon. For one thing, it's free. Like the Garden of the Gods, North Cheyenne Canyon is a Colorado Springs city park. And as in the Garden of the Gods, you're likely to see expert rock climbers challenging the 400-foot-high granite walls in the middle part of the canyon. The paved road twists steeply in places, to **Helen Hunt Falls,** a classic mountain waterfall that looks exactly like the one on Coors Beer labels.

Not far past the falls, the North Cheyenne Canyon road joins the narrow, unpaved **Gold Camp Road.** Originally the track bed for the Cripple Creek Short Line narrow-gauge railroad, which carried ore down from the goldfields at the turn of the century, the road runs through Pike National Forest around the south side of Pikes Peak for 36 slow miles to return to the pavement near Victor. For a shorter trip—and one affording some of the most spectacular views—return via North Cheyenne Canyon to Colorado Springs. The eight-mile trip follows the rim of the canyon, goes through two railroad tunnels and traverses the mountainside high above the city. Despite appearances, there *is* room for two vehicles to pass each other.

The Gold Camp Road comes back to town on 26th Street, across Route 24 from the Old Colorado City area. The road descends from the mountainside into Bear Creek Regional Park. The solar-heated **Bear Creek Nature Center,** at the northwest side of the park, has exhibits on the wildlife of the park's foothills and streamside forests, which can be explored on a network of nature trails. ~ 245 Bear Creek Road, Colorado Springs; 719-520-6387.

The most direct route between Colorado Springs and Cañon City is Route 115, which runs along the perimeter of a military reserve used for maneuvers by the mechanized infantry forces at Fort Carson army base. The 42-mile trip takes less than an hour. Nine miles outside of Colorado Springs, an iron sculpture of a beetle larger than a man marks the entrance to the private, eccentric little **May Natural History Museum.** The museum contains more than 7000 mounted insects of the tropics, some of them brightly colored and others incredibly large. Open May through September; winter visits by appointment. Admission. ~ Route 115, Colorado Springs; 719-576-0450.

As you drive along Route 115, the mountain ridge that rises steeply on your west is **Cheyenne Mountain.** From a distance it's easy to visualize why, in Ute Indian legend, the mountain represented the Dragon of Thirst, who ended a great primordial flood by drinking up the water that covered the earth and has lain sleeping ever since. Even stranger and absolutely true is the fact that tunnels inside the mountain house the **North American Air Defense Command Headquarters,** a Cold War–era control center for U.S. and Canadian missiles built on giant shock absorbers that theoretically would withstand the shock of a direct nuclear strike. Public tours of the facility are rare (though not unheard-of), but you can glimpse the massive steel-doored entrance to the facility from the highway about three miles south of the Colorado Springs city limit.

LODGING

The cheapest beds in the region are at the **Garden of the Gods Youth Hostel**, located near the south entrance to the Garden of the Gods. For AYH members only, the hostel is part of the large, crowded Garden of the Gods campground. It consists of 12 spartan dormitory cabins with four bunk beds each. Guests share the campground's restroom and shower facilities. ~ 3704 West Colorado Avenue, Colorado Springs; 719-475-9450. BUDGET.

There are a number of older, low-priced motels along West Colorado Avenue between Old Colorado City and Manitou Springs, relics from the pre-freeway era when this street was the main highway to Pikes Peak and points west. A good bet in this area is the **Garden of the Gods Motel**, a two-story motel offering the most ordinary rooms imaginable and an indoor heated swimming pool within easy walking distance of Old Colorado City. ~ 2922 West Colorado Avenue, Colorado Springs; 719-636-5271. BUDGET TO MODERATE.

The Antlers Doubletree Hotel stands on the site of an earlier Antlers Hotel built by the founder of Colorado Springs.

Located in the residential part of historic Old Colorado City, the **Holden House Bed and Breakfast Inn** has five suites in a Victorian-era Colonial Revival home and carriage house. Some suites feature fireplaces and Roman marble tubs large enough for two. ~ 1102 West Pikes Peak Avenue, Colorado Springs; phone/fax 719-471-3980. DELUXE.

Downtown Colorado Springs is dominated by the **Antlers Doubletree Hotel**, a modern 290-room high-rise. The hotel has a gleaming all-marble lobby and spacious guest rooms with king-sized beds and exceptional quality furnishings. All rooms have computer dataports, many have views of Pikes Peak, and some have whirlpool baths. ~ 4 South Cascade Avenue, Colorado Springs; 719-473-5600, fax 719-444-0417. ULTRA-DELUXE.

The finest bed and breakfast in downtown Colorado Springs is the **Hearthstone Inn**, an 1885 Victorian mansion built by a paper bag tycoon, located near Colorado College, the Colorado Springs Fine Arts Center and Monument Valley Park. The innkeepers annexed the neighboring building, built in 1885 as a tuberculosis sanatorium, and extensively remodeled both buildings to create an antique-filled 25-room hostelry that glows with warm elegance. Rates include a full breakfast. ~ 506 North Cascade Avenue, Colorado Springs; 719-473-4413, 800-521-1885, fax 719-473-1322. MODERATE TO ULTRA-DELUXE.

The **Broadmoor Hotel** has traditionally been considered the finest resort hotel in Colorado. Instead of slipping into decay like so many other grand hotels, for decades the Broadmoor has been pursuing an expansion program designed to keep up with the finest new resorts worldwide. Three hotel annexes have brought the total number of rooms to 700. Rooms in both the old and new parts of the hotel were recently redecorated with antiques, and the hotel's common areas are filled with original paintings by Toulouse-Lautrec and Maxfield Parrish as well as priceless oriental artworks. Among the recreational facilities are three golf courses, three swimming pools, 16 tennis courts, a spa, stables, and a hot-air balloon. ~ 1 Lake Avenue, Colorado Springs; 719-634-7711, 800-634-7711, fax 719-577-5700. ULTRA-DELUXE.

DINING   **Giuseppe's Depot** is a Colorado Springs classic. You'll find great pizzas and huge submarine sandwiches here, alongside more sophisticated fare such as rib-eye steaks, lasagna and snow crab, Key-lime pie and Kahlúa chocolate mousse as well as a good selection of wines. Windows overlook the railroad yards, where coal trains still rumble by. ~ 10 South Sierra Madre Street, Colorado Springs; 719-635-3111. BUDGET TO MODERATE.

Another old-time favorite, recently relocated from downtown to the city's main shopping mall, is **Michelle's**, a candy shop, soda fountain and café operated by a Greek family since 1950. The front part of the café is a shop displaying candies made on the premises. In the back part, people gorge themselves on big, elaborate concoctions of homemade ice cream. Though fewer than one out of ten patrons actually comes here to eat a meal, there is a limited but tasty lunch and dinner menu ranging from cheeseburgers to Greek hero sandwiches. ~ 750 Citadel Drive East, Colorado Springs; 719-597-9932. BUDGET.

Jose Muldoon's, a sort of cross between a Mexican restaurant and a fern bar, serves contemporary south-of-the-border fare—fajitas are a specialty—as well as a varied selection of steak, chicken and seafood options. Start your meal with the best gazpacho soup in town. The atmosphere in this half-bar, half-restaurant is dark and congenial, with a large courtyard patio for summer dining. ~ 222 North Tejon Street, Colorado Springs; 719-636-2311. BUDGET TO MODERATE.

A favorite hangout of the Colorado College crowd for more than 20 years, **Poor Richard's Feed and Read** is a blend of restaurant and bookstore. Dining is in a rambling series of cozy literature-lined rooms. Featured fare includes a full range of sandwiches and creative vegetarian choices. ~ 824H North Tejon Street, Colorado Springs; 632-7721. BUDGET.

The most exclusive restaurant in Colorado Springs is the Broadmoor Hotel's **Charles Court**. Located in the hotel's modern annex on the west side of the lake, Charles Court is decorated in elegant Tudor style and features fare that changes seasonally, including wild game entrées such as Colorado elk steaks. The presentation, by a serving staff that often seems to outnumber the diners, is impeccable, and the wine cellar—over 100,000 bottles representing

650 wineries—will impress even the most jaded connoisseur. ~ 1 Lake Avenue, Colorado Springs; 719-577-5774. ULTRA-DELUXE.

The **Mountain View Dining Room**, serves buffet-style gourmet dinners featuring six hot entrées plus vegetables, potatoes and rice, as well as an array of desserts including six different cakes and pies plus ice cream, brownies and petits fours—all you can eat at a fixed price. The view takes in not only the mountains but also the distant glow of Colorado Spring's city lights. It's perfect by candlelight. ~ Cheyenne Mountain Conference Resort, 3225 Broadmoor Valley Road, Colorado Springs; 719-576-4600. DELUXE.

If down-home food—and lots of it—sounds good to you, check out the **Hungry Farmer**, a huge restaurant on the north side of town that was designed to resemble a barn. Waiters wear overalls, waitresses wear granny dresses and the decor is way cuter than any real farmyard ever was. A bottomless bucket of thick, hearty soup, homemade oatmeal muffins and cinnamon rolls come with all meals. Entrées include seafood, steaks and country-style cooking. ~ 575 Garden of the Gods Road, Colorado Springs; 719-598-7622. MODERATE.

SHOPPING

Despite high-volume tourism, Colorado Springs and the Pikes Peak area have never developed the high-priced, arts-oriented retail shops that characterize so many Colorado resort areas.

Recently in Colorado Springs, **Old Colorado City**, a formerly rundown three-block area along Colorado Avenue, has blossomed into new life with an array of artisans' shops.

Simpich Character Dolls is both factory and gallery for these unique, individually made collectible dolls, which are sold nationwide; factory tours are available. ~ 2413 West Colorado Avenue, Colorado Springs; 719-636-3272.

Artist Michael Garman, famous in the world of cowboy art for his finely detailed sculptural miniatures of Old West street scenes, had his factory-like studio in Old Colorado City long before the neighborhood became trendy; today, his works are on display in the big **Michael Garman Gallery**. ~ 2416 West Colorado Avenue, Colorado Springs; 719-471-9391.

The **Pine Creek Art Gallery** exhibits paintings and sculpture by local artists. ~ 2419 West Colorado Avenue, Colorado Springs; 719-633-6767.

The **Candle Shoppe** features exquisite creations in wax. ~ 2421½ West Colorado Avenue, Colorado Springs; 719-633-4856.

El Dorado Fine Arts has art in all price ranges, from original oil paintings to posters and greeting cards. ~ 2504 West Colorado Avenue, Colorado Springs; 719-634-4075.

NIGHTLIFE Jeff Valdez' Comedy Corner is Colorado Springs' top comedy club and features adult humor. ~ 1305 North Academy Boulevard, Colorado Springs; 719-591-0707.

The top singles dance club is **Meadow Muffins**, a perennial favorite even though it presents deejay dance music only. ~ 2432 West Colorado Avenue, Colorado Springs; 719-633-0583. A lively alternative dance club that does have live bands is the student-oriented **The Club House Underground Pub**. ~ 130 East Kiowa Street, Colorado Springs; 719-633-0590.

For adults, the classic Colorado Springs hangout is the **Golden Bee**. A sing-along ragtime piano player encourages a party atmosphere; the crowd is a mix of the Broadmoor's well-heeled guests and Colorado Springs locals who come here for fun. This is where you can watch sophisticated women dripping in diamonds, as well as lawyers and bankers competing to see who can chug a "yard" of beer (a three-foot-tall carafe) the fastest. ~ Broadmoor Hotel, 1 Lake Avenue, Colorado Springs; 719-634-7711.

A long-established gay-friendly club is the **Hide N'Seek**, featuring deejay dance music. The dark, warehouselike club has one of the town's largest dancefloors. There is also a country bar and a restaurant. ~ 512 West Colorado Avenue, Colorado Springs; 719-634-9303.

PARKS **BEAR CREEK REGIONAL PARK AND BEAR CREEK CANYON PARK** Birdwatchers, equestrians and joggers meet on this network of trails among the scrub oak foothills on the west side of Colorado Springs. The visitors center, an experimental solar-powered structure, contains exhibits on bird and animal life found within the park boundaries, as well as live animals and relief maps of the park and the Pikes Peak area. While the west half of the park is rugged and wild, the east half has neat lawns, tennis courts and soccer and football fields. Bear Creek Canyon Park, adjoining the west side of Bear Creek Regional Park and continuing south to Gold Camp Road, follows the creek for about two miles and offers numerous parking areas and picnic sites. The area is especially beautiful in autumn, when the forest along the creek bursts into a riot of reds, oranges and golds. Facilities include picnic areas, restrooms, a visitors center, game fields and nature trails. ~ Located south of Route 24 between 21st Street and 26th Street, which becomes Bear Creek Canyon Road and joins the Gold Camp Road; 719-520-6387.

Pikes Peak Area

Besides the huge granite massif that dominates the skyline west of Colorado Springs, the Pikes Peak region includes an assortment of towns and scenic routes that surround the mountain on all sides. Manitou Springs, the quaint old tourist town at the foot of Pikes Peak's east face, is the natural starting point for exploring the town and the region. From there, the main highway skirts the north side of the mountain, following an old railroad route known as Ute Pass (though it is not a true pass because it has no summit). Other former railroad routes—the Gold Camp Road from Colorado Springs and the Phantom Canyon Road from Cañon City—provide access to the rugged forest and canyon country on the south side of the Peak. On the west side, the Cripple Creek District was once the richest goldfield in the Rockies, supporting a city that ranked as one of the region's largest at the turn of the century—long since abandoned but recently revived as a gambling center. Allow at least four days to explore all sides of Pikes Peak, beginning with an ascent to the summit.

About two miles west of Old Colorado City, **Manitou Springs** is the actual site of the 26 mineral springs for which Colorado Springs was named. Beginning in the 1870s, people from the East and even Europe began to flock to Manitou Springs for the dry mountain climate and the healing waters, which were thought to cure everything from tuberculosis to polio. In those days, the circular building in the center of town was a fashionable spa, and a geyser spurted at regular intervals on Manitou Avenue. Most of the springs have been capped or clogged by mineral deposits, though a few still trickle fizzy mineral water by the roadside. A small exhibit case in the **Manitou Springs City Hall** shows each spring's location, status and mineral content. ~ 606 Manitou Avenue, Manitou Springs; 719-685-5481.

SIGHTS

Today, a number of old-time tourist attractions live on in this quaintly old-fashioned town. Up the hill, easier to reach from the Route 24 bypass than from the town itself, the **Cave of the Winds** has been one of the Pikes Peak area's top commercial sites for more than a century. The cave is long, narrow and twisting, with plenty of stalactites, stalagmites, crystal formations and colored lights. Admission. ~ Cave of the Winds Road, Manitou Springs; 719-685-5444.

Just down the highway from the cave, the **Manitou Cliff Dwellings Museum** is a group of Anasazi cliff dwellings that were found in a canyon near Dolores in southwestern Colorado and moved to a sandstone cliff above Manitou Springs in the 1920s. It probably made sense at the time, when few travelers could reach the area of Dolores and Mesa Verde. Today, the most remarkable fact about these reconstructed cliff dwellings is that they were disassembled into tens of thousands of individual stones, each marked for position, and reassembled 300 miles away. Admission. ~ Route 24, Manitou Springs; 719-685-5242.

The best Manitou Springs tourist attractions are on Ruxton Avenue, which leads south up a canyon from the center of town.

HIDDEN ▶   **Miramont Castle** is a restored 1895 stone mansion built by a wealthy French priest who had come to Manitou Springs to seek a cure for his tuberculosis. It was opened to the public as a museum in the late 1970s. A fantasyland of eclectic architecture, the castle incorporates nine different styles—among them Romanesque, Gothic, Tudor and Byzantine. Some rooms have been restored with period furnishings, while others house miscellaneous collections such as dolls. Closed Monday. Admission. ~ 9 Capitol Hill Avenue, Manitou Springs; 719-685-1011.

At the end of Ruxton Avenue is the depot for the **Pikes Peak Cog Railway,** certainly the easiest way to climb the peak. The railroad uses Swiss-made two-car diesel trains to climb the otherwise-inaccessible west face of Pikes Peak. The trains run from May through October, twice daily during the spring and fall, as many as eight times a day during peak season. The round trip takes between three and four hours. Reservations are essential. Admission. ~ 515 Ruxton Avenue, Manitou Springs; 719-685-5401.

The Pikes Peak Cog Railway, the highest in the United States, climbs grades as steep as 26 percent.

Pikes Peak (14,110 feet) is not the highest mountain in the Colorado Rockies (Mount Elbert, between Leadville and Aspen, is 323 feet higher). It is not even the highest mountain with a road to the top. (Mount Evans, west of Denver, is 154 feet higher.) But Pikes Peak is certainly the most famous mountain in the Rockies. To early pioneers and prospectors its name was synonymous with gold, for the massive, solitary mountain marked the gateway to the goldfields around Fairplay and Leadville—though gold was not found on its slopes until about 35 years after the Pikes Peak gold rush.

Pikes Peak was the first major tourist attraction in Colorado. When Captain Zebulon Pike, the explorer for whom the mountain was named, failed to reach the summit on his 1810 expedition, undertaken to map the southern reaches of the Louisiana Purchase and the Mexican border, he declared that the mountain would never be climbed. But by the 1870s, thousands of visitors were climbing Pikes Peak on foot, on muleback and by horse-drawn carriage. A fancy resort hotel at the 11,000-foot level on the west side, its ruins now lost beneath the surface of a city reservoir, did a thriving business for decades. Cog railway tracks reached the summit in 1891, and two years later, Katherine Lee Bates wrote the lyrics to "America the Beautiful" on top of the peak.

In 1916, when gold-refinery tycoon and philanthropist Spencer Penrose converted the old carriage road up the peak to a graded automobile toll road, the assault on Captain Pike's "unclimbable" mountain began in earnest. Now, more than 250,000 people reach the summit of Pikes Peak each summer.

The **Pikes Peak Highway** turns off from Route 24 at the tiny town of Cascade, three miles west of Manitou Springs. The road is 19 miles long, paved with blacktop for the first seven miles and gravel for the last 12. It takes about two hours to drive to the summit. Only on the switchback climb from the house at Glen Cove to the top ridge is the road precipitous enough to make inexperienced mountain drivers wish there were guard rails. Accidents are rare, but breakdowns are common since some vehicles need fuel-system adjustments to run at such high altitudes. Motorists who are inexperienced at mountain driving would be well advised to take the cog train instead, which ascends the east face of the mountain at a straight, steep angle from Manitou Springs. Admission. ~ 719-684-9138.

Whichever mode of transportation you choose, morning is the best time to climb Pikes Peak. The view is clearer then because there's less smog over Colorado Springs and Denver, and the weather is more reliable in the morning. Even in August, afternoon lightning storms can bring snowdrifts, closing the road temporarily and stranding motorists on top until the snowplows come. Visitors to Pikes Peak soon learn what a climatic difference elevation makes. Temperatures at the summit fall below freezing every night and, even on the sunniest days, typically run 40 degrees lower than in Colorado Springs.

Above timberline, Pikes Peak's long ridgeline is carpeted with delicate arctic tundra—tiny plants and flowers that can grow in the thinnest layers of soil and survive severe cold. Visitors taking either the toll road or the cog railway are likely to see some of the Rocky Mountain bighorn sheep that graze on the tundra, as well as alpine rodents—big, rotund golden marmots and smaller animals called picas that look something like prairie dogs. The very top of the mountain is so high that not even tundra can grow; the only life native to the boulder-strewn summit is lichen.

The Pikes Peak summit has a large curio shop, snack bar and observation deck. From the top, on a clear day, you can see most of Colorado, from the Continental Divide to the boundaries of Kansas, Oklahoma and New Mexico. The eastern horizon is about 175 miles away. While on the summit, keep in mind that there is not much oxygen at 14,000 feet. Excessive exercise can cause altitude sickness—dizziness, nausea, fainting. Alcoholic beverages, which have a much more powerful effect at high altitudes, should be avoided. Another high-altitude effect many people experience is sleepiness on the way down the mountain.

In addition to the interpretive exhibits at the visitors center on Pikes Peak's summit, two new small museums tell more about the mountain and its history. The **Pikes Peak Auto Hill Climb Race Car Museum** traces the traditional Fourth of July road race to the summit, presents video views of what driving in the race is like, and displays some of the cars that have raced up the peak in past years. Admission. ~ 135 Manitou Avenue, Manitou Springs; 719-685-4400. The **Ute Pass Cultural Center** in the bedroom community of Woodland Park, 18 miles from Manitou Springs up Route 24 on the way to Cripple Creek, has a small art exhibit and a visitor information center. ~ 210 East Midland Avenue, Woodland Park; 719-687-5218.

The stretch of Route 24 between Manitou Springs and Woodland Park, commonly called **Ute Pass** although it is a canyon and not a true pass, follows the route of the Colorado Midland a narrow-gauge train that carried gold ore from Cripple Creek to Colorado Springs for processing. Tall smokestacks south of Route 24 between 8th and 21st streets mark the site of the former refinery. On the way up the "pass," the village of **Green Mountain Falls** is one of the region's prettiest mountain communities. The waterfall for which it is named is well hidden on a secluded dirt road without signs, but the lake in the center of town makes a good picnic spot.

No tour of the Pikes Peak region is complete without a visit to the **Cripple Creek–Victor Historic District**, located at 9600 feet above sea level on the west slope of Pikes Peak, about an hour's drive from Colorado Springs. To get there, take Route 24 west for 25 miles to the crossroads town of Divide, then Route 67 south for 18 miles. In the summer tourist season and on weekends year-round, expect long lines of traffic at the one-lane, stoplight-controlled tunnel on Route 67.

The town of **Cripple Creek** was founded in 1891 after a local rancher spotted gold nuggets in the mountain stream of the same name. The discovery touched off the last great gold rush in the lower 48 United States, and by 1900, the Cripple Creek metropolitan area had become the largest city in Colorado, with a population of more than 60,000 including nearby Victor and several smaller settlements. The district boasted 150 saloons, 91 lawyers, and 15 newspapers. The mines of the Cripple Creek district produced some 625 tons of gold, worth more than eight billion dollars at today's gold prices.

Twenty years after the town was founded, most of the mines in the Cripple Creek district had closed down. Little by little, the 100 or so blocks of residential neighborhoods vanished as the few remaining residents tore down abandoned buildings for firewood until only bare, grassy hillsides remained. A stark reminder of the transitory nature of mortals' works and wealth set against a background of Pikes Peak's massive, timeless crags, Cripple Creek gradually developed a low-key tourism economy, and by the late 1960s a number of shops had opened along the main street to sell arts and crafts, antiques and curios.

In 1991, the Colorado legislature legalized casino gambling in Cripple Creek. The idea was to generate money to preserve the

Gold Camp
Luck

Greed, more than any other factor, attracted settlers to Colorado. From 1858 through the 1890s, newspapers regularly carried stories of prospectors who ventured into the mountains, spotted a flash in a streambed or rock cliff, and came back rich beyond their wildest imaginings. Never mind that of the hundreds of thousands of people who risked everything to seek their fortunes in the goldfields, only a few hundred found the wealth they hoped for, or that most of those few did it through retail commerce, real estate deals or speculative stock issues, rather than by actually finding silver or gold. Still, every once in a while, against all odds, people actually did "strike it rich."

Every junior-high student in Colorado learns how Horace Tabor was fleeced into trading his store for a worthless Leadville gold mine, only to discover that it contained the richest silver vein in the Rockies. (Then, as the richest man in Colorado, he became a U.S. Senator only to lose his fortune when the price of silver crashed). The same mining boom also made a rich man of prospector Leadville Johnny Brown. (Rebuffed by Denver high society, Brown used his wealth to build the city's most elegant hotel, the Brown Palace, and divorced his wife, who later survived the sinking of the *Titanic*, earning national notoriety.)

The Cripple Creek District, too, spawned its share of get-rich-quick tales. Between 1893, when Cripple Creek became a town, and 1899, four local storekeepers, two druggists, two real estate agents, two schoolteachers, a lawyer, a butcher, a sawmill owner, a coal delivery man, a race horse trainer and a former sheriff from Iowa all became overnight millionaires by discovering veins of gold.

Most famous of all Cripple Creek prospectors was Winfield Scott Stratton, a Colorado Springs carpenter who used to spend his summers exploring various gold districts around Colorado. After years of fruitless searching, Stratton promised his wife that he would give up his daydreams and stay home and attend to his family and trade. He settled down and specialized in making hand-carved fireplace mantles that are valued as antiques today, but within a few years Stratton succumbed to temptation and went to take a second look at a claim he had once staked in Cripple Creek. On his second day there, he discovered the vein that would become the Independence Mine, the largest in Cripple Creek History. Stratton later sold the mine to British investors for $11 million. Though he built a hospital and bought bicycles for all the city's working women, Stratton's fortune earned interest faster than he could give the money away, and he is remembered as the most generous philanthropist in Colorado Springs history.

historic buildings, many of which were crumbling away with neglect. When the casinos opened in 1993, the interior of every building on Bennett Avenue had been spruced up with pseudo-Victorian glitz. Slot machines and blackjack tables had displaced almost every other business in town, and huge tracts of vacant land had become parking lots. How gambling will ultimately reshape Cripple Creek's character is anybody's guess. Meanwhile, wild donkeys, great-grandchildren of beasts that pulled ore carts in the old days, still wander the streets, and several tourist attractions from the pre-casino days continue to operate.

The two-story **Cripple Creek District Museum**, at the east end of town, offers a look at the mining district's heyday, including its seamy or otherwise unpleasant aspects: fast money, deadly epidemics, labor violence, gambling and prostitution. One of the most interesting exhibits is a model showing the vast underground network, many miles of tunnels reaching thousands of feet into the earth, in just one of the district's 500 gold mines. Open weekends only in winter. Admission. ~ Bennett Avenue, Cripple Creek; 719-689-2634.

Near the museum, the **Cripple Creek and Victor Narrow Gauge Railroad** takes passengers on a 45-minute narrated trip through the goldfields in open railcars pulled by an old-time steam locomotive. The old mines and other abandoned buildings along the way are off-limits to sightseers these days. A mining company is recovering gold from the low-grade ore found in mine tailings through a highly toxic cyanide leaching process. The train operates May through mid-October. Admission. ~ 520 East Carr Street, Cripple Creek; 719-689-2640.

About a mile out of town, the **Molly Kathleen Gold Mine** offers tours into a gold mine. An elevator drops visitors down a shaft to a tunnel 1000 feet underground to see where miners blasted and drilled along a gold vein. Everyone who takes the tour receives a sample of gold ore. Closed November through April. Admission. ~ Route 67, Cripple Creek; 719-689-2465.

Seven miles south of Cripple Creek, at the other end of the mining district, lies **Victor**. By some legislative whim, gambling was legalized in Cripple Creek but not in Victor, so visitors to the small near–ghost town can get a good idea of what Cripple Creek was like before casinos. Among the town's points of historic interest are the city hall building, where soon-to-be world heavyweight boxing champion Jack Dempsey trained while making his living as a prizefighter in the bars of the Cripple Creek district, and a saloon with a mine entrance inside.

Victor's main attraction is the **Victor-Lowell Thomas Museum**, which contains newspaper articles, photos and memorabilia on the life and worldwide travels of the journalist-adventurer who grew up here and began his distinguished career as a cub reporter on the *Victor Record*. The museum also has an exhibit on miners and promoters who struck it rich in the Cripple Creek District. Lowell Thomas buffs can also see the outside of his modest boyhood home at 225 South 6th Street and visit the Victor Record Building, a weekly newspaper office with a thick patina of history, at 118 South 4th Street. Admission. ~ 3rd Street at Victor Avenue, Victor; 719-689-3211.

From the west end of Bennett Avenue in Cripple Creek, unpaved County Road 1 passes the perfect little volcanic cone of **Mount Pisgah** and runs through ranchland for about 20 miles and intersects Route 24 at Florissant, eight miles west of the main Cripple Creek turnoff at Divide. The road past Mount Pisgah takes motorists to **Florissant Fossil Beds National Monument,** a 6000-acre expanse where volcanic ash covered a sequoia forest 35 million years ago, preserving 1100 species of butterflies, dragonflies, beetles, bees and other prehistoric bugs, as well as plants, fish, birds and mammals, and providing the most detailed information anywhere on the natural history of the Eocene era. The monument's most striking feature is a forest of giant petrified tree stumps. Equally interesting is the visitors center's display of remarkably detailed small fossils found in the monument. Admission. ~ Florissant; 719-748-3253.

◀ HIDDEN

Manitou Springs is full of small ma-and-pa motels, cottages and guest houses dating back to the early 20th century, when this little town in the shadow of Pikes Peak was one of the most popular tourist resorts in the region. Some are rundown and only marginally acceptable by modern standards; most are remarkably affordable. One of the nicer old cabin compounds is **Town-n-Country Cottages,** which has ten recently renovated Spanish-style one- to three-room cabins with full baths and furnished kitchens. The

LODGING

✔ CHECK THESE OUT—UNIQUE LODGING

- *Budget to moderate:* Once the county poor farm, the **River Run Inn** offers both hostel and B&B accommodations in a rural setting near the Arkansas River. *page 230*
  - *Moderate:* Sidestep into Cripple Creek's clattering casino strip into the genuine Victorian ambience of the venerable **Imperial Hotel.** *page 221*
    - *Moderate to ultra-deluxe:* Hide out at Manitou Springs' **Red Crags B&B,** one of Theodore Roosevelt's favorite hideaways—even before they installed the jacuzzi. *page 220*
      - *Ultra-deluxe:* Check into the **Broadmoor Hotel** and check out the meticulously preserved Roaring Twenties elegance. *page 209*

Budget: under $50 Moderate: $50–$90 Deluxe: $90–$130 Ultra-deluxe: over $130

four-acre grounds have an outdoor swimming pool, a hot tub, barbecue grills, a laundromat, a game room and a children's playground. A stream runs through the property, and there is easy access to hiking trails. ~ 123 Crystal Park Road, Manitou Springs; 719-685-5427. MODERATE.

Santa Fe–style architecture sets the recently refurbished **El Colorado Lodge** apart from other long-established Manitou Springs motels. Most of the 26 guest cabins have rough-hewn beam ceilings and fireplaces, and all have light, cheerful color schemes with earthtone accents. Eight have kitchenettes complete with dishes and utensils. The heated outdoor swimming pool is the largest one in town. ~ 23 Manitou Avenue, Manitou Springs; 719-685-5485, 800-782-2246. MODERATE.

Situated in the middle of the Manitou Springs Historic District, the **Two Sisters Inn** offers four guest rooms in a charming Victorian bungalow that was originally a boardinghouse for the town's schoolteachers, plus a separate "honeymoon cottage." The atmosphere here is light and airy, and fresh flowers are everywhere. Works by local artists are on exhibit in the lobby, and the parlor has a large fireplace and antique piano. Rates include a gourmet three-course breakfast, formally served with crystal and silver. ~ 10 Otoe Place, Manitou Springs; 719-685-9684. MODERATE TO DELUXE.

Built in 1871, the **Red Crags B&B** was a favorite vacation spot of President Theodore Roosevelt. The eight guest rooms, including five suites, which were renovated in 1991, feature Victorian-era antique decor. All have private baths and king-size European-style beds with down mattresses, and five have fireplaces. The private patio has a Pikes Peak view and a jacuzzi. The landscaping of the two-acre grounds includes a duck pond and herb gardens. Rates include a full breakfast. ~ 302 El Paso Boulevard, Manitou Springs; 719-685-1920, 800-721-2248, fax 719-685-1073. MODERATE TO ULTRA-DELUXE.

Setting the standard for luxury accommodations in Manitou Springs, the **Rockledge Country Inn** opened in 1997 in a historic 20-room Tudor-style mansion built in 1912 as the summer home of an oil tycoon. It's situated on three-and-a-half terraced, landscaped, gated acres. The spacious guest suites have feather beds and spectacular mountain views, and some have fireplaces. The main living room has an 1875 Steinway grand piano, and there is more room for lounging in the solarium and on the large, secluded patio. Typical of the full gourmet breakfasts served is a Rocky Mountain trout quiche served with fruit juice, new potatoes and fruit cobbler. Colorado wines and hors d'ouvres are served each evening. ~ 328 El Paso Boulevard, Manitou Springs; 719-685-4515, fax 719-685-1031. ULTRA-DELUXE.

For low-priced lodging with a touch of antique atmosphere, check out the **Buffalo Lodge**, on the boundary between Colorado Springs and Manitou Springs. The venerable old creekside lodge has 46 units ranging from small, threadbare motel rooms with dark and dreary wood paneling to contemporary, recently remodeled accommodations, plus a large, beautifully rustic lobby right out of a century past. ~ 2 El Paso Boulevard, Colorado Springs; 719-634-2851, 800-235-7416, fax 719-634-2851 ext. 101. MODERATE TO DELUXE.

For gay-friendly accommodations in the vicinity of Colorado Springs (a city that has gained a homophobic reputation in recent years), contact the **Pikes Peak Paradise B&B**. This six-bedroom inn on a dirt backroad in the ponderosa pine forest 25 minutes west of the city resembles a Southern mansion and offers a romantic atmosphere with plenty of privacy. Amenities include a sundeck, fireplaces and hot tubs in some rooms. A full breakfast is included. Clientele is half gay, half straight. ~ 236 Pinecrest Road, Woodland Park; 719-687-6656, fax 719-687-9008. DELUXE TO ULTRA-DELUXE.

The **Imperial Hotel** was Cripple Creek's most elegant hotel when it was built in 1896 at the peak of the gold boom. When the city was largely abandoned, the hotel kept its doors open by presenting authentic Victorian melodramas that have been imitated throughout the West. While the melodrama is still presented nightly for most of the year, the big draw these days is gambling. The Imperial's casino occupies drawing rooms on three floors of the hotel. Most of the 29 guest rooms and suites have been remodeled with original period oil paintings and antique or period furnishings; 11 have private baths. ~ 123 North 3rd Street, Cripple Creek; 719-689-7777, 800-235-2922, fax 719-689-1020. MODERATE.

In the heart of the historic mining district but several miles away from the gambling action, the **Victor Hotel** was built in 1892 as a bank with hotel rooms upstairs. Now entirely a hotel, it features original woodwork and furnishings in its lobby and 30 rooms with period furnishings. The original Otis birdcage elevator, the first elevator in the Cripple Creek district when it was installed in 1899, is still in use. ~ 4th Street at Victor Avenue, Victor; 719-689-3553, 800-748-0870, fax 719-689-3979. MODERATE TO DELUXE.

DINING

A long-standing favorite for fine dining in Manitou Springs is the **Craftwood Inn**, with its romantic ambience in a lovely 1912 Tudor-style home that was once a woodcrafter's studio and shop. The à la carte menu specializes in wild game—caribou, elk, pheasant, venison, quail, duck, rabbit, antelope and Colorado mountain bass—but also has some excellent vegetarian dishes, plus unique desserts such as jalapeño white-chocolate mousse and white chocolate ravioli. The owner is a connoisseur of wines, so the wine list contains some of the most expensive selections anywhere. ~ 404 El Paso Boulevard, Manitou Springs; 719-685-9000. DELUXE.

Fine dining is also offered at the **Briarhurst Manor**, serving contemporary international cuisine in a turn-of-the-century mansion that is one of Manitou Springs' historic showpieces. The ambience is lavish with polished hardwood, ceramic fireplaces and wall tapestries. House specialties include rack of Colorado lamb and clay-baked rainbow trout. Dinner only. ~ 404 Manitou Avenue, Manitou Springs; 719-685-1864. DELUXE.

Casual dining beside a shady creek is offered at the **Stagecoach Steak & Ale House**, housed in the building that was originally the stage stop for Manitou Springs in the 1870s. Rustic Victorian-era decor sets the stage for such fare as buffalo steaks, prime rib, rotisseried chicken, and an assortment of pastas and vegetarian entrées. Dinner only. ~ 702 Manitou Avenue, Manitou Springs; 719-685-9400. MODERATE.

International and vegetarian cuisine is the focus of the **Adams Mountain Café**. The restaurant–coffee shop maintains a friendly, casual atmosphere amid Victorian antique furnishings. Typical of the international no-meat offerings is orzo Mediterranean (orzo with broccoli, sun-dried tomatoes, onions, cucumbers, dill and garlic). White poultry and shrimp are also served. Desserts such as chocolate-hazelnut torte and a list of fine wines, beers and gourmet coffees round out the menu. ~ 110 Cañon Avenue, Manitou Springs; 719-685-1430. MODERATE.

Cripple Creek restaurants tend to be loud little places installed as afterthoughts in the back corners of casinos, where slot ma-

---

✔ **CHECK THESE OUT—UNIQUE DINING**

- *Budget:* Take a spoonful of world-famous chili at **Zeke's**, whose doors open at 3:30 a.m. to serve breakfast to gold miners on the way to work. *page 223*
- *Moderate:* Relish the international dishes—sans meat—at **Adams Mountain Café**, a casual Victorian restaurant that serves the region's best vegetarian food. *page 222*
- *Deluxe:* Book a table for two at the **Mountain View Dining Room**, where a mountainside location and a gourmet buffet add up to a great spot for a romantic dinner. *page 211*
- *Ultra-deluxe:* Feast on caviar and elk steaks with a lakefront view at the Broadmoor Hotel's elegant **Charles Court**. *page 210*

Budget: under $8   Moderate: $8–$16   Deluxe: $16–$24   Ultra-deluxe: over $24

chines make for a more profitable use of floor space than dining tables. Food at least gets equal billing with games of chance at the **Old Chicago Casino**, a location of the Old Chicago Pizza chain found up and down the Front Range. The Old Chicago has been designed to accommodate diners and slot machines in the same space—with the result that bus-tour groups tend to descend on it at conventional lunch hours. The best deal in town is the all-you-can-eat pizza, soup, appetizer and salad bar. ~ 419 East Bennett Avenue, Cripple Creek; 719-689-7880. BUDGET.

The old-fashioned dining room in the **Imperial Hotel** has been in operation for a full century, ever since the gold mining era, and continues to serve prime rib and continental entrées in an atmosphere of Victorian elegance, oblivious to the clatter of slot machines elsewhere in the hotel. The Imperial also offers hearty sandwiches in its Red Rooster bar. ~ 123 North 3rd Street, Cripple Creek; 719-689-7777. MODERATE.

Zeke's is the oldest continuously operating business in the Cripple Creek district; the owners' ancestors started their first restaurant in Victor in 1888, even before the start of the gold boom, and moved to the present location in 1899. The walls are of old red bricks and the tables, each different, are wooden and old. It still opens at 3:30 a.m. to serve breakfast to gold miners on their way to work, and serves breakfast, lunch and dinner all day; miners also come here to drink after work, keeping the doors open until 2 a.m. The menu ranges from hamburgers and hot dogs to full meals such as pork steak with mashed potatoes and mixed vegetables. The chili is said to be world famous—that is, Lowell Thomas once praised it in a newspaper column. ~ 108 South 3rd Street, Victor; 719-689-2109. BUDGET.

SHOPPING

The region supports a fair number of artists and craftspeople, found in highest concentration in Manitou Springs, adjoining the western city limit of Colorado Springs along Manitou Avenue (Business Route 24). You can see a representative sampling of local arts and crafts at the **Commonwheel Artists Co-op**, one of the region's longest-established co-op galleries. ~ 102 Cañon Avenue, Manitou Springs; 719-685-1008. The newer **Business of Art Center** houses galleries, shops and studios featuring local artists' works in all media. ~ 513 Manitou Avenue, Manitou Springs; 719-685-1861.

NIGHTLIFE

In summer, the top nighttime tourist attraction in the Colorado Springs area is **Laser Canyon**. You may have seen laser light shows before; you may even have seen better ones—this program seems a bit "dumbed down" for mass appeal with an uncomfortable mix of educational lecture, flag-waving old-time pop songs and a too-brief taste of hard rock—but this is probably the only place where you'll see computer-animated laser imaging projected onto an 800-foot-high limestone canyon wall. Spectacular. Admission. ~ Cave of the Winds, Manitou Springs; fax 719-634-2887.

On the other side of Pikes Peak, Cripple Creek is one of the three historic mining towns where casino gambling ($5-per-bet limit) is legal. All of its 25 gambling casinos are located along three blocks of Bennett Avenue. The reigning queen is the relatively classy **Midnight Rose**, with six blackjack tables, four poker tables and 325 video poker and slot machines. ~ 256 East Bennett Avenue, Cripple Creek; 719-689-0303. **Bronco Billy's Sports Bar & Casino** features not only blackjack tables and slot machines but also a sports bar with 45 TV sets and a 70-inch big-screen showing sporting events nonstop. ~ 233 East Bennett Avenue, Cripple Creek; 719-689-2142. **Womack's Casino** is the only casino in town that features off-track betting. ~ 200 East Bennett Avenue, Cripple Creek; 719-689-3242. The flashy **Aspen Mine & Casino** offers a touch of Las Vegas gimmickry with its naturelike decor, which features artificial trees and rocks, a trout pond and a replica gold slough. ~ 166 East Bennett Avenue, Cripple Creek; 719-689-0770.

For gaming in an authentic Victorian setting, you can't beat the casino in the **Imperial Hotel** where blackjack tables and banks of slot machines are scattered through a number of intimate parlor rooms. It is traditional to have a drink in each of the Imperial's five turn-of-the-century-style bars. One might suspect that this tradition originated with the hotel's management in the early days of tourism, since the 9500-foot altitude doubles the potency of alcoholic beverages and makes driving back to Colorado Springs both hazardous and illegal. The hotel, a century-old Cripple Creek classic, also features the **Imperial Melodrama**, a dinner theater that has been presenting authentic productions of Victorian-era plays for more than 35 years; call 800-235-2922 for reservations. ~ 123 North 3rd Street, Cripple Creek; 719-689-2922.

PARKS

PIKE NATIONAL FOREST 🏃 🚲 🛶 🏕 ⚓ This forest, which includes all of Pikes Peak as well as the Rampart Range between Colorado Springs and Denver, encompasses more than a million acres of pine, aspen and fir forests and alpine tundra. More visitors use it for recreation than any other national forest in Colorado. In the winter, the U.S. Forest Service operates a small downhill ski area beside the Pikes Peak Highway; cross-country skiing is also popular on trails near Colorado Springs. You may fish for rainbow trout in Rampart Reservoir. Facilities include picnic areas, restrooms, jeep and bike trails and a ski area. ~ Primary access to Pike National Forest is via the Pikes Peak Highway, the Gold Camp Road between Colorado Springs and Cripple Creek, and the Rampart Range Road between Colorado Springs and Sedalia. The

Crags Campground is two and a half miles in on Forest Road 383, four miles south of Divide off of Route 67; 719-636-1602.

▲ Camping opportunities are limited on Pikes Peak itself. On the west side of the peak along the route to Cripple Creek, the Crags Campground has 17 RV/tent sites (no hookups); closed November to mid-May; $8 per night. Other national forest campgrounds are located along the Rampart Range Road north of Woodland Park. Official campgrounds along the Gold Camp Road have been closed, but there are several spots suitable for informal RV camping and hike-in tent camping along this route.

MUELLER STATE PARK AND WILDLIFE AREA 🚶 ⏤ This 12,000-acre mountain park provides camping in the vicinity of Cripple Creek. It also has an 80-mile network of hiking trails through a variety of habitats ranging from aspen and conifer forests to spectacular rock formations and open meadows ablaze with wildflowers. Abundant wildlife includes deer, elk, wild turkeys, bears and bighorn sheep. Fishing is good for rainbow trout in Fourmile Creek. There are picnic areas, restrooms and showers. Day-use fee, $4. ~ Located three and a half miles west of Divide off Route 67; 719-687-2366.

▲ There are 22 walk-in tent sites, $7 per night; and 110 RV/tent sites with electrical hookups, $10 per night.

Cañon City Area

Cañon City, a quiet ranching town on the Arkansas River, is named for the geological wonder that has become its claim to fame and fortune. The Royal Gorge is owned by the municipal government, and visitor admission fees have provided the town's main source of revenue since 1929. Despite hundreds of thousands of visitors each year, Cañon City has retained so much of its old-fashioned, small-town character that as you wander along the downtown sidewalks you may feel as if you'd stumbled into a Norman Rockwell painting.

SIGHTS

It is possible to make a loop tour and see the Cripple Creek district and the Royal Gorge in the same day by taking the steep, narrow, unpaved and spectacularly scenic road that starts near Victor and winds between the reddish granite walls of **Phantom Canyon** to reach Route 50 at Florence, a few miles east of Cañon City. The 35-mile drive takes about two and a half hours. Like the Gold Camp Road, the Phantom Canyon Road was originally a narrow-gauge railroad route. In their haste to build the first railroad to the Cripple Creek district in 1893, the engineers cut a few corners, and on the second Florence-to-Cripple Creek run the train tumbled off a trestle into the canyon. By the time the tracks were reopened, the Midland Railroad route from Colorado Springs had won the race to the goldfields.

The **Royal Gorge** is one of the deepest canyons in Colorado, 1053 feet from the rim to the Arkansas River at the bottom. Visitors can descend to river level on an incline railway or glide across the gorge on an aerial tramway. The canyon's main attraction, however, is the world's highest suspension bridge, built in 1929. Clatter across it by car or simply walk out to the middle for a swaying, dizzying view of the gorge. The scrub oak–covered parkland surrounding the canyon rim is home to many tourist-friendly mule deer. Admission. ~ 719-275-7507.

Just outside the Royal Gorge entrance gate is **Buckskin Joe**, a movie-set town of pioneer buildings collected from around the state and placed below the stunning backdrop of the Sangre de Cristo Range. Some of the buildings came from a real town called Buckskin Joe, 80 miles to the northwest near present-day Alma. When not in use as a film location, Buckskin Joe does a roaring business as a stagecoaches-and-shootouts tourist theme park. Admission. ~ County Road 3A; 719-275-5149.

Motorists who enjoy mountain driving should not miss **Skyline Drive**, a three-mile scenic detour on the way back from Royal Gorge to Cañon City. Built in 1915 by an automobile club to prove the feasibility of asphalt highways, it was the first paved road west of the Mississippi. The narrow one-way road runs above the town along the top of a hogback ridge with 800-foot drop-offs on both sides.

The **Colorado Territorial Prison Museum** was in use as a state maximum-security facility until the late 1970s, when the Colorado Supreme Court ruled that to confine prisoners there was "cruel and unusual punishment." Since then, the old stone prison has been opened to the public, providing a close-up look at the section where women prisoners were held and an antique electric chair that was used for more than 100 executions. Open daily in summer, Friday through Sunday off-season. Admission. ~ 201 North 1st Street, Cañon City; 719-269-3015.

In town, the **Cañon City Municipal Museum** has a log cabin and a settler's stone house from the 1880s, as well as a mixed bag of Indian artifacts, fossils, guns, antiques and big-game hunters' trophies. Closed Sunday and Monday in winter. Admission. ~ 612 Royal Gorge Boulevard, Cañon City; 719-269-9018.

To reach Route 25 from Cañon City, take Route 50 east for 39 miles to Pueblo.

LODGING   Cañon City has little to offer in the way of lodging, since most travelers visit on day trips from the Colorado Springs area. One good place to spend the night is the modern **Cañon Inn**. Located six miles from Royal Gorge, this motor inn has 152 contemporary, oversized rooms with all standard amenities. Facilities include six indoor hot tubs and an outdoor heated swimming pool. ~ Route

50 at Dozier Street, Cañon City; 719-275-8676, fax 719-275-8675. MODERATE.

The **Lemon Drop Inn** is a small bed and breakfast in an older home in Cañon City's downtown area. It has a large, shaded yard, a sun porch and covered patio, and a large central living room. The three guest rooms are individually decorated with antiques; the most unusual of the three is strewn with turn-of-the-century children's toys. Rates include a continental breakfast of seasonal fruits and home-baked muffins and breads. ~ 1131 Harrison Avenue, Cañon City; 719-269-8387. MODERATE.

A daydream on Elm Street, the **Deweese Lodge**, dates back to 1896 and features four guest rooms with shared baths in the main house, as well as a suitelike guest house. The lodge has a large veranda furnished with rocking chairs, ideal for watching the world go by on lazy afternoons. Rates include breakfast. ~ 1226 Elm Street, Cañon City; 719-269-1881. MODERATE.

In Cañon City, fine dining is found at **Merlino's Belvedere**, operated by an Italian family of long-time residents. The emphasis is on Italian food—veal parmesan, fettuccine—but the menu also includes salmon, shrimp, trout, prime rib, filet mignon and great desserts (try the "chocolate suicide cake"). ~ 1330 Elm Avenue, Cañon City; 719-275-5558. MODERATE TO DELUXE.

DINING

Ortega's is a longtime favorite out of the many family-owned Mexican restaurants in the Cañon City area. The atmosphere is Southwestern and modest, and the specialty of the house is *chile rellenos*. They also serve standard Mexican combination plates and New Mexican–style dishes, as well as imported beer and margaritas. Closed Monday and Tuesday. ~ 2301 East Main Street, Cañon City; 719-275-9437. BUDGET.

North of Penrose, the **Juniper Valley Ranch Dining Room** has been serving the same menu since it opened in 1951, and it continues to be so popular that you'll want to phone ahead for reservations. Dinner specialties include skillet fried chicken and baked ham, served family-style in a rustic ranch house setting. The dinner prices include beverages and homemade desserts. Closed December through April. ~ Route 115, 15 miles north of Penrose; 719-576-0741. MODERATE.

As is true in most of Colorado's older tourist areas, Cañon City has more than its share of rock shops where you can buy crystals, geodes, arrowheads, turquoise, gold ore and other geological curiosities. One of the best, located in front of Buckskin Joe on the way to Royal Gorge, is **The Mother Lode**, which has mineral specimens from around the world, rock carvings and gemstone jewelry, as well as clothing, beadwork, drums and other items made by Lakota Sioux craftspeople. Closed Wednesday. ~ Royal Gorge Road, Cañon City; 719-269-1460.

SHOPPING

The carriage house of a turn-of-the-century mansion now serves as a mall where dealers sell antiques, local handmade quilts and a quilting supply shop at the **Carriage House Antique Emporium.** Closed Monday. ~ 840 South 1st Street, Cañon City; 719-269-9428.

In the neighboring town of Florence, you'll find 25 antique dealers under one roof at **Oil City Merchants Antique Shoppes.** Among the wares featured are hardwood furniture, 1920s lighting, glassware and art glass, pottery, cowboy tools and Victoriana. ~ 126 West Main Street, Florence; 719-784-6582.

PARKS

SAN ISABEL NATIONAL FOREST 🏃 🛶 This long, narrow strip of national forest contains the eastern slope of the Sangre de Cristo Range southwest of Cañon City as well as the Wet Mountains to the south. Much of the forest is hard to reach because the Sangre de Cristos are so steep that not even jeep trails climb them. The Sangre de Cristo Wilderness, reaching from the north end of the range near the town of Salida as far south as the Great Sand Dunes, encompasses 226,000 acres. It was the largest of the wilderness areas created by the 1993 Wilderness Act. There are hiking trails and a ski area. ~ The easiest access to the Sangre de Cristo portion of San Isabel National Forest is via several unpaved roads that run west from the town of Westcliffe into the mountains. To get to Westcliffe, take Route 50 west to Route 69 south. To reach Alvarado Campground from Westcliffe, continue south on Route 69 for three miles, then head west on County Road 140 for five miles. Wet Mountain access is via Route 165; 719-269-8500.

▲ Among the few forest service campgrounds in the area is Alvarado Campground, with 30 RV-only sites and 17 RV/tent sites (no hookups); open late May to mid-September; $8 per night.

▼▼▼▼▼▼▼▼▼▼▼▼
South Park Area

South Park is a sparsely populated basin of high ranchlands between Pikes Peak and the Collegiate Peaks. Despite its windswept emptiness, South Park is where three key highways converge, an important crossroads for motorists touring Colorado. From Buena Vista, Route 24 heads east toward Cripple Creek and Colorado Springs and north toward Leadville and Breckenridge, while Route 285 goes north to Fairplay and, eventually, Denver, or south to Salida. From Salida, Route 50 follows the Arkansas River east down a long canyon to Cañon City and Pueblo, and west over Monarch Pass to Gunnison, while Route 285 continues south across the San Luis Valley.

SIGHTS

Salida, at the south end of South Park, is an older town that has recently broken the tourism barrier to become the most popular travelers' destination in the area. The main industry in this unpre-

tentious little Victorian-era town is whitewater rafting on the Arkansas River, with dozens of local outfitters running river trips through Browns Canyon and downriver ◆◆◆◆◆◆◆◆◆◆◆◆◆◆◆◆◆◆◆◆◆◆◆◆◆◆◆◆◆◆◆◆◆
toward the Royal Gorge and Cañon City. Skiing at nearby Monarch Ski Area also contributes to the town's rising popularity. The four-block-long historic district, consisting of red brick two-story buildings with Victorian-era stone ornamentation, takes visitors back to an earlier time. The small, free **Salida Museum**, located next to the visitor information center at the main highway turnoff, contains displays on the town's early history, including mining equipment and ranching gear. Closed in winter. ~ Route 50 and I Street, Salida; 719-539-4602.

The Collegiate Peaks are named for the Ivy League schools for good reason: their mountaineering teams were the first to reach the summits in the early years of the 20th century.

The **Salida Hot Springs Pool** uses geothermal water piped from springs five miles away in the high mountains to heat a municipal swimming pool that is claimed to be the largest spring-fed pool in the state. There are also six individual European-style hot baths and a 100-degree therapeutic soaking pool. The main pool is also used for kayak instruction. Admission. ~ 410 West Rainbow Boulevard, Salida; 719-539-6738.

To the north of Salida is **Buena Vista**, ranch center for South Park and home of the Colorado State Reformatory. The town may not look like much, but its setting, where the high plains of South Park meet the solid wall of the **Collegiate Peaks**, defies comparison. Colorado's greatest concentration of 14,000-foot peaks stands in a row just west of Buena Vista: Mount Oxford (14,153 feet), Mount Harvard (14,420 feet), Mount Columbia (14,075 feet), Mount Yale (14,196 feet) and Mount Princeton (14,197 feet). In the southernmost part of the Collegiate range is **Mount Princeton Hot Springs**, where geothermal swimming pools are open to the public. Admission. ~ 15870 County Road 162, Nathrop; 719-395-2447.

Continuing north on Route 285, Fairplay is the site of **South Park City**, an open-air museum that gives visitors glimpses into the details of everyday life during the gold-rush era. More than 30 buildings have been moved here from abandoned mining towns in the area and filled with antiques and artifacts of the time to create the quintessential Colorado ghost town. Among the historic structures are miners' cabins, a bank, a general store, a stagecoach station and a brewery. This is not one of those movie-set/tourist-trap assemblages of old western buildings; it's well worth visiting for the powerful sense of the past it evokes. Closed mid-October to mid-May. Admission. ~ Fairplay; 719-836-2387.

North of Fairplay at the tiny town of Alma, take unpaved County Road 8 and then Forest Road 415 for a total distance of

HIDDEN ▶   about six miles to the **Bristlecone Pine Scenic Area**, one of several alpine areas in Colorado where these stunted, slow-growing trees are twisted by the wind into fantastic and grotesque shapes. The trees are some of the oldest living organisms on earth. Some have been determined to be almost 5000 years old—twice as old as California's giant redwoods.

HIDDEN ▶   A favorite jeep route in the South Park region, **Mosquito Pass Road** lumbers from Alma over a 13,188-foot pass, then descends into Leadville (see Chapter Four). The first seven miles of the road, past the remains of old mines and the ghost town of Park City, are usually fine for passenger cars; the last three miles to the pass summit are steep and rocky and can be negotiated only by high-clearance, four-wheel-drive vehicles.

LODGING   Salida's historic district has recently sprouted an impressive number of bed and breakfasts. Noteworthy among them is the **Gazebo Country Inn**, a 1901 Victorian home built for a prominent Salida merchant during the railroad era. Set in a quiet residential neighborhood of shade trees and white picket fences, the two-story inn has flower gardens and a redwood deck with views of the surrounding 14,000-foot mountains. The three guest rooms are accented with floral prints and down comforters. Rates include a full breakfast. ~ 507 East Third Street, Salida; 719-539-7806, 800-565-7806.

The **River Run Inn**, situated on the bank of the Arkansas River, once served as the county poor farm, where, for more than 50 years, indigents were sent to work for room and board. Today, it has been refurbished in light, contemporary style as a combination hostel–bed-and-breakfast inn, with a 13-bed dormitory on the top floor and seven individual guest rooms—some with shared baths, others private. The countryside location offers trout fishing and great mountain views. ~ 8495 County Road 160, Salida; 719-539-3818, 800-385-6925, fax 719-539-3818. BUDGET TO MODERATE.

HIDDEN ▶   Nestled among the evergreens at the foot of the dramatic Chalk Cliffs, **Mount Princeton Hot Springs Resort** has been the site of one hotel after another since 1870. In the 1920s a magnificent four-story hotel that then stood at the springs was one of the most elegant hot-spring spas in the West. Today, a modern lodge and adjacent motel offer pleasant, spacious accommodations, a dining room and a spacious sun deck. Four of the largest among many hot springs in the vicinity feed the resort's three outdoor swimming pools and two private hot tubs. Undeveloped hot springs that line the creek and hillsides nearby include Hortense Spring, the hottest hot spring in Colorado—a scalding 183°F. To find this secluded resort, drive eight miles south from Buena Vista on Route 285 to Nathrop and turn west on the well-marked county road; the resort is five miles up the road. ~ 15870 County Road 162, Nath-rop; 719-395-2447, fax 719-395-6249. MODERATE.

Open only during the summer months, the **Trout City Inn** is located on 9346-foot Trout Creek Pass eight miles east of Buena Vista. A century-old narrow-gauge train station and two old-time railroad cars have been refurbished to create four guest accommodations so authentically decorated in elegant Victorian fashion and in such a remote location that they're the next-best thing to a time machine. A full breakfast is included in the rates. ~ Route 24/285, Buena Vista; 719-395-8433. MODERATE.

In Salida, try **Country Bounty** for huge portions of home cookin'. This family-style restaurant features a long and varied menu that ranges from fresh-caught Arkansas River trout, homemade soups and Mexican combination plates to specialties such as almond chicken Shanghai in a sesame-ginger sauce. The ambience is more like a gift shop than a restaurant, with country crafts, Indian jewelry and curios—all with price tags—wherever you look. ~ 413 West Rainbow Boulevard, Salida; 719-539-3546. BUDGET TO MODERATE.

DINING

The **Laughing Ladies Café** offers intriguing international specialties, as well as vegetarian entrées, thick steaks with butter-garlic sauce, fresh bakery goods, and brew-pub beers. The atmosphere is Victorian and friendly. ~ 128 West 1st Street, Salida; 719-539-6209. BUDGET TO MODERATE.

Near the main highway, away from the historic district, the family-style **Windmill Restaurant** offers a selection ranging from fajitas and Tex-Mex taco salads to steak and seafood, as well as an all-you-can-eat soup and salad bar. The main attraction here is the decor, featuring an extensive collection of old-time advertising memorabilia. ~ 720 East Route 50, Salida; 719-539-3594. BUDGET.

The restaurant choice elsewhere in South Park is more limited but far from hopeless. The hands-down favorite in Buena Vista is **Casa Del Sol**, an outstanding Mexican restaurant that features dishes made from regional recipes collected throughout Mexico, from seafood quesadillas to *enchiladas suizas* and *pollo en mole*. Mexican guitar music, kachina and chile ristra decor and summer outdoor dining add spice to the homey atmosphere. ~ 303 Route 24, Buena Vista; 719-395-8810. MODERATE.

ARKANSAS HEADWATERS RECREATION AREA

PARKS

Established through a unique partnership between the federal Bureau of Land Management and the Colorado state parks, this recreation area spans the first 148 miles of the Arkansas River, from its origin just below Leadville's Turquoise Lake to Pueblo Reservoir. Highways trace the entire length of the river, just above the bank in some places and miles away in others, making this one of the most popular rivers in the West for recreational use. More commercial rafting outfitters use it than any other stretch of river in the United States, and on weekends in June and July, when the flow is highest, hundreds of private canoes and kayaks also shoot its challenging rapids. The most remote part of the river, Browns Canyon, is home to many wildlife species, including mule deer, mountain lions, bobcats and peregrine falcons. The section of the river below Salida, from Wellsville to Parkdale, is bighorn sheep habitat. There are picnic areas and restrooms. Day-use fee, $2. ~ Route 25 follows the river from Leadville to Buena Vista, Route 285 from Buena Vista to Salida, and Route 50 from Salida to Pueblo. Access to the remote Browns Canyon area is via the three-mile unpaved Hecla Junction Road, which leaves Route 285 midway between Buena Vista and Salida; 719-539-7289.

> Fishermen rate flyfishing on the Arkansas as the world's best for brown trout.

▲ There are a total of 100 RV/tent sites (no hookups) in four campgrounds—Ruby Mountain and Hecla Junction upriver from Salida, Rincon downriver from Salida and Five Points above Cañon City and Railroad Bridge; $7 per night.

PIKE NATIONAL FOREST 🏃 ⤵ Much of the east half of South Park is part of Pike National Forest. The 15,000-acre wilderness area includes scenic Elevenmile Canyon and the roadless Lost Creek Wilderness, an area of rugged terrain with spectacular sandstone and granite formations and abundant wildlife. Fishing is available for northern pike in Tarryall Reservoir. Day-use fee, $3. There are jeep trails here. ~ Trailheads for the Lost Creek Wilderness can be reached on County Road 77, which runs between Route 24 north of Buena Vista and Route 285 at Jefferson, passing small Tarryall Reservoir on the way. Elevenmile Canyon Road runs from Route 24 at Lake George to Elevenmile Reservoir—a distance of 11 miles; 719-836-2031.

▲ There are seven forest service campgrounds along Elevenmile Canyon Road. Among them are Spruce Grove Campground, with 20 RV/tent sites (no hookups) and 8 tent-only sites; and Blue Mountain Campground, with 20 RV/tent sites (no hookups) and one tent-only site. Both are open April through October; $9 per night.

SAN ISABEL NATIONAL FOREST 🏃 🏇 ⤵ The vast Collegiate Peaks Wilderness, which covers 159,000 acres west of Buena Vista, is divided equally between Pike and San Isabel national forests. This forest also includes large expanses of pine woods east of Buena Vista and Salida. You may fish for rainbow trout in Chalk Creek, Cottonwood Creek, Browns Creek and other area streams. There are picnic areas, restrooms and jeep trails. ~ The main access to this part of the national forest is on Chalk Creek Road (Forest Road 211), which leaves Route 285 at Nathrop and passes Mount Princeton Hot Springs. All public campgrounds in the area are along this road; 719-539-3591.

▲ There are four national forest campgrounds along Chalk Creek at the base of Mount Princeton, including Cascade Campground, with 23 RV/tent sites; and Mount Princeton Campground, with 17 RV/tent sites. Both are open mid-May to mid-September and cost $8 per night.

▼▼▼▼▼▼▼▼▼▼▼▼▼▼▼

Outdoor Adventures

FISHING

The upper **Arkansas River** is a favorite fishing area. It's particularly known for brown trout, and rainbow, cutthroat and brook trout are abundant in many of the river's tributary streams. **Cottonwood Lake**, off Cottonwood Pass Road west of Buena Vista, is legendary for big rainbow trout. Tarryall Reservoir is stocked with northern pike. Fishing tackle is sold in Salida at **Homestead Sports Center**, which is also a good source of information on fishing spots and guides. ~ 228 North F Street, Salida; 719-539-3529.

RIVER RUNNING

The Salida area, on the southern edge of South Park near the headwaters of the Arkansas River, is one of the top whitewater rafting areas in Colorado. Nearly 100 tour operators operate there, including **Rocky Mountain Tours**. ~ 12847 South Route 24/285, Buena Vista; 719-395-4101. Also contact **Dvorak Kayaking & Rafting Expeditions** for rafting information. ~ 17921 Route 285, Nathrop; 719-539-6851. Trips are also available though **Canyon Marine**. ~ 129 West Rainbow Boulevard, Salida; 719-539-7476. You may also try **Moondance River Expeditions, Ltd.** in Salida. ~ 310 West 1st Street, Salida; 719-539-2113. Rafting companies operating from the Cañon City area include **Arkansas River Outfitters**. ~ 719-275-3229. There's also **Brown's Royal Gorge Rafting Tours**. ~ 719-275-5161. You can contact **Royal Gorge River Adventures** for more rafting information. ~ 719-269-3700. **Sierra Outfitters** also offers tours in this area. ~ 719-275-0128.

SKIING

PIKES PEAK AREA The Forest Service operates a small ski hill with a T-bar lift, open only when natural snowfall permits, about eight miles up the Pikes Peak Highway. For real downhill skiing, the closest ski areas are at Breckenridge, 150 miles away (see Chapter Four), and Monarch, 120 miles away (see Chapter Seven).

The best cross-country skiing is found at **The Crags** and **Mueller State Park**, both off Route 68 on the west side of Pikes Peak en route to Cripple Creek.

Ski Rentals In Colorado Springs, cross-country skis, telemarking skis and snowshoes are available at **Mountain Chalet**. ~ 226 North Tejon Street; 719-633-0732.

ICE SKATING

Colorado Springs has a downtown skating rink under an atrium at the **Plaza Ice Chalet**. ~ 111 South Tejon Street; 719-633-2423. **The Broadmoor Ice Arena** is open to the public for limited hours; this is where many Olympic gold-medal winners, such as Peggy Fleming, trained under Broadmoor Hotel sponsorship. ~ Broadmoor Hotel, Colorado Springs; 719-634-7711.

GOLF

COLORADO SPRINGS AREA   Public courses in Colorado Springs include the 18-hole **Patty Jewett Golf Course**, a municipal course with cart and club rentals and a close-in location. ~ 900 East Española Street; 719-578-6825. The 18-hole **Pine Creek Golf Club** boasts generous fairway landing areas, subtly breaking greens, dramatic elevation changes, bunkers, trees, creeks and lakes. ~ 9850 Divot Trail; 719-594-9999. There's also the 18-hole **Valley Hi Municipal Golf Course**. ~ 610 South Chelton Road; 719-578-6351.

CAÑON CITY AREA   In Cañon City, the nine-hole **Shadow Hills Country Club Golf Course** is open to the public on weekdays, but is members-only until 3 p.m. on weekends. ~ 1232 County Road 143; 719-275-0603.

SOUTH PARK AREA   **Collegiate Peaks Golf Course** has a nine-hole course with cart and club rentals. ~ 28775 Fairway Drive, Buena Vista; 719-395-8189. There's also a nine-hole course at **Salida Golf Club**. ~ Crestone and Grant streets, Salida; 719-539-6373.

TENNIS

Colorado Springs has four public tennis courts at **Monument Valley Park**. ~ Monument Creek; 719-578-6636. There are also four courts at **Bear Creek Regional Park**. ~ 21st and Argus streets. Four more public courts are located at **Memorial Park**. ~ East Pikes Peak Avenue at Hancock Street; 719-578-6676. All are first-come, first-served, and are lighted for night play.

RIDING STABLES & LLAMA TREKS

COLORADO SPRINGS AREA   Horses for riding in the Garden of the Gods may be rented at **Academy Riding Stables**, which also offers easy one- and two-hour guided trips, often with 50 or more riders. ~ 4 El Paso Boulevard, Colorado Springs; 719-633-5667.

CAÑON CITY AREA   Near Cañon City, public stables are located on **Indian Springs Ranch**, which offers rentals and organized group trips. ~ Indian Springs; 719-372-3907.

SOUTH PARK AREA   Horse rentals and guided hour-long to all-day trail rides on forested mountain slopes are available at **Mount Princeton Riding Stable**, located three miles west of Nathrop. ~ Nathrop; 719-395-2361. Overnight llama treks are offered by **Spruce Ridge Llama Treks**. ~ 4141 County Road 210, Salida; 719-539-4182.

PIKES PEAK AREA Several multiple-use trails off **Gold Camp** **BIKING**
Road above the junction with North Cheyenne Canyon Road are
popular for mountain biking. A great area for dirt-road bike touring is the **Rampart Range Road** between the Garden of the Gods
and the mountain town of Woodland Park. West of Cañon City,
the three-mile **Tunnel Drive**, which leads to an overlook near
Royal Gorge, has been closed to motor vehicles and is now a popular bike route.

SOUTH PARK AREA In the Fairplay area, mountain bikers use
the 35 miles of marked trails in the **Fairplay State Snowmobile**
Trail System, two and a half miles north of town on Forest Road
659. Around Salida, popular rides include **Bighorn Sheep Canyon**,
which starts in downtown Salida and follows the Arkansas River
for 12 miles to Coaldale.

Bike Rentals In Colorado Springs, mountain bikes are for rent
at **Criterium Bike Shop**. ~ 6510 Corporate Drive; 719-599-0149.
Team Telecycle also has mountain bikes. ~ 615 South Baldwin
Street, Woodland Park; 719-687-6165. **Headwaters Outdoor**
Equipment rents front-suspension mountain bikes in Salida. ~ 228
North F Street; 719-539-4506.

All distances listed for hiking trails are one way unless otherwise **HIKING**
noted.

COLORADO SPRINGS AREA On the southwestern edge of Colorado Springs, North Cheyenne Canyon has several outstanding,
easy-to-reach hiking trails. The **Mount Cutler Trail** (1.75 miles)
climbs 500 feet from the middle part of the canyon up to the
ridge between North and South Cheyenne canyons for a view of
Seven Falls. The **Columbine Trail** (5 miles) runs the length of the
North Cheyenne Canyon from its lower end all the way to Helen
Hunt Falls.

✔ **CHECK THESE OUT—UNIQUE OUTDOOR ADVENTURES**

- Experience a wet and wild whitewater trip down the Arkansas River
  and discover why more people go rafting here than on any other river
  in America. *page 233*
- Hike among the mountain sheep that often greet climbers on the
  Barr Trail from Manitou Springs to Pikes Peak's summit. *page 236*
- Ice skate where Peggy Fleming and other Olympic champions
  trained, at the Broadmoor Ice Arena in Colorado Springs. *page 234*
- Ride a mountain bike (motor vehicles are banned) on Tunnel
  Drive near Cañon City for a rarely seen view of Royal Gorge.
  page 235

PIKES PEAK AREA   The ultimate Colorado Springs–area hike is the **Barr Trail** (17 miles) from Manitou Springs to the summit of Pikes Peak. The first three miles of the trail, from the Pikes Peak Cog Railway parking lot on Ruxton Avenue to the top of Mount Manitou, is the steepest portion. From there it's an easy ridgeline walk to Barr Camp at timberline on the east face of Pikes Peak. The last few miles of switchbacks, up rocky alpine slopes, are difficult not so much because the trail is steep but because the air is thin. There is also a short trail up Pikes Peak from The Crags, a National Forest campground on a marked dirt road off Route 67 on the west face of the peak near Cripple Creek.

Near Cripple Creek, Mueller State Park has a 85-mile network of hiking trails, ranging from the easy, spectacular **Outlook Ridge Trail** (2 miles) to the long, strenuous **Four Mile Overlook Trail** (9 miles), which commands dramatic views of remote Four Mile Canyon.

SOUTH PARK AREA   In the Collegiate Peaks, a longer and more challenging ascent that requires no special equipment is the 8.5-mile trail that goes to the summit of **Mount Harvard** (14,420 feet). The upper portion of the climb follows the Colorado Trail, which runs 420 miles from Denver to Durango.

Another popular hiking route, the **Browns Pass Trail** starts from the Denny Creek Trailhead 12 miles west of Buena Vista and climbs four miles to a pass on the Continental Divide, then descends for half a mile to a century-old prospector's cabin.

▼▼▼▼▼▼▼▼▼▼▼▼
Transportation

CAR

Colorado Springs is 70 miles south of Denver on **Route 25**. From Colorado Springs, **Route 24** heads west toward South Park, with turnoffs to Pikes Peak and Cripple Creek. **Route 115** goes south from Colorado Springs to the Cañon City area.

AIR

Colorado Springs Airport is served by America West, American Airlines, Continental Airlines, Delta Airlines, Mesa Airlines and Trans World Airlines. Built about the same time, the Colorado Springs Airport has been competing aggressively with the problem-ridden Denver International Airport for airline hub routes; as a result, airfares are often significantly lower if you fly into Colorado Springs instead of Denver. **Airport Shuttle Service** shuttles airline passengers to and from major hotels. ~ 719-578-5232. **Colorado Springs Transit** provides low-cost bus service to and from the airport. ~ 719-475-9733.

BUS

TNM&O Coaches, a Greyhound affiliate, provides service to Colorado Springs. ~ 120 South Weber Street; 719-635-1505.

Among the many car-rental agencies at or near the Colorado Springs airport are **A-Courtesy Rent A Car** (800-441-1816), **Alamo Rent A Car** (800-327-9633), **Avis Rent A Car** (800-331-1212), **Budget Rent A Car** (800-527-0700), **Dollar Rent A Car** (800-800-4000), **Enterprise Rent A Car** (800-325-8007), **Hertz Rent A Car** (800-654-3131) and **National Interrent** (800-328-4567).

CAR RENTALS

Colorado Springs municipal buses are operated by **Colorado Springs Transit.** ~ 719-475-9733.

PUBLIC TRANSIT

Yellow Cab is the local taxi company in Colorado Springs. ~ 719-634-5000.

TAXIS

SEVEN

South Central Colorado

Colorado changes character south of the Arkansas River. The slender green valleys of the north give way to turquoise-gray sagebrush desert. Spring sandstorms whip across the arid flats and wash against the steep slopes of the Sangre de Cristo Range like typhoon waves on a rocky shore, piling dunes to heights unknown elsewhere in America. Forbidding and fascinating, this strange landscape speaks of the awesome scope and power of nature wherever you look. At the heart of the region, the San Luis Valley is the oldest, poorest, driest, coldest part of the state—a perfect place to search for "Hidden Colorado."

The towns are different, too. Other than Pueblo, there is no community in south central Colorado that could be characterized as a city. Alamosa, the largest town after Pueblo, has a population of less than 8000. The names of most towns, as well as rivers, mountains and other landmarks, are Spanish, the language still spoken by about half the people who live in the region. Their forefathers arrived in neighboring New Mexico by wagon train from Mexico City more than two centuries before Zebulon Pike led the first United States expedition into what is now Colorado. Gradually, generation by generation, the descendants of these Spanish immigrants moved northward along the Río Grande from Santa Fe and Taos. Their spirit endures in the arts and crafts, religion and language of the region, and in an austere rural way of life not far removed from the pioneer tradition.

The land south of the Arkansas River and east of the San Juan Mountains belonged to Mexico until 1848, when it became United States territory in the treaty that ended the Mexican War. No battles were ever fought here, though; the fighting took place more than a thousand miles to the south, where American troops invaded Mexico and seized Mexico City. At the time, there were not yet any Mexicans in the region that is now southern Colorado. Apache and Comanche Indian refugees who had been driven out of Texas by non-Indian settlers had laid claim to the mountains, prairies and desert of southern Colorado as their new homeland and sought to keep it by waging a campaign of terror against anyone who tried to start a farm or ranch farther north than Taos. The soldiers sent to secure United States ownership of New Mexico also provided protection from Indian raids, making it safe for settlers from New Mexico to homestead in southern Colorado.

Even today, south central Colorado is sparsely inhabited. The rapid growth that has swollen northern Colorado's population into the millions has bypassed south central Colorado completely. No significant gold strike was ever discovered in the Sangre de Cristos—only coal, which held out the dismal promise of life as a mine laborer without the corresponding possibility of striking it rich. The lack of water limited agriculture to family farms operating at subsistence level, and cattle quickly overgrazed the fragile grasslands, transforming them into desert with hardly a trace of fertile soil. Today, the economy of the region still depends mainly on small vegetable farms and, more and more, on specialty agriculture including herb farms and llama and bison ranches.

Tourism in south central Colorado bears little resemblance to the major industry that has brought such prosperity to resort towns in the northern part of the state. Although there are expanses of mountain wilderness with abundant wildlife, they are so remote and inaccessible that few hikers or hunters ever venture into them. Restaurants and motels tend to be simple, unpretentious little places with prices to match. Yet travelers who take the time to explore the Sangre de Cristos, the San Luis Valley, and the Gunnison River area discover scenery and recreational opportunities as exciting in their way as any to be found in the better-known and more crowded Colorado tourist areas.

South central Colorado has something to offer just about every traveler. The underrated Great Sand Dunes National Monument merits a ranking alongside the Grand Canyon and Carlsbad Caverns as one of the premier natural wonders of the American Southwest. History echoes in the whistle of the steam locomotive that pulls the Cumbres and Toltec narrow-gauge passenger train, as well as in the artsy little revival mining town of Creede and the ghost-town remains of other such communities that did not survive. Although most of the region covered in this chapter has no ski slopes, the two exceptions—Monarch and Crested Butte—afford more relaxed alternatives to northern Colorado resort scenes such as Aspen and Vail. The annual crane migration draws birders to wildlife refuges along the Rio Grande, and fishing and boating lure water sports enthusiasts to Blue Mesa Reservoir, Colorado's largest lake. Mountain biking was born on the jeep trails around Crested Butte, where fat-tire bicycles now seem to outnumber cars.

▼▼▼▼▼▼▼▼▼▼

Pueblo Area

Pueblo is Colorado's third-largest city; it was the second largest before Colorado Spring's prodigious growth spurt in the early 1970s. Pueblo thrived because in 1875 the Colorado Fuel and Iron Company (later CF&I Steel), which dominated coal mining in Colorado for generations, chose this location as the site of its huge steel mill. Today, it is the only Front Range city with a declining population. Except for specialty steel manufacturing on a very small scale, the mill has not operated since 1982. The mill's smokestacks stand abandoned now, and nothing moves in the network of conveyors and catwalks that link the buildings and coke ovens on the east side of Route 25. The shut-down improved air quality, but the economy has not yet fully recovered.

SIGHTS

Certainly Pueblo's top sightseeing highlight is **Rosemont**. This three-story, 37-room stone mansion, one of the grandest in Colorado, was built for a banker in 1893. On display in the servants' quarters, the McClelland Collection of curiosities from around the world strikes a fun-loving counterpoint to the opulence of Rosemont's polished wood-and-marble interiors. Look for the rose motif, which appears somewhere in each room of the home. Closed Monday. Admission. ~ 419 West 14th Street, Pueblo; 719-545-5290.

Tourism has not figured much in Pueblo's development over the years. It has a plain but comfy hometown feel, and the main points of interest are meant primarily for residents to enjoy. The story of the town's early years awaits at the free **Pueblo County Historical Museum** in the Union Avenue Historic District. The museum's collection of Pueblo paraphernalia features an impressive collection of locally made saddles. Open Tuesday through Saturday afternoons. ~ 217 South Grand Avenue, Pueblo; 719-543-6772.

At the northeast end of Pueblo's historic district, the modern **Sangre de Cristo Arts and Conference Center** has three galleries that show changing exhibits, works by regional artists and shows on national tour, as well as a permanent collection of Western art. There are also a children's museum and a theater that presents local theater and dance productions. Closed Sunday. Admission. ~ 210 North Santa Fe Avenue, Pueblo; 719-543-0130.

On Pueblo's southwest side near the state fairgrounds is **El Pueblo Museum**. Operated by the Colorado Historical Society, the museum is a re-creation of the adobe Fort Pueblo trading post, built on the site in 1842. Plains Indian artifacts, buffalo robes and long, black-powder rifles are on display. Admission. ~ 324 West 1st Street, Pueblo; 719-583-0453.

To the northwest, on the way out to Lake Pueblo, is Pueblo's **City Park**, with green lawn and picnic tables surrounding a duck pond, as well as a children's playground, a baseball diamond and tennis courts. The park is the home of the **Pueblo Zoo**. The small zoo features an "ecocenter" containing artificial environments that range from tropical rainforest to penguin habitat. There are also a children's petting zoo and a sizable collection of snakes and other reptiles. City Park also has a restored antique carousel that children can ride for a small charge. Admission. ~ Pueblo and Goodnight boulevards, Pueblo; 719-561-9664.

Hose Company No. 3, Pueblo's firefighters museum, shows kids of all ages the workings of a traditional fire station, and fea-

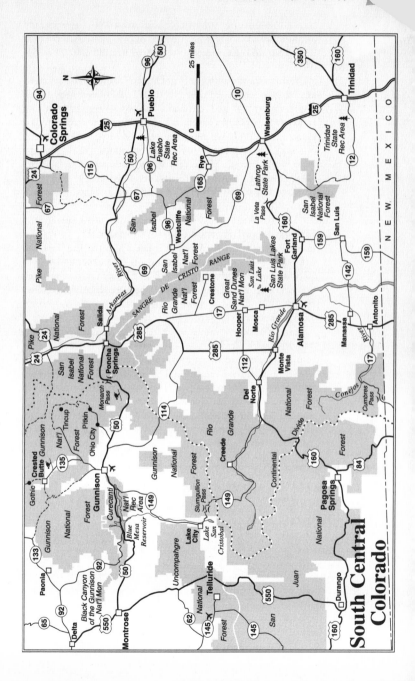

South Central Colorado

tures an old-time, hand-drawn fire hose cart, a 1917 fire truck, and memorabilia including tributes to acts of bravery by local firemen. Closed Saturday and Sunday. ~ 102 Broadway, Pueblo; 719-254-6737.

Perhaps the most unusual sight in Pueblo, even more astonishing than the abandoned steel mill, is the **Pueblo Levee Mural Project**. Sixty feet high and four and a half miles long, the levee that conducts the Arkansas River through Pueblo was a graffiti-riddled eyesore until 1980, when the city began inviting individuals and organizations to paint sections of a continuous mural along the levee every Cinco de Mayo, recycling surplus paint that has been collected as toxic waste. The result is one of the largest community-participation artworks ever made—and it's growing longer each year.

The free **Weisbrod Aircraft Museum** and **International B-24 Museum**, located on opposite sides of the road at the airport, contain major collections of World War II–era aircraft. The Weisbrod Museum has 26 airplanes, including a B-29 bomber and an RB-37, with interpretive plaques. The B-24 Museum traces the development of the B-24 Liberator, one of the most successful bombers of World War II, and its crewmen who trained in Pueblo. ~ Pueblo Airport, Pueblo; 719-948-9219.

From Pueblo, the mountains barely break the western skyline. Motorists with plenty of time can leave Route 25 on a scenic detour that takes three times longer than the drive from Pueblo to Walsenburg on the interstate and takes you as close to the mountains as it's possible to go by car. Take Route 9-6 west from Pueblo for 52 miles, across the low Wet Mountains, to the small ranching town of **Westcliffe**, the all-but-undiscovered base camp for recreation along the steep eastern slope of the Sangre de Cristos. The range is a jagged, impassable wall of granite that runs unbroken

✦✦✦

✔ CHECK THESE OUT—UNIQUE SIGHTS

for 75 miles without a single road over it. Route 69 heads southeast along the base of the mountain range, returning to Route 25
at Walsenburg, 57 miles away.

Twenty-four miles west of Route 25 south of Pueblo near the
small town of Rye is the unique **Bishop Castle**, a project that
owner Jim Bishop has been working on since 1969. Built of stone
and iron, the three-story castle features medieval walls, flying but-
tresses, and a 130-foot-tall tower. Future plans call for a moat and
a drawbridge. Bishop, who has dedicated the project to the spirit
of working men around the world, asserts that the castle is the
largest structure ever built in the United States by a single individual. ~ County Road 75, Rye; 719-564-4366.

LODGING

With only a couple of notable exceptions, lodging options in
Pueblo consist of name-brand motor inns and a scattering of little
ma-and-pa motels, mostly clustered around Route 25 Exit 101
(the junction with Route 50 westbound) at the north end of town.
That's where you'll find the city's largest hotel, the **Holiday Inn
of Pueblo**, which bills itself as the city's only full-service hotel,
with amenities that include a laundromat and room service, not
to mention business communications links and a fitness center.
The 192 rooms are contemporary, with cheerful color schemes,
refrigerators and current pay-per-view movies on TV. There are
an indoor swimming pool and a cocktail lounge. ~ 4001 North
Elizabeth Street, Pueblo; 719-543-8050, 800-465-4329, fax 719-
545-2271. MODERATE.

Small, low-priced motels are found side-by-side with the major
motor inns along Elizabeth Street, paralleling Route 25 between
Exits 101 and 102. The **Rambler National 9** has 29 clean units
with TVs and in-room phones. Most units have two double beds,
and some have bathtubs. There is an outdoor heated swimming
pool. ~ 4400 North Elizabeth Street, Pueblo; 719-543-4173.
BUDGET.

A veranda, a winding staircase, inlaid wood floors and stained
glass are among the elegant architectural features of the **Abriendo
Inn**, a 1906 foursquare-style brick mansion centrally located in
Pueblo's historic district. Built by Pueblo brewery owner Martin
Walter, each of the ten rooms is individually decorated with Victorian and Asian antiques. Some rooms feature handcrafted four-
poster beds, leaded and beveled windows, armoires and hand-
crocheted bedspreads. Rates include a full gourmet breakfast. ~
300 West Abriendo Avenue, Pueblo; 719-544-2703, fax 719-542-
6544. MODERATE.

The **Inn at Pueblo West**, a Best Western affiliate, is an attractive Spanish-style 80-room resort hotel located eight miles west
of the city. Guest rooms are exceptionally spacious and feature

bright, contemporary decor. Guests enjoy the use of a nearby golf course. ~ 201 South McCulloch Boulevard, Pueblo; 719-547-2111, 800-448-1972, fax 919-547-0385. MODERATE.

DINING   You'll find Continental cuisine at affordable prices at **La Renaissance**, which has been operating in a converted 1886 church since the early 1970s. High ceilings and stained glass add a touch of class to the casual ambience. Specialties include baby back ribs and slow-roasted prime rib. Lunch on weekdays only. Closed Sunday. ~ 217 East Routt Avenue, Pueblo; 719-543-6367. MODERATE.

Ianne's Whisky Ridge is a good Italian restaurant with white linen tablecloths and a seductive menu featuring such selections as pasta primavera, chicken piccata, veal Marsala, linguini, scampi, calamari and escargot. Dinner only. ~ 4333 Thatcher Avenue, Pueblo; 719-564-8551. MODERATE.

The **Gold Dust Saloon** serves what are reputed to be the best cheeseburgers and fries in town, as well as homemade soups, salads, sandwiches and big pitchers of beer, in a neighborhood-style bar and grill with Old West decor. You also get free peanuts so that you can contribute to the crunchy drifts of shells that cover the floor, sometimes ankle-deep. Closed Sunday. ~ 130 South Union Avenue, Pueblo; 719-545-0741. BUDGET.

There are plenty of good Mexican restaurants in Pueblo, most of them hidden away in neighborhoods where tourists are rarely seen. A family-run local favorite that has been in business for 60 years at the same easy-to-find location is **El Valle Restaurant & Lounge**, just off Route 25 Exit 97A. The food is authentically Mexican, with house specialties that range from shrimp burritos to *menudo* (tripe stew), and the portions are huge. Closed Wednesday and Thursday. ~ 208 West Northern Street, Pueblo; 719-564-9983. BUDGET TO MODERATE.

SHOPPING   Artists and crafters have discovered that Pueblo offers low rents and a central location between the Denver and Santa Fe art markets, and new studios, galleries and gourmet shops are revitalizing the neighborhood around Union Avenue, Pueblo's original main street, and the Pueblo Union Depot. Local arts and crafts are shown at **Heritage House Art**. ~ 320 South Union Avenue; 719-545-2691. **Earth 'n Art** also has a selection of crafts. ~ 111 West B Street; 719-544-6224. You'll find custom gold and silver jewelry at **Skystone and Silver**. ~ 310 South Victoria; 719-544-5959. Southwestern Indian jewelry can be found at **Avanyu**. ~ 313 South Union Avenue; 719-543-8112.

You can hunt for antiques at **Granny's Attic**. ~ 103 West B Street; 719-545-5245. **Tivoli's** also has a selection of antiques. ~ 325 South Union Avenue; 719-545-1448. Crafts studios include **The Mountain Weavery**. ~ 311½ South Union Avenue; 719-545-

2297. Other shops deal in old and rare books, flower arrangements and antique radios.

NIGHTLIFE

Peppers Pueblo Hot Spot, bills itself as the hottest nightclub between Denver and Albuquerque, although not everyone would agree. The club features mainly recorded music with occasional live bands. The sound is '50s, '60s and '70s pop except on Thursday, College Night, when techno-alternative music is the main attraction. Nationally known comedy acts are featured on Saturday nights. Cover. ~ 4109 Club Manor Drive, Pueblo; 719-542- 8629.

The **Gold Dust Saloon** attracts an intriguing cross-section of Puebloans with its rowdy pub atmosphere (dartboards on the walls and peanut shells on the floor). Several TVs located around the pub blare sporting events most evenings and weekends. ~ 130 South Union Avenue, Pueblo; 719-545-0741.

Located next to the now-defunct CF&I steel mill, **Gus's Place** was the after-work hangout for generations of steelworkers. Today the bar is spruced up and decorated with so much CF&I memorabilia that it's virtually a steel mill museum. ~ 1201 Elm Street; 719-542-0756. Another long-time Pueblo favorite, the **Irish Pub and Grille**—a bar attached to an Italian restaurant, despite its name—draws a largely professional after-work crowd that slops over into the late evening in a mellow, conversational atmosphere. ~ 108 West 3rd Street, Pueblo; 719-542-9974.

As for the performing arts, Pueblo supports several local groups including the **Broadway Theater League.** ~ 719-545-4721. There's also the **Impossible Playhouse.** ~ 719-542-6969. The **Pueblo Choral Society** holds performances. ~ 719-544-4455. You may see the **Pueblo Symphony** and the **Sangre de Christo Ballet Theatre** at the **Sangre de Cristo Arts and Conference Center.** ~ 210 North Santa Fe Avenue, Pueblo; 719-543-0130.

LAKE PUEBLO STATE RECREATION AREA

PARKS

Surrounded by arid prairie and limestone cliffs, with moun-

MEET AN EAGLE FACE-TO-FACE

Part of the Pueblo Greenway and Nature Center, the **Raptor Center of Pueblo** rescues injured eagles, hawks, falcons and owls that are reported or brought in to the center. Most are victims of gunshot wounds. One of the few raptor rehabilitation facilities in the United States, the center succeeds in returning about half the birds it treats to the wild. Handlers introduce some of the nonreleasable birds to visitors in the center's "Birds of Prey" educational program. Call 719-549-2327 for program times.

tain views to the west, windswept Pueblo Reservoir is a favorite sailing and windsurfing lake. Swimming is prohibited in the lake but permitted in the Rock Canyon area below Pueblo Dam. Fishing is good for bass, carp, catfish and other lake species. The recreation area also takes in a wide strip of wild land around the lake, providing habitat for coyotes, deer, wild turkeys and many other denizens of the high plains. This backcountry is accessible via a number of hiking and horse trails. There are picnic area, restrooms, marinas, cruise boats and a visitors center. Day-use fee, $4. ~ Located four miles west of Pueblo, with access from Route 50 at the town of Pueblo West via Nichols Road or McCulloch Boulevard; also accessible from Route 96; 719-561-9320.

▲ There are 221 RV/tent sites (no hookups); $7 to $10 per night. They are usually full on weekends; call 800-678-2267 for reservations.

PUEBLO GREENWAY AND NATURE CENTER 🚶 🚴 The Pueblo Greenway, which follows the banks of the Arkansas River west from Pueblo Boulevard to Lake Pueblo, is a popular cycling and jogging path. Midway along the greenway, the nature center has exhibits about flora and fauna of this prairie and riparian habitat designed with kids in mind. There are nature trails and restrooms. ~ Located a mile west of Pueblo Boulevard at 5200 Nature Center Road; 719-549-2414.

▼▼▼▼▼▼▼▼▼▼▼▼▼▼▼▼▼▼
Walsenburg–Trinidad Area

Motorists heading south from Pueblo on Route 25 will find a landscape so vast and empty that it strikes a startling contrast to the busy, heavily populated Front Range corridor of northern Colorado. Walsenburg and Trinidad are the only two towns on the 100-mile route from Pueblo to the New Mexico state line, and neither is generally regarded as a tourist destination. Those who prefer to avoid the interstate and stick to secondary highways will discover leisurely, scenic backroads along the base of the Sangre de Cristo Range.

SIGHTS

Aside from the lake and trails of Lathrop State Park, **Walsenburg** has little but fuel and fast food to entice travelers off the interstate. But the massive stonework of its old courthouse, high school and other buildings, quarried locally in the early 20th century, when Walsenburg was an important railroad junction, gives this unpretentious little town far from anyplace else a rare feeling of permanence.

West of Walsenburg, on the way up La Veta Pass where Route 160 crosses the mountains to Alamosa, the main sight in the small town of La Veta is the **Fort Francisco Museum**, built in 1862 as one of several army outposts designed to protect settlers in south central Colorado from Comanche attacks. The plaza-like fort is now an open-air museum with a collection of period buildings including a blacksmith shop, a schoolhouse and a saloon. ~ Route 160, La Veta; 719-742-3676.

Southwest from Walsenburg, the **Highway of Legends Scenic Byway** (Route 12) loops around the back side of the Spanish Peaks and returns to the interstate at Trinidad.

The **Spanish Peaks** (12,683 feet and 13,626 feet) are the easternmost mountains in the Rockies except for Pikes Peak. Formed by volcanic activity independent of the upheavals that created the Sangre de Cristo Range, the twin peaks are almost disconnected from the main mountain range. The 82-mile paved highway reaches only 9941 feet in elevation as it passes between the Spanish Peaks and the Sangre de Cristos. Along the route lie lakes like mirrors, crumbled adobe ruins, abandoned mines and mills, modern vacation cabins, some of Colorado's most colorful fields of wildflowers and the strange natural formations called the **Great Dikes**, hundreds of narrow rock walls up to 100 feet high and 14 miles long. At Stonewall Gap, the road goes through a natural gateway in the dikes.

The first towns in the region were established in the early 1850s, several years before the "Pikes Peak or Bust" gold rush brought the first wave of settlers to northern Colorado.

A few miles farther up the road, eight miles outside of Trinidad, the **Cokedale National Historic District** preserves the largest of more than 50 coal-mining camps that once brought prosperity to the Spanish Peaks area. Cokedale had a population of 1500 before the company town's owner and sole employer, the American Smelting and Refining Company, shut down its coke ovens here in 1947. Well-preserved homes, small and now mostly abandoned, are scattered through the ghost town. They are overshadowed by the remains of huge ovens that were used to heat coal, refining it into a fuel that burned longer and hotter for use in making steel. Beside the ovens, giant heaps of black slag, a byproduct of the coking process, give visitors some idea of the quantities of coal that were refined here.

Located in the foothills and canyons below Raton Pass, the low, often stormy summit that marks Colorado's boundary with New Mexico, **Trinidad** got its start in the 1830s as a way station on the Santa Fe Trail and became a busy railhead for shipping coal from area mines. The center of town, now preserved as the **Corazon de Trinidad National Historic District**, presents a distinctive blend of New Mexican adobe construction with Colorado's architecture.

Trinidad's historic district has several museums. Be sure to check out the **Baca House, Bloom House and Pioneer Museum**. The main attractions are two mansions—the Baca House, an 1870

Territorial-style adobe hacienda that belonged to a Mexican cattle baron, and the Bloom House, a three-story Victorian mansion built in 1881 for the town banker. The contrast between the two exemplifies the cultural clash that shaped Trinidad's unique personality. The houses are furnished with antiques of the period, and behind the Baca House, a small museum in the former carriage house contains local memorabilia including substantial collections of weapons, historical photographs, and Indian artifacts. Other exhibits tell the history of the Santa Fe Trail, which connected Kansas City with the capital of New Mexico, and honor Colorado's Hispanic heritage. Admission. ~ 300 East Main Street, Trinidad; 719-846-7217.

In a restored 1906 department-store building, the free **A. R. Mitchell Memorial Museum and Gallery** displays a large collection of works by celebrated local artist Arthur Roy Mitchell depicting life in the Old West, along with paintings by other cowboy artists of the early and mid-20th century. Within the Mitchell Museum, the **Aultman Collection** displays a large exhibit of historic pictures by a longtime local photographer along with his old-time cameras and darkroom equipment. ~ 150 East Main Street, Trinidad; 719-846-4224.

The **Trinidad Children's Museum** is housed in Firehouse #1, the town's original fire station. In addition to firefighting memorabilia, the museum contains the usual hands-on educational exhibits aimed at grade-school kids. ~ 314 North Commercial Street, Trinidad; 719-846-7721.

Located on the Trinidad State Junior College Campus, the free **Louden-Henritz Museum of Archaeology** contains exhibits about prehistoric human life in the area. Of special interest is a diorama re-creating Trinchera Cave, which was occupied by nomadic Indians for an estimated 3000 years. The museum also has large collections of arrowheads, fossils and geological samples. ~ Freudenthal Memorial Library, Trinidad; 719-846-5508.

LODGING   The frontage strip between downtown Walsenburg and the north interstate exit has several nondescript motels, of which perhaps the nicest is **The Best Western Rambler Motel**. This motor inn has 32 rooms decorated in cool earthtone color schemes, and there's a heated pool. ~ Route 25 Exit 52, Walsenburg; 719-738-1121, 800-528-1234. MODERATE.

Travelers won't be disappointed with the spacious, contemporary rooms at the 55-unit **Best Western Trinidad Inn**. This motor inn with its hillside location commands a view of Trinidad and the interstate. Many of the bright, spacious rooms overlook the municipal golf course. It has an outdoor swimming pool, a jacuzzi and an exercise room. ~ 900 West Adams Street, Trinidad; phone/fax 719-846-2215, 800-955-2215. MODERATE.

The **Days Inn** has 62 clean motel rooms in cheerful color schemes. The two-level complex has an outdoor heated pool, spa, exercise room and restaurant. The rooms are standard fare, but lower in price than most of the comparable motels clustered around the town's interstate exits. ~ 702 West Main Street, Trinidad; phone/fax 719-846-2271. MODERATE.

DINING

Other than fast-food fare, the best dining bet in Walsenburg is the **Iron Horse**, a family restaurant located in the city's old armory and decorated with small-town memorabilia. Specialties include barbecued ribs and pasta. ~ 503 West 7th Street, Walsenburg; 719-738-9966. BUDGET TO MODERATE.

The selection is a little better in Trinidad. The **El Paso Café** offers Mexican food as authentic as you're likely to find in this largely Hispanic town, featuring an outstanding combination plate and a *comida corrida* (blue plate special) that changes daily. The prices are hard to beat. ~ 1101 East Main Street, Trinidad; 719-846-8522. BUDGET.

Chef Liu's Chinese Restaurant, another long-time local favorite, serves Cantonese and spicy Szechuan dishes, including a number of vegetarian options, in a dimly lit restaurant accented in red and gold hues. ~ 1423 Santa Fe Trail, Trinidad; 719-846-3333. BUDGET TO MODERATE.

Nana & Nono's Pasta House serves fettuccini, spaghetti and other pasta entrées with a full range of tantalizing sauces. An unpretentious blend of Italian and Mexican decorations sets the stage for low-priced romantic dinners in this cheerful, student-oriented restaurant. ~ 415 University, Trinidad; 719-846-2696. BUDGET.

PARKS

SAN ISABEL NATIONAL FOREST 🕺🛶 A 19,000-acre detached unit of San Isabel National Forest surrounds the Spanish Peaks. The Peaks themselves became the Spanish Peaks Wilderness with the passage of the 1993 Wilderness Act. There are hiking trails around and between the two peaks, and a trail leads to the summit of West Spanish Peak. You may fish for rainbow and brown trout in Cucharas Creek and other area streams. ~ Access to the Spanish Peaks is by the Highway of Legends Scenic Byway (Route 12), which circles both mountains; 719-742-3681.

▲ Along Cucharas Creek, west of Route 12 on Forest Road 413, are Blue Lake and Bear Lake Campgrounds, totalling 30 tent and RV sites (no hookups). Purgatoire Campground, located on the north fork of the Purgatoire River, has 23 RV/tent sites (no hookups). All three campgrounds are open late May to mid-September; sites cost $8 per night.

LATHROP STATE PARK 🕺🚲🚣🏊🛶🚤 The park's twin lakes, Martin Lake and Horseshoe Lake, are quite small, but that doesn't stop Walsenburg area residents from flocking here for waterskiing, sailboarding and fishing. A hiking trail wanders among rock formations on its way up to a hogback ridge, and the campground offers a view across Martin Lake to the Spanish Peaks. Its convenience to Route 25 makes Lathrop State Park a welcome oasis on a long, desolate highway drive. Fishing is good for rainbow trout, bass, catfish, walleye and tiger muskie. There are picnic areas, restrooms, showers, a visitors center and a golf course. Day-use fee, $4. ~ Located off Route 160, three miles west of Walsenburg; 719-738-2376.

▲ There are 100 RV/tent sites (most with hookups); $7 to $12 per night. For reservations, call 800-678-2267.

TRINIDAD STATE RECREATION AREA 🏃🚣🛶🚤⛵ Trinidad Lake, which hides old coal mines in its depths, offers fishing, boating and windsurfing in the pretty Purgatoire River Valley above the town of Trinidad. Nine miles of backcountry hiking trails within the park take you among hills studded with piñon and juniper. They connect with a vast network of jeep roads and trails into the surrounding San Isabel National Forest. The lake is populated with rainbow trout, walleye, largemouth bass, channel catfish and bullheads. There are picnic areas and restrooms. Day-use fee, $4. ~ Located four miles west of Trinidad on Route 12; 719-846-6951.

▲ There are 62 RV/tent sites (most with hookups); $12 per night. The campground closes from mid-October through March. For reservations, call 800-678-2267.

▼▼▼▼▼▼▼▼▼▼▼▼
Alamosa Area

The San Luis Valley is probably the least-visited area in the Colorado Rockies. The **San Luis Valley**, an oval of flat land 120 miles long and 60 miles wide surrounded by soaring mountain peaks, was settled in the 1800s by Spanish colonists from nearby Taos. Most people of the valley, descendants of Spanish New Mexican pioneers, live on truck farms along the Rio Grande or in small, poor villages near the foot of the mountains. The valley's inhospitable climate discourages newcomers. Alamosa's winter low temperatures often register as the coldest in Colorado, and the wind blows all year long.

SIGHTS

Visitors to **Alamosa**, the valley's largest town, may find little more than a long stretch of roadside strip development, though a detour through the old, tree-lined residential neighborhood north of Route 160 reveals a number of Victorian-vintage homes. Founded as the northern terminus of the Denver & Rio Grande Railway's "Chili Line," which followed the Rio Grande Valley south to Espanola, New Mexico, much of Alamosa was erected almost overnight with plain, portable buildings brought here on flatbed rail cars. Since then, the railroad has declined, the weather has continued to be as notoriously bad as ever year-round, and Alamosa has remained a plain, utilitarian town whose most notable feature is the low rents that have attracted a growing community of artists and crafters in recent years.

One of the most extraordinary natural phenomena in the state lies 36 miles northeast of Alamosa. **Great Sand Dunes National Monument** is a 50-square-mile expanse of shifting sand, carried by windstorms and deposited over millions of years in this notch at the foot of the Sangre de Cristo Range. Rising 900 feet high, they are the largest sand dunes in the United States. In the summer months, visitors by the thousands flock here to climb the dunes or just play on the half-mile-wide "beach" along the broad, shallow, constantly shifting streams of chilly mountain water where Medano Creek makes its way across the sand. A four-wheel-drive road provides access to primitive campgrounds in remote areas of the dunes. Admission. ~ 11999 Route 150, Mosca; 719-378-2312.

One of the more unlikely attractions in the area is the **San Luis Valley Alligator Farm**, also known as the Two Mile Creek Wildlife Habitat. Located 17 miles north of Alamosa, this colony of more than 80 'gators is the northernmost and highest-altitude outdoor alligator colony in the world. The alligators were brought in to provide a means for disposal of the tons of waste created by a fish processing plant at the facility, which produces tilapia fillets that are shipped fresh to cities throughout the United States and Canada. Both fish and reptiles are able to survive the subzero San Luis Valley winters because the water in which they live is warmed by hot springs. Admission. ~ Route 17, Hooper; 719-589-3032.

◄ HIDDEN

Alamosa National Wildlife Refuge, located three miles east of town on a meandering stretch of the Rio Grande, protects wetlands that provide migratory habitat for ducks, egrets and herons, and, in the winter months, bald and golden eagles. There is a nature trail along the river and a 12-mile-long auto tour loop. ~ Route 160, Alamosa; 719-589-4021.

Off Route 160 east of the turnoff to Great Sand Dunes, **Fort Garland Museum** preserves the old U.S. Army fort established in 1858, shortly after the United States won the territory at the end of the Mexican War. Active for 25 years, the fort was the final command in the military career of Colonel Kit Carson, the Southwest's most notorious Indian fighter. The only real test of the fort's effectiveness at peacekeeping came in 1863, when, a family known as "the bloody Espinozas" mounted a reign of terror in the valley after the Virgin Mary appeared in a vision and told them to drive the Anglos out of the San Luis Valley. The buildings house exhibits of 19th-century military uniforms, weapons and everyday items Closed Tuesday and Wednesday. Admission. ~ Fort Garland; 719-379-3512.

South of Fort Garland, little San Luis is the oldest town in Colorado. **The San Luis Museum, Cultural and Commercial Center** presents the folk art and history of the valley's people. Exhibits include an outstanding collection of carved wooden saints, known as *bultos*, and a reconstruction of a traditional *penitente* chapel. ~ 402 Church Place, San Luis; 719-672-3611.

HIDDEN ►

Beginning at a trailhead near the junction of Routes 159 and 142 in San Luis, a 1.25-mile walking trail leads up past a series of life-size bronze statues by local sculptor Humberto Maestas depicting the **Stations of the Cross.** The 14 life-sized sculptures depict scenes from the Passion—Christ's trial and suffering leading to His crucifixion. On Good Friday and Easter weekend, hundreds of pilgrims walk from other San Luis Valley communities to perform devotions at the stations along this path. At the path's terminus, the top of the mesa, a Crucifixion scene looms over the valley.

HIDDEN ►

A few miles away, the even smaller town of **Manassa** is locally famous as the birthplace of boxer Jack Dempsey, who as a teenager fought for prize money in mining-camp saloons from Durango to the Cripple Creek district and went on to win the world's heavyweight title in 1919. The **Jack Dempsey Museum** exhibits a collection of Dempsey mementos contributed by residents. Manassa was established in the mid-1870s as the first Mormon colony in the region, and its population (988 people) is still entirely Mormon. The San Luis Valley as a whole has a Mormon population of about 3500—who make up most of the area's non-Hispanic residents. Closed October through May. ~ 401 Main Street, Manassa; 719-843-5207.

At the southwestern edge of the valley, Antonito is the northern terminus of the **Cumbres & Toltec Scenic Railroad.** Two separate narrow-gauge steam trains run each morning from Antonito, Colorado, and Chama, New Mexico, climbing by sweeping loops through forests of aspen up to Osier, a mountain ghost town that is inaccessible by car. In the afternoon, passengers can return along the same route or, for a higher fare, continue all the way to Chama and take a van back in the evening. The 64-mile Antonito-to-Chama trip is America's longest and highest narrow-gauge steam train route operating today. The train runs from Memorial Day to mid-October. ~ 719-376-5483.

Motorists can take a scenic drive different from, but comparable to, the train route by taking paved Route 17 over La Manga Pass (10,230 feet) to the summit of **Cumbres Pass** (10,022 feet), where the narrow-gauge tracks parallel the road for several miles. The ghost town of Cumbres, near the summit of the pass, was home to railroad workers who kept the trains running year-round back in the 1880s.

Colorado's
Hispanic Heritage

Colorado's largest ethnic subculture, accounting for more than 15 percent of the population, is Hispanic. The Latino heritage in Colorado dates back more than two centuries. All of present-day Colorado became Spanish territory in 1762, when France ceded the Louisiana Territory (which reached from the Mississippi River to the Pacific) to the King of Spain. Acquisition of the vast new territory inspired the government of Spanish colonial Nuevo Mexico to send the first European explorers into Colorado.

In 1765, Don Juan Maria de Rivera led an expedition through the San Juan Mountains to the Gunnison River in search of gold and silver—which they did not find. In 1786, Don Juan Bautista de Anza, governor of the Spanish colony of Nuevo Mexico, led an army of almost 600 Spanish soldiers from Santa Fe north through the San Luis Valley and down the Arkansas River, where he picked the site for the town of San Carlos (present-day Pueblo). Unfortunately, this first settlement failed within a year.

No permanent Spanish settlement was ever established in Colorado by Spain, or later by Mexico. But within a few years after it became U.S. Territory in 1848 as part of the treaty of Guadalupe Hidalgo ending the Mexican War, Spanish-speaking settlers began moving into southern Colorado, and through most of the 1850s more Coloradans spoke Spanish than English. It was during this era that most towns, rivers and mountains in southern Colorado received the Spanish names by which they are known today.

A second wave of Spanish-speaking inhabitants came to Colorado in the 1920s, as the growth of the sugar-beet industry created a big demand for seasonal farm labor. With no immigration restrictions between Mexico and the United States, contractors brought thousands of Mexican workers north to Colorado each summer, and many stayed. But as the Great Depression brought unemployment, a racist backlash against Mexicans swept through Colorado. The Ku Klux Klan vowed to drive Catholics (meaning Hispanics) out of the state, and Mexicans were increasingly segregated into barrios in the Front Range cities and into separate satellite towns, often lacking public utilities, on the outskirts of mountain towns.

Only since the 1960s have Chicano activists made progress toward ending the discrimination. Today, the Mexican holiday Cinco de Mayo is one of the biggest holiday celebrations in Denver and other Colorado communities. Spanish is taught in Colorado public schools from the second grade on. And Hispanic candidates have won the offices of mayor of Denver and governor of Colorado.

Motorists going west toward Wolf Creek Pass and Durango on Route 160 pass through the towns of Monte Vista and Del Norte. Monte Vista is best known for the **Monte Vista National Wildlife Refuge**, well known among birders as a stopover for as many as 20,000 sandhill and whooping cranes migrating south to New Mexico each October and November. Bald eagles and thousands of ducks spend the winter months in these wetlands. ~ Route 15, Monte Vista; 719-589-4021.

Del Norte's **Rio Grande County Museum** focuses on the multicultural history of American Indians, Spanish settlers and Anglo trappers and traders along the upper Rio Grande. Exhibits range from ancient petroglyphs to relics from the failed 1848 expedition of mountain man John C. Fremont, who lost 11 of his 33 men to hypothermia in a fruitless wintertime search for a year-round route over the Continental Divide. The museum also hosts history and nature lectures and local art programs. Admission. ~ 580 Oak Street, Del Norte; 719-657-2847.

HIDDEN ►

Toward the north end of the San Luis Valley, the tiny, remote village of **Crestone** has become a New Age phenomenon. The old mining town's population had shrunk to 61 by 1978, when developers bought a nearby ranch and subdivided it into homesite lots. Inspired by a vision of international spiritual harmony (not to mention the tax advantages), the promoters donated lots to be used as spiritual retreats by Carmelite nuns, Tibetan Buddhists and other groups including the Sri Aurobindo Learning Center, the Crestone Mountain Zen Center, the Haidakhandi Universal Ashram, the Naropa Institute and Lindesfarne Temple, as well as several environmental projects. In 1996, renowned Tibetan shaman Kardum Sonam came to Crestone to consecrate the 41-foot-tall Stupa of Many Auspicious Doors, one of the largest Buddhist stupas in the Western Hemisphere. Today, Crestone has a year-round population of 500 and hosts spiritual conferences that draw thousands of participants from throughout the world.

LODGING

Alamosa's hotel and restaurant selection is on the slim side. A welcome find is the **Cottonwood Inn Bed & Breakfast & Gallery**, a big pink-and-gray Victorian several blocks from the main highway in a quiet, shady neighborhood. It has nine antique-furnished guest rooms, most with private baths, including four suites. The common areas feature changing exhibits by local artists. ~ 123 San Juan Avenue, Alamosa; 719-589-6437, 800-955-2623, fax 719-589-3882. MODERATE TO DELUXE.

The **Alamosa Lamplighter Motel** is actually two motels under the same management but several blocks apart, with a total of 70 guest rooms. The rooms, which are about as conventional as motel rooms get, are a bargain when you consider that the rent includes the use of the indoor swimming pool and sauna at the main motel and the jacuzzi in the annex. There is also a restaurant on the premises. ~ 425 Main Street, Alamosa; 719-589-6636, 800-359-2138, fax 719-589-3831. MODERATE.

Other lodging options in Alamosa consist of a scattering of motels and motor inns along Route 160. For example, modern, spacious, air-conditioned lodgings and an indoor swimming pool, hot tub and sauna, can be found at the 121-unit **Best Western Alamosa Inn**. The recently remodeled rooms, available with two double beds or one king-size, are clean and contemporary. Most face the interior pool area instead of the highway and are quieter than an average motel room. ~ 1919 Main Street, Alamosa; 719-589-2567, 800-528-1234, fax 719-589-0767. MODERATE.

The most luxurious accommodations in the San Luis Valley are at the **Great Sand Dunes Country Inn at Zapata Ranch**, just three miles from the national monument entrance. Seclusion is part of the allure of this log building complex dating back to the 1880s. The inn doesn't provide phones, television sets or newspapers, but it does have a golf course, pool, jacuzzi, mountain bikes and miles of hiking trails, along with majestic views of the Great Sand Dunes. Fifteen guest rooms feature handmade pine furniture, Indian-design fabrics and Mexican tile bathrooms, adding up to a feel of rustic elegance. The inn's greatest pride is its bison herd—one of the largest in existence anywhere—that grazes on Zapata Ranch's 100,000 acres. Daily tours take guests close to the mighty beasts. Rates include breakfast. Closed November through February. ~ 5303 Route 150, Mosca; 719-378-2356, 800-284-9213, fax 719-378-2428. ULTRA-DELUXE.

Travelers can spend the night in a nunnery at **El Convento Bed & Breakfast**. Set in the center of a small village that dates back to the Spanish Colonial era, this historic building served as a Catholic school and convent before the church decided to remodel it and

◆◆

✔ CHECK THESE OUT—UNIQUE LODGING

- *Moderate:* Spend the night in a former nunnery at **El Convento Bed & Breakfast** in the Spanish Colonial village of San Luis. *page 255*
- *Moderate:* Enjoy affordable elegance at the **Abriendo Inn**, a turn-of-the-century mansion in Pueblo's historic district. *page 243*
- *Deluxe:* Chuckle at the eccentric surroundings at the **Claim Jumper**, a B&B with design quirks such as a man-eating fish and an in-house putting green. *page 267*
- *Ultra-deluxe:* Sleep with the buffalo in a luxurious log lodge at the **Great Sand Dunes Country Inn at Zapata Ranch**. *page 255*

Budget: under $50 Moderate: $50–$90 Deluxe: $90–$130 Ultra-deluxe: over $130

open it to the public as a bed and breakfast. The four rooms are decorated in authentic Southwestern style, with handcrafted furniture and *horno* fireplaces. ~ 512 Church Place, San Luis; 719-672-4223. MODERATE.

At the other end of the valley, the **Best Western Movie Manor Motel** harks back to the 1950s and the height of America's infatuation with automobiles. In all 60 units of this otherwise-ordinary motel, big picture windows look out onto the big screen of the Star Drive-In Theater next door. The movie soundtrack plays through speakers installed in each room. Although the drive-in operates during the summer months only, the motel is open year-round. ~ 2830 West Route 160, Monte Vista; 719-852-5921, 800-771-9468, fax 719-852-0122. MODERATE.

DINING

In Alamosa, you can get breakfast all day—until the 2 p.m. closing hour—at **Bauer's Campus Pancake House and Restaurant**, which caters to the students at Adams State College. Giant cinnamon rolls are the most popular item on the menu. The restaurant also serves weekday lunch specials. Closed Tuesday. ~ 435 Poncha Avenue, Alamosa; 719-589-4202. BUDGET.

A good carry-out option is **Lara's First Street To-Go Café**, featuring homemade Italian entrées along with steaks, shrimp and lobster and Mexican combination plates. ~ 2040 1st Street, Alamosa; 719-589-6769. BUDGET.

A local favorite, **Taqueria Calvillo** serves authentic Mexican food such as chile rellenos, tacos and enchiladas, using homemade tortillas and fresh sauces. Closed Tuesday. ~ 119 Broadway, Alamosa; 719-587-5500. BUDGET.

Enchiladas and hot chili stew are everyday fare for many local people in the San Luis Valley. Mexican restaurants in the area serve good, spicy food at low prices in a simple atmosphere. One such restaurant, **El Charro Café**, has been run by the same family for more than 50 years. No alcohol. ~ 421 6th Street, Alamosa; 719-589-2262. BUDGET.

Diners who prefer their Mexican food with margaritas or imported beer might try **Alberto's**, where a house specialty is *chiles rellenos*—green chili peppers stuffed with cheese. The decor features touches of Old Mexico. ~ 1019 6th Street, Alamosa; 719-589-0277. BUDGET.

For fine dining in the San Luis Valley, the top choice is the **Great Sand Dunes Country Inn at Zapata Ranch**. Since Zapata Ranch raises bison, the restaurant's specialty is bison steaks and roasts. Patrons can also opt for pasta, seafood or vegetarian dishes. The small restaurant commands a majestic view of the Great Sand Dunes. ~ 5303 Route 150, Mosca; 719-378-2356. MODERATE.

In San Luis, just about the only place to eat is a good one—
Emma's Hacienda. The same family has been operating this tiny
restaurant for almost 50 years, and it's as homey as any restaurant
around. The menu features traditional regional fare, from chicken
and cheese enchiladas to green-chile burgers. ~ San Luis; 719-672-
9902. BUDGET.

Crestone's top dining establishment is the **Roadkill Café**, where   ◄ HIDDEN
the house specialty is cheeseburgers made from your choice of
ground buffalo or tempeh. The highlight of the unpretentious
decor is a bulletin board announcing current improbable events
around the "town." ~ Alder Street, Crestone; 719-256-4599.
BUDGET.

A fair number of contemporary artists and craftspeople make   **SHOPPING**
their homes in the San Luis Valley, where the cost of living is low.
While most sell their work in other localities, some also show at
galleries in Alamosa. **Firedworks Gallery** exhibits paintings, pottery and weavings by the studio-gallery's owners and other area
artists. ~ 608 Main Street, Alamosa; 719-589-6064. A block down
the street, **Gallery West** features paintings, sculptures, graphics,
ceramics and fiber art by San Luis Valley artists. ~ 718 Main
Street, Alamosa; 719-589-2275.

Traditional arts and crafts from Spanish colonial times, including tinwork and religious wood carving, are still practiced.
The most noteworthy folk-art specialty of the San Luis Valley is
pictorial quilting. Examples are found in museums around the
West, and examples can usually be purchased in the area. A good
place to shop for local arts and crafts is **Centro Artesano**. This
little gallery run by the Catholic church shares the building with
El Convento Bed & Breakfast, providing exhibit space for the
valley's traditional artisans. ~ 512 Church Place, San Luis.

Another church-sponsored gallery, the **San Juan Art Center**,
is located in the Chapel of San Juan Bautista in the small village
of La Garita, eight miles off Route 285 at the foot of the mountains on the northwest side of the San Luis Valley. Open in summer only.

Alamosa's nightlife is pretty much limited to the lounges of the   **NIGHTLIFE**
two biggest motor inns such as **Clancy's** at the Holiday Inn. ~
333 Santa Fe Avenue, Alamosa; 719-589-5833. The other lounge
is **Alamosa Inn Restaurant and Lounge,** which features Monday
night football and the rest of the week . . . TV. ~ 1901 Main Avenue,
Alamosa; 719-589-4943.

RIO GRANDE NATIONAL FOREST 🏃 🚣 This horseshoe-shaped,   **PARKS**
two-million-acre national forest surrounds the San Luis Valley.

The eastern part, which runs along the western slope of the Sangre de Cristo Range, is virtually roadless. Much of it has recently been designated the Southern Sangre de Cristo Wilderness. Most trails are only a few miles long, following gulches up the slope of the high, jagged, unbroken wall of 13,000-foot peaks. You may fish for trout in area streams. There are jeep trails. ~ The easiest trail access is from the Mosca Pass trailhead, off Route 150 in Great Sand Dunes National Monument; 719-852-5941.

SAN LUIS LAKES STATE PARK Shallow, natural San Luis Lake, just west of the Great Sand Dunes, is a locally popular spot for waterskiing, fishing, sailing and windsurfing. The north portion of the lake, as well as the wetlands and smaller Head Lake, are off-limits to boats but laced with wide, level trails for nature lovers to observe wildlife such as migrating whooping cranes and bald eagles, as well as native waterfowl, songbirds, coyotes and pronghorns. Fishing is excellent year-round for trout. The park adjoins the second-largest bison ranch in the United States. Facilities include picnic areas with tables and restrooms. Day-use fee, $4. ~ Located ten miles east of Mosca on Six Mile Lane; 719-378-2020.

▲ There are 51 RV/tent sites with electric hookups, tables and fireplaces, drinking water, showers and laundry facilities; $12 per night. For reservations, call 800-678-2267.

▼▼▼▼▼▼▼▼▼▼▼▼▼▼▼
Creede–Lake City Area

The San Juans of southwestern Colorado are the largest, wildest and least populated mountains in the state. Compared to the western side of this vast range, where adventurous Durango and Telluride visitors often mob old mining roads with hundreds of mountain bikes and four-wheel-drive vehicles, the eastern side adjoining the San Luis Valley has a refreshingly undiscovered feel. The area's main towns—unexpectedly artsy little Creede and the even tinier Texan stronghold of Lake City—are short on development and long on personality. The Silver Thread Scenic Byway, which connects the two towns, takes motorists through some of the most spectacular mountain scenery anywhere.

SIGHTS

Following the Rio Grande toward its source high in the mountains by way of paved Route 149 brings travelers to **Creede**, one of several spectacularly situated, spruced-up old mining towns turned mountain hideaways in the San Juans. (Others include Telluride, Ouray and Silverton, which are covered in Chapter Eight.) Creede is the only one east of the Continental Divide. Founded in 1889 upon the discovery of the richest silver lode in Colorado, Creede is also remembered in history as one of the wildest Western boomtowns. Such legendary characters as the

James Gang, "Calamity Jane" Canary, "Poker Annie" Tubbs, con artist "Soapy" Smith and lawman Bat Masterson passed through Creede during its heyday. The boom lasted for only four years, but unlike other similar mine camps, Creede was never completely abandoned. A self-guided auto tour takes visitors to the steep, narrow canyon above town and several of the mines on which Creede's fortunes rose and fell a century ago. Creede is also home to the finest summer repertory theater in south central Colorado.

A magnificent scenic drive, the 48-mile **Silver Thread Scenic Byway** (Route 149) climbs from Creede to meander gently through lush green mountain meadows where streams flow together to form the headwaters of the Rio Grande. The only difficult part of the drive on the byway is the steep descent from 11,361-foot Slumgullion Pass. Stop at the overlook near the top of the pass for a look at **Slumgullion Slide**, where a huge mudslide eight centuries ago slipped down the slopes below Slumgullion Pass to block the valley and dam the river, forming **Lake San Cristobal**, the second-largest natural body of water in Colorado. Its namesake, the tiny village of **Lake City**, is the Hinsdale County seat—and, in fact, the only town in the county, which otherwise consists of national forest land. Lake City had its beginnings in 1875 as a gold camp, and many wooden storefronts and churches date back to that period. By 1960 it had declined to only six residents, but burgeoning tourism has boosted Lake City's present-day population to 223.

Lake City is the starting point for another national forest scenic route, the **Alpine Loop Backcountry Byway**. This narrow, unpaved   ◀ HIDDEN
63-mile mountain road is very rocky and steep in places, suitable only for four-wheel-drive vehicles and mountain bikes. Passenger cars can take the first stage of the loop, Engineer Pass Road, as far as the site of **Capitol City**. Local ore processor George T. Lee, who founded the town, believed it was destined to become the state

THE "OTHER" RED MEAT . . .

Lake City is best known as the home of Colorado's most macabre historical figure, Alferd Packer, who was convicted of murdering—and eating—five prospectors who had hired him as a guide in 1874. Cannibal jokes have had a place in Colorado culture ever since: The official name of the main student dining hall at the University of Colorado in Boulder (thanks to a student vote a generation ago) is the Alferd E. Packer Memorial Cafeteria, and prominent Coloradans often receive invitations to join a venerable social club called The Friends of Alferd E. Packer. The club's motto: "Serving our fellow man since 1874."

capital, but today the site contains only scattered traces of the lavish governor's mansion that Lee built there soon after Colorado attained statehood.

From Capitol City the road deteriorates quickly as it climbs to the 12,800-foot summit of Engineer Pass and descends the wind-blasted south face of Engineer Peak to the early-day mining district of **Mineral Point** and **Animas Forks**, strewn with rusty mementos of past prosperity. To return to Lake City, take the road from Animas Forks west over Cinnamon Pass (12,620 feet). The return route passes the site of **Sherman**, which was destroyed when a dirt dam burst upriver. Little remains of the town. The road between Sherman and Lake San Cristobal is easily passable by passenger car.

LODGING   Creede has a few small bed and breakfasts in the upstairs rooms of refurbished historic buildings on the main street near the repertory theater. **The Creede Hotel** has been in operation for more than a century and was the only lodging in town until 1992. The four guest rooms in the main house are rather sparsely furnished with mining-era antiques. Two other buildings, with four additional units, have been renovated and opened as bed and breakfasts. Closed mid-October through April. ~ Main Street, Creede; 719-658-2608. MODERATE.

The Old Firehouse No. 1 B&B, decorated with firefighting memorabilia and historic photos of old-time Creede, has four guest rooms and a sitting room with a library and games. On the ground floor is an old-fashioned soda fountain. Open in summer only. ~ Main Street, Creede; 719-658-0212. MODERATE. Across the street, **Blessings** offers four antique-filled rooms with private baths. Open in summer only. ~ Main Street, Creede; 719-658-0215. MODERATE.

The tiny hideaway town of Lake City offers a fine selection of vacation accommodations. Foremost among them is **Crystal Lodge**, secluded in fir-and-aspen forest on the Lake Fork of the Gunnison River near Lake San Cristobal. The lodge offers 18 simple, wood-paneled guest rooms, including five with full kitchens and four housekeeping cabins. The dining room serves the best gourmet meals in town. Amenities include hiking trails, a hot tub and a sundeck with a spectacular view of nearby Crystal Peak. Closed November and April. ~ Route 149 South, Lake City; 970-944-2201, 800-984-1234; fax 970-944-2503. MODERATE TO DELUXE.

A long-established riverbank cabin complex, **Texan Resort**, nestled at the base of a maroon-colored canyon wall on the Lake Fork of the Gunnison River, has 15 housekeeping cabins with full kitchen facilities as well as outdoor barbecue grills. It's an easy walk to a 65-foot waterfall nearby. ~ Route 149 South, Lake City; 970-944-2246. MODERATE.

For travelers who prefer to stay in town, the **Cinnamon Inn Bed & Breakfast** has five guest rooms, including a luxury suite, in an 1878 two-story Victorian residence that belonged to the town jeweler in Lake City's heyday. Each room is individually decorated with period furnishings. A full country breakfast is included in the room rates. ~ 426 Gunnison Avenue, Lake City; 970-944-2641, 800-337-2335. DELUXE.

In Creede, the place to eat is the **Creede Hotel Dining Room**. This little restaurant on the ground floor of a frontier Victorian-style bed and breakfast near the repertory theater serves a full menu of homemade entrées each evening, including tamari-honey chicken, prime rib, baked salmon and fettuccine Alfredo. Can you resist the pecan brandy apple pie? Make reservations well in advance for theater nights. Breakfast, lunch and dinner daily from mid-May through October; dinner only on the weekends the rest of the year. ~ Main Street, Creede; 719-658-2608. MODERATE.

DINING

Eighteen miles southwest of Creede, a rustic-elegant restaurant stands secluded in the heart of Rio Grande National Forest. The **Bristol Inn** serves lobster, roast beef and quail with a Continental flair. It is busiest around noon on Sundays, when an early dinner provides a tantalizing excuse for people all over south central Colorado to go for a drive in the mountains. The inn has an art gallery that exhibits works in various media by 11 local artists. Reservations required. Dinner only. Closed Monday and Tuesday. ~ 39542 Route 149, Creede; 719-658-2455. MODERATE TO DELUXE.

Creede has a mini-arts district on its main street near the repertory theater. **Rare Things**, a studio-gallery, spotlights a horse-hair jewelry collection. ~ Main Street, Creede; 719-658-2376. There's also **Abbey Lane Gallery**. ~ Main Street, Creede; 719-658-2736. And right down the street is **Quiller Gallery**, which features watercolor landscapes. ~ Main Street; 719-658-2741. Latin American folk art is the focus at **Captive Inca**. ~ Main Street, Creede; 719-658-2662.

SHOPPING

Culture in the Rockies pops up in some of the most unlikely places. The **Creede Repertory Theater** has been staging plays in the remote mining town seasonally for more than 30 years. It has gained a reputation as the top summer-stock company in the southern Colorado Rockies. Theater professionals from coast to coast vie for roles in a schedule of plays ranging from Shakespearean tragedies to Broadway musicals. Order tickets well in advance; contact CRT Box Office, P.O. Box 269, Creede, CO 81130. ~ 160 Creede Avenue, Creede; 719-658-2540.

NIGHTLIFE

PARKS

RIO GRANDE NATIONAL FOREST 🏃 🚤 🚤 🚣 The west side of this national forest covers the eastern slope of the San Juans, offering boundless hiking possibilities in the vast Weminuche Wilderness and the smaller La Garita Wilderness, both in the vicinity of Creede. Forest roads off the paved Silver Thread Scenic Byway (Route 149) provide access to campgrounds and natural and artificial lakes in the high country. Fishing is good for trout in Rio Grande Reservoir, Tucker Ponds, Poso Creek and many other lakes and creeks; the upper Conejos River is famous for rainbow trout and kokanee salmon. There are picnic areas, restrooms and an archery range. ~ Main access roads to the national forest are Route 160 below Wolf Creek Pass, and the Silver Thread Scenic Byway (Route 149) beyond Creede. Silver Thread Campground is 25 miles southwest of Creede on Route 149. Big Blue Campground is on Forest Road 868, nine miles northwest of Route 149 north of Lake City; 719-852-5941 or 719-641-0471.

▲ There are seven campgrounds in the Creede area, including Silver Thread Campground, with 11 RV/tent sites (no hookups); closed mid-September through May; $9 per night. The five campgrounds in the Lake City area include Big Blue Campground, with 11 RV/tent sites (no hookups); closed November to mid-June; $4 per night.

▼▼▼▼▼▼▼▼▼▼▼▼▼▼▼▼▼▼▼▼▼
Gunnison–Crested Butte Area

From Lake City, Route 149 follows the Lake Fork of the Gunnison River northeast through a red-cliff gorge and then descends arid foothills to Curecanti National Recreation Area, joining Route 50 in the Gunnison area. In the summer, many visitors to the Gunnison area come for the fishing, as well as other water sports, on Blue Mesa Reservoir, Colorado's largest reservoir. In nearby Crested Butte, mountain biking is the most popular summer sport. Gunnison National Forest surrounds Gunnison and Crested Butte with jeep roads to old mining camps and a network of foot trails that could keep a hiker busy all summer. In the winter, Crested Butte enjoys a wealthier lifestyle as a famous ski resort. Motorists can also reach the Gunnison area on Route 50 from Cañon City and Salida up a series of switchbacks to the summit of Monarch Pass (11,846 feet)—a hard pull for those who are headed for Curecanti National Recreation Area with boats in tow.

SIGHTS

The town of **Gunnison** is situated among dry hills beside a raging whitewater stretch of the Gunnison River. Gunnison has been the site of **Western State College** since 1911. The campus is located at the east edge of town. ~ 600 North Adams Street, Gunnison; 970-943-0120.

Nearby, the **Pioneer Museum** occupies several buildings, including Gunnison's original one-room schoolhouse. On exhibit are a restored narrow-gauge steam train, early-day automobiles and assorted collections of arrowheads, rocks, farming tools and other memorabilia dating as far back as 1874, when Gunnison was founded as a transportation and supply center for mining camps in the surrounding mountains. Admission. ~ Route 50, Gunnison; 970-641-4530.

A few miles west of Gunnison, **Curecanti National Recreation Area** encompasses the three basins of 20-mile-long Blue Mesa Reservoir, the largest manmade lake in Colorado, as well as the smaller and more secluded Morrow Point Reservoir and long, narrow Crystal Lake, which winds through the upper part of the Gunnison River Gorge. In the summer, the National Park Service operates daily boat cruises with naturalist guides on Morrow Point Reservoir (reservations required; 970-641-0402). ~ Route 50; 970-641-0406.

Downriver from Curecanti National Recreation Area, beyond the dam that impounds Crystal Lake, lies **Black Canyon of the Gunnison National Monument**, which contains the most spectacular 12 miles of the Gunnison River Gorge. The canyon's dark gray cliffs of schist and gneiss, almost 3000 feet deep, rise so steeply that in some places the canyon is deeper than its width from rim to rim. The south rim, easily accessed from Route 50 via a paved park road, has a large campground, a visitors center and numerous overlooks and short hiking trails. The more remote north rim is reached only by a long unpaved road from the little town of Crawford on Route 92. ~ Montrose; 970-249-1915.

North of Gunnison on Route 135 is the historic district of **Crested Butte**, which began in 1879 as a way station on the road between Gunnison and Aspen. It became a mining town when Colorado Fuel & Iron, the Rockefeller family's steel company, discovered large deposits of coal there. Coal mining continued in Crested Butte until the 1950s, saving the beautiful frontier Vic-

THE BIRTHPLACE OF MOUNTAIN BIKES

In the 1970s, according to local legend, a bunch of Crested Butte locals made a friendly wager: they would race to Aspen on jeep roads over a 12,700-foot pass on the crest of the Sawatch Range—but instead of jeeps they would ride old-fashioned newspaper bicycles. The race evolved into Fat Tire Bike Week, the world's largest mountain-bike gathering, held each July, and the legend gave rise to Crested Butte's reputation as a mountain biking mecca.

torian town from the decay and abandonment that erased so many other Colorado mining towns from the map. Ski-resort development came within a few years after the mines closed. The historic district retains a lot of authenticity and old-time charm beneath new coats of paint. Across the valley, not quite adjoining the old town, is **Mount Crested Butte**, a development of custom homes and luxury condominiums that stands in dramatic contrast to the old town. Among the modern town's part-time residents is former President Gerald Ford, who put Crested Butte in the news during his brief administration in the mid-1970s.

In its day—from 1881 to 1910—the Alpine Tunnel was recognized as an engineering masterpiece, especially since the monumental amount of heavy labor was done in the rarefied air 11,500 feet above sea level.

Mountain bikes seem to outnumber cars for most of the summer around Crested Butte. To find out why, one needs only look at a Gunnison National Forest map (buy one—$4 plus tax—from the ranger station at 216 North Colorado Street, Gunnison; 970-641-0471 or any of several Crested Butte cycle shops) and marvel at the array of dirt roads and jeep trails that lead into the surrounding mountains.

One of the most spectacular routes that is accessible by passenger car is the unpaved **Kebler Pass Road**, which starts at the west end of White Rock Avenue in Crested Butte and goes 31 miles over Kebler Pass (10,000 feet) to Paonia Reservoir. Following an abandoned railroad bed, the road offers panoramic views of the high peaks of the West Elk Wilderness and provides access to aspen forests, alpine meadows and fishing lakes such as **Lost Lake** and **Lake Irwin**. Near Lake Irwin, a graveyard is just about all that remains of **Irwin**, a silver-mining town that was founded in 1879, flourished briefly with a peak population of almost 5000 and was abandoned by 1884. The saloons, stores and banks have long since been stripped for firewood and their rubble sunk in the soggy marsh that was once the main street.

Some of Colorado's most picturesque old mining towns can be found in the Sawatch Range east of Gunnison and Crested Butte. Eight miles north of Crested Butte on unpaved Forest Road 317 is the site of **Gothic**, a gold-prospecting town that boomed between 1879 and 1881 to 4000 people and 400 buildings—mostly boardinghouses, saloons and bordellos. Unfortunately, none of the eager prospectors who swarmed over the mountainsides around Gothic ever found gold in sufficient quantities to mine, and the town was abandoned in a few years. For the past 60 years, the townsite has been owned by the **Rocky Mountain Biological Laboratory**, which conducts environmental studies there. A number of the old buildings remain standing along the main road, and there are campgrounds nearby. Guides from the laboratory lead flora and fauna tours around Gothic several days a week during the summer. ~ 970-349-7231.

Other old mining towns in varying states of disrepair lie secluded in the mountains east of Gunnison and Crested Butte. **Pitkin**, a notoriously lawless silver-mining town of 1500 people, lasted less than 20 years—from 1879 to 1898—before the mines played out and a rash of fires destroyed the business district. Yet the town was never entirely abandoned; as of the 1990 census, it had a full-time population of 58. Along the paved road to Pitkin, which turns off Route 50 about 12 miles east of Gunnison, lie the ruins of **Ohio City**, a more enduring gold and silver town where mining continued until World War II. A few scattered structures there have been kept up as summer homes.

A mile or so past Pitkin, a rocky dirt road branches off and climbs an old railroad grade for ten miles to the west portal of the **Alpine Tunnel**. It took 18 months for a work crew of 400 men to dig this 1771-foot tunnel through the sheer wall of granite that is the crest of the Sawatch Range. Today, the scope of the accomplishment remains evident even though both portals of the tunnel have collapsed. Nearby are the ruins of Woodstock, where railroad workers lived until 1884, when it was wiped out by an avalanche.

◄ *HIDDEN*

Visitors traveling in high-clearance vehicles can continue on the unpaved road from Pitkin over 12,000-foot Cumberland Pass to **Tincup**, one of the most remote mountain communities in the state. Like Pitkin, Tincup earned a reputation in the early mining days as a wide-open, violent town. With a population of 3000, it had 20 saloons and four graveyards. Abandoned in 1918, Tincup was all but forgotten until the 1950s, when radio host Pete Smythe started broadcasting his popular talk show from "East Tincup" (meaning Denver) and rekindled interest in the old ghost town. Now Tincup has a country store, a church and a cluster of summer homes. The original town is preserved as a historic district.

◄ *HIDDEN*

Beyond Tincup, the road descends to **Taylor Park Reservoir**, a large lake with fishing and boating facilities and campgrounds in a high mountain valley. A paved road follows Taylor Canyon down to join Route 135 between Crested Butte and Gunnison.

For affordable elegance in Gunnison, the best bet is the **Mary Lawrence Inn**. This five-unit bed and breakfast, located in a two-story former rooming house built in 1885 and situated on a tree-shaded side street, has lovingly decorated theme rooms—Victorian, Southwestern Indian, flowery and downright lovely. A gourmet breakfast is included in the room rate. ~ 601 North Taylor Street, Gunnison; 970-641-3343, fax 970-641-6719. MODERATE TO DELUXE.

LODGING

Most of your other lodging choices in Gunnison are the standard-issue motels and motor inns lying along Tomichi Avenue (Route 50). There are independent places such as the plain-and-simple 24-unit **ABC Motel**. ~ 212 East Tomichi Avenue, Gunnison; 970-641-2400, 800-341-8000. BUDGET TO MODERATE. There is also the reasonably-priced luxury of the Southwestern-style, 49-unit **Best Western Tomichi Village**. Rates include continental breakfast. ~ Route 50 East, Gunnison; 970-641-1131, 800-528-1234, fax 970-641-9554. BUDGET TO MODERATE.

One of the nicer guest ranches in the Gunnison–Crested Butte area is **Waunita Hot Springs Ranch**. Set among the pines at 9000 feet in the mountains 27 miles northeast of Gunnison, the ranch has a picture-perfect hot-spring pool. No nude bathing here—the staff is cheerfully Christian and holds nondenominational church services on summer Sundays. The rooms are simple, with wood paneling; designed for families and groups, many have bunk beds. The lodge is heated geothermally with water from the springs. The family-oriented ranch has a petting farm and group activities that include fishing, hiking, horseback riding, river trips, hayrides and four-wheel-drive excursions. Rates include all meals and all activities in summer. Open in winter for cross-country-ski and snowmobile groups, with a two-night minimum. ~ 8007 County Road 887, Gunnison; 970-641-1266. DELUXE.

Luxurious lodging is not why people come to **Irwin Lodge**; isolation is. Situated in the Elk Mountains at 10,700 feet and overlooking Lake Irwin, the lodge is reached via ten miles of unpaved forest roads (transportation is provided from Crested Butte). The barnlike lodge has 24 very simple, spacious rooms with queen-size beds and foldout couches. The rooms open off the long, narrow common room with its 30-foot ceiling. Although snow closes the road to the lodge for about five months of the year, the lodge stays open as a very exclusive ski resort. Sno-Cats carry skiers from the lodge to 2500 acres of remote ski bowls. Après-ski amenities include a giant fireplace and two 20-person jacuzzis. Summer rates for bed and breakfast are in the deluxe price range, while winter rates including all meals, skiing and transportation are ultra-deluxe (three-night minimum stay). ~ 318 Elk Avenue, Crested Butte, CO 81224; 970-349-5308.

Several modern ski lodges and condominium complexes lie at the foot of the Mount Crested Butte ski area. The largest of the lodges, the **Crested Butte Marriott Hotel**, offers 262 bright, contemporary guest rooms and suites with whirlpool baths as well as balconies, refrigerators, king-size beds and queen-size fold-out sofas. The lodge has an indoor swimming pool, outdoor hot tubs, a sauna and a spa. ~ Gothic Road, Mount Crested Butte; 970-349-4000, 800-642-4422, fax 970-349-4466. ULTRA-DELUXE.

Nearby, the **Nordic Inn** offers cozy, ski-from-your-doorstep lodging, with 27 guest units plus two chalets in a distinctive Scandinavian-style lodge. After a day on the slopes, guests relax around the large fireplace that dominates the lobby or soak in the hot tub. Rates include a generous continental breakfast. ~ 14 Treasury Road, Mount Crested Butte; 970-349-5542, 800-542-7669, fax 970-349-6487. ULTRA-DELUXE.

Condominium rentals at Mount Crested Butte are available through **Crested Butte Accommodations**. ~ 800-821-3718.

Lodgings are generally smaller and more homelike in the old town of Crested Butte, about three miles from the slopes. In the winter, shuttle buses run constantly from town to the ski area. In fact, staying in town offers a wider selection of restaurants and nightlife within walking distance. One good choice is the **Crested Butte Club**, a seven-room bed and breakfast in a frontier-style building with a false facade on the town's main street. Originally a social club for Croatian immigrants who worked in the coal mines a century ago, the 1886 building is listed on the National Register of Historic Places. The rooms are large and lavishly decorated in Victorian style, with flowery furniture, old-fashioned fireplaces and copper bathtubs, as well as such modern amenities as four-poster waterbeds. This bed and breakfast is also a health club, so guests have access to a lap pool, steam rooms, weights and exercise machines, as well as aerobic and fitness classes. ~ 512 2nd Street, Crested Butte; 970-349-6655, 800-782-6037, fax 970-349-7580. ULTRA-DELUXE.

The **Claim Jumper**, is whimsical, fun and the most eccentric bed and breakfast in town. The decor—satirical taxidermy and creative clutter that includes a jukebox, a man-eating fish and an in-room putting green—exudes a slightly warped sense of humor, making this six-unit inn a place travelers either love or hate. Each room has its own theme—cowboys, gold miners, sailing ships or sports. ~ 704 White Rock Avenue, Crested Butte; 970-349-6471. DELUXE.

Accommodations in Crested Butte can be hard to find during the winter months. Travelers can save a lot of calls in search of a vacancy by telephoning **Mount Crested Butte Central Reservations**. ~ 800-544-8448. You may also contact the **Crested Butte Chamber of Commerce**. ~ 970-349-6438.

DINING

The established favorite for fine dining in Gunnison is the **Cattlemen Inn**. The decor is ranch-style, and the menu offers a full assortment of hand-cut steaks, from sirloin and rib eye to T-bone and filet mignon, as well as chicken and seafood entrées. ~ 301 West Tomichi Avenue, Gunnison; 970-641-1061. MODERATE TO DELUXE.

The Trough, west of Gunnison on the way to Curecanti National Recreation Area, serves steak, wild game and seafood favorites in a relaxed, casual environment of natural wood and dim lighting. Swordfish, salmon and catch-of-the-day specials make this the best place in the area to satisfy a craving for fish. ~ 37550 West Route 50, Gunnison; 970-641-3724. MODERATE TO DELUXE.

Inexpensive meals, from chicken-fried steak to chimichangas, can be found at the **Sundae Shoppe Restaurant**. The restaurant exhibits local arts and crafts, including a kitsch collage of handmade clocks with faces depicting unicorns, owls, Elvis and the Pope, to name just a few. As the name suggests, the restaurant doubles as a soda fountain and offers a tantalizing array of banana splits, hot-fudge sundaes, chocolate malts and pies. Closed Sunday. ~ 901 West Tomichi Avenue, Gunnison; 970-641-5051. BUDGET TO MODERATE.

The cuisine scene is considerably more interesting in Crested Butte. For starters, the little resort town boasts more French cuisine than the rest of south central Colorado put together. Top of the line is **Le Bosquet**, a small French restaurant decorated in pink hues, lace and photos of French provincial life. The menu features such entrées as elk medallions in cabernet sauce and grilled duck breast in raspberry-mint sauce. ~ Majestic Plaza, 6th Street and Belleview Avenue, Crested Butte; 970-349-5808. DELUXE.

Another French restaurant, **Soupçon**—pronounced "soup's on"—has a more rustic ambience—it's in a historic log cabin in the alley behind Kochevar's Bar. The frontier feel of the restaurant sets off the sheer elegance of the cuisine. The gourmet menu, which changes daily, typically features fresh fish and lamb entrées. Classic appetizers include escargot, caviar and duckling mousse. ~ 127 Elk Avenue, Crested Butte; 970-349-5448. DELUXE.

◆◆◆

✔ CHECK THESE OUT—UNIQUE DINING

- *Budget:* Visit San Luis' **Emma's Hacienda**, where they've been serving green-chile burgers and enchiladas for more than 50 years. *page 257*
- *Moderate to deluxe:* Order some stomach-filling surf-and-turf fare at the **Wooden Nickel**, Crested Butte's oldest restaurant. *page 269*
- *Moderate to deluxe:* Spend a leisurely Sunday in the mountains at the **Bristol Inn**, whose Continental menu features delicacies like lobster and quail. *page 261*
- *Deluxe:* Indulge in haute cuisine such as elk medallions in cabernet sauce at the small French eatery **Le Bosquet**. *page 268*

Budget: under $8   Moderate: $8–$16   Deluxe: $16–$24   Ultra-deluxe: over $24

Karolina's Kitchen, adjoining Kochevar's Bar, serves assorted soups, salads, sandwiches and steaks in a historic building that once served as Crested Butte's blacksmith shop. Vintage photographs and fragments of old-time machinery and equipment, including a moonshine still, decorate the wall. ~ 127 Elk Avenue, Crested Butte; 970-349-6756. MODERATE.

The two-story **Timberline** features a variety of creative Continental dishes, from venison medallions to herb-seasoned pasta in butter sauce and smoked trout. Framed food and wine posters complement the pink-and-gray decor. ~ 21 Elk Avenue, Crested Butte; 970-349-9831. DELUXE.

Located in a picturesque Old West false-front building, the **Slogar Bar & Restaurant** serves delicious home-style fried chicken with all the fixings—cole slaw, fresh vegetables, mashed potatoes and flaky biscuits. Dinner only. ~ 517 2nd Street, Crested Butte; 970-349-5765. MODERATE.

The **Wooden Nickel** is the oldest restaurant in the Crested Butte historic district. The original restaurant on the site had been in business for 56 years when it burned to the ground in 1985, so the same owners built this modern restaurant on the same spot. The decor is a clutter of antiques and oddities, including an intricate wooden ship over the fireplace and a number of deer heads. The menu offers just about anything people are likely to crave after a day on the ski slopes, from jalapeño cheese potato skins to steak and lobster. Dinner only. ~ 222 Elk Avenue, Crested Butte; 970-349-6350. MODERATE TO DELUXE.

An affordable and often lively place for breakfast or lunch is the **Paradise Cafe**. The small restaurant, which occupies part of the large, tourist-oriented general store known as the Company Store, has eclectic decor reminiscent of the South Seas and offers a menu of health-conscious breakfasts and overstuffed deli sandwiches. ~ 303 Elk Avenue, Crested Butte; 970-349-6233. BUDGET.

For Mexican food in Crested Butte, it's **Donita's Cantina**. This cozy restaurant and lounge, built around a big rock fireplace, features not only predictable taco-and-burrito fare but also such unconventional options as spinach enchiladas. Portions are large and prices are reasonable. ~ 330 Elk Avenue, Crested Butte; 970-349-6674. MODERATE.

SHOPPING

Shopping possibilities in Gunnison are limited for the most part to hunting and fishing supplies. The town has one art gallery, **The Great Wall**, specializing in limited-edition Southwestern lithographs. ~ 125 North Main Street, Gunnison; 970-641-4680. The **Gunnison Rockery** carries Indian-style jewelry, decorative rocks and other souvenir items. ~ 107 North Main Street, Gunnison; 970-641-1503.

Crested Butte offers a larger range of shops and galleries. **Paragon Art Gallery** shows works by craftspeople and local artists. ~ 132 Elk Avenue, Crested Butte; 970-349-6484.

In Crested Butte, another good bet for gifts is the **Rocky Mountain Chocolate Factory**, which creates attractive gift baskets of handmade chocolates and cookies. ~ 314 Elk Avenue, Crested Butte; 970-349-0933.

NIGHTLIFE Surprisingly, for a college town Gunnison is practically devoid of nightlife. **The Trough** has comedy shows on Thursday and live rock bands Friday and Saturday nights. ~ 37550 West Route 50, Gunnison; 970-641-3724.

Up the hill in Crested Butte, rowdy après-ski clubs line the main street and rock on all year long. **Kochevar's Bar** retains the feel of an Old West saloon; memorabilia on the walls recall the days when the place was a casino and house of ill repute. Today, pool tables and occasional bands keep the bar lively well past midnight. ~ 127 Elk Avenue, Crested Butte; 970-349-6745.

A block down the street, the **Idle Spur** is a spacious bar and restaurant with a large stone fireplace in the middle. Rock bands play in the back room on Thursday, Friday and Saturday nights. ~ 226 Elk Avenue, Crested Butte; 970-349-5026.

A bit more upscale, the **Wooden Nickel** gradually metamorphoses from restaurant to rock-and-roll bar as the evening wears on. ~ 222 Elk Avenue, Crested Butte; 970-349-9945.

Well-heeled après-ski revelers gather for happy hour at **The Rafters** and party on into the night once the live rock bands get warmed up. ~ Ski Area Central, Mount Crested Butte; 970-349-2298. For mellower surroundings at the foot of the ski slopes, visit the **Dugout Lounge** in the Grand Butte Hotel. Both places are packed elbow-to-elbow during ski season but are pretty dead during the summer months. ~ Mount Crested Butte; 970-349-4041.

PARKS **GUNNISON NATIONAL FOREST** 🚶 🚴 ⛴ 🚤 ⛵ This 1.7 million-acre forest contains 27 mountain peaks over 12,000 feet high. The forest surrounds the towns of Gunnison and Crested Butte, reaching south to include Slumgullion Pass and the mountains above Lake City. On the north, it borders three other national forests—Grand Mesa, White River and San Isabel—in the highest and most remote part of the Colorado Rockies. The West Elk Wilderness, an expanse of granite peaks and alpine ridges southwest of Crested Butte, is a popular backpacking area. East of Gunnison and Crested Butte, the Sawatch Range was a major mining district in the late 19th century. Today, unpaved forest roads and jeep trails lead back to ghost towns and hidden fishing lakes throughout the district. A bowl in the mountains east of Crested Butte forms the spectacular setting for Taylor Park

Reservoir, a popular boating and fishing lake. Fishing is good for trout in Taylor Park Reservoir, Spring Creek Reservoir, Lake Irwin, Lost Lake and many smaller lakes and streams. Facilities include boat ramps at Taylor Park and Spring Creek reservoirs, and picnic areas with tables in Taylor Canyon. ~ Paved routes that provide access to the national forest include Taylor Canyon (Forest Road 742), from Route 135 north of Gunnison to Taylor Park Reservoir; and Quartz Creek (76 Road) from Route 50 east of Gunnison to the ghost town of Pitkin. The unpaved Kebler Pass Road winds through alpine lake country to connect Route 135 at Crested Butte with Route 133 near Paonia to form the West Elk Scenic Loop. Lake Irwin Campground is seven miles west of Crested Butte on County Road 2, then three miles north on Forest Road 826. Lost Lake Campground is 15 miles west on Route 135, then three miles south on Forest Road 706; 970-641-0471.

▲ There are several campgrounds in the Crested Butte area, including the Lake Irwin Campground, with 32 RV/tent sites (no hookups; no drinking water); closed October through May; $8 per night; and Lost Lake Campground, with 10 RV/tent sites (no hookups; no drinking water); closed mid-November to late June; free.

CURECANTI NATIONAL RECREATION AREA

Colorado's largest lake, Blue Mesa Reservoir, is the centerpiece of this boating and fishing area, which also encompasses two smaller reservoirs, Morrow Point Reservoir and Crystal Lake. Blue Mesa Reservoir is used for waterskiing and speedboating; boating on both of the smaller lakes, which have no boat ramps, is limited to hand-carried craft. Fishing is good for rainbow, brook, brown and mackinaw trout and kokanee salmon. An area of Blue Mesa Reservoir called the Bay of Chickens is a favorite windsurfing area. The recreation area also includes many miles of backcountry in the foothills around the lake, although the water is very cold for swimming. There are restrooms, picnic areas and groceries. ~ Located along Route 50 from about 5 to 25 miles west of Gunnison; there are numerous turnoffs to areas of the lakeshore; 970-641-2337.

▲ Permitted in eight campgrounds totaling 352 RV/tent sites (no hookups); $8 to $9 per night.

Outdoor Adventures

FISHING

Hundreds of lakes, rivers and mountain streams throughout south central Colorado offer great fishing for several species of trout; most areas are stocked annually by the Colorado Division of Wildlife. Rainbow and brown trout are the most common, and some areas have kokanee (freshwater salmon). There is bass fishing on some of the larger reservoirs.

Most fishing east of the mountains is in warm-water reservoirs such as Pueblo Reservoir near Pueblo and Trinidad Lake near Trinidad. The catch in these lakes can include largemouth bass, channel catfish, pike, bluegill, carp, bullhead, perch and crappie.

ALAMOSA AREA   West of Antonito, at the southern end of the San Luis Valley, the **Conejos River** is highly regarded by fly-fishermen.

GUNNISON–CRESTED BUTTE AREA   Between Gunnison and Crested Butte, the **Roaring Judy State Wildlife Area** permits fly-fishing in the East River, both upstream and downstream from the state fish hatchery there. It is a catch-and-release area, so all fish under 12 inches long must be returned to the water. **Willowfly Anglers** offers trout-fishing float trips on the upper Gunnison River. ~ 130 County Road 742, Almont, CO 81229; 970-641-1303. The Curecanti National Recreation Area includes Blue Mesa Reservoir and two other reservoirs on the Gunnison River that are stocked with fish. Eight tributary creeks offer good rainbow, brown, brook and cutthroat trout fishing. Fishing guides, as well as bait, tackle and information, are available in Gunnison at **High Mountain Drifter**. ~ 115 South Wisconsin Street, Gunnison; 970-641-4243.

BOATING   **ALAMOSA AREA**   Near Alamosa, the shallow, natural San Luis Lake (the largest of several lakes in San Luis Lakes State Park) is a locally popular spot for waterskiing, fishing, sailing and wind-surfing. There are no boat rentals, though.

GUNNISON–CRESTED BUTTE AREA   A few miles west of Gunnison, Curecanti National Recreation Area offers water sports on 20-mile-long Blue Mesa Reservoir. ~ Route 50; 970-641-0406. The recreation area has two rental concessions with identical rates. You can rent a fishing boat, pontoon boat or cruiser at **Elk Creek Marina** on Route 50 or **Lake Fork Marina** on Route 92; call the recreation area headquarters for information. A more secluded recreational lake is Taylor Park Reservoir, in the mountains east of Crested Butte. Boat rentals there are available through **Taylor Park Boat House**. ~ Taylor Park; 970-641-2922.

RIVER RUNNING   Scenic River Tours runs the Gunnison and Upper Taylor rivers, with trips ranging from the gentle and sublime to fast-action whitewater thrills, including expeditions through the Black Canyon of the Gunnison. ~ 703 West Tomichi Avenue, Gunnison; 970-641-3131.

BALLOON RIDES   **Big Horn Balloon Company** takes passengers on hour-long early-morning flights among the mountain crags that surround the ski resort of Crested Butte. It bills itself as the world's highest-altitude balloon operation. ~ P.O. Box 361, Crested Butte, CO 81224; 970-349-6335.

Located 28 miles north of Gunnison, **Crested Butte Ski Area,** a midsize winter resort, offers excellent downhill skiing for beginners through experts. The total vertical drop is 2775 feet, and there are eight chairlifts. Many consider the north face, where telemarking was invented, to be Colorado's ultimate "extreme skiing" run. The resort rents skis. The ski area is open Thanksgiving to early April. ~ 12 Snowmass Road, Crested Butte; 970-349-2222.

DOWNHILL SKIING

    Monarch Ski Area, 43 miles east of Gunnison, is only about one-third the size of Crested Butte. Since the ski lifts start beside the summit of Monarch Pass (11,312 feet), you ski above timberline on the highest part of the mountain. The vertical drop is 1160 feet. The resort is used mainly by weekenders from Colorado Springs and Denver, but the four chairlifts run almost empty on winter weekdays. Half the trails are suitable for beginners; 25 percent are intermediate and 25 percent are expert. Ski rentals are available. Open Thanksgiving to late March. ~ Route 50, Monarch Pass; 970-539-3573.

Ski Rentals In Mount Crested Butte, **Flatiron Sports** rents downhill and cross-country skis. ~ 10 Crested Butte Way; 970-349-6656.

More than 20 kilometers of groomed cross-country ski trails, maintained by the Crested Butte Nordic Council, start from the outskirts of Crested Butte. For equipment rentals, maps and information on other cross-country ski routes in the area, go to **Alternative Ski & Sport.** ~ 309 6th Street, Crested Butte; 970-349-1320.

CROSS-COUNTRY SKIING

PUEBLO AREA Pueblo's newest and best public course is the 18-hole **Walking Stick Golf Course.** Designed by Arthur Hill, the course rambles over rolling hills on the city's west side. It has cart and club rentals, a restaurant and a bar. ~ 4301 Walking Stick Boulevard; 719-584-3400. You can also rent a cart and clubs for the day at the 27-hole **City Park Golf Course.** ~ 3900 Thatcher Avenue; 719-561-4946. The public is also welcome at the privately owned 18-hole **Pueblo West Golf Club.** ~ Route 50 at McCullock Boulevard; 719-547-2280.

GOLF

WALSENBURG–TRINIDAD AREA The nine-hole golf course at **Walsenburg Golf Club** has a beautiful location adjoining Lathrop State Park. ~ Route 160 West; 719-738-2730. Trinidad also has a nine-hole course, the **Trinidad Municipal Golf Course.** ~ 1415 Nolan Drive; 719-846-4015.

ALAMOSA AREA Golfers visiting the Alamosa area have the unique opportunity to play the game on a buffalo ranch: the 18-hole **Great Sand Dunes Golf Course,** located at Zapata Ranch, offers spectacular views of the sand dunes and mountains along with epic solitude. Green fees include cart use; club rentals are available. ~ 5303 Route 150, Mosca; 719-378-2357. Also in the region is the 18-hole **Alamosa Golf Club**. ~ 6678 North River Road, Alamosa; 719-589-9515.

GUNNISON–CRESTED BUTTE AREA   On the outskirts of Gunnison, the 18-hole **Dos Rios Golf Club** is open to the public in the summer months; cart and club rentals are available. ~ Route 50, Gunnison; 970-641-1482. Near the foot of the ski slopes at Crested Butte, the 18-hole golf course at **Skyland Resort** is ranked as one of the best in America. The spectacular mountain setting is one of the reasons former U.S. President Gerald Ford says it's his favorite golf course. Cart usage is included in the greens fee; club rentals are available. ~ 385 Country Club Drive, Mount Crested Butte; 970-349-6131.

TENNIS

Pueblo has a 17-court tennis complex in **City Park**. ~ 800 Goodnight Avenue; 719-566-1745. Crested Butte has three municipal tennis courts in **Town Park**, open to the public at no charge on a first-come, first-served basis.

RIDING STABLES

Near Gunnison, guided private and group rides are available at **Monarch Valley Ranch**. ~ Route 50, Gunnison; 970-641-6177. Horse rentals and guided daytrips are also offered at **Just Horsin' Around**. ~ P.O. Box 173, Gunnison, CO 81230; 970-349-9822. One-hour to all-day guided trail rides on Crested Butte Mountain are offered by **Lazy F Bar Outfitters**, located two miles past the Crested Butte Airport. ~ 2991 County Road 738, Gunnison; 970-349-7593.

PACK TRIPS & LLAMA TREKS

GUNNISON–CRESTED BUTTE AREA   Multiday horse pack trips into the West Elk and Raggeds wilderness areas can be arranged at **Teocalli Outfitters**. ~ Route 135, Almont; 970-349-5675.

BIKING

PUEBLO AREA   The **Pueblo Greenway** offers 30 miles of multiuse trails suitable for biking along the Arkansas River, from Lake Pueblo east through Pueblo.

ALAMOSA AREA   The flat, straight roads of the **San Luis Valley** make the area ideal for bicycle touring. Besides the main highways, a grid of farm roads crisscrosses the valley with very little traffic.

CREEDE–LAKE CITY AREA   There are national forest jeep roads suitable for mountain biking in the **Cumbres Pass** area west of Antonito. For information, contact the Rio Grande National Forest Headquarters. ~ 1803 West Route 160, Monte Vista; 719-852-5941. In the Creede area, contact Rio Grande National

Forest, Creede Ranger District for information. ~ P.O. Box 270, Creede, CO 81130; 719-658-2556.

GUNNISON–CRESTED BUTTE AREA   Since the sport was invented in Crested Butte in the late 1970s, mountain biking has become Colorado's most popular summertime sport. World-class, organized events include Crested Butte's Fat Tire Bike Week in July. Some popular mountain-biking routes in the area are **Kebler Pass Road** and the roads from **Pitkin** to the west portal of the **Alpine Tunnel** and over Cumberland Pass to **Tincup** and **Taylor Park Reservoir**. For details on these and many other forest roads that make good bike routes, get a Gunnison National Forest map from the ranger station. ~ 216 North Colorado Street, Gunnison; 970-641-0471.

Bike Rentals   In Alamosa, **Kristi Mountain Sports** provides bike rentals for road and all-terrain touring. ~ 7565 West Route 160; 719-589-9759. In Creede, **San Juan Sports** rents mountain bikes. ~ 102 Main Street; 719-658-2359. In Gunnison, mountain bike rentals are at **Tomichi Cycles**. ~ 134 West Tomichi Avenue; 970-641-9069. Bicycling is a big industry in Crested Butte, where rentals are available at half a dozen shops including **Paradise Bikes & Skis**. ~ 232 Elk Avenue, Crested Butte; 970-349-6324. **Flatiron Sports** also provides rentals here. ~ 10 Crested Butte Way; 970-349-6656. Or you may contact **Crested Butte Sports Ski & Bike Shop**. ~ 35 Emmons Road; 970-349-7516.

All distances listed for hiking trails are one way unless otherwise noted.

HIKING

WALSENBURG–TRINIDAD AREA   In San Isabel National Forest, the short, steep **West Spanish Peak Trail** (3 miles) to the 13,626-foot summit west of Trinidad is one of several outstanding trails among the Spanish Peaks. A longer but easier trail, the **Wahatoya Trail** (10 miles), climbs over the saddle between the two peaks;

✔ **CHECK THESE OUT—UNIQUE OUTDOOR ADVENTURES**

- Test your fly-fishing prowess at the Roaring Judy State Wildlife Area where a trout is a "keeper" as long as it's over a foot long! *page 272*
- Schuss down the North Face at Crested Butte Ski Area, considered by experts to be America's ultimate "extreme skiing" run. *page 273*
- Play golf on a buffalo ranch amid spectacular scenery at the Great Sand Dunes Golf Course (but beware the world's largest sand trap). *page 274*
- Ride the road where mountain biking was invented—Kebler Pass between Crested Butte and Aspen. *page 275*

the distance from the trailhead on Huahatolla Valley Road to the upper ridge is four miles, and from there it is possible to leave the established trail and scramble across rocky alpine terrain to the summit of **East Spanish Peak**.

ALAMOSA AREA   Although no permanent trails mar the sands of **Great Sand Dunes National Monument**, it is virtually impossible to get lost. Yet the dunes are so vast that hikers with plenty of water can explore the dune field for days (backcountry hiking permit required). Also in the national monument, the **Mosca Pass Trail** (3.5 miles) climbs to the crest of the Sangre de Cristo Range for spectacular views of the San Luis and Wet Mountain valleys.

CREEDE–LAKE CITY AREA   Various trailheads in the vicinity of Creede provide access to the Weminuche Wilderness. They range from the fairly easy climb to Ruby Lake on the **Fern Creek Trail** (3.5 miles) to the 80-mile stretch of the **Continental Divide Trail** that crosses the wilderness from Stony Pass to Wolf Creek Pass.

GUNNISON–CRESTED BUTTE AREA   Curecanti National Recreation Area has hiking trails through a wide range of habitats: the lush streamside greenery of the five-mile **Neversink Trail**; the dry, rugged **Curecanti Needle Trail** (2.5 miles) to the base of the spire-like rock formation for which it is named; and the steep **Curecanti Creek Trail** (2 miles) down to Morrow Point Reservoir in the Black Canyon of the Gunnison. Within **Black Canyon of the Gunnison National Monument**, four trails, ranging in distance from one to three miles, descend from the rim to the river; a high-clearance vehicle is necessary to reach the trailheads.

Hikers can explore the West Elk Wilderness west of Gunnison and Crested Butte on the **Mill Creek Trail** (15 miles), which climbs to heights of over 12,000 feet. There is an extensive network of interconnecting trails from **Cement Creek**, seven miles south of Crested Butte. Perhaps the ultimate hike in the Crested Butte area is the **Conundrum Trail** (14 miles), which starts above the ghost town of Gothic and crosses the Continental Divide to Conundrum Hot Springs and, from there, descends toward Aspen.

▼▼▼▼▼▼▼▼▼▼▼
Transportation

CAR

South central Colorado has two main east–west highways, each of which crosses the Continental Divide over a high switchback pass. **Route 50** exits from Route 25 at Pueblo, winding its way over Monarch Pass (11,312 feet) and then descending into the Gunnison–Crested Butte area. **Route 160** exits from Route 25 at Walsenburg and, after an easy climb over La Veta Pass (9413 feet), descends into the San Luis Valley and the Alamosa area, then continues over Wolf Creek Pass (elevation 10,850 feet).

Several north–south highways connect Route 50 with Route 160. The straightest and fastest roads are **Route 285** and **Route**

17, both of which run the length of the San Luis Valley, meeting Route 50 at Poncha Springs and Route 160 at Salida. **Route 149**, also known as the Scenic Thread Scenic Byway, meets Route 50 at Gunnison, goes through Lake City and Creede and intersects Route 160 at Del Norte.

AIR

The **Pueblo Memorial Airport** has America West, Continental Express and Trans World Airlines flights; both **City Cab** (719-543-2525) and **City Bus** provide airport ground transportation.

Mesa Airlines/United Express has flights between Denver and **Alamosa Municipal Airport**. Visitors arriving by air may wish to arrange shuttle service through their lodging; no public transportation is available in Alamosa.

Continental Express, Mesa Airlines/United Express and Sky-west/Delta Connection fly into **Gunnison County Airport**. The airport, which serves both Gunnison and Crested Butte, also handles ski-trip flights from other parts of the United States during the winter months. Airport shuttle service is furnished by **Alpine Express**. ~ 970-641-5074.

TRAIN

Amtrak's "Southwest Limited" crosses southern Colorado with a stop in Trinidad on its route between Chicago and Los Angeles. Call for schedule information and reservations. ~ 800-872-7245.

BUS

TNM&O Coaches, a Greyhound affiliate, provides service to Pueblo. ~ 116 North Main Street; 719-544-6295. They also service Trinidad. ~ 639 West Main Street; 719-846-7271.

Greyhound Bus Lines has bus service to Gunnison. ~ 800-231-2222.

CAR RENTALS

In Pueblo's airport, try **Avis Rent A Car** (800-331-1212), **Budget Rent A Car** (800-527-0700) and **Hertz Rent A Car** (800-654-3131).

Rental cars are scarce in the Alamosa area. Try **L & M Auto Rentals**. ~ Alamosa Municipal Airport, Alamosa; 719-589-4651. Or contact **Whitlock Motors**. ~ 1313 Route 160, Monte Vista; 719-852-5152.

Agencies at the Gunnison County Airport include **Avis Rent A Car** (800-331-1212), **Budget Rent A Car** (800-527-0700) and **Hertz Rent A Car** (800-654-3131). Four-wheel drives can be rented in Crested Butte at **Whetstone Automotive 4-Wheel-Drive Rental**. ~ 301 Belleview Avenue; 970-349-7374. **Flatiron Sports** also rents four-wheel-drives. ~ 10 Crested Butte Way; 800-821-4331. In Lake City, **Rocky Mountain Jeep Rental** provides jeeps. ~ 549 South Gunnison Avenue, Wade's Addition; 970-944-2262. Also try **Lake City Auto & Jeep Rentals**. ~ 809 Route 149; 970-944-2311.

PUBLIC TRANSIT   Pueblo public transportation is provided by **City Bus**. ~ 719-542-4306.

TAXIS   Taxi service is provided in Pueblo by **Pueblo City Cab**. ~ 210 West 2nd Street; 719-543-2525. In Gunnison try **Alpine Express**. ~ Gunnison County Airport; 970-641-5074. In Crested Butte taxi service is available through **Town Taxi**. ~ 26 Cinnamon Mountain Road; 970-349-5543.

EIGHT

Southwestern Colorado

Stone towers stand silent watch over hidden canyons littered with painted pot shards and marked with shamanic petro-glyphs, remnants of an ancient civilization that arose among the juniper-covered mesas a thousand years ago and then vanished; today, only wild horses live in the canyons. Unknowable and often baffling even to archaeologists, the mysteries of these ruins tug at a visitor's imagination. Meanwhile, an hour's drive up the highway, tourists line up to board the old-time steam train that will carry them on an all-day excursion through Colorado's most dramatic mountain scenery, inching across sheer cliffs and dizzying trestles to a born-again Victorian-era mining town high in the San Juan Mountains.

The San Juans are so vast that they can accommodate every kind of recreation. As motorists take in the thrill-a-minute scenery along the 200-mile highway loop coined the San Juan Skyway, mountain bikers and off-roaders explore the web of hundreds of miles of dirt wagon roads and railroad beds leading to forgotten ghost towns that once yielded fortunes in gold and silver. Elsewhere in the same mountains, Colorado's largest wilderness areas offer backcountry trails where hikers can go for a week or more without crossing a single road, paved or otherwise. Mountain climbers liken the challenges presented by the jagged, spirelike peaks to those found in the Swiss Alps. And in an even more remote part of the mountains, many people believe, the last grizzly bears in Colorado make their home far from the reach of human eyes.

Southwestern Colorado emerged as a tourist area much later than the state's other major destinations. At the time the Pikes Peak region, Estes Park and Aspen began striking it rich in the tourist business, about the most exciting thing happening in this distant corner of the state was the pinto bean crop. Surrounded on three sides by Indian reservations and on the fourth by high mountains, the Durango area was almost three hundred miles from any larger town. To reach it, motorists had to maneuver their way over steep Wolf Creek Pass, one of the last highways in Colorado to be paved. The region was so hard to reach that during the 1920s an archaeologist actually disassembled an ancient cliff dwelling in McElmo Canyon stone by stone and reassembled it on a cliff face above Manitou Springs west of Colorado Springs—so that visitors could see for themselves a cliff dwelling of the Ancestral Pueblo culture whose empire spanned the Four Corners region, without making the long, arduous journey all the way to the southwestern mesas. The Ancestral Puebloans were known to archaeologists as Anasazi (Navajo for "ancient enemies") until 1997, when their Hopi descendants persuaded the U.S. government to declare the term Anasazi politically incorrect and change it at all national parks and monuments.

As roads improved, attendance figures grew gradually at Mesa Verde National Park, site of the most elaborate cliff dwellings. But it was not until the late 1970s, with the opening of the Durango & Silverton Narrow-Gauge Railroad and the emergence of Telluride as Colorado's most out-of-the-way ski resort in winter and leading music and art festival venue in summer, that visitors began coming to Durango in numbers comparable to other Colorado tourist destinations.

Tourists may be more common these days, but much of the region has retained its traditional character. In fact, southwestern Colorado is the only part of the state where Indians live on tribal land today. The Ute people who live south of the Durango area—and formerly claimed the entire region as their homeland—add an additional dimension to the local cultural heritage. Although their reservation appears small on the map, it and the adjoining Navajo and Hopi reservations form a bloc of Indian lands larger than the states of Massachusetts, Connecticut and Vermont combined. Nor are Indians the only distinctive subcultures that help shape southwestern Colorado's unique character. Buckskin-clad mountain men still live in the wild San Juans, and the hills east of Durango are home to a traditional rural community of Basque sheepherders.

Pagosa Springs Area

One of the largest and hottest geothermal springs in the United States, the Great Pagosa Hot Spring has been held sacred in American Indian tradition since ancient times for the curative power of its sulphurous mineral water. It was used for healing by Ute, Navajo and Apache people, and probably in earlier times by the Ancestral Pueblo people living at nearby Chimney Rock. The town of Pagosa Springs sprang up in connection with developers' attempts to convert the spring into a European-style spa (the water's mineral content is similar to that of the famous Karlsbad Spa in the Czech Republic), but none of the spas flourished until recent times, when basking in geothermals pools became the preferred après-ski pastime for skiers at nearby Wolf Creek Ski Area. Though the area has seen steady, modest development in recent years, its vast mountains and cozy town center seem "undiscovered" compared to most areas of southwestern Colorado.

SIGHTS   Motorists coming from the eastern slope on Route 160 reach the Durango area by way of **Wolf Creek Pass** (10,850 feet), one of

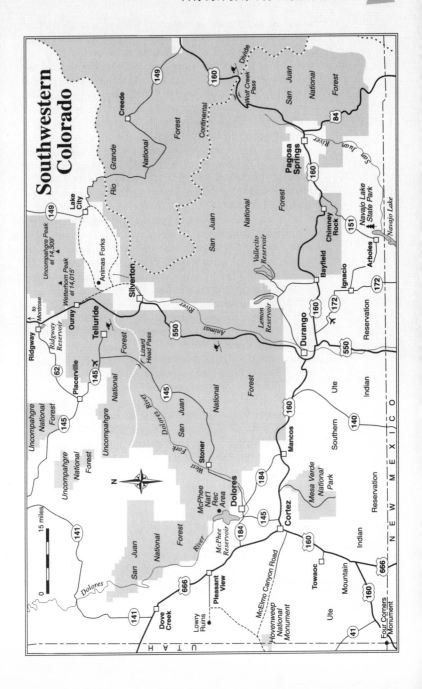

Southwestern Colorado

the highest and steepest passes on any U.S. highway. At the foot of the winding descent down the west side of the pass lies **Pagosa Springs**, a likable little town named for the steamy, slightly sulfurous **Great Pagosa Hot Spring** located behind the visitors information center in the middle of town. The depth of the spring is unknown; it has been plumbed to 850 feet without reaching the bottom. The bathing area, operated as a spa by the Spring Inn, is arranged in a series of cooling pools that dilute the scalding 154°F spring, said to be the hottest natural mineral spring in the world.

"Pagosa" is the Ute word for "healing water," and the springs were traditionally used as a gathering place and wintering ground by nomadic Indians of the region, who built a 50-foot-long pool to mix the scalding geothermal water with chilly river water for bathing. In 1878 the U.S. Army built a fort here, and 13 years later the town was established by developers who hoped to popularize it as a hot springs spa. But Wolf Creek Pass presented a formidable barrier that inspired travelers to visit other, easier-to-reach spas instead. The Pagosa Springs economy has traditionally depended on timber cutting in the surrounding national forest, and as logging operations in the area have been phased out in favor of recreational uses, the town has evolved into a low-key resort area. The history of the hot springs and the area's Ute Indian inhabitants and early settlers is recalled in displays of photos and artifacts at the **San Juan Historical Society Pioneer Museum**. Other exhibits include a one-horse open sleigh and a fully equipped blacksmith shop. ~ 1st and Pagosa streets, Pagosa Springs; 970-264-4424.

Two miles west of town is the **Fred Harman Art Museum**, exhibiting collected works by the late Pagosa Springs artist whose cowboy comic strip, "Red Ryder," was syndicated worldwide in the 1950s. ~ Route 160, Pagosa Springs; 970-731-5785.

Between Pagosa Springs and Durango, three miles off Route 160 on the road to Navajo Lake, the **Chimney Rock Archaeological Area** is open to visitors from mid-May to mid-September by

---

✔ CHECK THESE OUT—UNIQUE SIGHTS

- Take a look at **Great Pagosa Hot Spring**, one of the largest, hottest, deepest geothermal springs in the United States. *page 282*
- Hop aboard the famous **Durango & Silverton Narrow-Gauge Railroad**, which chugs along the edge of the vast San Juan Wilderness, affording unforgettable scenery. *page 286*
- Explore hidden Ancestral Pueblo sites such as the strangely haunting towers of **Hovenweep National Monument**. *page 297*
- Ride Telluride's free public **gondola** for fantastic mountain views and great hiking, biking and cross-country skiing trails. *page 300*

guided tour only; the rest of the year, only group reservations are offered. Nine hundred years ago, this ancient Ancestral Pueblo site was the most distant "outlier," or colony, of the huge settlement at Chaco Canyon in New Mexico. Archaeologists believe that mostly single men lived at the Chimney Rock pueblo, which served as both a ceremonial center and a lumber camp from which logs were floated down the Piedra River for use as roof beams in Chaco Canyon. Admission. ~ Route 151; 970-264-2268.

LODGING

In Pagosa Springs, the classiest place to stay is three and a half miles west of town at the 100-room **Pagosa Lodge**. The lodge is on a private lake in a resort community of custom-built vacation homes and condominiums with a golf course, tennis courts and a swimming pool, all under a spectacular mountain skyline. Touches of Southwestern decor and furnishings as tasteful as they are durable brighten the rather condominium-like guest rooms. ~ 3505 West Route 160, Pagosa Springs; 970-731-4141, 800-523-7704. MODERATE TO DELUXE.

Right in the center of town, the **Spring Inn** has 20 standard double-bed, phone, shower, cable TV motel rooms, two suites and one big difference: guests have unlimited use of the inn's 13 outdoor geothermal pools set in a landscaped fantasy oasis on the bank of the San Juan River. It's one of the best hot-springs facilities in southern Colorado. ~ 165 Hot Springs Boulevard, Pagosa Springs; 970-264-4168, 800-225-0934, fax 970-264-4707. MODERATE.

Guests can also soak in hot-spring pools at the **Oak Ridge Motor Inn**, a conventional mid-range establishment where the rooms have air conditioning and offer a choice of two double beds or one queen-size. ~ 158 Hot Springs Boulevard, Pagosa Springs; 970-264-4173, fax 970-264-4472. MODERATE.

There are individual geothermal tubs at the nearby, no-frills **Spa Motel**, where the rooms are tidy, well lit and close to the pool. ~ 317 Hot Springs Boulevard, Pagosa Springs; 970-264-5910, 800-832-5523, fax 970-261-6063. BUDGET.

The 10,000-square-foot **Echo Manor Inn**, known among locals as "the castle," was a typical Queen Anne–style residence until a previous owner—inspired by a visit to Disneyland, so the story goes—started building on towers, gables and sprawling additions, creating an architectural curiosity of such mammoth proportions that cars often stop on the highway to take snapshots. The lodge has a game room, a sun deck, a hot tub and a fantastic view of the San Juans. There are nine rooms, each individually decorated in country style with antiques and a handmade quilt, and there is a three-bedroom suite with a kitchen and fireplace. ~ 3366 Route 84, Pagosa Springs; 970-264-5646, fax 970-264-4617. MODERATE TO DELUXE.

DINING

Most Pagosa Springs restaurants are several miles out of town. **Ole Miners**, east of Pagosa Springs, specializes in surf and turf. There is a wider selection of seafood here than in most other southern Colorado restaurants—including lobster, Alaskan King crab, rainbow trout, catfish, flounder and shrimp. The restaurant is designed for privacy, with cozy dining nooks containing one or two tables each, separated by rough-hewn wood dividers. The decor is like a mining museum, with shovels, rusty machinery, old photographs and an antique bathtub that serves as a salad bar. Dinner only. ~ 3825 East Route 160, three miles east of Pagosa Springs; 970-264-5981. DELUXE.

At the **Branding Iron Bar-B-Q**, next door to Ole Miners, the menu is simple: your choice of Texas-style barbecued beef, pork ribs, sausage or chicken, served with potatoes, pinto beans and corn-on-the-cob, plus pecan pie for dessert. The simple dining room has rustic pine-paneled walls decorated with branding irons and Indian rugs, and there is more seating on the small outdoor patio. Closed November through April; closed Sunday. ~ 4101 East Route 160, three miles east of Pagosa Springs; 970-264-4268. BUDGET.

The **Green House**, a contemporary two-story restaurant with picture windows that provide great views of Pagosa Peak and the nearby airport, offers something for everybody; choose from filet mignon, steak Diane, grilled salmon, roast turkey or pizza, as well as homemade soups and spinach salad. ~ Piedra Road, three miles west of Pagosa Springs; 970-731-2021. MODERATE TO DELUXE.

PARKS

SAN JUAN NATIONAL FOREST 🏃 🛶 🚤 🎣 This two-million-acre forest includes a 130-mile expanse of mountains north of Pagosa Springs and Durango, from the Continental Divide on the east to the Dolores River on the west. The part of the forest around Pagosa Springs includes Williams Reservoir and portions of two major wilderness areas—the 459,000-acre Weminuche Wilderness to the north and the 128,000-acre South San Juan Wilderness to the east. Fishing is good for rainbow trout, brook trout and kokanee salmon in Williams Creek Reservoir. There are picnic areas, restrooms and pack trails. ~ There is trail access to the national forest from Route 160. Major trailheads for the South San Juan Wilderness are near East Fork Campground, ten miles northeast of Pagosa Springs off Route 160, and Forest Roads 662/665 east of Pagosa Springs. Access to Weminuche Wilderness trailheads and Williams Creek Reservoir is via Forest Road 631, which leaves the main highway two miles west of town. The distance to the reservoir is 22 miles; 970-274-4874.

▲ Of the eight forest service campgrounds in the Pagosa Springs area, the closest to town is East Fork Campground, with

26 RV/tent sites (no hookups); open mid-May to mid-November; $7 per night. At Williams Creek Reservoir, Williams Creek Campground has 69 RV/tent sites (no hookups); open mid-May to mid-November; $7 to $9 per night; reservations recommended on weekends—call 800-280-2267, fax 301-722-9802.

NAVAJO LAKE STATE PARK 🛶 🚤 ⛴ Thirty-five-mile-long Navajo Lake wanders among pine-forested hills and reaches into a hundred hidden side canyons. The reservoir was created in 1962 when the San Juan River was dammed to provide irrigation for the Navajo Indian Reservation. Most of the lake lies in New Mexico, where there is another state park of the same name. At the opposite end of the lake from the dam, Colorado's Navajo Lake State Park combines a wild, remote feel with a few modern conveniences such as an airstrip for fly-in campers and the largest boat ramp in the state (80 feet wide and a quarter-mile long). Fishing and waterskiing are the main water sports. The lake is populated by bluegill, catfish, crappie, largemouth bass, kokanee salmon and rainbow, brown and brook trout. The visitors center displays Ancestral Pueblo and Ute artifacts found in the canyons that were flooded by the lake. Wildlife in the park includes bald eagles, wild turkeys, beaver, mink, foxes, deer and elk. Mountain lions inhabit the backcountry but are rarely seen. Facilities include picnic area with tables and restrooms, boat ramp, airstrip, marina with boat, ski and fishing tackle rentals and groceries. Food and lodging are two miles away in Arboles. Day-use fee, $4. ~ Located two miles south of Arboles and Route 151. Navajo Lake State Park is 35 miles south of Pagosa Springs and 45 miles southeast of Durango; 970-883-2208.

▲ The 71-site campground is situated on a peninsula so that most sites have water frontage; $7 to $10 per night ($4 per night in the primitive tent area). There are showers, flush toilets and a dump station; four sites have electric hookups.

▼▼▼▼▼▼▼▼▼▼
Durango Area

Durango is the largest town in southwestern Colorado and the natural hub for exploring the Four Corners area. The San Juans, the most spectacular mountains in the central Rockies, dominate the region's skyline wherever you go. The Durango area is a full day's drive from any major population center, giving it an off-the-beaten-path feel.

In spite of its rather isolated location, Durango boasts one of Colorado's most popular tourist attractions—the narrow-gauge railroad to Silverton. The town also serves as a base camp for the many thousands of outdoor enthusiasts who each year venture into the San Juan Mountains by car, jeep or mountain bike or on horseback or foot to gaze with awe upon a panorama of unvanquished mountain crags that has often been likened to the Swiss Alps.

SIGHTS   About 25 miles northeast of Durango is **Vallecito Reservoir**, a popular boating and fishing area. The shore is lined with campgrounds, marinas, motels, lodges, bed and breakfasts, restaurants and cocktail lounges. Not far away is the less-developed Lemon Reservoir. Both reservoirs are manmade.

Routes 501 and 240 make for a pretty back-road trip between Bayfield and Durango through sheep-ranching country. Many of the sheepherders in this area are Basques who retain their unique language and many traditions brought from the Pyrenees between Spain and France.

Durango got its start in 1880 as a smelter town where gold and silver ore from the mining camps in the San Juan Mountains was refined. Within two years the boom town rivaled Denver as the richest city in Colorado. Although the gold-mining era ended, the town slid into poverty and many structures in Durango were abandoned, the solidly built, elaborately ornamented red-brick buildings downtown endured through the decades. Good times began returning to Durango in the mid-1950s, when Fort Lewis College was established there and the popularity of nearby Mesa Verde National Park began to grow and boosted the local economy. When the Durango & Silverton Narrow-Gauge Railroad was revived in 1981, the town saw a surge of tourism that lifted it to a new level of prosperity. Today, Durango throbs with youthful exuberance thanks to the college students who make up a sizable part of its population. The town also has far more than its share of latter-day mountain men, old and young, who live in the wilderness of the San Juans, at least during the warm months, and who come into town for supplies and celebrations.

Each morning from May through October, the **Durango & Silverton Narrow-Gauge Railroad** fills Durango's downtown historic district with steam and tumult as it loads passengers for the 45-mile trip to Silverton in the heart of the San Juan Mountains. Though steam locomotives pull sightseeing trains through many parts of the West these days, the Durango & Silverton trip, with its trestles hundreds of feet above the Animas River and its thrilling climb along a narrow shelf cut into the sheer Animas River Canyon wall, remains unsurpassed. The trip to Silverton takes three hours. Passengers have a three-hour stay, plenty of time for lunch and shopping. The two-hour return trip arrives in Durango at dinnertime. Passengers can choose to spend one or more nights in Silverton before returning to Durango. One-way tickets allow backpackers to get off the train at the Needleton or Elk Park trailhead and trek into the Weminuche Wilderness. The Durango & Silverton Narrow-Gauge Railroad is one of the most popular tourist attractions in Colorado, carrying more than 200,000 passengers a year; reservations are essential and should be made at least a month in advance. Admission. ~ 479 Main Avenue, Durango; 970-247-2733.

North of Durango up the Animas River Canyon, Route 550 passes the ski resort of **Purgatory**. In the summer months, the ski lift carries thrill seekers up the slopes to career down an **alpine slide** on vehicles that look like a cross between a sled and a skateboard. Admission. ~ Route 550, Durango; 970-247-9000.

The perfect ending to a Durango day is a relaxing dip in **Trimble Hot Springs**. The original resort on the site was built in 1883. Recently rebuilt and reopened, the present hot springs have an Olympic-size swimming pool and a smaller, hotter pool; the water comes from underground at 119°F and is diluted to 104° before being piped into the pool. The hot springs are open late into the evening year-round and are especially popular in the winter months, when people stop there on the way back to Durango from the Purgatory ski slopes. Admission. ~ 6475 County Road 203, Durango; 970-247-0111.

LODGING

The shores of Vallecito Reservoir, northeast of Durango, are lined with cabins, most of them in small rental-cabin compounds referred to as lodges. For instance, try **Circle S Lodge**, situated at the north end of the lake near the edge of the Weminuche Wilderness. The 14 cabins are spacious enough to accommodate up to nine people and have carpeting, kitchenettes and fireplaces. ~ 18022 County Road 501, Bayfield; 970-884-2473, fax 970-884-2470. DELUXE.

Farther along the east shore of the lake, two miles past the end of the pavement, **Elk Point Lodge** offers nine cabins, most with fireplaces, and also rents horses and boats. The cabins vary

---

✔ **CHECK THESE OUT—UNIQUE LODGING**

- *Budget:* Beat the high cost of mountain hideaways at the **Teller House Hotel**, a former miners' boardinghouse turned Victorian hostel. *page 308*
- *Moderate:* Stay at Pagosa Springs' **Spring Inn** and enjoy 13 steamy geothermal pools at the Inn's spa. *page 283*
- *Moderate to ultra-deluxe:* Experience the good life at the **China Clipper**, an elegant mansion in small-town Ouray. *page 307*
- *Ultra-deluxe:* Find out why the **Lightner Creek Inn** is one of the state's finest B&Bs when you stroll the acres of manicured lawns then retire to an exquisitely decorated bedroom. *page 290*

Budget: under $50   Moderate: $50–$90   Deluxe: $90–$130   Ultra-deluxe: over $130

in size and range in price. ~ 21730 County Road 501, Bayfield; 970-884-2482. BUDGET TO DELUXE.

At the top of the list of Durango's restored historic lodgings is the **Strater Hotel**, which has been in continuous operation since 1887, when it was one of the most luxurious hotels in the West. Beautifully maintained, the interior of the five-story hotel now glows with a soft patina of authentic frontier elegance. Twelve-foot-high mirrors and gold-papered walls brighten the lobby, where a big writing desk looks out upon Main Avenue. Since the second coming of the railroad brought prosperity back to Durango, the guest rooms have been upgraded to grand-hotel quality with flowery carpets and ornate 100-year-old walnut furnishings. Rates include breakfast. ~ 699 Main Avenue, Durango; 970-247-4431, 800-247-4431, fax 970-259-2208. DELUXE TO ULTRA-DELUXE.

Rates at Durango motels drop by 50 percent or more in the winter—a great bargain for skiers at nearby Purgatory.

A block down the street stands Durango's other historic landmark hostelry, the **General Palmer Hotel**. The hotel's namesake, Denver & Rio Grande Railroad owner William Jackson Palmer, founded the town of Durango, as well as other Colorado towns including Colorado Springs. The hotel, which dates back to 1898, was recently restored with period antiques and reproductions. It looks brighter and shinier than the Strater though somehow less genuinely old. The long, narrow lobby has brass fittings, dark wood trim, pink wallpaper, overstuffed armchairs, loveseats, rocking chairs and carpeting in Victorian floral patterns. There is a library with a picture window on Main Avenue, as well as a window display room full of teddy bears. Each room is individually decorated and features a full- or queen-size poster bed, pewter bed or brass bed. ~ 567 Main Avenue, Durango; 970-247-4747, 800-523-3358, fax 970-247-1332. DELUXE TO ULTRA-DELUXE.

Renovated in 1995, the **Jarvis Suite Hotel**, in a former theater listed on the National Register of Historic Places, offers 22 sunny, modern suites, each with a fully equipped kitchen. The location, within easy walking distance of the railroad station and downtown galleries and restaurants, is ideal. ~ 125 West 10th Street, Durango; 970-259-6190, 800-824-1024, fax 970-259-6190. MODERATE TO DELUXE.

For a low-priced Victorian atmosphere, try the **Central Hotel and Hostel**. This 1892 hotel is upstairs from a downtown pool hall known as the El Rancho Tavern, where Jack Dempsey won $50 in a prizefight in 1915, four years before he claimed the world's heavyweight championship title; the event is commemorated in a mural painted on the side of the building. The hotel had sunken into musty decrepitude before new management and an influx of adventure-oriented budget travelers arrived to rejuvenate it. Today it's one of the best youth hostels in Colorado, with both dormitory accommodations and a handful of sparely decorated private rooms. Youthful exuberance abounds here, but prize fights in the bar are a thing of the past. ~ 975 Main Avenue, Durango; 970-382-3910. BUDGET.

The largest hotel in Durango, with 154 guest rooms, the **Doubletree Hotel Durango** feels more like a big-city business travelers' hotel than a vacation retreat. Rooms are colorful, contemporary and extraordinarily spacious. The motor inn has an indoor swimming pool, a spa and an exercise room. ~ 501 Camino del Rio, Durango; 970-259-6580, 800-547-8010, fax 970-259-4398. DELUXE.

For those who prefer more conventional roadside lodging, the three-mile-long commercial strip along Route 550 on the northern outskirts of Durango is lined with standard highwayside motels. There are enough choices that travelers should be able to spot a few "vacancy" signs even during peak season. While in-season rates for private rooms aren't cheap anywhere in Durango, more reasonable rates can be found at well-maintained independent motels such as the **Caboose Motel**. ~ 3363 Main Avenue, Durango; 970-247-1191, fax 970-247-1191. BUDGET TO MODERATE. The **Alpine Motel** is another choice. ~ 3515 North Main Avenue, Durango; 970-247-4042, 800-818-4042. MODERATE.

Farther from downtown—but more convenient to the ski slopes at Purgatory—the **Iron Horse Inn** is Durango's other large, upscale motor inn. Each of the 140 guest accommodations is a suite with a loft bedroom and a fireplace. An indoor swimming pool, a sauna and a whirlpool are on the premises. Rooms facing the railroad tracks are more desirable; the steam train comes by only twice a day, while the highway keeps on rolling all night long with big trucks roaring slowly up the canyon. ~ 5800 North Main Avenue, Durango; 970-259-1010, 800-748-2990, fax 970-385-4791. MODERATE TO DELUXE.

Durango also has more than 20 bed-and-breakfast inns. In the historic residential neighborhood adjoining downtown, just five blocks from the narrow-gauge railroad station, the **Gable House** has antique-furnished guest rooms, each with its own private entrance, in a large, three-story Queen Anne Victorian home with a beautifully landscaped yard. The inn is open during the summer months only. ~ 805 East 5th Avenue, Durango; 970-247-4982. MODERATE.

The **New Rochester Hotel**, one of Durango's oldest hotels, has been in operation since 1892, when—under the name Peeple's Hotel—it rivaled the Strater and the General Palmer in prestige. It continued to thrive until the 1950s, then became a boarding-house, a residential hotel and finally a flophouse with the cheapest rates in town—but no heat. New owners rescued the hotel in 1993, converting its 33 old rooms to 15 spacious ones individually renovated in the spirit of various movies filmed in the Durango area, including *How the West Was Won, Butch Cassidy and the Sundance Kid* and *City Slickers.* The hotel lobby is like a cowboy movie museum, its walls festooned with vintage posters and publicity stills. ~ 721 East 2nd Avenue, Durango; 970-385-1920, 800-664-1920. DELUXE TO ULTRA-DELUXE.

The **Leland House Bed & Breakfast Suites**, a circa-1927 apartment building across the street from the New Rochester Hotel and under the same management, has one ultra-deluxe-priced, one-bedroom suite with full kitchen and living room and a plainer deluxe-priced single room with kitchenette and private bath, both decorated with pre-Depression antiques from around Colorado. ~ 721 East 2nd Avenue, Durango; 970-385-1920, 800-664-1920, fax 970-385-1967. DELUXE.

Away from downtown, Durango-area bed and breakfasts tend to be modern, luxurious and located in spectacular settings. Consider, for example, the **River House Bed & Breakfast**, which overlooks the Animas River from a county road just north of town. As late sleepers soon discover, the narrow-gauge train steams right past the house a little before nine each morning. Gourmet breakfasts are served in a sunny 928-square-foot atrium with a waterfall. Other features include a living room with fireplace and wet bar, a snooker table, a sauna and an exercise room. Some of the individually decorated guest rooms have skylights or clawfoot tubs, and one is entirely lined with shelves of books. ~ 495 Animas View Drive, Durango; 970-247-4775. MODERATE.

Also north of town, the **Apple Orchard Inn** was recently transformed by new owners into one of the area's most spectacular B&Bs, with six lavishly decorated cottages on landscaped grounds with river-fed streams and a small private lake. The farmhouse-style main lodge has three more rooms, a sitting room with a river-rock fireplace and original artwork. All rooms and cottages have elegant country furnishings including featherbeds, down comforters and armoires; some cottages have fireplaces and jacuzzis. Memorable breakfasts are prepared by the European-trained chef, co-owner. ~ 7758 County Road 203, Durango; 970-247-0751, 800-426-0751, fax 970-385-6976. DELUXE TO ULTRA-DELUXE.

A few miles west of town, the award-winning **Lightner Creek Inn** is regularly cited as one of the finest bed and breakfasts in the state. The imposing white inn stands amid acres and acres of carefully manicured lawn complete with a duck pond and gazebo, looking like a Connecticut country estate magically transported to the Rockies. The four guest rooms and carriage house suite feature brass beds, cute stuffed toys and an overwhelming plethora of floral patterns. The breakfast here is exceptional. ~ 999 County Road 207, Durango; 970-259-1226. ULTRA-DELUXE.

Eleven miles southeast of Durango, on a county road a mile from the highway to Ignacio on the Southern Ute Indian Reservation, **Penny's Place Bed & Breakfast** is a modern home with a glass-roofed solarium over the hot tub, a fireplace and a deck looking out on the La Plata Mountains. A spiral staircase leads up to the master suite, which even has its own laundry facilities. Other guest rooms offer a choice of a four-poster bed or a queen-size brass bed. ~ 1041 County Road 307, Durango; 970-247-8928. MODERATE.

Several of the finest guest ranches in the state are located in the vicinity of Durango. **Colorado Trails Ranch**, near Vallecito Reservoir, boasts one of the finest Western and English-style riding instruction programs offered anywhere. It also has a Western village complete with opera house and trading post. The family-oriented ranch offers activity programs organized by age group and supervised by full-time counselors. Other amenities include a heated swimming pool, tennis courts, a fishing pond and archery, rifle target and trap ranges. Guest accommodations are in individual cabins with modern furnishings, carpeting and private baths. Rates include all meals. Open in the summer only. ~ P.O. Box 848, Durango, CO 81302; 970-247-5055. DELUXE.

Perhaps the ultimate resort ranch experience in southwestern Colorado is to be found at **Tall Timber**. With just ten modern, split-level suites in duplexes secluded in a shimmering forest of aspens, the resort is so exclusive that it can't be reached by road—only by the narrow-gauge train or helicopter. The suites have high vaulted ceilings, loft bedrooms and marble baths. Among the resort's amenities are a riding stable, a nine-hole golf course, tennis courts, a solar-heated swimming pool, an exercise room and a riverside jacuzzi. San Juan National Forest surrounds the lodge and offers boundless opportunities for hiking and fishing. Rates, as you might expect, are high—as much as $1600 per person for a three-night minimum stay. Meals are included in the rate. ~ P.O. Box 90, Durango, CO 81302; 970-259-4813. ULTRA-DELUXE.

North of Durango, just three miles from Purgatory Ski Area, is the 325-unit **Tamarron Resort**. Built for $50 million in the early 1970s, Tamarron has become known as one of the state's top resorts, with a golf course that ranks among the best in the Rocky Mountain region. The resort also offers tennis courts, nature trails, riding stables, an indoor-outdoor pool and exercise rooms, as well as easy access to the ski slopes and miles of groomed ski trails. Guest rooms, decorated in pastel hues and Southwestern patterns, are on the small side but still include king-size beds and kitchenettes. Three-bedroom condominiums are also available. ~ Route 550, Purgatory; 970-259-2000, 800-678-1000, fax 970-259-0745. ULTRA-DELUXE.

DINING

Besides the array of family-style restaurants and familiar fast-food places along the three-mile-long Route 550 commercial strip on the northern outskirts of Durango, you'll find a good selection of places to eat in the downtown historic district. In a turn-of-the-century red-brick building next to the narrow-gauge train station, the **Palace Restaurant** offers mesquite-grilled chicken breast and a variety of other dishes such as honey duck and brandy pepper steak in an elegant Victorian-style ambience. ~ 1 Depot Place, Durango; 970-247-2018. MODERATE TO DELUXE.

Family dining meets 19th-century elegance in the stately old Strater Hotel at **Henry's at the Strater**, with its Tiffany lightshades, ornate moldings and trim and red leatherette booths. The menu presents standard steak, chicken, fish and pasta entrées, and there is a prime-rib buffet with a 25-item salad bar. ~ 699 Main Avenue, Durango; 970-247-4431. MODERATE TO DELUXE.

Francisco's Restaurante y Cantina, established in 1968 by a family from northern New Mexico, is one of the best Mexican restaurants in Colorado and certainly the most popular restaurant in Durango, with seating for 250 people amid a labyrinth of adobe walls and Santa Fe–style decor. Try the enchiladas Durango, beef wrapped in blue-corn tortillas and smothered in green chili. Besides Mexican food, entrées include steak, chicken, trout and lobster. ~ 619 Main Avenue, Durango; 970-247-4098. MODERATE.

Downtown Durango has more than its share of breakfast places, all designed to entice visitors before they board the narrow-gauge train. The unpretentious-looking **Carver Brewing Company** serves healthy breakfast specials such as granola pancakes. For dinner try the fajitas—beef or chicken fried in tequila salsa with green chili and onions, served with black beans, black olives and sour cream. Vegetarian entrées are also featured, and four varieties of home-brewed beer are available. ~ 1022 Main Avenue, Durango; 970-259-2545. BUDGET.

SHOPPING

At first glance, Main Avenue in Durango's nine-block downtown historic district seems to consist entirely of sporting goods stores. Look closer and you'll find that there are also a lot of factory outlet stores.

The tourism boom that has turned once-sleepy little Durango into prime retail space has also spawned a growing number of art galleries. They exhibit traditional American Indian art as well as works by area artists and craftspeople reflecting the full range of visual and spiritual imagery to be found in the Four Corners area. The largest gallery in town, **Toh-Atin**, offers high-quality Indian arts and crafts from around the Southwest, including fine selections of both replica Ancestral Pueblo pottery and authentic modern Pueblo pottery. ~ 145 West 9th Street, Durango; 970-247-8277. The gallery has a second store, **Toh-Atin's Art on Main**, just

around the corner. ~ 865 Main Avenue, Durango; 970-247-4540.
The **New West Gallery** displays sculptures and paintings of Southwestern subjects as well as an overwhelming selection of turquoise-
and-silver jewelry. ~ 747 Main Avenue, Durango; 970-259-5777.
One of the most distinctive traditional folk art galleries in town
is the **Martin+Roll Gallery**, featuring Navajo weavings, Spanish
colonial antiques, Huichol bead art and Edward Curtis photogra-
vures among its many delights. ~ 635 East 2nd Avenue, Durango;
970-247-2211.

Among the dozen or so contemporary galleries in Durango is
Piedra's Gallery, which exhibits a wide assortment of works by
local artists and artisans, including designer jewelry, ceramics,
gift items handcrafted of wood and numbered lithographs. ~ 846
Main Avenue, Durango; 970-247-9395.

Termar Gallery offers an array of Indian, Spanish and Anglo
fine arts, jewelry and pottery, as well as works by many of the best-
known Southwestern artists. ~ 780 Main Avenue, Durango; 970-
247-3728.

Railroad memorabilia and rare books can be found at **Southwest Book Trader**. ~ 175 East 5th Street, Durango; 970-247-8479.

Former Presidents Ronald Reagan and George Bush are
among the distinguished clientele of **O'Farrell Hat Company**,
where custom-fitted hats are made the old-fashioned way, by
hand. ~ 598 Main Avenue, Durango; 970-259-2517.

In the Strater Hotel, the **Diamond Circle Theatre** presents a campy   **NIGHTLIFE**
rendition of Victorian melodrama nightly during the summer sea-
son. Also here is the **Diamond Belle Saloon**, which has a ragtime
piano player and is frequently a site for sing-alongs. ~ 699 Main
Avenue, Durango; 970-247-4431.

Farquahrts, a student hangout, serves pizzas as well as drinks
and features bluegrass or folk music early in the week and gutsy
rock as the weekend draws near. ~ 725 Main Avenue, Durango;
970-247-9861. **The Pelican's Nest**, upstairs from the West Antique
Shop, features live jazz nightly except Monday. ~ 656 Main Avenue, Durango.

SAN JUAN NATIONAL FOREST 🚶 🚴 🐎 🎿 🏠 ≈ ⚓ 🛶   **PARKS**
🚤 🚤 ⛵ This vast national forest encompasses all the mountains north of Durango (see "San Juan Skyway Area Parks" later
in this chapter), as well as the popular recreation area of Vallecito Reservoir. Fishing is good for rainbow and brown trout and
kokanee salmon in the Animas River, Vallecito Reservoir and
Lemon Reservoir. There are picnic tables, restrooms, pack trails
and jeep trails. ~ The main roads for forest access from the Durango area include the San Juan Skyway (Route 550), Vallecito
Road (County Road 501) to Vallecito Reservoir from Bayfield,

and Junction Creek Road (Forest Road 171) from the north side of Durango; 970-884-2512.

▲ The closest forest service campground to Durango is Junction Creek Campground, five miles north of town on Junction Creek Road (Forest Road 171), with 34 RV/tent sites (no hookups); closed mid-November through April; $8 per night. Most forest service campgrounds in the area are at Vallecito Reservoir, including Graham Creek Campground, with 25 RV/tent sites (no hookups); closed mid-November through April; $8 per night.

▼▼▼▼▼▼▼▼▼▼▼▼▼
Mesa Verde Area

With the explosive growth of tourism in southwestern Colorado in recent years, Mesa Verde has emerged as one of the most-visited places in the U.S. national park system. Park Service officials say more European visitors visit Mesa Verde than the Grand Canyon, Yellowstone or Yosemite. The spectacle of these unique ancient ruins is well worth braving the crowds for. Once you've been there and done that, why not head for one of the smaller, more remote archaeological sites in the area, such as Hovenweep or Lowry Ruins, where you're likely to find yourself alone with ancient spirits?

SIGHTS

West of Durango off Route 160, **Mesa Verde National Park** protects one of the greatest wonders of pre–Columbian America—a community of castlelike stone pueblos built in niches high up the sheer cliffs of the mesa. Mesa Verde is the northernmost site of the ancient Ancestral Pueblo people, whose civilization dominated the Southwest for centuries and who evolved into the modern-day Pueblo Indians. Visitors drive up a long, steep road on the north side of the mesa to the nearly level top, then drive all the way to the south end of the mesa where the cliff dwellings are located, a half-hour's drive from the entrance. The miniature forest of juniper and piñon on the mesa top, plus some spectacular views of the distant mountains and the surrounding desert 3000 feet below set the stage for a visit to what may be the biggest mystery in Colorado's past. Admission. ~ 970-529-4465.

Although there are thousands of Ancestral Pueblo ruins in southwestern Colorado and neighboring New Mexico, Arizona and Utah, no other cliff dwellings rival those at Mesa Verde in size or architectural elegance. The people who built them had started a permanent community on top of Mesa Verde around 500 A.D., when they learned to cultivate corn and abandoned their previous nomadic way of life. Around 950 A.D., faced with the pressures of a growing population, they built an extensive system of irrigation ditches and reservoirs that allowed them to cultivate more land. After living in individual pit houses for six centuries, around 1100 A.D. they began building large pueblos on the mesa top. Examples of both the pit houses and the pueblos have been excavated and restored to provide visitors with a look at both stages of development.

Around 1200 A.D., for reasons archaeologists cannot agree on, the Mesa Verde people moved off the mesa top and into new dwellings built into the overhanging cliffs in canyons that sliced into the sides of the mesa. Experts who date Indian ruins by analyzing the tree rings of roof beams to see when they were cut have determined that almost all the great Mesa Verde cliff dwellings were built at the same time. Construction took just a few years, and they were not added on to later. Nobody knows for sure why they suddenly decided to build these unique dwellings. For many years, the theory was that warfare drove the people off the mesa top because the cliff dwellings were easier to defend. But no extraordinary numbers of burials have been found that would indicate battles, and no burials reveal evidence of wounds from warfare. A more recent theory is that after inhabiting the mesa for 700 years, they may have been running out of firewood. The cliff dwellings, experts point out, might be easier to heat than the older pueblos.

> In addition to corn, the Ancestral Pueblo grew beans, squash and tobacco and raised turkeys for meat.

Then comes the biggest mystery of all. About 100 years after the Ancestral Pueblo moved into the cliff dwellings, they abandoned them and left Mesa Verde for good. Most experts believe the Mesa Verde people migrated southward around 1300 A.D., briefly inhabiting the abandoned pueblos at Aztec and Chaco Canyon—which had been abandoned 50 years before by another Ancestral Pueblo group—and then establishing Acoma Pueblo on a high mesa near Grants, New Mexico. The reason they left Mesa Verde has been a subject of ceaseless speculation among archaeologists. War? Disease? Again, no large number of burials or corpses has been found that would indicate such a catastrophe. Drought or famine? Abandoned storerooms containing corn and beans make the food shortage theory doubtful. Again, the most appealing theory is that their civilization ended in an energy crisis when they burned the last wood on the mesa. This theory, however, does not explain why the people walked away leaving weapons, jewelry and kitchen utensils around as if they would be back by nightfall.

The main ruins area at Mesa Verde is below the rim of Chapin Mesa, 21 miles from the park entrance. There is an **archaeology museum** at the starting point of the two six-mile loop drives that take motorists and cyclists along canyon rims to sites such as **Cliff Palace** and **Balcony House**. Exploring the largest ruins involves some climbing on ladders and narrow trails. An unpaved road from Far View Visitors Center leads to the more remote pueblo sites of **Step House** and **Long House** on Wetherill Mesa. Public access to most parts of Mesa Verde is restricted to protect unexcavated archaeological sites. The strict visitor controls makes the park seem very crowded much of the time, but the expanse of land untouched by humans harbors an abundance of wild animals, which often show themselves by the roadside. Keep your eyes peeled for mule deer and wild horses. Mountain lions, bears and bighorn sheep are also spotted sometimes, and the mesa provides habitat for more than 160 species of birds.

The town of **Dolores**, located 17 miles northwest of Mesa Verde's entrance gate via Route 160 West and Route 145, seems so low-key that you may wonder whether anybody lives there. In truth, things have livened up a lot since the completion of **McPhee Reservoir**, just west of town, boosted the bait-and-tackle business. Near the lake is the Bureau of Land Management's **Anasazi Heritage Center** (the name was not changed when the National Park Service expunged the word "Anasazi" elsewhere as politically incorrect), which displays Pueblo Indian artifacts from the classic period (11th to 13th centuries) that were found in canyons now flooded by the reservoir. Nearby are two partially excavated Ancestral Pueblo sites. ~ Route 184, Dolores; 970-882-4811.

In Dolores you can see **Galloping Goose #5**, a gasoline-powered hybrid—part Buick passenger bus and part boxcar—that carried passengers on the narrow-gauge trail routes of the San Juans from 1931 to 1951. The local historical society has been working since 1987 to restore the strange vehicle so that it can run again on a track up Lost Canyon.

For most travelers, Dolores is a stop on the San Juan Skyway, from which Route 145 will take them to Telluride (see "San Juan Skyway Area" later in this chapter). But if you want to explore more ancient Ancestral Pueblo ruins—or just want to go around the mountains instead of over them—Route 666 takes you northwest to **Dove Creek**, from which a long and not particularly interesting Route 141 will lead you to either Grand Junction or Montrose. A dirt-road detour on 10.00 Road just south of town will bring you to a remote campground on the rim of the **Dolores River Canyon** for a panoramic view of the red canyon walls and the wild river far below.

HIDDEN ▶ The main point of interest worth searching the maze of parallel farm roads in the Dove Creek area for is **Lowry Ruins**, a small Ancestral Pueblo located about eight miles west of the hamlet of Pleasant View on a straight dirt road marked by small but plentiful signs. The three-story pueblo, built in stages over a period of 30 years in the late 11th century, contained 40 rooms and eight round kivas believed to have been used for religious rituals. Entering one of the rooms at the front of the pueblo, you descend into a lower room behind it and another behind and below that one, to find yourself on the rim of a large kiva built beneath the center of the pueblo. Traces of stucco murals that decorated the kiva walls are still visible. Down the hill from the main pueblo, a very large great pueblo stands alone. The size of the great kiva and the number of smaller ones is out of proportion to the size of the pueblo, which could only have housed about 100 people. Archaeologists believe it must have served as a ceremonial and government center. Some speculate that it may not have been lived in by families at all but by an elite group of priests. The site was abandoned around 1150 A.D. after only 80 years of use. It has no visitors center or other facilities. ~ Pleasant View; no phone.

From Lowry Ruins or from Route 666 near Pleasant View, several dirt roads are marked with small signs that keep you aimed in the right direction for **Hovenweep National Monument,**   ◄ *HIDDEN* which straddles the Colorado–Utah state line. One of the least-visited National Park Service units in Colorado, Hovenweep is far enough off the beaten path so that you're likely to have the place completely to yourself—a welcome change from the crowds of Mesa Verde for anyone who wants to contemplate the mysteries of the Ancestral Pueblo in solitude and silence. Admission. ~ McElmo Route.

The main ruins, the **Square Tower group,** has a ranger station and campground (but no food, water, firewood or gasoline; stock up on what you may need before venturing out here). An interpretive trail leads around the canyon rim to several small pueblos and the most distinctive feature of the Hovenweep ruins: several tall, square towers both at the bottom of the canyon and along the rim. They are unique to the Hovenweep sites, and their function is unknown. There are also five other ruins groups in Hovenweep—the Holly, Hackberry Canyon, Cutthroat Castle, Goodman Point and Cajon sites. All are in remote locations along rough back roads that are not well marked and may require high-clearance or four-wheel-drive vehicles at some times of the year. Ask for a map and check on current road conditions at the Square Tower Ruins ranger station. The partially unpaved **McElmo Can-**   ◄ *HIDDEN* **yon Road** from Hovenweep National Monument takes you 40 miles east through a lonely red-rock canyon to join Route 160 near Cortez.

South of Mesa Verde are the adjoining **Southern Ute and Ute Mountain Indian reservations,** the only Indian lands in Colorado. In addition to **Navajo Lake** and the **Ute Mountain Casino** in Towaoc, visitor attractions on the Ute reservations include the **Southern Ute Indian Cultural Center,** the only tribally owned and operated museum in Colorado, with exhibits of Ute beadwork, leatherwork and other arts and crafts as well as ancient Ancestral Pueblo artifacts found on the reservation. Admission. ~ Ignacio; 970-563-4531.

There's also the **Ute Mountain Tribal Park,** a remote group of Ancestral Pueblo cliff-dwelling ruins that can be visited only with an Indian guide on a fairly strenuous hike or mountain-bike tour. The most interesting feature of these cliff dwellings is a kiva containing one of the few surviving examples of Ancestral Pueblo ceremonial murals. ~ Towaoc; 970-565-3751 ext. 282.

In the southwestern corner of the Ute Mountain Indian Reservation is the spot where the Colorado–Utah and Colorado–New Mexico state lines intersect, the only place in the United States where four states touch one another (Arizona is the fourth state). The **Four Corners Monument**, a large plaque inlaid in concrete just off Route 160 in the middle of nowhere says so. Navajos sell jewelry from the tailgates of pickup trucks in the monument parking lot. There is nothing else around.

LODGING   The only lodging in Mesa Verde National Park is at **Far View Lodge** on the summit of Navajo Hill, commanding a spectacular panoramic view out over the valleys that lie to the south, clear to the huge rock formation known as Shiprock in New Mexico and the Lukachukai Mountains in the Navajo lands of Arizona. The lodge's 150 rooms are in duplex and four-plex units scattered across juniper-covered hillsides. The spacious rooms are decorated in Ancestral Pueblo motifs and have private sun porches. Closed mid-October to mid-April. ~ 970-529-4421, 800-449-2288, fax 970-529-4411. MODERATE TO DELUXE.

DINING   The sleepy little town of Dolores boasts one of the finest restaurants along the San Juan Skyway, the **Old Germany Restaurant & Lounge**. In a renovated turn-of-the-century home, the restaurant is decorated with memorabilia imported from Bavaria, including 800-year-old antiques. The food is also authentically Bavarian. Savor a delicacy such as *paprikaschnitzel* sausage or sauerbraten with German potato salad. ~ 200 South 8th Street, Dolores; 970-882-7549. BUDGET TO MODERATE.

In Mancos, a good place to stop and eat after visiting Mesa Verde is **Candy's Country Cafe**. This little diner—nine tables and a lunch counter in a concrete-block building—serves up hefty helpings of good down-home food, from "wagon wheels and axle grease" (biscuits and gravy) to "pigbutt" (ham steak). ~ 121 Railroad Avenue, Mancos; 970-533-7941. BUDGET.

SHOPPING   In Mesa Verde National Park, curio concessions at Morefield Campground, Far View Visitors Center and Chapin Mesa sell a full range of T-shirts and trinkets as well as a good selection of books on the region's natural history and Indian cultures. Among the more interesting gift items are Navajo and Zuni jewelry and reproductions of Mesa Verde–style pottery manufactured by non-Indians. Here and elsewhere in southwestern Colorado you will also find Ute Mountain pottery, manufactured near Towaoc by the Ute people. This factory-made pottery is not a traditional Ute craft; like most nomadic Indians, ancestral Utes made their vessels of less fragile materials like leather and gourds. But it is pretty. You can see the pottery made and buy it from the source, at the **Ute Mountain Pottery Plant**. ~ 156 Route 160, Towaoc; 970-565-8548.

NIGHTLIFE

The only gambling hall in southwestern Colorado today is the **Ute Mountain Casino** in Towaoc, the capital of the Ute Mountain Indian Reservation. Although the gambling goes on seven days a week until 4 a.m., no alcoholic beverages are allowed to be served on tribal land. Shuttle buses run to the reservation from Cortez, Dolores and Mancos; for information, call 970-565-8800.

PARKS

MANCOS STATE PARK A three-mile road winds into the mountains above Mancos to the reservoir that provides the small town with drinking and irrigation water. The lake is open to nonmotorized boating and fishing (rainbow and brown trout). A four-mile trail runs from the lake along slopes and ridgelines bright with wildflowers to join a larger trail network in the adjoining San Juan National Forest. The park is open in the winter for cross-country skiing. There are restrooms and a picnic area with tables. Day-use fee, $4. ~ From Mancos, go north on Route 184 for one-half mile, then right on County Road 42 for four miles and left on County Road N; 970-883-2208.

▲ There are 24 RV/tent sites (no hookups) and 9 tent-only sites scattered along the lakeshore; $7 per night. Drinking water is available.

San Juan Skyway Area

To experience the San Juans by car, drive the 231-mile San Juan Skyway, which follows paved Routes 160, 184, 145, 62 and 550 to form a loop beginning and ending in Durango. The route is clearly marked with "Scenic Byway" signs. In fact, the San Juan Skyway was one of the first routes selected under a 1988 federal law directing the National Forest Service to designate the most scenic driving routes in national forests as scenic byways. But you don't really need special road signs to tell you that you're on one of America's most spectacular drives.

I recommend traveling the San Juan Skyway clockwise, mainly because drivers unaccustomed to edgy mountain roads will find that the road that climbs south from Ouray is much easier to drive uphill than downhill. (If I had to choose either the Dolores–Telluride leg of the trip or the Ouray–Silverton leg as a one-way route between Durango and the Gunnison or Grand Junction area, it would be a hard decision indeed; the whole loop route is filled with variety and scenic beauty on a grand scale. However, the segment between Ouray and Silverton has what is probably the most breathtaking scenery.)

SIGHTS   First, drive west from Durango on Route 160 to Mancos, the small town near the turnoff to Mesa Verde National Park; from there, go northwest on Route 184 to Dolores (see the "Mesa Verde Area" in this chapter). Follow Route 145 north from Dolores. At the tiny community of Stoner a side road turns off to follow the **West Fork of the Dolores River**, a popular fishing area. Unpaved forest roads provide access to the aspen-covered plateau above the rim of Dolores Canyon. Route 145, the main highway up the East Fork of the river, is equally scenic. Past Stoner, the highway begins its long climb into the high mountains and ultimately to the summit of **Lizard Head Pass** (10,222 feet), where there is a trailhead for a hiking trail to the top ridgeline of Lizard Head Peak, the mountain with the 400-foot spire of granite on top. Rock climbers rate the monolith as one of the most difficult technical ascents on earth.

Past Lizard Head Pass, a side trip along the San Juan Skyway brings you to **Telluride**. No other ski town in Colorado is as far from a major city. This fact alone has made the town irresistible to skiers who want to *really* escape the outside world. In fact, only Aspen, in its glitzier way, can rival Telluride for away-from-it-allness. But when it comes to mountain scenery, Telluride, set in a basin surrounded by peaks over 13,000 feet high, actually has Aspen beat. Out past the end of 1st Street, Ingram Falls plunges hundreds of feet down craggy cliffs that stand like castle walls. All around, snow-capped mountain turrets protect the town and its residents from the outside world.

For the best view imaginable, ride the **gondola**. It sweeps sightseers, hikers, bikers and cross-country skiers 2000 feet up to the top of Coonskin Ridge, providing easy access to the surrounding peaks, and then swoops down the other side of the ridge to

THE MOST CELEBRATIONS PER-CAPITA IN THE WEST

Telluride's 300-inch annual snowfall makes the town a skiers' mecca. During the summer, Telluride is the festival capital of Colorado. In the mid-1970s, residents hatched a plan to boost the local economy during the no-snow season by hosting the Telluride Bluegrass Festival. It drew huge crowds, and spinoffs in the form of a jazz festival and a film festival came quickly. Today, all three have attained international stature, and other festivals completely fill the town's calendar from mid-May through September except for one weekend in July, when the annual Telluride Nothing Festival packs 'em in.

Mountain Village, an exclusive Euro-style condo development, spa and shopping area that makes for a striking contrast to Victorian-style Telluride. Built as a unique municipal public transportation project, the gondola is free to all. It runs nonstop year-round except for the off-season months of April and mid-October to mid-November, when it shuts down for inspection and servicing.

Telluride was founded in 1875 as a gold-mining camp. The town's rebirth started in 1971, when plans to build a ski area there were unveiled. Even before the first ski lift was running, a motley assortment of ski bums, trust-fund babies, realtors, lawyers and Aspen dropouts had moved into the near-deserted old mining town to buy up abandoned buildings for back taxes. Many of the newcomers had seen resort money swallow the souls of other historic Colorado gold-rush towns, so the new city fathers promptly adopted rigid preservation laws. Today, the historic district is free of new buildings, and turn-of-the-century structures have been refurbished instead of replaced. Historic landmark buildings include the **Sheridan Opera House**, where Sarah Bernhardt once performed and William Jennings Bryan made a speech, and the **Bank of Telluride**, the first bank Butch Cassidy ever robbed. The bygone glory of the gold era is recalled at the **San Miguel County Historical Museum**. Stop in to find out about the days when Telluride supported 26 saloons and 12 houses of ill repute and the miners returned home on winter days by sledding on shovels from the mines down the mountainside to town. Closed in spring and fall. ~ 317 North 1st Street, Telluride; 970-728-3344.

Visitors can drive up to the old **Idarado Mine and Mill**, the town's biggest employer for more than 50 years in the late 19th and early 20th centuries. Nearby, **Bridal Veil Falls** has the longest vertical drop of any waterfall in Colorado—365 feet.

North of Telluride, Route 145 descends from the mountains. To continue on the San Juan Skyway loop route, turn east on Route 62 at Placerville and then south on Route 550 at Ridgway. Route 550 goes all the way back to Durango.

Last Dollar Road (Forest Road 638), an unpaved route that ◀ HIDDEN
turns off the main road three miles west of Telluride and runs north over high mesa country to rejoin the San Juan Skyway near Ridgway, is a favorite with four-wheel-drivers—especially in the fall—because of the picturesque old ranch buildings and dazzling stands of aspen along the way. The first few miles from the Telluride end are the roughest, and motorists in low-clearance two-wheel-drive cars should inquire locally before trying it. An abbreviated version of the trip can be made from the Ridgway end, taking a left fork that returns you to the highway before reaching the rugged, rocky stretch of Last Dollar Road.

Most motorists on the San Juan Skyway barely notice the little town of **Ridgway** as they drive through it. Situated in the center of a broad bowl-shaped ranching valley walled in by distant mountain ridgelines, its charms present themselves less dramatically than other towns along the route. Yet a milder climate, longer hours of direct sunlight and a central location within half an hour's drive of Telluride, Ouray and Montrose give Ridgway a quiet appeal. More celebrities have homes here than in any other town on the San Juan Skyway; General Norman Schwartzkopf owns a vacation home in the area, actor Dennis Weaver lives here and operates a restaurant and an environmental foundation, and designer Ralph Lauren owns a vast cattle ranch just west of town.

In the farming community of **Montrose**, is the **Ute Indian Museum**. Landscaped with columbines of many colors, the museum occupies land that was once the farm of Chief Ouray, the great statesman of the Ute people. He is remembered for negotiating an 1873 treaty with the U.S. government that established a Ute homeland in the San Juan Mountains. Soon after Ouray's death in 1880, the treaty was broken and his people were forced into the badlands of Utah to make way for gold prospectors. Visitors to the museum can see beaded costumes and artifacts, photographs of Ouray and other Ute leaders and a bigger-than-life copy of the broken treaty. Admission. ~ 17253 Chipeta Road, Montrose; 970-249-3098.

Chipeta Park, a grassy expanse adjoining the museum, is named for Chief Ouray's wife. The highway re-enters the mountains through the Uncompahgre River Canyon, whose maroon walls rise so steeply that mountain streams plunge over the rim and fall hundreds of feet before splashing against the cliffs. The deepest part of the canyon is the dramatic setting for the village of Ouray.

With neither a ski area nor a railroad, **Ouray** has been spared the kind of industrial tourism that has swallowed other Colorado mining towns whole. The town's slightly old-fashioned charm is as authentic as can be. Most buildings in town date back to the turn of the century and before. Some have been refurbished and painted in rainbow color schemes; others, such as the shell of the grand old Ouray Hotel, built in 1887 and closed in 1964, stand vacant. Main Street has endured good and bad times, and local businesses keep on keeping the spirit of small-town Colorado alive.

Ouray's special claim to fame is its hot springs. At the northern edge of town, the municipal **Ouray Hot Springs Pool** has an Olympic-size swimming pool and a smaller, hotter (104°F) pool. Admission. ~ Route 550, Ouray; 970-325-4638. Other options include the private outdoor hot tub, available to the public by the hour with reservations, at the European-style **Wiesbaden Hot Springs Spa**. Admission. ~ 625 5th Street, Ouray; 970-325-4347.

At **Orvis Hot Springs** between Ridgway and Ouray, you'll find a sand-bottomed natural pool with a hot waterfall and a smaller, very hot pool (both bathing suits–optional) as well as an indoor pool (suits required). Admission. ~ 1585 County Road 3, Ridgway; 970-626-5324.

Waterfalls are another Ouray specialty. A dozen or more of them plummet down the cliffs surrounding the town. The most accessible is Lower Cascade Falls, reached by a half-mile trail that starts a few blocks uphill from Main Street. Farther up the cliffs, the same stream takes an earlier and even longer fall at **Upper Cascade Falls,** reached by a steep trail two and a half miles long that begins at the natural amphitheater south of town. The most spectacular of Ouray's waterfalls is **Box Canyon Falls and Park.** The 285-foot-high falls have sliced a canyon so narrow that visitors who walk into its misty depths along the narrow boardwalks and turn-of-the-century steel bridge feel as if they're in a cave filled to overflowing with the noise and spray of down-rushing water. Admission. ~ Route 550 South, Ouray; 970-325-4981.

Ouray is also an excellent base for exploring old mining roads by mountain bike or four-wheel-drive vehicle. **Engineer Pass Road** leads to the early-day mining district around Mineral Point and Animas Forks, one of Colorado's best ghost towns, to join the **Alpine Loop Backcountry Byway** (see "Creede–Lake City Area" in Chapter Seven). From there other jeep roads go to Lake City and Silverton. Another great four-wheel-drive trip is on rugged **Camp Bird Road,** which leads past the abandoned mines and ghost towns of what was once the busiest gold and silver district of the San Juans to Yankee Boy Basin, a broad expanse of alpine meadows that bursts with red, yellow and purple wildflowers in summer.

◀ *HIDDEN*

◀ *HIDDEN*

◀ *HIDDEN*

An easier way to explore the Ouray district's mining heritage is to tour the **Bachelor-Syracuse Mine.** Mine carts take visitors two-thirds of a mile into the mountain to see where hard-rock miners followed veins of gold and silver ore for a hundred years before the mine ceased operations in 1984. Admission. ~ County Road 14, Ouray; 970-325-4500.

Mining is also the focus of the small **Ouray County Museum.** Exhibits include an ore train and a re-creation of an assay office, as well as several rooms of Victorian-era antiques and an old-time law office. The building that houses the museum was originally a hospital, and several upstairs rooms have been restored to offer a glimpse of 19th-century health care. Admission. ~ 420 6th Avenue, Ouray; 970-325-4576.

South of Ouray, Route 550 climbs steep cliffs in a sweeping series of switchbacks and finally reaches the summit of **Red Mountain Pass** (11,008 feet), the highest point on the San Juan Skyway.

Well above timberline, this part of the route offers the most spectacular views of the remote Needle Mountains in the Weminuche Wilderness to the east. Long before the Forest Service dubbed it part of the San Juan Skyway, the stretch of Route 550 between Ouray and Silverton was known as the **Million Dollar Highway**. Some say the name came from the high cost of building the road back in the days when a million dollars was a lot of money for road construction, while others say the road's foundation, built with mine tailings, contains $1 million worth of gold ore. It may well be the most scenic 23 miles of highway in America.

> Silverton's mines have never shut down but continue producing silver, lead, zinc and other minerals, giving rise to the local motto, "The town that never quit."

Silverton was founded in 1874 as the center of what would prove to be one of the wealthiest mining districts in southwestern Colorado. Large deposits of gold, silver, copper and lead were located here, but the town could be reached only by crossing high mountain passes, so only limited amounts of ore could be shipped out until the **Denver & Rio Grande Railroad** (now the Durango & Silverton Narrow-Gauge Railroad) reached the town in 1882. As Silverton boomed to a population of 4000 in the next few years, it saw the construction of elegant false-front Victorian buildings along Main Street. The boom faded slowly, until finally the last of the mines closed during World War II. Nearly abandoned, the town became nothing more than a roadside curiosity on Route 550. Motion-picture companies occasionally slapped fresh coats of paint on the old buildings and used Main Street as an Old West location. The revival of the Durango & Silverton Narrow-Gauge Railroad as a scenic train for tourists brought a new wave of prosperity to Silverton, whose sidewalks and curio shops bustle with train passengers every day from about 11 a.m. to 2 p.m. The rest of the time, the town is very quiet.

The **San Juan County Museum** is housed in the former county jail adjacent to the county courthouse. The memorabilia and photographs on display there recount the mining era in Silverton and several other mining towns that have since faded into oblivion. There are displays about mining, including an exhibit of minerals from local mines, and railroads, including one of the last railcars remaining from the days when the Denver and Rio Grande ran narrow-gauge trains between Durango and Silverton, but perhaps the most interesting aspect of the museum is the old jail itself, with its colorful anecdotes of mine camp law and order. Admission. ~ 1559 Greene Street, Silverton; 970-387-5838.

On the hillside west of Silverton stands **Christ of the Mines**, a larger-than-life statue of Jesus with outstretched arms, carved from a 12-ton block of marble. The sculpture is dedicated to the protection of miners, although it was only erected in 1959, long after the mining era had ended in most Colorado towns. Tenth Street leads out of town and climbs the hillside to the statue.

Besides allowing you to stroll the streets and browse through the town during off-hours, driving to Silverton lets you explore back roads in the surrounding national forest. A short distance north of town, Main Street becomes Forest Road 586. The pavement soon ends, but the road continues past the scattered remains of the old mining towns of Howardsville and Eureka. It is passable without four-wheel-drive as far as **Animas Forks**, one of the most picturesque ghost towns in the San Juans thanks to its dramatic timberline setting. Beyond that, rough roads suited only for four-wheel-drive vehicles and mountain bikes climb to join the Alpine Loop Backcountry Byway in the heart of the San Juans.

◀ *HIDDEN*

Telluride's grand old hotel, the three-story red-brick **New Sheridan Hotel**, operated for 30 years—from 1895 to 1925—and then stood abandoned for more than a half-century. Thanks to a meticulous restoration completed in 1977, the hotel's lobby and guest rooms have recaptured the glory of bygone days with rich, warm period decor. The guest accommodations vary in size from rather small rooms with shared baths to larger rooms with private baths and a single opulent suite with impressive views of the town and the mountains. Room rates vary wildly, from the ultra-deluxe range with a five-night minimum stay during peak ski season to the budget range with no minimum stay on summer weeknights. ~ 231 West Colorado Avenue, Telluride; 970-728-4351, 800-200-1891, fax 970-728-5024. DELUXE TO ULTRA-DELUXE.

LODGING

A great Telluride bed and breakfast is **San Sophia**. Although situated in the historic district, San Sophia is of recent vintage, designed and built as an inn, with gabled dormers and a central tower. The 16 guest rooms, each named after a gold mine, have soothing pastel interiors appointed with brass beds, etched mirrors, stained-glass windows and extra-large bathtubs. A full gourmet breakfast and afternoon wine and hors d'oeuvres are included in the rates. Closed mid-October to mid-November and mid-April to mid-May. ~ 330 West Pacific Avenue, Telluride; 970-728-3001, 800-537-4781, fax 970-728-6226. DELUXE TO ULTRA-DELUXE.

The **Alpine Inn**, an eight-room Victorian bed and breakfast beautifully restored and furnished with period antiques, has an ideal location on the main street of town, within easy walking distance of the public gondola. Fresh-baked breakfast goodies are served in a sunny dining room or on the big open-air deck. ~ 440 West Colorado Avenue, Telluride; 970-728-6282, 800-707-3344, fax 970-728-3424. MODERATE TO ULTRA-DELUXE.

The **Bear Creek Bed & Breakfast** is located on the upper floors of a historic brick building at the east end of Telluride's main street, making it the closest accommodation to the stage area for the various summer music festivals. The eight rooms are newly refurbished in contemporary style, and the rooftop hot tub is one of the best spots in town from which to watch the sunset. ~ 221 East Colorado Avenue, Telluride; 970-728-6681, 800-338-7064, fax 970-728-3636. MODERATE TO ULTRA-DELUXE.

Another Telluride bed and breakfast, **Pennington's Mountain Village**, ranks as one of the most luxurious and expensive B&Bs in Colorado. It is located by the 12th fairway of the golf course in Telluride Mountain Village, the newly built area on the mesa five miles from the historic district. The inn's ridgeline site affords spectacular panoramic views from every window and balcony. A magnificent circular staircase leads up to 12 guest rooms, each with its own whirlpool bath and private deck. The rooms are decorated in French country style. Common areas include a sunken library and sitting room with a big fireplace and a game room with a pool table. ~ 100 Pennington Court, Telluride; 970-728-5337, 800-543-1437, fax 970-728-5338. ULTRA-DELUXE.

Although Telluride lodging tends to be very expensive in peak season, there is one affordable hostelry in town—the **Oak Street Inn**. This hostel, situated in a building that was originally a Methodist church and affiliated with American Youth Hostels (AYH), provides very plain private rooms and also has six-bed dormitory rooms at youth hostel prices. All rooms have shared baths. The best features are the coed sauna and the upstairs TV lounge where a young, enthusiastic crowd often hangs out. Closed mid-April to mid-May. ~ 134 North Oak Street, Telluride; 970-728-3383. BUDGET.

Santa Fe–style charm sets the **Chipeta Sun Lodge** in Ridgway apart from other bed-and-breakfast accommodations along the San Juan Skyway. The 12-unit inn, built in 1994, is warmed by passive solar heat from the two-story picture windows that fill the south wall of the spacious lobby. Guest rooms have queen- or king-size beds with down comforters, rustic Southwestern furniture and Mexican-tile private baths, including one with a private spa tub. Centrally located between Telluride, Montrose and Ouray, this is a great base camp for touring the area—and it's surprisingly affordable compared to other San Juan Skyway B&Bs. ~ 304 South Lena, Ridgway; 970-626-3737, 800-633-5868, fax 970-626-3715. MODERATE.

Ouray offers affordable luxury in lodging along the San Juan Skyway. Even during the peak summer season, rates here are less than they would be for comparable accommodations in Telluride. In winter, skiers can actually save hundreds of dollars on lodging by staying in Ouray and driving an hour to Telluride Ski Area. Many Ouray inns participate in a continuing co-promotion campaign that gives visitors who stay there during the winter discounts on Telluride lift tickets and free admission to Ouray's municipal hot springs.

Ouray's original landmark hostelry, the Beaumont Hotel (circa 1887), kept its doors open until 1964, then closed them for good. The shell of the elegant old building still dominates Main Street, and maybe someday investors will come along to restore it. In the meantime, two smaller historic hotels operate in town. Back in the 1880s, the **St. Elmo Hotel** was a low-rent boardinghouse for mine laborers' families, but times have changed. Today, this intimate nine-room hotel is full of antiques and period reproductions, stained glass, polished wood and brass trim. Guest rooms, each one individually decorated, have brass beds, lace curtains and ornate mining-era wallpaper. ~ 426 Main Street, Ouray; 970-325-4951. MODERATE.

The **Historic Western Hotel** opened as a hotel in 1891 and operated as a boardinghouse for mine workers until World War II. Closed but never quite abandoned—it served for a while as office space and a local museum—the three-story wood-frame hotel with its grandiose whitewashed facade is mostly original, refurbished but not rebuilt. The period antiques that grace the 14 small guest rooms and the common areas are genuine but not fancy; they speak with eloquence of daily life in the Old West. Most rooms have shared baths. The hotel is undergoing a room-by-room interior renovation. Closed November. ~ 210 7th Avenue, Ouray; 970-325-4645, 888-624-8403. MODERATE.

The most elegant of Ouray's bed-and-breakfast inns, the **China Clipper** is a three-story, 7800-square-foot mansion on a quiet residential street. The sitting room and elegant formal dining room are accented with antiques and mementos from the owners' Asian travels. Ten individually decorated guest rooms have queen-size beds and private baths, and some have fireplaces and two-person jacuzzis. The house has a hot tub for guests' use in a pretty enclosed garden. ~ 525 2nd Street, Ouray; 970-325-0565, 800-315-0565, fax 970-325-4190. MODERATE TO ULTRA-DELUXE.

A more modest Ouray B&B, **The Manor** is a tastefully restored 1890 Georgian Revival home with seven guest rooms. All are on the second and third floors, with mountain views. Decor is simple and evocative of the Old West, though now they have queen-size European featherbeds and down comforters. ~ 317 2nd Street, Ouray; 970-325-4754, 800-628-6946. MODERATE.

Box Canyon Lodge & Hot Springs is essentially a standard midrange motel with a spectacularly scenic location and one other distinction: It has outdoor hot tubs fed by natural mineral springs located on the property. The clean, modern guest rooms hint at European sensibilities in their decor and furnishings. There are also two luxury suites with fireplaces and fully equipped kitchens. ~ 45 3rd Avenue, Ouray; 970-325-4981, 800-327-5080. MODERATE.

A different kind of hot-spring experience awaits at the **Wiesbaden Hot Springs Spa and Lodgings**. Originally started as Mother Buchanan's Bathhouse in 1879 and later used as a hospital, the place was converted into a European-style spa in the late 1970s. The lodgings are small, conventional motel rooms, apartments and cottages, most of them redecorated with Old World antiques. Guests have full use of the spa facilities, which include a natural vapor cave, a sauna and soaking pool, an outdoor swimming pool and a fully equipped exercise room. ~ 625 5th Street, Ouray; 970-325-4347, fax 970-325-4845. MODERATE TO DELUXE.

In Silverton, the historic landmark hotel is the 40-room **Grand Imperial Hotel**. Its understated elegance shows in the lobby with its leather-upholstered sofas and in the rooms with their brass beds, crystal chandeliers and oak bathroom fittings. The Old West–style saloon on the main floor is open only during daytime hours when the train is in town. The hotel itself is open only from mid-March through September. ~ 1219 Greene Street, Silverton; 970-387-5527. MODERATE.

The **Wyman Hotel and Inn** is a restored 1902 building of local red sandstone with high ceilings and arched windows. The 19 guest rooms are comfortably furnished with king- or queen-size beds, period pieces and antiques, and all have private baths and TVs with VCRs. Rates include a full gourmet breakfast. ~ 1371 Greene Street, Silverton; 970-387-5372, 800-609-7845, fax 970-387-5745. MODERATE TO DELUXE.

There are also a number of smaller, bed-and-breakfast-style lodgings around Silverton. **Smedley's** has just three suites above an ice-cream parlor. The guest suites have period furniture and full kitchens. ~ 1314 Greene Street, Silverton; phone/fax 970-387-5423, 800-342-4388. MODERATE.

The same innkeepers operate the **Teller House Hotel**, a former miners' boardinghouse. You'll find five shared-bath guest rooms and four private-bath accommodations, all decorated in early Victorian. ~ 1250 Greene Street, Silverton; phone/fax 970-387-5423, 800-342-4388. BUDGET.

Nearby is the **Wingate House**, an ornate mansard-roofed Victorian home filled with floral patterns and lace. The four antique-furnished guest rooms share two baths. ~ 1045 Snowden Street, Silverton; phone/fax 970-387-5520, call before faxing. MODERATE TO DELUXE.

DINING

Telluride has about two dozen restaurants, many of which are designed for an upscale resort clientele. Poshest of them all is **La Marmotte**, where Continental cuisine and fine wines are served in an intimate environment that looks much like an old wine cellar but in fact was once the town icehouse. Closed in winter. ~ 150 West San Juan Avenue, Telluride; 970-728-6232. DELUXE.

The **Cosmopolitan,** in the newly restored, very Victorian Columbia Hotel, serves a broad range of meals for all tastes and budgets, from pizzas to chicken cordon bleu and wild-mushroom calzones. Eat in the elegant dining room or outside on the deck with a view of the ski slopes. ~ 300 West San Juan Avenue, Telluride; 970-728-1292. MODERATE TO DELUXE.

One of the liveliest restaurants in Telluride is the **Floradora Saloon,** specializing in beef and offering a large salad bar as well. The Old West saloon atmosphere makes the Floradora a perfect après-ski spot. Lunch only. Closed October and November. ~ 103 West Colorado Avenue, Telluride; 970-728-3888. BUDGET.

Two blocks down the main street, **BJ's Bluegrass Café** serves gourmet pizzas, pasta and overstuffed sandwiches on an outdoor deck with one of the best views in town. ~ 300 West Colorado Avenue, Telluride; 970-728-5335. BUDGET.

Top of the line in Ouray is the **Bon Ton Restaurant,** serving northern Italian fare in an atmosphere that emphasizes the historic Victorian building with its bare brick walls and cut-glass accents. Although the menu may have changed over the years, the restaurant has been in continuous operation since the 1880s. The Sunday brunch is the best in town. ~ 426 Main Street, Ouray; 970-325-4951. DELUXE.

Another good place to dine is **Pricco's Restaurant.** Victorian woodwork complements the exposed brick interior of the restaurant. The specialty of the house is a surf-and-turf plate of shrimp scampi and rib-eye steak. ~ 736 Main Street, Ouray; 970-325-4040. MODERATE.

The **Piñon Restaurant** is a modern little café with a tavern upstairs. Try the vegetarian burrito, stuffed with black beans, zucchini, carrots, onions and celery, or the trout with piñon nuts. ~ 737 Main Street, Ouray; 970-325-4334. MODERATE.

✔ **CHECK THESE OUT—UNIQUE DINING**

- *Budget:* Eat healthy and sip gourmet coffee or homemade beer with the Durango locals at **Carver Brewing Company.** *page 292*
- *Moderate to deluxe:* Peek out at Pagosa Peak while dining on filet mignon or grilled salmon at the two-story **Green House.** *page 284*
- *Deluxe:* Enjoy the northern Italian fare and the Victorian ambience at the historic **Bon Ton Restaurant,** which has been in business in Ouray for more than a century. *page 309*
- *Deluxe:* Savor the Continental cuisine and fine wines at **La Marmotte,** perhaps the poshest restaurant in the region. *page 308*

Budget: under $8   Moderate: $8–$16   Deluxe: $16–$24   Ultra-deluxe: over $24

In Silverton, the **French Bakery Restaurant** in the Teller House Hotel tantalizes guests and passersby alike with the wafting smell of baking bread. It serves omelettes and croissants, sandwiches, soups and full dinners. Its location near the narrow-gauge train depot makes it a lunchtime favorite. ~ 1250 Greene Street, Silverton; 970-387-5423. MODERATE.

Another good place for breakfast, lunch or dinner is the **Pickle Barrel**, which was operating as a restaurant long before the railroad started running again. In a building that dates back to 1880 and was originally a general store, the restaurant serves sandwiches, steak and trout. Closed in winter. ~ 1304 Greene Street, Silverton; 970-387-5713. BUDGET TO MODERATE.

SHOPPING   Telluride has plenty of T-shirt shops and pricey sporting goods stores. It also has a handful of quite upmarket art galleries. As in Durango, the galleries in Telluride feature predominantly American Indian arts and Southwest-style paintings and sculptures, including some pieces that cost as much as a car. A good places to gaze longingly at such artworks is the **Telluride Gallery of Fine Art**. ~ 130 East Colorado Avenue, Telluride; 970-728-3300. The **McNair Gallery** features American Indian artwork and has a fascinating collection of historical photographs. ~ 209 East Colorado Avenue, Telluride; 970-728-3617. The **Brody Art Gallery** also displays American Indian artwork. ~ 575 West Colorado Avenue, Telluride; 970-728-3734.

Souvenir shopping in Ouray offers an intriguing ambience. Some of the stores along Main Street look as if they haven't changed in 50 years. Check out, for example, **Ouray V & S Variety**, a traditional small-town general store. ~ 700 Main Street, Ouray; 970-325-4469. In recent years, many artists and craftspeople have settled in Ouray because living is cheaper there than in most southwestern Colorado towns. Their work is exhibited in a half-dozen Main Street galleries, including the **Artist's Guild of Ouray County**. ~ 735 Main Street, Ouray; 970-325-0270. There's also the **Ouray Gallery**. ~ 512 Main Street, Ouray; 970-325-4110. And don't miss the remarkable hand-turned wooden vessels and

HASTY HARVEST

Silverton's extremely short growing season—less than two weeks—means local gardeners can successfully grow only one crop: rhubarb. The community celebrates an annual Rhubarb Festival in August, and rhubarb pie is a specialty in many restaurants.

furniture of master craftsman Bob Willis at **Willis Woodworks**. ~   ◀ HIDDEN
306 6th Avenue, Ouray; 970-325-0426.

Silverton's main industry is curio shops, which cluster along
Greene Street between 11th and 14th streets. None stands out.
You can also find San Juan Mountains guidebooks and maps as
well as hiking and camping gear. **Silverton Mountain Pottery** has
original stoneware handmade in Silverton from local clay. ~ Blair
Street, Silverton.

Telluride's most venerable drinking establishment is the **Sheridan**   **NIGHTLIFE**
Bar, a dignified old hotel bar that harks back to the Victorian era
but can become rowdy during ski season. ~ 225 West Colorado
Avenue, Telluride; 970-728-3911. For really loud fun, though, the
place to go is the **Fly Me to the Moon Saloon**. It presents live rock,
R&B or reggae bands nightly during the ski and festival seasons
and has an underground dancefloor. Cover. ~ 132 East Colorado
Avenue, Telluride; 970-728-6666.

For an authentic Old West atmosphere complete with modern-
day mountain men (and women), spend an hour or two in the
Silver Eagle Saloon. ~ 617 Main Street, Ouray; 970-325-4161.

MCPHEE NATIONAL RECREATION AREA   **PARKS**
Completed in 1987, McPhee Reservoir flooded the lower
portion of the Dolores River Canyon and a network of tributary
canyons to create a long, narrow lake that provides almost boundless opportunities for backcountry boating and fishing. Before it
was flooded, the canyon was the site of a number of Ancestral
Pueblo ruins and home to a wide assortment of wildlife. Archaeological surveys performed during the dam's construction yielded
numerous artifacts, many of which are on exhibit at the Bureau of
Land Management's Anasazi Heritage Center nearby. A "mitiga-
tion area" surrounding the lake protects habitat for birds and animals, including bobcats, coyotes, mountain lions, ospreys, beavers and mule deer, that previously lived in the canyons where the
lake is today. Fishing is good for rainbow, brown and cutthroat
trout as well as largemouth bass. There are picnic areas with tables, drinking water, restrooms, boat ramps and hiking trails. ~
Located 12 miles west of Dolores off Route 184; 970-882-1435.

▲ McPhee Campground, on the lake's western shore, and
House Creek Campground, on the eastern shore, have 133 RV/tent
sites (some with electric hookups) with drinking water and dump-
ing stations; $12 per night.

RIDGWAY STATE PARK   Recreational facilities are located in two separate areas along the shoreline of
80,000-acre Ridgway Reservoir. The main recreational site, on a
promontory at the lake's south shore, has a boat ramp, a public

swimming beach, two campgrounds and four miles of hiking trails. The mile-long, paved main trail leads to the Dallas Creek Recreation Site, at the east end of the reservoir where both Dallas Creek and the Uncompahgre River flow in. The Dallas Creek site has picnic areas, as well as walkways and bridges that provide pedestrian access to the lake's north shore. There are rainbow and brown trout and ice fishing is available in the winter. Facilities include picnic areas with tables and restrooms, and a marina (970-626-5094) with boat rentals, which is open Friday through Sunday only. Day use fee $4. ~ Located five miles north of Ridgway on Route 550, about midway between Telluride and Ouray; 970-626-5822.

▲ The Dakota Terrace and Elk Ridge campgrounds offer a total of 177 RV/tent sites and 10 walk-in tent sites; $7 to $10 per night. Most have electric hookups. There are showers, flush toilets and laundry facilities as well as a dump station. Pa-co-chu-puk has 42 RV sites (full hookups), showers and flush toilets; $12 per night.

SAN JUAN NATIONAL FOREST

San Juan National Forest surrounds the San Juan Skyway and includes the jagged, lofty Needle Mountains, which rise to the east of the Skyway, and the narrow-gauge railroad in the vast Weminuche Wilderness. Parts of the Lizard Head and South San Juan wilderness areas also lie within San Juan National Forest. The San Juan Mountains were a rich gold-mining district in the 1870s to 1920s, containing numerous mines, camps and wagon roads and narrow-gauge tracks; today, more than 2000 miles of unpaved forest roads, many of which require four-wheel-drive vehicles or are suitable for mountain biking, provide access to many areas of the forest. For serious backpackers, San Juan National Forest is one of the most popular playgrounds in the Rocky Mountains. Fishing is good for rainbow and other trout in more than 90 natural lakes and 280 streams throughout the forest. Facilities include picnic areas, restrooms, pack trails and jeep trails. ~ Access is via the San Juan Skyway Scenic Byway—Route 145 between Dolores and Lizard Head Pass and Route 550 between Durango and Silverton. Purgatory Campground, South Mineral Campground and most other campgrounds and trailheads are found along these highways; 970-247-4874.

▲ Among the numerous campgrounds along the San Juan Skyway is Purgatory Campground, located near Purgatory Ski Area midway between Durango and Silverton, with 14 RV/tent sites (no hookups); closed mid-September to mid-May; $10 per night. South Mineral Campground near Silverton has 23 RV/tent sites (no hookups); closed mid-October to late May; $10 per night.

UNCOMPAHGRE NATIONAL FOREST (SOUTHERN UNIT)

This part of Uncompahgre National Forest (see also "Grand Junction Area Parks" in Chapter Five) encompasses the mountains around Telluride and Ouray. Big Blue Wilderness contains Uncompahgre Peak (14,309 feet) and Wetterhorn Peak (14,015 feet) near Ouray. Other areas (without roads) include the Mount Sneffels and the Lizard Head wilderness areas, both near Telluride. All are destinations for serious mountain-climbing expeditions. There are picnic areas, restrooms, hiking trails, pack trails and jeep trails. Best in July and August for rainbow, brown and brook trout, especially in Owl Creek and Beaver Lake east of Ridgway. ~ Access is via the San Juan Scenic Skyway—Route 145 between Lizard Head Pass and Telluride and Route 550 between Ouray and Silverton. Most trailheads and campgrounds, including Matterhorn, Sunshine and Amphitheater campgrounds, are along these highways; 970-327-4261.

▲ Matterhorn and Sunshine Campgrounds near Telluride offer 38 RV/tent sites (no hookups; open Memorial Day through September; $10 to $14 per night. Amphitheater Campground near Ouray has 30 RV/tent sites (no hookups); closed late September to late May; $12 per night.

Outdoor Adventures

FISHING

PAGOSA SPRINGS AREA The east and west forks of the San Juan River above Pagosa Springs are known for especially good trout fishing, with rainbow and brown trout at lower elevations and cutthroat trout higher upstream. A broad spectrum of fishing options, from largemouth bass in the shallows to kokanee salmon in the deeps, can be found at Navajo Lake State Park.

DURANGO AREA Directly east of Durango, Vallecito Reservoir, a large fishing lake, offers bass fishing.

SAN JUAN SKYWAY AREA The Dolores River is reputed to be one of the finest dry flyfishing areas in the West. In particular, the stretch of river below McPhee Reservoir teems with large rainbow and brown trout and Snake River cutthroats. Guides for wading or horseback flyfishing expeditions on the Dolores River and its tributaries can be arranged through West Fork Guide Service. ~ P.O. Box 300, Dolores, CO 81323; 970-882-7959.

They say 12- to 18-inch rainbow and brown trout are the norm in the San Miguel River near Telluride. Telluride Flyfishers offers combination flyfishing schools. ~ 150 West Colorado Avenue, Telluride; 970-728-4477. For fishing guide services, call Hank Hotz. ~ 970-249-4441.

BOATING

PAGOSA SPRINGS AREA On Navajo Lake, San Juan Marina has a full spectrum of rentals, from little fishing skiffs to 24-foot pontoon boats and 50-foot houseboats. ~ 1526 County Road 982; 970-883-2343.

DURANGO AREA Vallecitos Reservoir, east of Durango, is the most popular lake in the Durango region for water sports. Aluminum fishing boat and pontoon boat rentals are available at the north end of the lake at **Angler's Wharf**. ~ 17250 County Road 501, Bayfield; 970-884-9477. **Mountain Marina** also provides rentals. ~ 14810 County Road 501, Bayfield; 970-884-9450.

SAN JUAN SKYWAY AREA You can rent fishing boats, pontoon boats on McPhee Reservoir at **McPhee Marina**. ~ 25021 Route 184, Lewis; 970-882-2257.

RIVER RUNNING

PAGOSA SPRINGS AREA Pagosa Rafting and Wilderness Journeys offers raft trips on the San Juan River as well as special two- and three-day expeditions. ~ P.O. Box 222, Pagosa Springs, CO 81147; 970-731-4081.

DURANGO AREA Durango rafting companies run the lower Animas River south from town past old mining ruins, down a series of wet-and-wild rapids and through the Southern Ute Reservation. Contact **Mountain Waters Rafting**. ~ 108 West 6th Street, Durango; 970-259-4191. **Flexible Flyers Rafting** also provides trips. ~ 2344 County Road 255, Durango; 970-247-4628.

BALLOON RIDES & GLIDING

For a unique perspective on the spectacular San Juan Mountains, try drifting silently on the updrafts above the mountain slopes in a glider or hot-air balloon. Both are among the pricier thrills to be found in the region; the cost of a glider ride—including glider rental, pilot and tow plane, is about the same as hot-air ballooning. Either way, you'll come away with an experience that's sure to remain a vivid memory.

PAGOSA SPRINGS AREA **Rocky Mountain Balloon Adventures** offers hot-air balloon flights above lush meadows in the San Juan Mountains and champagne afterward. Advance reservations are essential; often, one day's notice is all that's necessary. ~ P.O. Box 4095, Pagosa Springs, CO 81147; 970-731-5315.

DURANGO AREA Scenic glider rides over Durango and the Animas Valley can be arranged through the **Durango Soaring Club**. ~ Val-Air Gliderport, Route 550, Durango; 970-247-9037.

SAN JUAN SKYWAY AREA Glider rides among the spectacular mountains that surround Telluride are offered by **Telluride Soaring**. ~ Telluride airport, Telluride; 970-728-5424. **San Juan Balloon Adventures** offers one-hour balloon flights over the Ridgway Valley every morning year-round (weather permitting) from Ridgway. There's a good chance of spotting wildlife, and passengers enjoy a champagne breakfast when they land. ~ P.O. Box 66, Ridgway, CO 81421; 970-626-5495.

PAGOSA SPRINGS AREA Wolf Creek Ski Area receives more snowfall than any other ski area in the state—over 400 inches a year. The ski area near the Wolf Creek Pass summit is located 70 miles west of Alamosa and 80 miles east of Durango. It has a vertical drop of 1425 feet and four chairlifts as well as a magic carpet and a Snow Cat shuttle to transport people back from the ungroomed trails of the "outback" area. There are 20 percent beginners' runs, 35 percent intermediate, 25 percent advanced and 20 percent expert. Snowboarding is permitted. Open Thanksgiving through April. There is a rental shop at the base. ~ Route 160, Wolf Creek Pass; 970-731-5605.

DURANGO AREA What you see from the highway of **Purgatory Ski Area** is just a hint of the complex 75-mile groomed trail network that works its way around the broad side of the mountain, making this relatively small ski area, with its 2029-foot vertical drop, wider than it is high. There are 11 chairlifts. Located 29 miles north of Durango, the ski area has rentals, child care and a ski school. There are 20 percent beginners' runs, 50 percent intermediate, and 30 percent advanced or expert. Snowboarding is allowed on most runs. Open Thanksgiving to late April. ~ Route 550; 970-247-9000.

SAN JUAN SKYWAY AREA Telluride Ski Area has a reputation as an "experts only" ski mountain. Developers in the early 1970s ran into financial problems after completing only the incredibly steep runs on the front side of the mountain. Today, 75 percent of the runs are for beginning and intermediate skiers, but these runs are hidden on the back side of the mountain. The vertical drop is an awesome 3165 feet. There are ten chairlifts and a gondola, as well as a new snowboarding park. The Plunge and Spiral Stairs running down the front face are the longest, steepest mogul runs in Colorado. There are ski rentals and a ski school. This ski resort

✔ **CHECK THESE OUT—UNIQUE OUTDOOR ADVENTURES**

- Discover why anglers consider the Dolores River one of the finest dry flyfishing areas in the West. *page 313*
- Rent a houseboat and cruise from Colorado to New Mexico and back on Navajo Lake. *page 313*
- Try Colorado's latest winter sport, ice climbing, on the 140-foot frozen waterfalls of the Ouray Ice Park. *page 316*
- Rent a llama to carry your gear and keep you company as you trek into the vast San Juan Wilderness for up to two weeks. *page 318*

offers the most spectacular mountain scenery in the state. Open
from Thanksgiving through April. ~ Route 145, Telluride; 970-
728-4424.

Ski Rentals   In Telluride, downhill and cross-country equipment
can be rented at **Telluride Sports**. ~ 150 West Colorado Avenue;
970-728-4477. **Paragon Sports** also rents equipment. ~ 213 West
Colorado Avenue; 970-728-4525. The best place to rent cross-
country skis is **Telluride Nordic Center**. ~ Town Park; 970-728-
3404.

CROSS-
COUNTRY
SKIING

DURANGO AREA   Purgatory Ski Touring Center offers rentals,
cross-country ski lessons and more than 15 kilometers of groomed
trails. ~ Route 550, Purgatory; 970-247-9000 ext. 3196.

SAN JUAN SKYWAY AREA   Telluride Nordic Center maintains 30
kilometers of groomed trails and offers rentals. ~ 136 Country
Club Drive, Telluride; 970-728-5989. In Ouray, cross-country ski
rentals and information about groomed trails in the national forest can be obtained at **Ouray Mountain Sports**. ~ 722 Main Street,
Ouray; 970-325-4284.

   For more information on renting equipment, see the ski-rental
section in "Downhill Skiing" above.

ICE
CLIMBING

From November through May, ice-climbing enthusiasts from all
over the world come to Ouray to pit their strength and skill against
the 140-foot-tall frozen manmade waterfalls in **Ouray Ice Park**.
For equipment rentals and event information, visit **Ouray Mountain Sports**. ~ 722 Main Street, Ouray; 970-325-4284.

GOLF

PAGOSA SPRINGS AREA   The **Pagosa Pines Golf Club**, located at
the Fairfield Resort west of Pagosa Springs, features three nine-
hole mountain courses designed by Johnny Bulla. Each course is
different, and there is a reduced fee for playing any two in tandem.
Club and cart rentals are available. ~ 1 Pines Club Place, Pagosa
Springs; 970-731-4755.

DURANGO AREA   In Durango, the 18-hole **Hillcrest Golf Course**
has spectacular mountain views from a mesa top overlooking
Durango. There are cart and club rentals and a driving range. ~
2300 Rim Drive; 970-247-1499. Also near Durango is the semiprivate 18-hole **Dalton Ranch & Golf Club**, designed by Ken Dye,
dramatically set among the red cliffs of the Animas Valley. ~ 435
County Road 252; 970-247-7921. A scenic mountain course designed by Arthur Hills, the **Cliffs Golf Course** at the prestigious
Tamarron Hilton Resort is open to nonguests on a standby basis—
only guests can reserve tee times in advance. Greens fees for nonguests are among the highest in the state. ~ 40292 Route 550
North, Durango; 970-259-2000.

SAN JUAN SKYWAY AREA The Fairway Pines Golf Club in Ridgway, an 18-hole championship course, is open to the public. It is set at 8000-feet elevation on a broad mesa, surrounded by mountain skylines. Cart and club rentals are available, and there is a driving range. ~ 117 Ponderosa Drive, Ridgway; 970-626-5284.

Near Pagosa Springs, hard-surface tennis courts and racquets are rented to the public at **Fairfield Pagosa Resort,** summer only, reservations required. ~ Route 160, Pagosa Springs; 970-731-4123 ext. 2078. In Durango, **Fort Lewis College** has 12 asphalt tennis courts, which are open to the public when they're not in use for school activities. ~ College Heights; 970-247-7571. Telluride, Ouray and Silverton each have two municipal tennis courts in their respective town parks.

TENNIS

PAGOSA SPRINGS AREA Wolf Creek Outfitters leads guided horseback rides, ranging in length from an hour to all day, into the high country around Wolf Creek Pass. ~ West Fork Road, Pagosa Springs; 970-264-5332.

RIDING STABLES

DURANGO AREA Vallecito Reservoir has several riding stables. **Outlaw West Livery/Elk Point Lodge** offers guided rides. ~ County Road 501, Bayfield; 970-884-9631 or 970-884-2070 in the winter.

Just north of Durango, **Red Mountain Ranch** has hour-long, all-day and overnight guided rides into the San Juan wilderness on the Hermosa Trail. ~ 27846 Route 550, Durango; 970-247-9796.

MESA VERDE AREA Near the entrance of Mesa Verde National Park, the **Mesa Verde Riding Stable** guides small-group tours of up to ten people, ranging from hour-long to all-day, and rents horses by the day for personal use in the park's hilly piñon and juniper woodlands. ~ Route 160 West, Mancos; 970-533-7269. In Dolores, you can ride at **Circle K Ranch.** ~ 26913 Route 145; 970-562-3808.

SAN JUAN SKYWAY AREA Horses and tours are available in Telluride at **Many Ponies Outfit.** ~ 122 South Townsend Avenue; 970-728-6278. **Telluride Horseback** organizes guided one and two-hour trail rides for up to 30 people on Turkey Creek Mesa near Wilson Peak as well as all-day and overnight trips by advance arrangement. ~ 9025 Route 145; 970-728-9611. **Deep Creek Sleighs & Wagon Rides** offers horse-drawn sleigh and wagon rides with dinner nightly. ~ 133 West Colorado Avenue; 970-325-4014.

Ouray Livery Barn rents horses for independent riding. ~ 834 Main Street, Ouray; 970-325-4606. In Silverton, Silverado Outfitters leads breakfast and dinner rides. ~ Mineral Street; 970-387-5668.

PACK TRIPS & LLAMA TREKS

A pack trip into the southern Colorado Rockies can turn a vacation into an adventure. For those who want to hike long distances into the high country but don't want to be burdened with backpacks, llama trekking may be just the ticket. Besides being an extraordinary hiking companion, the llama carries your lunch, camera gear and fishing tackle—up to about a 40-pound load.

DURANGO AREA In Bayfield, **Outlaw West Livery** has guided rides of varying lengths, including seven-day full-service pack trips in the Weminuche Wilderness. ~ County Road 501A; 970-884-9631. **Red Mountain Ranch** offers overnight and three-day pack trips to ancient pueblo ruins in the red-rock country and rents llamas for wilderness treks of up to two weeks. ~ 27846 Route 550, Durango; 970-247-9796. **Engine Creek Outfitters & Cascade Stables** also offers trips. ~ 50827 Route 150, Durango; 970-259-2556. Near Durango, the **Buckhorn Llama Company** takes visitors on trips into the high San Juans. ~ 1834 County Road 207, Durango; 970-259-5965.

SAN JUAN SKYWAY AREA In Silverton, **Silverado Outfitters** lead ten-day horse pack trips on the Colorado and Continental Divide trails. ~ Mineral Street; 970-387-5668.

BIKING

PAGOSA SPRINGS AREA An easy ride near Pagosa Springs, the **Turkey Springs Trail** (6 miles) offers views of Pagosa Peak. A more challenging route, the **Willow Draw Trail** (16 miles), starts at Pagosa Springs City Park and climbs high into the hills before the thrilling downhill run back into town.

DURANGO AREA The chairlift at **Purgatory Ski Area** is equipped in the summer to take riders and their bikes to the summit, where they can ride the four-mile **Harris Park Loop** across the alpine **Hermosa Creek Valley** on the back side of the mountain. Admission. ~ Route 550, Durango; 970-247-9000. A longer and more challenging ride, the **Hermosa Creek Trail** (23 miles) takes cyclists through high meadows and along the rim of the Hermosa Cliffs. Just up the highway from Purgatory, the graded **Lime Creek Road** (11 miles) makes for a gentle ride through aspen forests with sweeping panoramic views of the surrounding mountains.

SAN JUAN SKYWAY AREA Telluride's gondola is equipped to let you transport a mountain bike to the high ridge above town for access to more than 100 miles of alpine trails. Unpaved **Ilium Road** is a favorite among mountain bikers in the Telluride area. The eight-mile road takes you to historic mining sites and waterfalls in a deep canyon. For an ultimate all-terrain biking experience, the trail to **Bear Creek Falls** climbs 1100 feet in elevation on its way to one of the most beautiful canyons in the area. **Ingram Falls Road** is a steep three-mile ascent to Bridal Veil Falls, at the upper end of the canyon overlooking town. For a week-long mountain-bike trek, the **San Juan Hut System,** a series of six shelters along a 215-mile bike route between Telluride and Moab, Utah, crosses varied terrain from alpine tundra to slickrock desert.

Unpaved, rugged four-wheel-drive roads leading to abandoned mines in the San Juan Mountains make for challenging mountain-bike trips. Around Ouray, great mountain-bike routes include the jeep trail from near Amphitheater campground up to the Portland and Chief Ouray mines. Another starts above Lake Lenore on the way to the Bachelor Mine and runs past the Wedge Mine to the Bridge of Heaven.

Bike Rentals In Pagosa Springs, you'll find bicycles at **Juan's Mountain Sports.** ~ 155 Hot Springs Boulevard; 970-264-4730. In Durango, try **Hassle Free Sports.** ~ 2615 Main Avenue; 970-259-3874. There's also **Mountain Bike Specialists.** ~ 949 Main Avenue; 970-247-4066. Places to rent bicycles in Telluride include **Telluride Sports.** ~ 150 West Colorado Avenue; 970-728-4477. Or you can contact **Paragon Ski and Sport.** ~ 217 West Colorado Avenue; 970-728-4525. In Ouray, there's **Downhill Biking.** ~ 722 Main Street; 970-325-4284.

All distances listed for hiking trails are one way unless otherwise noted.

HIKING

DURANGO AREA Durango has an overwhelming number of hiking options. The ultimate trail in the area is the **Colorado Trail** (469 miles), which goes all the way from Durango to Denver, following the Continental Divide most of the way. The first segment of the trail goes from Durango to Silverton, a distance of about 70 miles through the rugged La Plata Mountains.

Another magnificently ambitious hike is the **Needle Creek Trail,** which starts at the ghost town of Needleton, a stop on the Durango & Silverton Narrow-Gauge Railroad route. The trail climbs into the jagged peaks of the Weminuche Wilderness to join a network of other trails, including the spectacular **Chicago Basin** route, which follows alpine valleys all the way to Creede—a 75-mile trip that takes about a week. Backpackers without train tickets use a longer route to reach the high wilderness, starting at Vallecito Reservoir and taking the **Vallecito Trail** or the **Pine River Trail.** Still other trails into the Weminuche Wilderness start from Route 550.

Among the many day-hike options in the Durango area are **Red Creek Trail** (6 miles), on Missionary Ridge above town, and **Twin Buttes Trail** (4 miles), overlooking town.

SAN JUAN SKYWAY AREA Telluride is hiker's heaven in the summertime. Short, challenging trails like the steep one-mile climb to **Bridal Veil Falls** start from the outskirts of town. For an all-day or overnight hike, the **Bear Creek Trail** passes another waterfall and climbs high in the mountains to join the **Wasatch Trail**

for a descent to Bridal Veil Falls, making a strenuous ten-mile loop. For mountaintop vistas without the pain, hikers can ride the chairlift (which operates all year) up the Telluride ski slopes and hike along at 10,500-foot elevation alpine ridges.

In Ouray, short hikes include the **Lower Cascade Falls Trail** (.5 mile), which starts just a few blocks from the center of town, and the steep **Upper Cascade Falls Trail** (2.5 miles), which starts from the natural amphitheater south of town. For an all-day hike, try **Bear Creek Trail** (7.25 miles), which passes several old mining operations on its way to the summit of Engineer Pass.

Near Silverton, the **Highland Mary Lakes Trail** (2.5 miles) takes you through a landscape thoroughly probed by miners a century ago and leads up to a pair of alpine lakes. This trail joins the Canada-to-Mexico **Continental Divide Trail** as it passes through the Weminuche Wilderness. The **Molas Pass Trail** (3 miles) starts at Molas Lake on Route 550 and descends steeply to the Animas River and the Durango & Silverton train tracks a thousand feet below, offering breathtaking views and a hard climb back up to your car.

▼▼▼▼▼▼▼▼▼▼▼
Transportation

CAR

Route 160 goes over Wolf Creek Pass (10,850 feet) between Pagosa Springs and the Durango area.

Route 550 and Route 145 together are known as the San Juan Skyway Scenic Byway. Route 550 leaves Route 160 at Durango and goes through Silverton and Ouray. Route 145 leaves Route 160 at Mancos, a short drive west of Durango, and goes through Dolores and Telluride.

AIR

Daily commuter flights from Denver to **Durango–La Plata Airport** are provided by America West Express, Continental Express and Mesa Airlines/United Express. Airport shuttles are operated by **Durango Transportation Inc.** ~ 970-259-4818.

Continental Express, Mesa Airlines/United Express and Skywest/Delta Connection serve the **Telluride Regional Airport**; the Continental and Mesa flights also land at **Montrose Regional Airport**. Ground transportation at both airports is available during ski season from **Telluride Transit Company Airport Shuttle Service**. ~ 970-728-6000.

BUS

Greyhound Bus Lines has bus service to Durango. ~ 275 East 8th Avenue; 970-247-2755, 800-231-2222.

CAR RENTALS

Car-rental agencies at Durango–La Plata Airport include **Avis Rent A Car** (800-331-1212), **Budget Rent A Car** (800-527-0700), **Hertz Rent A Car** (800-654-3131) and **National Interrent** (800-328-4567). You can rent either a late-model used car or a four-wheel-drive vehicle at **Rent A Wreck**. ~ 21760 Route 160 West; 800-327-0116.

Along the San Juan Skyway, four-wheel-drive vehicles are for rent at **Telluride Outside 4 X 4 Rentals**. ~ 1982 West Highway 145, Telluride; 970-728-3895. They are also available at **Switzer-land of America Jeep Rentals**. ~ 226 7th Avenue, Ouray; 970-325-4484. **Colorado West Jeep Rentals** provides rentals. ~ 440 Main Street, Ouray; 970-325-4014. **Triangle Rent A Jeep** also rents four-wheel-drive vehicles. ~ 864 Greene Street, Silverton; 970-387-9990.

The **Durango Lift** provides in-town, fixed-route bus service during the summer months and shuttle service from Durango to the slopes at Purgatory during ski season. ~ 949 East 2nd Avenue, Durango; 970-259-5438.   **PUBLIC TRANSIT**

In Durango, the taxi company is **Durango Transportation**. ~ 547½ East 2nd Avenue; 970-259-4818. In Telluride, it's **Skip's Taxi**. ~ 129 West San Juan Avenue; 970-728-6667.   **TAXIS**

NINE

The Eastern Plains

Sunflowers, a common cash crop along the plains that make up Colorado's eastern state line, face Kansas in the morning. The flowers rotate in unison to follow the sun, pointing the way to the Rocky Mountains in the afternoon. This seemingly arcane bit of information can be important to know if you leave the main route without a compass to venture into the gridwork of forgotten two-lane blacktop highways and gravel farm-to-market roads that segment the prairie out past the horizon where the mountains cannot be seen and all directions look pretty much the same.

Forty percent of Colorado's land area lies east of the Rocky Mountains and the major Front Range population centers. If Colorado's arbitrary boundaries were redrawn according to geography, economy or cultural heritage, the eastern plains would belong to Kansas or perhaps Nebraska, certainly not to Colorado. The region is arid, nearly flat land used for cattle ranching and dryland farming, the main crops being corn and wheat. Tourism is not a significant factor in eastern Colorado's economy.

It's not that the plains of eastern Colorado are devoid of things to see or do. It's just that the distances are vast and the sights so modest that they can't begin to rival those found in any other part of the state. The information presented in this chapter is for motorists and bus passengers bound for Colorado's cities and resort areas from points east. Then, too, my search for points of interest in this nearly empty land has sometimes led me to special spots on the most remote reaches of the prairie where few people have set foot since the days of the pioneers. I include these spots for the benefit of the rare traveler driven by curiosity to seek out the most thoroughly "hidden" places in the entire state.

Three main highway routes cross the eastern plains. Route 76 follows the South Platte River from Nebraska, where it branches off Route 80, entering the northeast corner of Colorado and angling down toward Denver, where it merges with Route 70. Colorado's early Anglo settlers turned off the Oregon Trail, the main covered-wagon route west, following the Overland Trail southwest from Nebraska along this fork of the river to establish new communities at the foot of the Rocky Mountains.

Route 70 follows no river or historical trail. A path first used by stagecoaches in the 1850s, it is simply the most direct line across the Great Plains from Kansas City west to Denver. Burlington and Limon, the two main agricultural towns along the 200-mile stretch of divided highway between the Colorado–Kansas state line and Denver, seem to be affected little by the high-speed traffic flow along their outskirts. Only occasionally do highway travelers stop for longer than it takes to fill up with gas and fast food.

Route 50 traces the Arkansas River and the Santa Fe Trail, one of the most important historical routes of the 19th century. The first explorers from the United States to set foot in Colorado came this way, and the first goods traded between the United States and Mexico were carried in wagons along this route. Today, this is the least-used of the three routes because it is somewhat slower than the interstate highways and it does not go to Denver. Travelers bound for the southern part of Colorado from points east may find that this is the easiest—and most interesting—route.

The weather on the eastern plains tends to be more extreme than along the Front Range Corridor, which is sheltered by the rain shadow of the Rocky Mountains. The prairie slopes slightly downward from the foothills east to the state line. The elevations of Julesburg and Burlington, for instance, are more than 1000 feet lower than that of Denver, and Lamar, the lowest point in Colorado at 3500 feet above sea level, is nearly half a mile lower than Colorado Springs. The difference in elevation translates into hotter summer temperatures. Thermometers commonly read 100 degrees on summer afternoons; large thunderstorms, tornadoes and golfball-size hail are fairly common, alternating with the sometimes devastating dry spells that earned the region the name "Great American Desert" in the days before irrigation or wells. Winter weather, though variable, can also be severe. Snowstorms are typically accompanied by high winds that create blinding blizzard conditions and road-blocking snowdrifts.

Despite the apparent drawbacks of prairie life, as you cross Colorado's eastern plains you will see that people do live way out here. They may live so spread out that no ranch or farm house is within sight of any other, and they may routinely drive forty miles to the nearest town, which may consist of a grain silo and a convenience store that also sells diesel fuel, but the people of the prairie fight hard to survive the economic problems that threaten small farmers and ranchers throughout in the Great Plains and hold on to their ties with the land. In eastern Colorado it can truly be said that America's pioneer spirit lives on.

South Platte River Area

History (along with grain silos and cattle feed lots) reigns supreme in northeastern Colorado. Most historical points of interest in the area are left over from the period between 1860 and 1868, when the Overland Trail was the busiest route in the American West. The trail branched off the Oregon Trail in central

Nebraska to follow the South Platte River southwest to Denver and other newly founded towns along the Rocky Mountain foothills.

SIGHTS

In 1860, a year after Congress created Jefferson Territory (which would later be renamed Colorado), the Pony Express established the first courier service to the new territory by building a station at Julesburg—less than two miles from the Nebraska border. Mail arriving at the station might not be delivered promptly, though, because Pony Express did not extend its route farther into the territory until 1862. The station was closed in 1868, when the arrival of the railroad made the Pony Express obsolete. The ruins of the **Pony Express station**, located just west of town on Route 138, the old, empty highway across the river from Route 76, are one of the few points of interest in present-day Julesburg. The little farm town's past is the focus of the **Fort Sedgwick Depot Museum**, with its modest displays of American Indian and pioneer artifacts. ~ 202 West 1st Street, Julesburg; 970-474-2264. Other Overland Trail historic sites along Route 138 include the remains of the **Lillian Springs and Spring Hill stage coach stops** at the tiny town of **Crook**.

One early Oregon Trail pioneer described the **South Platte River** as "a mile wide and an inch deep." The South Platte looks much different than any of the other major rivers—such as the Arkansas, the Rio Grande and, of course, the Colorado—that originate in the Colorado Rockies. From the main highway, all that can be seen of the river is a skyline of tall trees in the middle distance. Fortunately, you can get a better look from any of the numerous bridges that span the river to reach towns on the other side, revealing the South Platte as a braid of many small channels that wind their ways among long, slender islands overgrown with bushes. Because the South Platte occasionally lets loose with a flood like a tidal wave, farms and buildings are set well away from its banks, leaving the river area wild and, in many places, so thickly tangled with vegetation as to be almost impenetrable.

You can get close to the river at any of several state wildlife areas designed for duck hunting in the fall and rarely visited at other times of year except by local fishermen. The biggest and best

HIDDEN ► is **Tamarack Ranch State Wildlife Area**, which takes in both banks of the river for almost 20 miles. The 10,600-acre wild area also includes a large tract of natural prairie, as well as plots of farmland where part of the crop is left for the birds. Notable among the many bird species seen at Tamarack Ranch year-round are wild turkeys and greater prairie chickens, an endangered species. Whitetailed and mule deer are also abundant. ~ Route 138, Crook; 970-474-2711.

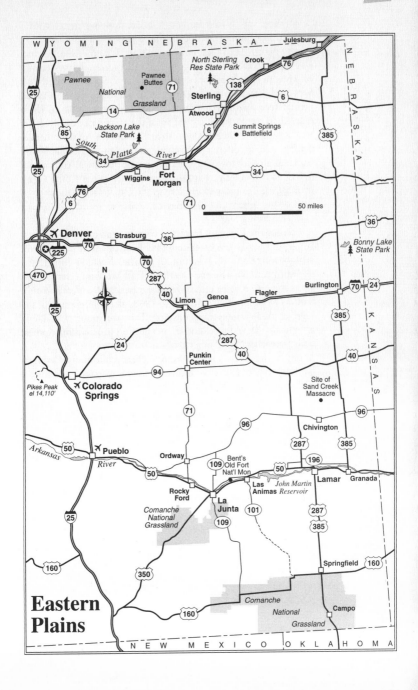

WYOMING   NEBRASKA   Julesburg

Pawnee

Pawnee Buttes   71   North Sterling Res State Park   Crook   76

National   138

Grassland   Sterling   6

14   Atwood

85   6

Jackson Lake State Park   Summit Springs Battlefield   385

25   South   Platte   River   34

76   Wiggins   Fort Morgan

6   71   0   50 miles

36

Denver   Strasburg   36   Bonny Lake State Park

225   70

470   70   Burlington   24

287   70

25   40   Limon   Genoa   Flagler   385

N   287

24   Punkin Center   40   40

94

Pikes Peak el 14,110'   Colorado Springs   Site of Sand Creek Massacre   96

71   96   Chivington

Arkansas   50   Pueblo   287   385

Ordway   Bent's Old Fort Nat'l Mon   50   196

River   50   109   John Martin Reservoir   Lamar   Granada

Rocky Ford   Las Animas

350   La Junta   101

Comanche National Grassland   109   287

385

160   Springfield   160

25

Comanche   Campo

Eastern Plains   350

160   National Grassland

NEW   MEXICO   OKLAHOMA

Sterling, an agriculture and railroad shipping center with a population of about 10,000, is the largest town on Colorado's eastern plains. The tallest building in town is a grain silo. Sterling was founded in 1873 by a group of settlers from Tennessee and Mississippi who abandoned the war-ravaged South to build new lives on the frontier. Sterling's most unusual sights are its so-called **Living Trees**, actually colossal wood sculptures, most of them more than ten feet tall, carved from the trunks of dead trees by local artist Brad Rhea. Sixteen (so far) of the fanciful sculptures—among them a golfer, a plainsman, giraffes and a mermaid—are scattered all over town in parks and public buildings. You can see one outside the **Visitors Information Center** at the Route 6 exit from Route 76 and pick up a map there that shows the way to each of the others and provides an excuse to spend a couple of hours exploring Sterling.

Across the highway from the visitors center stands an even larger sculpture—the **Overland Trail Monument**, a 20-foot-tall, 40-foot-long concrete rendition of a covered wagon pulled by a team of oxen. Nearby, the **Overland Trail Museum** offers a look at the migration route that brought thousands of settlers and gold hunters to Colorado from 1862 to 1868, when the coming of the railroad made wagon trains obsolete. The main museum building, a replica of an old fort, houses a collection of buckskin clothes, dolls, arrowheads and other artifacts from the pioneer era, as well as one of the world's largest branding-iron collections. Grounds landscaped with native wildflowers and prairie grasses and strewn with covered wagons and old-time farm machinery surround a cluster of historic buildings including a one-room schoolhouse, a blacksmith shop and a Lutheran church. Admission. ~ Route 6, Sterling; 970-522-5070.

HIDDEN ►
History buffs can also get directions at the Sterling Visitors Information Center to the small monument marking the **Summit**

✔ CHECK THESE OUT—UNIQUE SIGHTS

- Take a tour of Sterling in search of the 16 **Living Trees**—colossal wood sculptures that are scattered all over town. *page 326*
- Pause in Burlington for a look at the **Kit Carson County Carousel**, the only antique merry-go-round in the U.S. that still has its original paint. *page 330*
- Climb the **World's Wonder View Tower** in Genoa for a view of miles and miles of wide open ranchland. *page 331*
- Travel deep into Comanche National Grassland to discover the mysterious ancient artworks in **Picture Canyon**. *page 337*

Springs Battlefield southwest of Sterling near Atwood. The 1869 battle, which ended in the killings of 50 Cheyenne and Arapaho men and the rescue of two kidnapped pioneer women from Kansas, was the last armed conflict between U.S. army troops and American Indians in eastern Colorado.

Although most visitors arrive in Sterling with the impression that there's nothing but flat grasslands for a hundred miles in any direction, surprisingly dramatic scenery can be found at **Chimney**   ◄ HIDDEN
Canyons, 20 miles north on County Road 37 (7th Avenue) and then 8 miles west of town on County Road 70, where the plains give way to 250-foot chalk cliffs.

Fort Morgan, the next large town on the Platte River west of Sterling, was originally the site of a military fort that protected pioneers on the Overland Trail from 1864 to 1868. The cavalry outpost is the subject of a permanent exhibit at the **Fort Morgan Museum**, which also contains plains Indian artifacts, a fully equipped soda fountain from the 1920s, and a gallery commemorating 1930s and '40s big-band superstar Glenn Miller, whose boyhood home was in Fort Morgan. ~ 414 Main Street, Fort Morgan; 970-867-6331. Located at Route 76 and Main is **Riverside Park**, a 180-acre natural area by the South Platte with trails along the riverbank and through verdant woodlands. Adjacent to the park, the **James Marsh Arch Bridge** (Route 53) is the only rainbow arch–design bridge in the state, a source of pride for Fort Morgan and presumably a thrill for bridge architecture buffs.

Much of the arid prairie land that lies north of the South Platte River is within the boundaries of **Pawnee National Grassland**, the Great Plains equivalent of a national forest. The grasslands were formerly in private ownership, first as part of the vast domain of late-19th-century cattle baron John Wesley Iliff, later transformed into small, marginally productive dryland farms by homesteaders between 1910 and 1918. Brutal winters, a deadly influenza epidemic and finally the Dust Bowl drought of the 1930s forced the abandonment of virtually all farm and ranch land in the area. In the late '30s, the federal government began an ambitious reclamation plan to dig wells, construct small reservoirs called catch basins, replant the ruined meadow land with hardy crested wheatgrass from the Russian steppes, and plant stands of trees for windbreaks and wildlife habitat. Restoration of the prairie has been more pragmatic than environmentally aesthetic, and today the national grasslands are managed by the National Forest Service according to a "multiple use" philosophy under which the land is shared by birdwatchers, grazing cattle, oil rigs and Air Force missile silos.

For hiking and wildlife viewing, the best place in Pawnee National Grassland is **Pawnee Buttes**, twin white sandstone for-   ◄ HIDDEN mations rising 350 feet above the surrounding plain. Many fossil skeletons of prehistoric mammals have been found at the buttes. A hiking trail leads to the base of the buttes. Rock climbing is discouraged and, during the March-to-June raptor nesting season, prohibited. The buttes are also a major nesting area for golden eagles, Swainson's hawks and other species of hawks, falcons and kestrels. ~ To get there, follow Route 14 west from Sterling for 42 miles to County Road 103 (known as the Keota Turnoff) and carefully follow the signs to Pawnee Buttes, a circuitous 16-mile route from the main highway on paved county roads.

LODGING   Accommodations in the towns along Route 76 are limited to conventional motels and motor inns, most of them offering very reasonable rates compared to those in other parts of the state.

The **Platte Valley Inn**, a two-story, 59-unit motel, has clean, nicely furnished rooms with phones and cable TV. The swimming pool is a welcome sight after a long, hot drive across Nebraska. ~ Route 76 Exit 180, Julesburg; phone/fax 970-474-3336, 800-562-5166. MODERATE.

For a touch of cowtown class, stay at Sterling's **Ramada Inn**, a two-story complex with 100 spacious, contemporary guest rooms that serves as the area's main conference center. Facilities include an indoor swimming pool, sauna, hot tub and exercise room. ~ Route 76 at Route 6, Sterling; 970-522-2625, 800-835-7275, fax 970-522-1321. MODERATE.

A decent, inexpensive place to spend the night in Sterling is the 14-unit **Colonial Inn**, located across the street from a city park that contains several of the town's "Living Tree" sculptures. The rather plain rooms have cable TV and coffeemakers, and some have bathtubs. There's no swimming pool, but the motel has a children's playground and basketball court. ~ 915 South Division Street, Sterling; 970-522-3382. BUDGET.

In Fort Morgan, the **Econo Lodge** has an outdoor swimming pool and 42 comfortable guest rooms with cable TV. Overnight valet laundry service is available. ~ 1409 Barlow Road, Fort Morgan; 970-867-9481, fax 970-867-3145. BUDGET.

DINING   Look for home-style cooking in Julesburg at the **D & J Café**, a classic roadside diner serving sandwiches and full dinners ranging from spaghetti to chicken-fried steak, as well as daily specials. ~ 114 Cedar Street, Julesburg; 970-474-3556. BUDGET.

The restaurant scene in Sterling offers more variety than you'll find in other towns in the area. Spicy, authentic Mexican food can be found at the small, friendly **Cocina Alvarado**. ~ 715 West Main Street, Sterling; 970-522-8884. BUDGET.

Another very popular Mexican restaurant, **Delgado's Dugout** serves selections such as guacamole tostadas and beef-stuffed sopapillas in the low-ceilinged, romantically rustic basement of a building that was formerly Sterling's original Baptist church. ~ 116 Beech Street, Sterling; 970-522-0175. BUDGET.

Dim lighting and exotic decor set the stage for Mandarin and Szechuan cuisine at the **China Garden Restaurant**. ~ 126 West Main Street, Sterling; 970-522-1137. BUDGET TO MODERATE.

In Fort Morgan, a good dining bet is the **Fort Restaurant** in the Econo Lodge, where you'll find a family atmosphere and a varied menu with daily specials and an emphasis on heart-healthy selections. ~ 1409 Barlow Road, Fort Morgan; 970-867-9481. MODERATE.

SHOPPING

Far more than mountain towns, the eastern plains of Colorado are prime antiquing territory. Family treasures dating back to the pioneer era are often discovered in remote farmhouses and tiny prairie towns, and a number of dealers specialize in offering them to collectors. Arts and crafts traditions from pioneer times, including wheat weaving, tatting, quilting and wood carving, are alive and well and on display in gift shops or artists' cooperatives in several eastern Colorado towns.

Antiques & Artisans has a little bit of everything: furniture, ceramics, farm collectibles, country dolls, jewelry and vintage clothing. ~ 101 Cedar Street, Julesburg; 970-474-2363. Handcrafted gifts and antiques are found at **Heart of the Plains Antiques**. ~ 103 Main Street, Sterling; 970-521-9519. Antique hunters will also want to stop in next door at **Trimbach's Antiques & Art**. ~ 101 Main Street, Sterling; 970-521-9192. Fort Morgan has several shops, including **Another Time**. ~ 316 Main Street, Fort Morgan; 970-867-8515. Also noteworthy is **M & M Collectibles**. ~ 331 Ensign Street, Fort Morgan; 970-867-4780.

PARKS

NORTH STERLING RESERVOIR STATE PARK Impounded since the turn of the century, this 3000-acre manmade lake was the first large-scale irrigation project in eastern Colorado. It is one of Colorado's newest state parks, though, opened for recreational use in 1992. Sailing, waterskiing and fishing are the main recreational activities except during the November waterfowl hunting season, when the lake is closed to boaters. The state park also includes more than 1000 acres of wild prairie lands that offer opportunities for hiking and wildlife watching. The area provides habitat for deer, eagles, pelicans, coyotes and many species of water birds. Fishing is good for warm-water fish including walleye, crappie, perch, bass, bluegill, catfish and wiper. There are restrooms and a marina with boat rentals (970-522-1511). Day-use fee, $4. ~ Located 11 miles north of Sterling on County Road 33. Take 7th Avenue north from town and follow the signs; 970-522-3657.

▲ Elks Campground has 50 RV/tent sites with electric hook-ups; $12 per night. Chimney View has 54 RV/tent sites (no hook-ups) and Inlet Grove has 47 RV/tent sites (no hookups); $9 per night.

JACKSON LAKE STATE PARK 🔷 ⛴ 🎣 🚤 🏊 ⛵ This prairie reservoir northwest of Fort Morgan has sandy beaches and shore-front campsites. Although recreational boating, fishing, water-skiing and windsurfing are the main sports, the lake also has a reputation as a good birding spot during migration season, when bald eagles, long-eared owls, sandhill cranes and pelicans by the hundreds, as well as flocks of up to 20,000 ducks, stop over at the lake. (In the fall, duck hunters also congregate here.) The lake is populated by wiper, rainbow trout, walleye, perch, crappie, cat-fish, northern pike, bluegill, carp and bullhead. There are rest-rooms, a marina with boat rentals and picnic areas. Day-use fee, $4. ~ Located ten miles north of Wiggins. Take Route 39 north from Route 76 and follow the signs to the state park entrance; 970-645-2551.

▲ There are 262 RV/tent sites; $9 to $12 per night.

Route 70

▼▼▼▼▼▼▼▼▼▼

Route 70 is the fastest and, for the most part, least inter-esting route from the Great Plains to the Colorado Rockies.

It can take you 177 miles from the state line to downtown Denver in less than three hours, and you'll only have to turn the steering wheel twice. The highway does not follow a river. Instead, it traces the old Lawrence & Pikes Peak stagecoach route, which dates back to 1859. It slices straight through the least-populated area in the state, a land so empty that it is has come to be known as "the outback." Still, travelers who want to take their time and look around can find a handful of interesting sights.

SIGHTS

HIDDEN ▶

Motorists arriving in Colorado from the east on Route 70 reach **Burlington** 14 miles after leaving Kansas. A small town serving the ranches of sparsely populated Kit Carson County, Burlington boasts one of the most unusual little tourist attractions in the state. The **Kit Carson County Carousel** was built in 1905 and bought by the county commissioners in 1928 to serve as a center-piece for the county fair. Accused of squandering public funds on the merry-go-round, the commissioners were forced from office, and within a few years the county fair was discontinued and the carousel was shut down. Thanks to a 20-year, $250,000 restora-tion effort, the carousel now operates from Memorial Day to Labor Day, carrying kids of all ages for just a quarter. Now a National Historic Landmark, it is the only antique carousel in the United States that still has its original paint. ~ County Fairgrounds, Burlington.

Burlington's **Old Town Museum** contains 23 historic structures gathered from plains towns of eastern Colorado and western Kansas, among them a jail, a saloon, a railroad depot, a newspaper office, a two-story farmhouse and an immense barn, all
restored with antique furnishings. The museum also has a 25,000-
square-foot indoor exhibit area where antique vehicles and farm
implements are displayed. Admission. ~ 420 South 14th Street,
Burlington; 719-346-7382.

The **World's Wonder View Tower**, located in the tiny town of   ◄ HIDDEN
Genoa 11 miles east of Limon, was built in 1934 as a sightseeing
attraction for early-day motorists. When it was completed, the
U.S. Geological Survey determined that the tower was the highest
point between Denver and New York City. Promoters claimed
that people who climbed to the top of the 75-foot stone tower
could see six states—Colorado, Wyoming, Nebraska, Kansas,
Oklahoma and Texas. It's hard to judge, since all the land on the
distant horizon looks pretty much the same. There is an old-time
museum of curiosities containing two-headed calves and other
livestock mutations as well as collections of branding irons, old
guns and ranch memorabilia, more than 20,000 Indian artifacts
and a 75,000-year-old imperial mammoth skeleton found nearby.
Admission. ~ 30121 Frontage Road, Genoa; 719-763-2309.

Limon got its start in 1888, when it became the dividing point
for Rock Island Railroad routes to Denver and Colorado Springs.
Today it continues to serve as eastern Colorado's central shipping
hub, where Route 70 to Denver and Route
24 to Colorado Springs meet Routes 40,
71 and 287. For motorists driving west on
Route 70, the first glimpse of the Rockies
comes when Pikes Peak springs into view on
the western horizon at Limon.

Although the terrain surrounding Limon may look flat, this
town of 1800 people is situated on one of the highest
points in the eastern
plains—officially 86 feet
higher than Denver.

Limon's original railroad depot has been restored to house the **Limon Heritage Museum and
Railroad Park**. Staffed entirely by volunteers, the
free, homegrown museum complex includes collections and cultural efforts started by private citizens
around the Limon area. Among them are the Don Bailey Saddle
Collection, Doug Morrison's scale model of the Limon railyards
circa 1940, the Gladys Liggett Memorial Little Theater, the Limon
Education Association's Pioneer Schoolhouse Museum and Dan
Houtz's American Indian Collection and Medicine Tipi. ~ Limon;
719-775-2373.

Between Limon and Denver, in the town of Strasburg, the free,
volunteer-operated **Comanche Crossing Museum** is a collection
of antique-furnished historic buildings surrounding the town's old
railroad depot, which now houses exhibits of everything from

bibles to barbed wire. With advance registration, second- through sixth-grade children can attend one of the teacher-supervised classroom sessions held in August in the museum's 1904 one-room schoolhouse. Closed in winter. ~ Strasburg; 303-622-4690.

LODGING   Burlington and Limon have more than a dozen motels each, and all of them offer budget room rates. You can almost always find a decent room in either town without advance reservations.

In Burlington, the 39-unit, single-story **Chapparal Motor Inn** has air-conditioned, blandly furnished guest rooms, a heated swimming pool and a hot tub. ~ 405 South Lincoln Street, Burlington; 719-346-5361. BUDGET.

In Limon, a good family bet is the two-story, 28-room **Safari Motel**. It offers a quiet location away from the highway with a heated pool, kids' playground and laundry room. Guest rooms are air-conditioned and have king- or queen-size beds, direct-dial phones and cable TV; two-bedroom family units are available. ~ 637 Main Street, Limon; 719-775-2363. BUDGET.

For something a little more atmospheric, spend the night at the **Midwest Country Inn**. This three-story, 32-room establishment combines all the amenities of a quality motor inn—cable TV, air-conditioning, direct-dial phones, and king- or queen-size beds—with touches of elegance in the antique-filled lobby and individually decorated rooms featuring handcrafted accents and designer fabrics. In trendier parts of the state, lodgings like this come at deluxe rates, but not out here on the prairie. ~ 795 Main Street, Limon; 719-775-2373, 888-610-6683. BUDGET.

DINING   In both Burlington and Limon, you'll find most of the familiar fast-food franchises that grace interstate highway exits from coast to coast. Aside from these, dining options are few.

If you're desperate for a romantic candlelight dinner on the prairie, your best bet is the **Burlington Country Club**. You don't have to be a member to eat here. The atmosphere is on the casual side, and the bill of fare is almost all beef—not surprisingly, since most patrons here are cattle ranchers. ~ 48640 Snead Drive, Burlington; 719-346-7266. MODERATE TO DELUXE.

For simpler fare, try **BJ's Restaurant**, a family-style place serving an assortment of breakfasts-all-day, burgers and other sandwiches, and a limited selection of full dinners. ~ 100 Rose Avenue, Burlington; 719-346-8322.

One of Limon's more satisfying eateries is the **Country Fare Restaurant**, located in Rip Griffin's Truck-Travel Center and open 24 hours a day. The varied menu, daily buffet, homemade pastries and salad bar confirm that the best highway food really is found where the most truck drivers stop. ~ Routes 70 and 24, Limon; 719-775-2811. BUDGET.

Hungry motorists passing through Limon may wish to skip the bevy of chain fast-food outlets and search out **JC's Deli & Bakery**, where luncheon specials feature sandwiches on fresh-baked bread. It has the ambience of roadside coffee shops where cowboys and highway workers gather to gab over breakfast, and the food is a cut above most such places. ~ 197 East Avenue, Limon; 719-775-8836. BUDGET.

When passing through Burlington, antique hunters will want to check out the **Old Town Emporium**, a shop located within the Old Town Museum. ~ 420 South 14th Street, Burlington; 719-346-8484.

SHOPPING

There's also a selection of antiques and gifts for sale at the **World's Wonder View Tower**. ~ 30121 Frontage Road, Genoa; 719-763-2309.

In Limon, **Treasures Unlimited** sells antiques, art and gift items on consignment for more than 60 local craftspeople and collectors. ~ 571 Main Street, Limon; 719-775-2057.

BONNY LAKE STATE PARK This large flood-control reservoir on the Republican River north of Burlington makes for a relaxing detour from Route 70. On weekends it is busy with fishermen, boaters and waterskiers from the surrounding area. On weekdays the lake is practically deserted, letting visitors experience this oasis and its abundant bird and animal life, including osprey and golden and bald eagles as well as deer, coyotes, badgers, bobcats and beavers. Some 250 bird species rest here during spring and fall migrations, and 30,000 to 50,000 birds including snow geese, Canada geese and pelicans winter here. In addition to the lake, the park encompasses more than 5000 acres of natural bluestem loess prairie land. A short nature trail near the North Cove campground has markers identifying many of the various plant species of the plains. There is swimming at two beaches; fishing is exceptional for northern pike, freshwater drum, walleye, white bass, largemouth and smallmouth bass, crappie, bluegill, bullhead, channel catfish and wipers. Facilities include a picnic area, restrooms, showers, laundry, a telephone and a marina with boat rentals. Day-use fee, $4. ~ Located 25 miles north of Burlington on Route 385; 970-354-7306.

PARKS

▲ There are four campgrounds totaling 200 RV/tent sites (26 with electric hookups); $7 to $12 per night. Reservations are advised on weekends; call 800-678-2267.

Unlike the other highway routes described in this chapter, Route 50 across eastern Colorado is not an interstate highway, nor does it form a direct link between major cities. To the east is Dodge City, Kan-

Arkansas River Area

sas; to the west is Pueblo, Colorado; and like these cities, the route that follows the Arkansas River across Colorado's eastern plains has far more historical significance than meets the eye today.

In 1806, U.S. Army Lieutenant Zebulon Pike and his party of 22 soldiers followed this route to become the first American explorers ever to set foot in what is now Colorado. Pike and his men ignored warnings from the local Pawnee that the region had long been claimed by Spain as part of colonial Nuevo Mexico, and they soon found themselves arrested by the Spanish army, to be held prisoner in Santa Fe and Chihuahua on espionage charges for six months and finally deported back to the United States. Subsequent explorations of Colorado followed the South Platte instead.

The Arkansas River route suddenly became important 15 years later, when Mexico gained independence from Spain and opened its borders for the first time to trade with the United States. As word of the new policy got out, merchants rushed to organize wagon expeditions along the Santa Fe Trail, earning enormous profits by trading hardware, textiles and other factory-made goods for Mexican gold, silver and furs. The wagon road that became Route 50 was known as the Mountain Branch of the Santa Fe Trail, longer but less hazardous than the hot, bone-dry Cimarron Cutoff route over the *llano* of eastern New Mexico. The Arkansas River route was the busiest road in what is now Colorado for the next forty years, reaching its height in the late 1850s with the "Pikes Peak or Bust" Gold Rush. Soon afterwards, the Atchinson, Topeka and Santa Fe Railroad began laying tracks, still used by Amtrak passenger trains today, along the old Santa Fe Trail route.

SIGHTS   Today, plenty of Santa Fe Trail history awaits the curious all along Route 50. The easternmost major town, 32 miles west of the Kansas state line, is **Lamar**. The largest town for more than 100 miles in any direction, Lamar boasts a population of 8300. Founded by the Santa Fe Railroad in 1886 as a cattle-shipping terminal, Lamar still retains a lot of old-time cowboy character. It's classic small-town America with broad-brimmed hats and gun racks in the rear windows of pickup trucks. The local economy still depends completely on ranching and the railroad.

The **Big Timbers Museum** displays collections of household antiques, ranch memorabilia, Indian artifacts, old guns and historical photographs from the Lamar area. The museum is named after the three-quarter-mile-wide Big Timbers cottonwood forest, which lines the Arkansas River for 45 miles up and downstream from Lamar and served as a landmark and oasis for travelers on the Santa Fe Trail. ~ Route 50 North at Route 196, Lamar; 719-336-2472.

The **Madonna of the Trail Monument,** a statue of a pioneer woman and her children, is one of 12 madonna monuments, each in a different state, placed by the Daughters of the American Revolution in 1928 to mark the 12 officially designated National Old Trails in the United States. Lamar was selected as the site for the Santa Fe Trail madonna monument because the Big Timbers was deemed the most significant landmark along the Santa Fe Trail. ~ Main and Beech streets, Lamar.

The area also offers the morbidly curious traveler a glimpse or two of the darker side of American history. From Granada, 17 miles east of Lamar, a short drive south on County Road 25 will bring you to the abandoned remains of **Amache**, one of the largest U.S. internment camps for Japanese Americans during World War II. If you take Route 385 north from Granada for 23 miles, turn west on Route 96 for 13 miles to the very small town of Chivington, and take County Road 54 north for about 10 miles to where it ends at a "T" intersection, you'll find a small monument on the **Site of the Sand Creek Massacre**, one of the most infamous episodes in 19th-century Colorado history. In 1864, state National Guard Colonel John Chivington led his regiment in a predawn "disciplinary action" intended to persuade the Cheyenne people to leave Colorado by attacking a camp occupied mainly by women and children. Chivington claimed his troops killed 1000 Indians there (historians' estimates run somewhat lower); Chivington's troops suffered no casualties. He was subsequently awarded a medal of honor by Colorado's territorial governor and court-martialed by the U.S. Army.

◄ HIDDEN

◄ HIDDEN

History buffs may also wish to visit the stone foundations of Old Fort Lyon and **Bent's New Fort (Fort Wise)**, located adjacent to one another, one mile south of Route 50 on a marked gravel road that turns off 12 miles west of Lamar. A trading post and Indian agency were established on the site in 1852 by William Bent, the younger of the two brothers who had previously operated Bent's Old Fort (see below) 35 miles to the west. Although the new enterprise never equalled the Bent brothers' original trading post, it served Santa Fe Trail travelers and troops at the army fort for more than a decade. With hostilities mounting between Indians and settlers, the Bent family saga culminated tragically in 1864 as George Bent, the son of William and his Cheyenne wife, Owl Woman, was forced into service as a scout for Colonel Chivington and eyewitnessed the slaughter of his Indian relatives at Sand Creek. The Bents turned over their fort to the army and left in disgust.

◄ HIDDEN

On the outskirts of Las Animas is the site of **Boggsville**, a sheep- and cattle-ranching community founded in 1862 that was the original county seat for 9000-square-mile Bent County. Two restored adobe ranch houses and dozens of historical markers line the trail system winding through the historic restoration district. Adobe bricks are made at the site to aid in the reconstruction of other buildings of the pioneer community, including a general store, stage stop, one-room schoolhouse and Kit Carson's last home. ~ Route 101, Las Animas; 719-384-8113.

The most interesting of all the historic sites along the Arkansas River is **Bent's Old Fort National Monument**, located between Las Animas and La Junta on the other side of the river from Route 50. This adobe fortress is a reconstruction of the original trading post established by brothers Charles and William Bent in 1833 as the first permanent Anglo settlement on the Santa Fe Trail and the headquarters for a vast commercial empire that served not only pioneers from the U.S. but also Mexican, Navajo, Southern Cheyenne, Arapaho, Ute, Northern Apache, Kiowa and Comanche people of the region. Bent's Old Fort operated until the late 1840s, when the Mexican War, increasing hostilities between Anglo settlers and Indians, the violent death of Charles Bent and finally a cholera epidemic drove William Bent and his family to abandon it. Today, the impressive complex has been fully restored, and antique furnishings and volunteers in period costume re-create the frontier way of life. Admission. ~ Route 194; 719-384-2596.

Indian rock art in the Picket Wire Canyonlands area is believed to date back as much as 4500 years.

HIDDEN ► In La Junta, the **Koshare Indian Museum** provides an ironic coda to the tragic history of Colorado's plains Indians. The Koshare Indian Dancers, a local troop of non-Indian Boy Scouts, have been performing since 1933. The proceeds from their performances are used to add to the collections in this museum of American Indian art objects and paintings depicting Indians. Admission. ~ 115 West 18th Street, La Junta; 719-384-4411.

The **Otero Museum**, located in the century-old Sciumato Grocery Store, has exhibits on the history of Otero County, focusing on the arrival of the railroads and growth of the sugar-beet industry, as well as a display about the World War Two Army Air Corps bomber base—one of the nation's largest—that was located near La Junta. Open afternoons only in summer, closed in the off-season. ~ 2nd and Anderson streets, La Junta; 719-384-7500.

South of the Arkansas River corridor lies a truly vast expanse of arid and almost completely uninhabited prairie, much of it contained within the 420,000 acres of **Comanche National Grassland** (719-384-2181). The most accessible area of the national grassland for recreational purposes is **Picket Wire Canyonlands**, a hiking and mountain-biking area south of La Junta. Visitors can see a large dinosaur-track site with more than 1300 tracks preserved in sandstone. In the canyonlands are the abandoned remnants of a Mexican mission and cemetery and an 1870s cattle ranch. ~ To get there, follow Route 109 south from La Junta for 13 miles; turn west on County Road 802 (David Canyon Road) and go eight miles; then turn south on County Road 25 (Rourke Road) and go six more miles to the canyonlands entrance. From

HIDDEN ►

there, four-wheel-drive vehicles can make it two miles in on rough Forest Road 500 before reaching a locked gate. Only hiking, horseback riding and mountain biking are allowed beyond the gate.

Deeper into Comanche National Grassland, in Colorado's southeast corner near the Oklahoma state line, **Picture Canyon** ◄HIDDEN is perhaps the most remote recreation area in Colorado. The canyon has natural arches and caves, abundant bird and animal life, and many Indian petroglyphs and pictographs. Unique rock art designs found here closely resemble a form of writing developed in ancient Ireland, leading some scholars to contend that Celtic explorers may have come here around 200 B.C. ~ To get there, follow Route 287 south from Springfield (which is 48 miles due south of Lamar) for 20 miles to the tiny crossroads of Campo; turn west on County Road J and go 10 miles to the marked turnoff for Picture Canyon.

Lamar's best accommodations are at the big **Cow Palace Inn**. The   **LODGING** only convention facility in this part of the state, this 100-room motor inn has modern, spacious rooms decorated in earth tones with king- or queen-size beds, direct-dial phones and cable TV. There are an indoor swimming pool, a hot tub and an indoor tropical garden. ~ 1301 North Main Street, Lamar; 719-336-7753, 800-678-0344, fax 719-336-9598. MODERATE.

Lamar also has a good selection of low-priced motels such as the **El Mar Budget Host Motel,** a 40-unit motel with clean, comfortable guest rooms, some with kitchenettes, and a heated pool. ~ 1210 South Main Street, Lamar; 719-336-4331, fax 719-336-7931. BUDGET.

Lodging options in La Junta are even more limited than in Lamar. A good choice among the handful of family-run motels in town, the **Mid-Town Motel** has a central location that would be wonderfully convenient if the town had much of anything to be convenient to. The 24 guest units are routine and clean. ~ 215 East 3rd Street, La Junta; 719-384-7741.

The closest thing to fine dining in Lamar is the dining room at   **DINING** the **Cow Palace Inn**, with both indoor and courtyard seating. As you might expect, the menu is mostly steak and potatoes; for vegetarian travelers, however, the impressively long salad bar is probably the best bet in the area. ~ 1301 North Main Street, Lamar; 719-336-7753. MODERATE TO DELUXE.

Lamar also has an exceptionally good Chinese restaurant, the **Green Garden**. All-red Oriental decor sets the stage for Mandarin and Szechuan specialties such as chicken, black mushroom and abalone soup, and velvet chicken and scallops. ~ 601 East Olive Street, Lamar; 719-336-3264. BUDGET.

In La Junta, try the **El Camino Inn**, a homey little Mexican restaurant that has been operated by the same family for more than 30 years. House specialties include spicy red enchiladas and *chiles rellenos*, green chile peppers stuffed with cheese, breaded and fried. ~ 816 West 3rd Street, La Junta; 719-384-2871. BUDGET.

SHOPPING   In Las Animas, **Colorado Originals** is a unique nonprofit gallery sponsored by the Bent County Development Foundation to promote arts and crafts of the region. Paintings, sculpture, wood carvings, quilts and stained glass, as well as antiques and food items, are displayed for sale. ~ 5th Street at Bent Avenue, Las Animas; 719-456-0200.

Rocky Ford, a small town 12 miles west of La Junta, grows cantaloupes that are reputed to be the best in the country. This claim to fame supports an abundance of roadside produce stands along Route 50, as, people come from as far away as Denver during the fall harvest season to buy the melons. The stands also sell watermelons, sweet corn and honey.

NIGHTLIFE   The Koshare Indian Dancers, Boy Scouts in American Indian garb, perform traditional dances on Friday and Saturday nights during the summer months at the kiva of the **Koshare Indian Museum** on the Otero Junior College campus in La Junta. ~ 115 West 18th Street, La Junta; 719-384-4411.

PARKS   **JOHN MARTIN RESERVOIR** This large flood-control reservoir managed by the U.S. Army Corps of Engineers is used for boating and water skiing. A 75-acre excavation originally dug to obtain earthfill for the dam was filled with water to create Lake Hasty, now used for swimming, canoeing, windsurfing and fishing. The lake is populated by rainbow trout, walleye, channel catfish, largemouth bass and bluegill. A fenced area north of the lake preserves a half-mile stretch of the original wagon ruts of the Santa Fe Trail. There is a visitors center, restrooms, a picnic area and playground. ~ From Route 50, 21 miles west of Lamar and 14 miles east of Las Animas, take Route 260 south for two miles to the park entrance.

▲ There are 65 RV/tent sites, including 12 with electric hookups; $5 to $7 per night.

Outdoor Adventures

FISHING   **SOUTH PLATTE RIVER AREA**   Once it leaves the mountains, the South Platte River runs so wide and shallow that it is an uninviting place for fish and fishermen alike. Fishing in the area focuses on several reservoirs: **Julesburg Reservoir** (commonly called Jumbo Lake) near Julesburg, **North Sterling Reservoir** near Sterling and **Jackson Lake** near Fort Morgan. All three lakes have good-sized catfish and walleye. The marina at Jackson Lake rents fishing boats and has bait and tackle. ~ 970-768-6011. North Sterling Reservoir's marina also has boat rentals. ~ 970-522-1511.

ROUTE 70 The only body of water in this part of the state, **Bonny Lake State Park** offers an assortment of warm-water fish including walleye, northern pike, freshwater drum, white bass, largemouth and smallmouth bass, crappie, bluegill, bullhead, channel catfish and wipers.

ARKANSAS RIVER AREA Its shoreline choked with tamarisk and scrub brush, the Arkansas River does not attract anglers in large numbers, though it is said to have some large native catfish. **Lake Hasty**, the manmade recreational lake adjoining John Martin Reservoir, is stocked with rainbow trout, walleye, channel catfish, largemouth bass and bluegill. Other area reservoirs that offer good warmwater fishing include **Adobe Creek Reservoir** (also called Blue Lake) north of Las Animas and a cluster of neighboring lakes—**Nee Skah, Nee Noshe and Nee Gronda reservoirs**—all north of Lamar.

BOATING

SOUTH PLATTE RIVER AREA North Sterling Reservoir (970-522-3657) near Sterling and **Jackson Lake** (970-645-2551) near Fort Morgan are popular areas for recreational boating, water-skiing and windsurfing. A favorite of sailboat enthusiasts, North Sterling Reservoir has a marina with boat rentals ranging from paddleboats to water-ski and pontoon boats, daily in summer and weekends only the rest of the year. ~ 970-522-3657.

ROUTE 70 Bonny Lake State Park attracts recreational boaters and waterskiers from all around this arid part of the Colorado and Kansas plains. There is a marina with fishing boats, pontoon boats and jet skis for rent. ~ 970-354-7306.

ARKANSAS RIVER AREA John Martin Reservoir offers a full range of water sports. The main reservoir is used for recreational

✔ **CHECK THESE OUT—UNIQUE OUTDOOR ADVENTURES**

- Slice the surface of Bonny Lake with waterskis or jet skis—the only skiing you'll be doing on the prairie. *page 339*
- Practice your swing at Sterling's inexpensive Riverview Golf Course—challenging because it boasts no fewer than 48 sand traps. *page 340*
- Hike the network of trails surrounding Pawnee Buttes, twin rock formations that were landmarks for early pioneers. *page 341*
- Ride a mountain bike in Picket Wire Canyonlands and discover dinosaur tracks, Indian pictographs and an abandoned ranch. *page 341*

boating and water skiing. Adjoining the reservoir is Lake Hasty, a smaller manmade lake that is off-limits to motorized boats and is used for canoeing and windsurfing. ~ 719-336-3476.

GOLF   **SOUTH PLATTE RIVER AREA** Platte River golf courses include the **Riverview Golf Course,** an 18-hole public course and driving range with cart and club rentals. Designed by Val Heim, the course takes advantage of the rolling prairie terrain, incorporating no fewer than 48 sand traps. ~ North Riverview Road, Sterling; 970-522-3035. There's also the 18-hole **Fort Morgan Municipal Golf Course,** where the front nine holes have been in use since 1929. Lined by mature shade trees, the traditional course has cart and club rentals. ~ Riverside Park, Fort Morgan; 970-867-5990.

ROUTE 70 In Burlington, there's the very hilly nine-hole **Prairie Pines Golf Course.** Cart and club rentals are available. ~ Route 385 North; 719-346-7266. You'll find nine more holes half an hour to the west at the **Flagler Golf Course.** ~ 1682 County Road 5, Flagler; no phone. There's another nine at the **Limon Municipal Golf Course.** Designed by Henry Hughes, the Limon course is laid out around two lakes and has challenging sand traps. Cart and club rentals are available. ~ Route 71 South, Limon; 719-775-9998.

ARKANSAS RIVER AREA Lamar has the **Spreading Antlers Golf Course,** a nine-hole course along Willow Creek with small greens and luxuriant bluegrass fairways, as well as a pro shop, carts and club rentals. ~ South Route 287; 719-336-5274. Other links along the Arkansas River include the **Las Animas Golf Course,** a level nine-hole course designed by Ray Hardy with five water hazards; cart and club rentals are available. ~ 220 Country Club Drive; 719-456-2511. You may also tee off at the nine-hole public **La Junta Municipal Golf Course;** cart and club rentals are available. ~ 27696 Harris Road; 719-384-7133. The challenging, hilly nine-hole course at the **Rocky Ford Golf Club** is also open to the public and has cart and club rentals. ~ 91 Play Park Hill; 719-254-7528.

TENNIS   You'll find two free asphalt-surfaced outdoor public tennis courts, lighted for night play, in Sterling at **Pioneer Park.** ~ West Main Street, Sterling; 970-322-9700.

BIKING   The prairie of eastern Colorado is crisscrossed by a gridwork of literally thousands of miles of straight, featureless, relatively level, infrequently used farm and ranch roads. A bike trip along any of them gives you a chance to fully appreciate the sights, sounds and scents of the high plains.

ARKANSAS RIVER AREA The most exciting mountain biking on the eastern plains is in **Picket Wire Canyonlands** south of La Junta. Eleven miles of multiple-use trails and primitive roads take you along the Purgatoire River to an old Mexican cemetery, dinosaur tracks, Indian rock art and the remains of a 19th-century cattle ranch.

Bike Rentals The best plan is to rent bikes in Boulder, Denver, Colorado Springs or Pueblo for a cycling expedition into the eastern plains. The nearest bike rentals to Picket Wire Canyonlands are in Pueblo at **Great Divide Ski, Bike & Hike**. ~ 4th Street and Santa Fe Avenue, Pueblo; 719-546-2453.

All distances listed for hiking trails are one way unless otherwise noted.

HIKING

SOUTH PLATTE RIVER AREA You'll find a network of short trails among the fascinating rock formations of Chimney Canyon north of Sterling. Farther north, a two-mile hiking trail leads to the foot of **Pawnee Buttes** in Pawnee National Grassland (see "South Platte River Area" earlier in this chapter).

ROUTE 70 There is little hiking here. Your best bet is a walk through the cottonwoods and natural prairie along the lakeshore in **Bonny Lake State Park**.

ARKANSAS RIVER AREA The **Picket Wire Canyonlands** trail described above under "Biking" also makes for a good all-day hike. On the route from La Junta to the canyonlands described elsewhere in this chapter, there is a scenic 2.25-mile loop trail in **Vogel Canyon**—watch for the marked entrance road off County Road 802 one mile west of the turnoff from Route 109. Along the Vogel Canyon trail you'll find Indian rock art and the ruins of an old homestead and a stage station. Farther southeast in Comanche National Grassland, a four-mile loop trail runs through **Picture Canyon**, offering a look at some of the best examples of Indian rock art in the state and an area of fantastic rock formations known as Hells Half Acre.

▾▾▾▾▾▾▾▾▾▾
Transportation

Route 76 follows the Platte River and the old Overland Trail through the towns of Julesburg, Sterling and Fort Morgan. **Route 70** runs through Burlington and Limon. The two interstate routes meet in Denver. **Route 50** follows the Arkansas River and the old Santa Fe Trail to Pueblo through Lamar, Las Animas and La Junta.

CAR

There is no commercial air service to the towns covered by this chapter. The nearest major airports are Denver and Colorado Springs.

AIR

TRAIN   Amtrak's "Southwest Chief," which provides service between Chicago and Los Angeles, traces the entire length of the old Santa Fe Trail, making stops in Lamar and La Junta. ~ 800-872-7245.

BUS   **Greyhound Bus Lines** (800-231-2222) buses go through Julesburg, Sterling and Fort Morgan on Route 76 and Burlington and Limon on Route 70. The driver can let you off at any of these towns on request; to make arrangements to board a bus on its way through any of these towns, you must call the bus terminal in Denver. ~ 303-293-6555.

            TNM&O Coaches (800-231-2222) has a bus route along Route 50 through Lamar and La Junta. To make arrangements to board a bus, call the terminal in Pueblo. ~ 719-544-6295.

Index

Lodging Index

Dining Index

Notes

Notes

HIDDEN GUIDES

Adventure travel or a relaxing vacation?—"Hidden" guidebooks are the only travel books in the business to provide detailed information on both. Aimed at environmentally aware travelers, our motto is "Adventure Travel Plus." These books combine details on unique hotels, restaurants and sightseeing with information on camping, sports and hiking for the outdoor enthusiast.

THE NEW KEY GUIDES

Based on the concept of ecotourism, The New Key Guides are dedicated to the preservation of Central America's rare and endangered species, architecture and archaeology. Filled with helpful tips, they give travelers everything they need to know about these exotic destinations.

ULTIMATE FAMILY GUIDES

These innovative guides present the best and most unique features of a family destination. Quality is the keynote. In addition to thoroughly covering each destination, they feature short articles and one-line "teasers" that are both fun and informative.

Ulysses Press books are available at bookstores everywhere. If any of the following titles are unavailable at your local bookstore, ask the bookseller to order them.

You can also order books directly from Ulysses Press
P.O. Box 3440, Berkeley, CA 94703
800-377-2542 or 510-601-8301
fax: 510-601-8307
e-mail: ulysses@ulyssespress.com

Order Form

HIDDEN GUIDEBOOKS

____ Hidden Arizona, $13.95

____ Hidden Bahamas, $12.95

____ Hidden Baja, $14.95

____ Hidden Boston and Cape Cod, $11.95

____ Hidden Carolinas, $16.95

____ Hidden Coast of California, $16.95

____ Hidden Colorado, $13.95

____ Hidden Florida, $16.95

____ Hidden Florida Keys & Everglades,
    $11.95

____ Hidden Hawaii, $16.95

____ Hidden Idaho, $13.95

____ Hidden Maui, $12.95

____ Hidden Montana, $13.95

____ Hidden New England, $17.95

____ Hidden New Mexico, $13.95

____ Hidden Oahu, $12.95

____ Hidden Oregon, $13.95

____ Hidden Pacific Northwest, $17.95

____ Hidden Rockies, $16.95

____ Hidden San Francisco and
    Northern California, $16.95

____ Hidden Southern California, $16.95

____ Hidden Southwest, $17.95

____ Hidden Tahiti, $16.95

____ Hidden Tennessee, $15.95

____ Hidden Utah, $13.95

____ Hidden Wyoming, $13.95

THE NEW KEY GUIDEBOOKS

____ The New Key to Belize, $14.95

____ The New Key to Cancún and
    the Yucatán, $14.95

____ The New Key to Costa Rica, $16.95

____ The New Key to Ecuador and
    the Galápagos, $16.95

____ The New Key to Guatemala, $14.95

ULTIMATE FAMILY GUIDEBOOKS

____ Disneyland and Beyond, $12.95

____ Disney World and Beyond, $13.95

Mark the book(s) you're ordering and enter the total cost here ⟹ [   ]

California residents add 8% sales tax here ⟹ [   ]

Shipping, check box for your preferred method and enter cost here ⟹ [   ]

❑ BOOK RATE   **FREE! FREE! FREE!**

❑ PRIORITY MAIL $3.00 First book, $1.00/each additional book

❑ UPS 2-DAY AIR $7.00 First book, $1.00/each additional book   [   ]

Billing, enter total amount due here and check method of payment ⟹ [   ]

❑ CHECK   ❑ MONEY ORDER

❑ VISA/MASTERCARD _____ EXP. DATE _____

NAME _____ PHONE _____

ADDRESS _____

_____

CITY _____ STATE _____ ZIP _____

MONEY-BACK GUARANTEE ON DIRECT ORDERS PLACED THROUGH ULYSSES PRESS.

ABOUT THE AUTHOR

RICHARD HARRIS has written or co-written eight other guide-books including Ulysses' bestselling *Hidden Southwest*. He has also served as contributing editor on guides to Mexico, New Mexico and other ports of call for John Muir Publications, Fodor's, Birnbaum and Access guides. He is a director of PENCenter USAWest and president of PEN New Mexico. When not traveling, Richard writes and lives in Santa Fe, New Mexico, with his shaggy 150-pound dog, Oso (that's "bear" in Spanish).

ABOUT THE ILLUSTRATOR

DOUG McCARTHY is the co-owner of Graphic Detail, a specialty graphics company in Berkeley. His illustrations appear in a number of Ulysses Press guides, including *Hidden Tennessee*, *Hidden Bahamas* and *The New Key to Ecuador and the Galápagos*. A native New Yorker, he lives in the San Francisco Bay area with his family.